"WE ARE IN CHARGE HERE"

"We Are In Charge Here"

Inuit Self-Government and the Nunatsiavut Assembly

GRAHAM WHITE

UNIVERSITY OF TORONTO PRESS
Toronto Buffalo London

ISBN 978-1-4875-5158-2 (cloth)   ISBN 978-1-4875-5274-9 (EPUB)
                                 ISBN 978-1-4875-5212-1 (PDF)

Library and Archives Canada Cataloguing in Publication

Title: "We are in charge here" : Inuit self-government and the Nunatsiavut Assembly /
    Graham White.
Names: White, Graham, 1948– author.
Description: Includes bibliographical references and index.
Identifiers: Canadiana (print) 20230133371 | Canadiana (ebook) 20230133592 |
    ISBN 9781487551582 (hardcover) | ISBN 9781487552749 (EPUB) |
    ISBN 9781487552121 (PDF)
Subjects: LCSH: Nunatsiavut. Assembly. | LCSH: Inuit – Newfoundland and
    Labrador – Labrador – Politics and government.
Classification: LCC E99.E7 W45 2023 | DDC 320.8089/971207182–dc23

We wish to acknowledge the land on which the University of Toronto Press
operates. This land is the traditional territory of the Wendat, the Anishnaabeg, the
Haudenosaunee, the Métis, and the Mississaugas of the Credit First Nation.

University of Toronto Press acknowledges the financial support of the Government of
Canada, the Canada Council for the Arts, and the Ontario Arts Council, an agency of
the Government of Ontario, for its publishing activities.

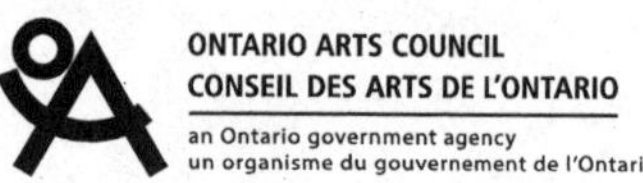

For Cathy, the love of my life

Contents

List of Figures, Tables, and Appendices ix

Preface and Acknowledgments xi

List of Abbreviations xv

Map 2

1 Inuit Self-Government and the Nunatsiavut Assembly 3
2 The Labrador Inuit: History, Society, Culture, and Political
   Institutions 14
3 Comprehensive Land Claims and Indigenous Self-Government 32
4 Governance in Nunatsiavut: Constitution, Organization, and Politics 47
5 The Assembly: Setting, Atmosphere, and Membership 73
6 The Assembly: Operations, Committees, and Services 105
7 Distinctive Features of the Nunatsiavut Assembly 124
8 Consensus, Consensus Government, and Inuit Influence 142
9 Assembly Effectiveness I: Representation and Policymaking 177
10 Assembly Effectiveness II: Accountability 202
11 Change, Continuity, and Self-Government in the Nunatsiavut
   Assembly 228

Notes 237

Index 273

Figures, Tables, and Appendices

Figures

5.1   The Assembly Building, Hopedale   78
5.2   The Assembly Chamber   79
5.3   Assembly meeting in boardroom, 2008   81
5.4   Assembly meeting, 2014   82

Tables

5.1   Number and duration of sessions, 2006–22   84
5.2   Length of members' service, 2006–22   90
5.3   Ministers' length of membership in NEC, 2006–22   92
5.4   Ministerial tenure, 2006–22   92
6.1   Standing and special committees, 2006–22   117
8.1   Voting cohesion of non-NEC members   166
8.2   Voting cohesion of non-NEC members   167
8.3   Voting of NEC and non-NEC members   168
9.1   Ordinary members' incumbency   183
10.1   NG/Assembly news releases, 1 January 2017–31 April 2022   205
10.2   Frequency of members' questions in question period   216
10.3   Frequency of supplementary questions   216
10.4   Original questions asked by type of member   217
10.5   Original questions by portfolio   218
10.6   Original questions with a local focus   220

x   Figures, Tables, and Appendices

Appendices

8.1   Split Votes   171
8.2   Individual Members' Votes in Split Votes   173
9.1   Characteristics of Legislation   199

Preface and Acknowledgments

In recent years, governments and individuals in Canada have committed themselves to "reconciliation" between Indigenous and non-Indigenous peoples. Understandings of just what reconciliation entails vary widely, but if it is to be more than pious phrases and good intentions, reconciliation must include meaningful expressions of what the United Nations Declaration on the Rights of Indigenous Peoples (UNDRIP) terms the right to self-determination and self-government.

According to UNDRIP, self-determination includes the right of Indigenous peoples to "freely determine their political status and freely pursue their economic, social and cultural development," pursuits that often take the form of self-government.[1] As discussed in chapter 3 of this volume, the term "self-government" is used in Canada to describe a wide range of governance arrangements, both prospective and aspirational as well as functioning, on-the-ground institutions. To date, the Canadian literature on self-government has been far more concerned with the former than with the latter. This book seeks to contribute to the understanding of self-government through a detailed analysis of the central political institution of an established self-government regime: the elected Assembly of the Nunatsiavut Government in northern Labrador. As the only Inuit self-government in Canada, Nunatsiavut is certainly unique, as, in their own ways, are the other Canadian Indigenous self-governments, so that studying it takes us only so far in the quest for understanding. Still, Nunatsiavut is the most populous self-government in Canada; in scale and complexity, its governance institutions go substantially beyond those found in most other current self-governments. It is therefore a worthwhile case study.

This book targets three quite distinct audiences. The first is the growing community of academics and practitioners interested in or directly involved with self-governments, existing and emerging. This community has at present a limited store of empirical analyses of the institutions of functioning self-governments on which to draw; I hope its members find *"We Are In Charge*

Here" of both intellectual and practical value. I also hope through this book to kindle the interest of a second audience, legislative scholars, by appealing to their abiding affinity for unusual constellations of parliamentary structures and processes, such as are found in the Nunatsiavut Assembly. It's important for Canadian academics who study legislatures, as, indeed, for the practitioners who work in them, to devote serious attention to the prospects for significant Indigenous involvement and influence in existing parliamentary institutions. I hope that this book will encourage reflection and research into such issues. Finally, I entertain the perhaps vain expectation that the elected and appointed officials of the Nunatsiavut Government and at least a few among the Nunatsiavut citizenry will learn something from these chapters. In that vein, I've aimed for clear, straightforward, jargon-free prose that won't put readers off too badly.

Given the differing perspectives and interests of these potential audiences, it is unlikely that every reader will find all parts of the book stimulating. This was brought home to me by the anonymous readers of the first draft of the manuscript, who clearly focussed on self-government rather than legislative studies and thus found the accounts of legislative rules and processes overly detailed, "pedantic," and "tedious." To be sure, substantial portions of the book will appeal mostly to those with a particular enthusiasm for legislatures. I don't apologize for this, but, in the spirit of accommodation, suggest that, other than hard-core legislative specialists, readers might want to skim or skip chapters 5 and 6, much of chapter 7, the analysis of "split votes" in chapter 8, and that of question period in chapter 10.

Research for *"We're In Charge Here"* was conducted as part of a SSHRC Partnership Grant for the "Tradition and Transition among the Labrador Inuit" project co-sponsored by the Nunatsiavut Government and Memorial University of Newfoundland, initially directed by Professor Tom Gordon and subsequently by Professor Lisa Rankin, both of Memorial. My friend and colleague Professor Christopher Alcantara of Western University and I were assigned the governance components of this sweeping and innovative project. Chris looked primarily at elections and representative processes through the study of the behaviour of Nunatsiavut politicians and voters.[2] As is evident from this book, I adopted an institutional perspective.

In addition to Tom, Lisa, and Chris, I owe thanks to a great many people for their help during my research, and especially during my trips to Nunatsiavut. In particular, I wish to express my thanks to Sheila Angnatok, Edward Blake-Rudkowski, Rexanne Crawford, Tyler Edmunds, Marjorie Flowers, Mark Gillette, Veryan Haysom, Alana Johns, Dave Lough, Loretta Michelin, Isabella Pain, Bert Pomeroy, Andrea Procter, Andrea Quigley, and Hans Rollman.

Though all members and staff of the assembly were generous with their time and remarkably candid in their observations, I must record a particular debt of gratitude to Mary Sillett, former clerk of the assembly, and to Tabea Onalik, her assistant. Mary and Tabea were unfailingly helpful in responding to my many requests for documents and in explaining aspects of the assembly I didn't understand or hadn't noticed.

More generally, I must add my heartfelt appreciation of how welcome I was made to feel as I wandered the halls of the assembly and was brought into conversations with members and staff. When lunch was ordered in, I was asked what I wanted. When sessions ended, I was offered rides back to the hotel. At the hotel I never found myself eating alone. *Nakummek.*

Thanks are also due the three anonymous referees whose constructive criticisms have greatly improved this book, as well as University of Toronto Press editor extraordinaire Daniel Quinlan, who was unfailingly supportive throughout the process, and model copy editor Ryan Perks, who significantly improved the book's readability while paying me the great compliment of not messing with my prose (much). Jason Edwards graciously agreed to permit the use of his stunning photograph of the Nunatsiavut Assembly Building for the book's cover.

The best for last: heartfelt gratitude for the support of my long-suffering wife, Cathy, who continues to abide my seemingly endless academic projects with good grace while only occasionally asking when I'm going to really "retire."

Finally, readers may notice that while I identify what strike me as shortcomings of the assembly and sometimes mention possibilities for change, I make no recommendations. If I've learned anything in more than thirty years of research in the North, it's that a non-Indigenous Toronto academic has no business telling northern Indigenous peoples how to run their affairs. I like to think I can offer food for thought, but it's not up to me to chart a way forward.

The book's title? Readers will find out where it comes from on page 194.

Abbreviations

AiP	Agreement-in-Principle
CLO	community liaison officer
CPI	Consumer Price Index
EA	environmental assessment
IBA	Impact and Benefit Agreement
ITC	Inuit Tapirisat of Canada (now Inuit Tapiriit Kanatami)
LIA	Labrador Inuit Association
LIL	Labrador Inuit Lands
LILCA	Labrador Inuit Land Claims Agreement
LISA	Labrador Inuit Settlement Area
LMA	Labrador Metis Association
LSC	Language Strategy Committee
MLA	member of the Legislative Assembly
NANL	Native Association of Newfoundland and Labrador
NCC	NunatuKavut Community Council
NEC	Nunatsiavut Executive Council
NEO	Nunatsiavut elections officer
NG	Nunatsiavut Government
NGC	Nunatsiavut Group of Companies
NWT	Northwest Territories
OK Society	OKâlaKatiget Society
TRHA	Torngat Regional Housing Association
UNDRIP	United Nations Declaration on the Rights of Indigenous Peoples

"WE ARE IN CHARGE HERE"

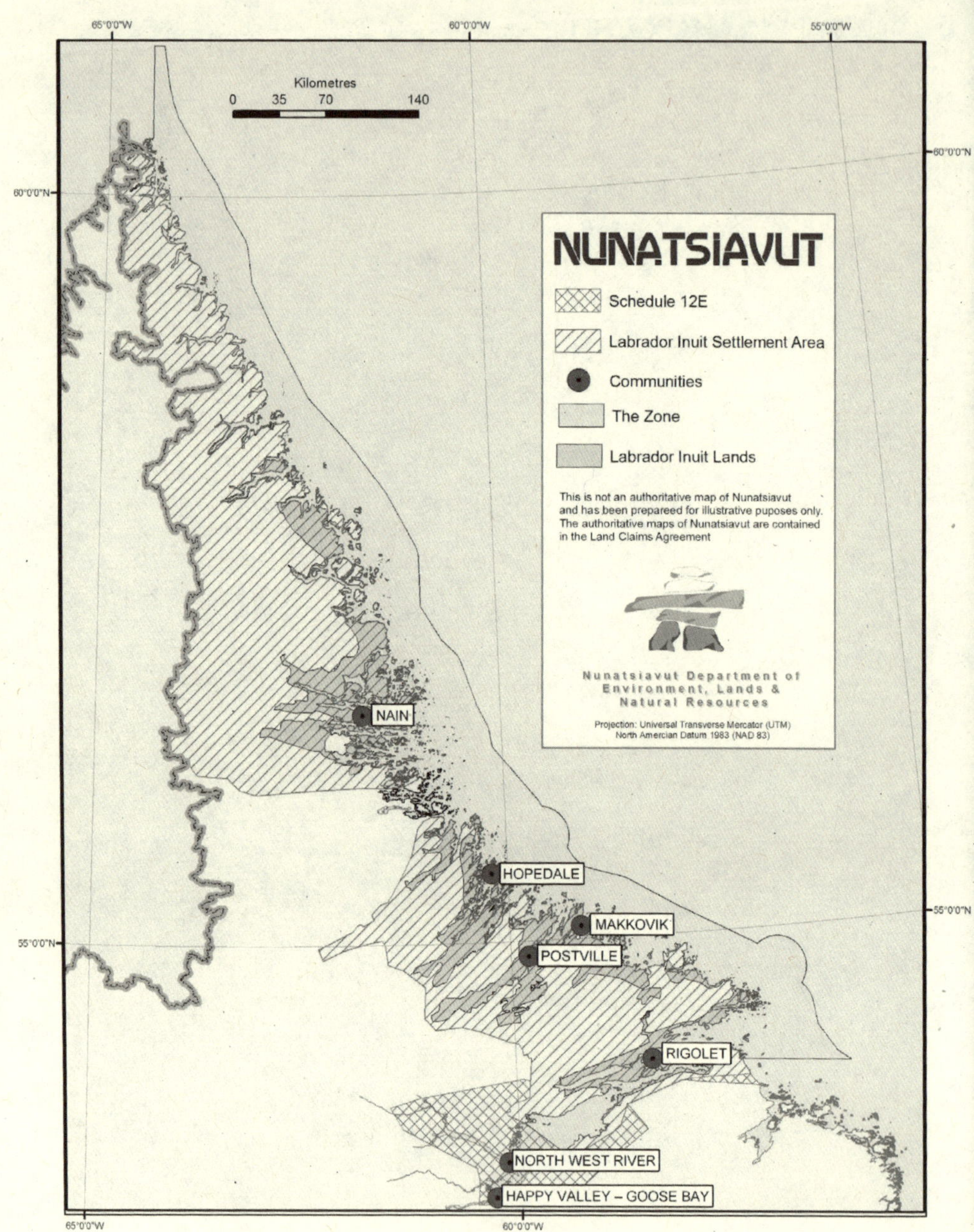

Map of Nunatsiavut. Courtesy of the Nunatsiavut Government

Chapter One

Inuit Self-Government and the Nunatsiavut Assembly

Introduction

While self-government has long been a widely held aspiration among Canada's Indigenous peoples, until recently no meaningful examples existed, as they had prior to contact with Europeans and well into the post-contact period. *Indian Act* band councils, tightly constrained by the federal government, were far from self-governing. Nor did non-status Indians, Métis, or Inuit have self-governing institutions with anything like substantial power. Beginning in limited ways with the 1975 James Bay and Northern Quebec Agreement, the federal *Cree-Naskapi Act* in 1984 and the 1986 *Sechelt Indian Band Self-Government Act*, and gaining momentum following Ottawa's 1995 declaration of its inherent right policy, a number of Indigenous nations and organizations have negotiated self-government agreements with the federal and territorial/provincial governments. Others are under negotiation.

As will be evident from the discussion in chapter 3, wide variation exists in how governments, Indigenous peoples, and observers conceive of self-government. The federal and provincial governments, for example, have a broad understanding of self-government, encompassing a wide range of actual and possible governance arrangements, including "public" governments, such as that of Nunavut, where Indigenous people may dominate numerically but all residents enjoy the same political rights,[1] and municipality-like status, as in the shíshálh (formerly Sechelt) Nation of British Columbia. Other self-government regimes, sometimes termed "ethnic governments," offer greater scope for Indigenous peoples to run their affairs in their own way, not least in limiting some services and political rights to Indigenous people.[2] It is with this last form of self-government that this book is concerned, and, as is common in academic analyses, it reserves the term "Indigenous self-government" for such regimes, save in the overview of institutional forms of Indigenous governance in chapter 3.

The nearly two dozen Indigenous self-governments operating in Canada in 2022 varied widely, reflecting the distinctive cultures and priorities of the Indigenous peoples involved as well as the circumstances of the negotiations that created them. Thus no single, straightforward model of Indigenous self-government exists. Rather, a wide range of actual and potential institutional arrangements is possible. Still, four key elements characterize all Indigenous self-government regimes. First, they exhibit substantial, though far from unlimited, governance authority. Second, although self-government models for landless urban Indigenous peoples have been proposed, all existing self-government regimes exercise authority over geographically bounded territories; this is of great moment given Indigenous people's spiritual relationship with the land. Third, criteria for membership, significantly termed "citizenship" in some self-government agreements, are to a substantial degree determined by Indigenous people and institutions. Fourth, they entail at least some exclusionary provisions, in that access to certain programs and services is restricted to Indigenous people and/or certain political rights are available only to Indigenous people.

With Indigenous self-government for many years an aspiration rather than a reality, the academic literature on it has largely focussed on normative arguments favouring self-government as well as possible institutional models. To date, analyses of functioning self-government regimes have been few and far between. As Indigenous self-governments become more prominent and more numerous, it is time for academics to shift towards examining the structure and operation of actual self-governments. Although the Canadian literature is overwhelmingly concerned with First Nations and Métis, in Canada and elsewhere, "Inuit peoples have been at the forefront of some of the most important developments in Indigenous self-government."[3] Accordingly, this book seeks to contribute to the study of Indigenous self-government through description and analysis of the Nunatsiavut Government (NG) in northern Labrador, which came into being in 2005 as a key element of the treaty between the Labrador Inuit and the governments of Canada and Newfoundland and Labrador: the Labrador Inuit Land Claims Agreement (LILCA). Measured in terms of numbers of members and size of administration, the NG is Canada's largest self-government.[4] Distinctive in many ways, Nunatsiavut – "Our Beautiful Land" in Inuttut, the local dialect of Inuktitut – is unique in that it is the only Inuit self-government in Canada; all other Indigenous self-governments entail First Nations.

This introductory chapter sets out the essential purpose of the book and offers a thumbnail sketch of Nunatsiavut that briefly examines the land covered by the treaty and the demography of the claim's beneficiaries. After describing the methods underpinning the research, it concludes with an outline of the book.

Focus on the Nunatsiavut Assembly

Examination of self-government in Nunatsiavut proceeds through an empirical focus on the design and operation of the assembly, the central democratic institution of the Nunatsiavut Government. Here, the elected representatives of Nunatsiavumiut[5] (the people of Nunatsiavut) meet to discuss the region's problems and prospects, to review and pass legislation, to allocate financial resources, and to hold the executive of the NG to account for its policies and administration. These functions are performed by all legislatures in democratic polities and thus warrant attention in a study of the Nunatsiavut Assembly. In addition, a key motivation for this book lies in another, deeper purpose, one that is specific to the Nunatsiavut Assembly: realization of the self-determination aspirations of the Labrador Inuit. This ambition was well captured by Tyler Edmunds, then NG minister of finance, who in November 2019 told the assembly that

> a key motivation for the founders of our Labrador Inuit Association, the negotiators of our *Land Claims Agreement* and those who voted to ratify the agreement has been the idea of recognition. What preface [*sic*: preceded?] us sitting in this Assembly was a stand and a fight to have a nation recognize that there is a distinct group of people in Northern Labrador and to have others know for themselves what we've always known, that we are Labrador Inuit … We are a self-determining Government, giving us the power to have greater control over our future and to create our own path forward. Every official around this table has a part to play. We are the instruments of self-determination. The voices of our communities, our departments, the voices of elected boards and councils or the voice of the Assembly itself, Mr. Speaker. We have a privilege to sit here and we have the power to speak to issues within these walls and outside. The rights that we are granted to speak on behalf of our communities and our respective bodies is how we will ensure that our Government is able to recognize how best we address the issues in our communities and to create realities where our people will be safe and connected to the culture and land. My call to the Assembly today is for each of us to remember that we are key in the implementation of our self-government models and that we recognize that we are the voice in the continuation of self-determination.[6]

The assembly is a quasi-Westminster legislature with some decidedly non-Westminster features and is explicitly designed and mandated to reflect and enhance Inuit culture. In terms of both design and operation, it is a site of intersection between Indigenous culture and traditions and Settler – that is, Euro-Canadian – constitutional order. As will become evident in later chapters, the melding of Inuit and Euro-Canadian approaches to governance exhibits both tensions and compatibility.

The premise of this book is that detailed study of the Nunatsiavut Assembly can offer valuable insight into the real-life workings of a prominent Indigenous self-government. No claim is made that the NG or the assembly are typical of self-governments elsewhere in Canada. Indeed, the relatively few actual Indigenous self-governments are characterized by a wide range of institutional arrangements and operating principles. The NG and its assembly form but a single case, though an instructive one.

The assembly is described and analysed in detail in later chapters; here, the salient features can be set out succinctly. Similar to the governance regimes in Nunavut and the Northwest Territories, it operates without political parties, as a so-called consensus government. Currently, it consists of eighteen members, who must be Inuit: a president, elected by all beneficiaries; ten ordinary members elected in "first-past-the-post" geographic constituencies; the AngajukKât (mayors) of the five Nunatsiavut Inuit community governments; and the chairs of the two Inuit community corporations. The Nunatsiavut Executive Council (NEC) – the cabinet – consists of the president, the first minister, and ministers, usually five in number. Aside from the president, only ordinary members are eligible to serve in the NEC. The assembly meets in Hopedale four or five times a year, usually for two-day sessions. A politically neutral speaker, who must be an ordinary member, presides. With minor variations, the assembly operates according to the tenets of Westminster parliamentary procedure, including both fundamental principles such as the confidence convention and routine practices such as question period.[7]

A full examination of Inuit self-government in Nunatsiavut would include analysis of the bureaucratic arm of the NG as well as the local Inuit community governments. Such a wide-ranging study is beyond the scope of an account of the assembly, which, as the central democratic governing institution in Nunatsiavut, plays a uniquely important role in the self-governing regime of the Labrador Inuit.

The overall objectives of this book are threefold. First, to examine in detail the operation of a key institution in a functioning Indigenous self-government regime in order to expand knowledge of the realities of self-government. Second, to better understand, within a self-government context, the intersection of Indigenous traditions and modes of governance with Western, Euro-Canadian governance precepts and institutions, most notably in terms of Inuit influences on the Westminster cabinet-parliamentary system. Third, to offer to Nunatsiavumiut a portrait of their key democratic institution that may be of use as self-government in Nunatsiavut proceeds. Prominent themes include

- the extent to which the assembly exhibits Inuit characteristics, as well as the nature of Inuit influences on the assembly;
- Euro-Canadian influences on assembly structure and operations;

- the nature of self-government as manifested in the organization and operation of the assembly;
- the assembly's role in furthering Nunatsiavut's promise and in dealing with its problems;
- the realities of "consensus government" – that is, the relationship between the assembly and the NEC, as well as the implications of that relationship for governance in Nunatsiavut; and
- changes in the assembly over its decade and a half of existence.

As mentioned in the preface/acknowledgments, *"We Are In Charge Here"* is directed at three distinct audiences: those interested in Indigenous self-government, those interested in legislatures, especially Westminster-style parliaments, and Labrador Inuit, especially those in the political elite.

Nunatsiavut: A Thumbnail Sketch

The Land

Contemplating the south shore of Labrador, Jacques Cartier was prompted to proclaim that this was "the land God gave to Cain"; doubtless he would have responded in similar fashion had he been passing the North Coast – Nunatsiavut (see map on page 2). As the easternmost outcropping of the Canadian Shield, this area exhibits the thin soil, granite barrens, low hills, and numerous lakes and bogs typical of the Shield. Boreal forest in southern Nunatsiavut gives way to subarctic tundra further north, with forests, primarily black spruce, becoming increasingly thin the further north one goes. The Torngat Mountains in the far north are the highest peaks in Canada east of the Rockies. The coast features rugged headlands and deep bays, with the cold Labrador Current bringing extensive land-fast ice in the winter and icebergs in summer. The weather is notoriously changeable; blizzards and fog can play havoc with transportation. Summer temperatures can reach into the twenties; on the other end of the spectrum, winter dips to minus twenty or minus thirty are common.

The Nunatsiavumiut

Present-day Labrador Inuit are descended from the Thule people, who moved across what is now northern Canada from west to east roughly a millennium ago, arriving in Labrador around the end of the fifteenth century. Prior to the arrival of the Thule, Labrador was occupied, perhaps for as long as thirty-five hundred years, by the Dorset people, and before them a Paleo-Eskimo people.[8] Strongly oriented to sea and its bounty of marine mammals, though also dependent on inland food sources, primarily caribou, the Inuit along the North

Coast of Labrador traditionally lived much as did other Inuit, save that their homeland was more heavily forested than those of other Inuit. Thus, Labrador Inuit share most important cultural characteristics with other Inuit across the Canadian Arctic. What has distinguished them has been their lengthy and extensive interaction with Europeans.

From the late sixteenth century on, Labrador Inuit intermittently encountered fishers, traders, missionaries, and whalers from Spain, France, and England. Profound change began in the 1760s with the arrival of Moravian missionaries from Germany. Supported by land grants from the British authorities, the Moravians established permanent communities that revolved around their missions and trading posts. "The Inuit of Labrador constitute a distinct regional group of Canada's Inuit with their own dialect of Inuktitut, their writing system and a unique history ... It is largely the distinct history of the Labrador Inuit as a people colonized by the Moravian missionaries, living in mission-centred communities, and subject to governmental policies made beyond the territory, that make the Labrador Inuit a distinct regional group in Canada."[9] Moravian influences on the Inuit were pervasive, expressed in both minor – fondness for brass band music – and substantial ways – extensive inculcation into Western, especially Christian, culture, widely seen as centrally important in shaping present-day Inuit identity. Labrador Inuit history and culture are examined more extensively in chapter 2.

The Claim and Its Beneficiaries

The population of Nunatsiavut is overwhelmingly Inuit, with non-Inuit comprising less than 10 per cent of the total. Within the settlement area are five communities: Nain, the administrative capital, is the largest, with 1,125 residents; Hopedale, the legislative capital, is home to 596 people; the population of Makkovik is 365; Rigolet stands at 327; and Postville is the smallest, with 188 residents.[10] Notable socio-cultural differences, carrying significant political implications, characterize Nunatsiavut's communities. John C. Kennedy has posited the concept of "Inuitness" in Labrador, referring to "knowledge and use of Inuttitut and to other cultural practices and beliefs that people of Inuit ancestry consider their own."[11] Kennedy identified a gradient of Inuitness, still evident today, with levels of Inuttut use and related cultural markers growing more prominent as one heads north, Nain and Hopedale being the most northern settlements.

All five communities are on the ocean but lack roads connecting them with other communities. Between the oftentimes problematic and unpredictable weather on the North Coast and the limited capacity of the local airstrips – none can accommodate planes significantly larger than a Twin Otter, and the Nain airstrip lacks runway lights for night landings – air travel can be difficult and expensive. Heavy or bulky freight can only be delivered by ocean-going cargo ships or ferries; after freeze-up, in late fall/early winter, even that option is not available. Accordingly, living costs are high. In recent years, residents of Nunatsiavut have complained repeatedly about inadequate and undependable cargo service.

As of March 2022, all told, 6,983 people were officially registered as LILCA beneficiaries (they are also called members), though only about 35 per cent (2,418) lived in Nunatsiavut proper.[12] Almost as many Nunatsiavut beneficiaries live in communities on or near the western end of Lake Melville, in southern Labrador – Happy Valley–Goose Bay, Mud Lake, Northwest River, and Sheshatshiu – which are outside the settlement area. Collectively, this area is known as Upper Lake Melville. Substantial numbers of Upper Lake Melville beneficiaries belong to either the NunaKatiget Inuit Community Corporation (Happy Valley–Goose Bay and Mud Lake; 1,878 beneficiaries) or the Sivunivut Inuit Community Corporation (Northwest River and Sheshatshiu; 259 beneficiaries). Creation of these and potentially other community corporations is contemplated in the LILCA, with details about their creation set out in the constitution; they are not local governments, as are the Inuit community governments in the five communities of Nunatsiavut proper. Rather, they are not-for-profit organizations designed to provide channels of information and representation for substantial concentrations of beneficiaries living outside the settlement area. Although the NG may delegate any of its jurisdictions, rights, and powers to them, in practice the services it provides through the community corporations are limited. Beneficiaries living in the Upper Lake Melville area are represented in the assembly by ordinary members as well as by the elected chairs of the community corporations. NG services extend to these beneficiaries, though they commonly complain that residents in the settlement area receive better services.

Some 2,428 beneficiaries living in Canada outside Nunatsiavut and Upper Lake Melville – more than a third of the total – are also covered by the LILCA. They elect members to the Nunatsiavut Assembly and are eligible for the most important programs and services offered by the NG, such as educational support, on the same basis as beneficiaries living in the settlement area. Elsewhere, some Canadian self-government agreements provide for services and political representation for citizens living outside their settlement areas. Citizens of the Nisga'a Nation living in certain British Columbia centres, for example, have representation in the Nisga'a Lisims Government and may receive services. Similarly, citizens of self-governing Yukon First Nations are entitled to services and a degree of representation so long as they live in the territory. Overall, however, none of these arrangements are nearly as encompassing as those of Nunatsiavut, which provide extensive programs and services to beneficiaries living anywhere in Canada.

As elsewhere in Inuit Nunangat (the Inuit homeland, encompassing Nunatsiavut, Nunavut, Nunavik in northern Quebec and the Inuvialuit Settlement Region in the Northwest Territories), the demographic profile of Nunatsiavumiut skews towards youth. As in other Inuit regions, inadequate housing and limited economic opportunities, partially reflecting weak infrastructure, contribute to social problems. Compared to the rest of Inuit Nunangat, levels of educational attainment tend to be higher in Nunatsiavut, but rates of Inuttut use are far lower; according to Statistics Canada, as of 2016 only about 25 per cent of Inuit in Nunatsiavut could conduct a conversation in Inuttut, and in fact, some NG officials suggest that this figure substantially overestimates fluency in Inuttut.[13] Language facility among beneficiaries outside Nunatsiavut is likely substantially lower.

In common with other regions of Inuit Nunangat, the Nunatsiavut economy is heavily dependent on public sector employment; this includes the NG, the Inuit community governments, and the federal and provincial governments (staff of the nursing stations and schools are provincial employees). Other important sectors of the economy in the settlement area include mining, primarily at the Vale nickel mine at Voisey's Bay, fishing, construction, transportation, and services. Data from the 2017 Aboriginal Peoples Survey indicate high rates of unemployment and non-participation in the labour force among Nunatsiavut Inuit.[14] A key player in the Nunatsiavut economy, representing important prospects for strengthening and diversifying the economy while providing training and employment to beneficiaries, is the Nunatsiavut Group of Companies (NGC). Wholly owned by the Labrador Inuit Capital Strategy Trust, an arm's-length economic development agency of the NG, NGC owns or has holdings in companies engaged in construction, transportation (including Air Borealis, the airline serving the North Coast), fisheries, logistics, and real estate. Nearly half the workforce employed by NGC companies in 2020 were beneficiaries.[15]

Methods

For a thinly populated, remote part of Canada, the people and history of the North Coast of Labrador have generated a rich literature, though much of the best analysis is found in unpublished theses. Considerable ethnographic and archaeological research has been conducted in Labrador in recent decades, with some truly remarkable accounts of post-contact Labrador Inuit society derived from the extensive, highly detailed written records of the Moravian missionaries who loomed so large in what was to become Nunatsiavut from the late eighteenth century on. Chapter 2 draws heavily on these literatures, with their insights also informing analyses in later chapters.

"We Are In Charge Here" covers the first four assembly sessions, the Fourth Assembly having been dissolved in April 2022. Beyond relying on the surprisingly

fulsome secondary literature on the Labrador Inuit, for information and insight I drew on a range of sources and methods. These include documents produced by the NG, most notably the full *Hansard* transcriptions of assembly sessions available on the NG website. I benefited enormously from the willingness of assembly members, NG staff, and others to respond candidly to questions in formal interviews and informal conversations. These interviews and discussions primarily occurred during three field trips to Hopedale between late 2017 and late 2019 to observe assembly sessions. In an instructive encounter with the realities of life in Nunatsiavut, one of the sessions was cancelled because bad weather prevented members and NG staff from arriving in Hopedale. On different trips, I spent time in Nain and in Happy Valley–Goose Bay meeting with NG officials. The 2016 Inuit Studies Conference in St. John's provided the opportunity for conversations with various NG officials and observers of Nunatsiavut politics. I listened to several sessions via the audio feed of assembly proceedings available through the NG website and watched the video streams of the March 2021 and January 2022 virtual sessions. Through the courtesy of the Clerk's Office, I viewed a number of video recordings of entire sessions, going back to 2008.[16] I reviewed the last half-dozen years of the stories and interviews posted on the OKâlaKatiget Society website. The "OK Society," as it's known (or sometimes just "OK"), is a non-profit communications service based in Nain, and an important source of information across Nunatsiavut; it is discussed at length in chapter 10. Finally, I monitored the NG website and its Facebook page and listened, mostly via podcast but occasionally live, to the daily CBC Radio show *Labrador Morning*.

As noted, the assembly produces and publishes a full *Hansard*. While I can't claim to have read every page, I did read a great many passages, brief and extended, of assembly debate, going back to the Transitional Assembly in 2006. In four separate rounds of reviewing *Hansard*, I at least scanned every page. Overall, the *Hansards* are invaluable resources, though they exhibit shortcomings, most of a minor, inconsequential nature, such as typographical errors or inaccurate renderings of what was actually said: "tenants" for "tenets," "coach here" for "co-chair," "for a set" for "assent," and so on. A more significant shortcoming is that, on occasion, the transcripts are incomplete; by way of illustration, the final page of *Hansard* for the June 2013 session clearly indicates that the assembly was adjourning for lunch and would return at 2:00 p.m., but no further transcript is provided.[17] Such apparent gaps occur several times in the assembly's first few years.

I conducted twenty-eight formal interviews with current and former members of the assembly, with current and former NG staff and with journalists, almost all in person, a few by telephone. In all instances, the interviews were done on a "not for attribution" basis; respondents were assured that no direct quotations or paraphrases from the interviews would be used in a way that might identify them. In several instances, interviewees were subsequently contacted by email for additional information. I also benefited a good deal from informal conversations with members and staff in the hallways of the assembly building and in the dining room of the Amaguk Inn, where most the members stay while in Hopedale. While none of these conversations are quoted in the book, they did provide useful background and context.

I also made use of interviews conducted by research assistants. In 2016 and 2017, Andrew Merrell conducted twenty-eight interviews, mostly in person but some by telephone, with candidates in Nunatsiavut elections, primarily ordinary member elections; a number of these interviewees either served in the assembly at the time of their interviews or had done so previously. Nicole McMahon conducted four telephone interviews with assembly members; Nicole and I jointly conducted a personal interview with one member. Some of Andrew's respondents agreed to have their comments attributed to them, but I have treated all interviews with the same regard for confidentiality. All otherwise unattributed quotations are taken from the interviews. Generally, I have not distinguished interviews with current and former assembly members and NG staff. It is accordingly important to recognize that a comment attributed to, say, "a Canada Constituency member" might have been made by either a current or former member.

The research was approved by the Nunatsiavut Government Research Advisory Committee.

Organization of the Book

The balance of the book unfolds as follows. Given the emphasis placed on the assembly as an institution of Inuit self-government, chapter 2 provides important context through an account of the distinctive cultural and political experiences of the Labrador Inuit, along with a more generic look at Inuit political culture. Chapter 3 explores, both conceptually and empirically, comprehensive land claims and the complex topic of self-government, with special reference to the Nunatsiavut experience. Chapter 4 sets out context for analysis of the assembly, beginning with a summary of the Nunatsiavut Constitution and the governance elements of the claim, emphasizing its self-government aspects as well as important distinctive features such as provisions to enhance the role of women in Nunatsiavut society and politics. The chapter also provides an overview of the institutions of government in Nunatsiavut as well as electoral processes and outcomes and briefly examines the sometimes fraught nature of beneficiary status. Chapter 5 looks at the assembly's setting, atmosphere, and members, including the variations among different categories of members and members' interpersonal relations. Chapter 6 outlines the basic structure and operations of the assembly, including procedures, committees, and services for members.

Chapter 7 reviews a range of processes and practices distinctive to the Nunatsiavut Assembly, such as the unusual frequency with which members are expelled from the assembly or dismissed from cabinet. Consensus government is the focus of chapter 8, encompassing relations between the NEC and non-NEC members as well as Inuit influences on the assembly. Chapters 9 and 10 examine the effectiveness of the assembly in terms of representation, policy influence, and accountability. Finally, after assessing the changes and continuities that have characterized the assembly, chapter 11 returns to the questions raised in the present chapter, especially with respect to the assembly's role in realizing Nunatsiavut's self-government aspirations.

Chapter Two

The Labrador Inuit: History, Society, Culture, and Political Institutions

Every society is a good deal more complex than it first appears. This truism certainly applies to Labrador Inuit society, the apparent simplicity of which conceals a variety of cultural and political components, including a highly distinctive history of interaction with Europeans, complex relations with people explicitly called "Settlers," who increasingly over time have had Inuit forebears, and a long history of formal political institutions quite unlike anything found elsewhere in the Inuit regions of Canada. "Despite the relatively low number of beneficiaries," two long-time observers of Nunatsiavut have written, "the diversity of social, cultural, and economic aspects is remarkable," not least because each Nunatsiavut community "has its own distinct social history, economy and land-use patterns … [Moreover] economic strategies, ties with other parts of Labrador, Quebec, and Newfoundland, and immigration patterns all differ widely, both between and within each community."[1]

By way of providing context for an analysis of the Nunatsiavut Assembly, this chapter examines the history, society, and culture of the Labrador Inuit, together with their political institutions, from the arrival in the eighteenth century of Moravian missionaries to the recent past, including the development of the Labrador Inuit Association (LIA) in the 1970s and the ethnic politics surrounding LIA's land claim. It begins with an account of the Moravians' experiences with and influence on the Inuit, followed by an overview of the complex social and political issues arising from the emergence of Settlers and their interactions with Inuit – issues that remain prominent to this day. The next section offers an overview of Inuit political culture generally and the notably distinct political culture of the Labrador Inuit and their political institutions. A final section briefly summarizes the politics of the North Coast from Newfoundland's entry into Confederation in 1949 to the finalization of the land claim.

The Pre-Moravian Period

Indigenous occupation of what is today Nunatsiavut by waves of various Paleo-Eskimo groups can be traced back over five thousand years.[2] Present-day Inuit are descendants of the Thule people, who migrated to the North Coast of Labrador, likely from southern Baffin Island, in the late fifteenth or early sixteenth centuries.[3] Recent scholarship suggests that contact between the Thule and the previous inhabitants, the Dorset people, was unlikely. More significantly, Lisa Rankin argues that the Thule migration to Labrador came "as a result of a decrease in their access to European metal and other items following the collapse of the Norse colonies in Greenland, and the coincidental beginning of the availability of such items on the southern coast of Labrador."[4] Thus, long before their first encounters with the Moravians, Labrador Inuit had substantial experience of Europeans and their ways.

Prominent anthropologist Diamond Jenness was convinced of the "extinction" of the Inuit of southern Labrador,[5] but recent research has confirmed "a lengthy and significant Inuit presence" in the region.[6] For reasons rooted more in the politics of land claims than in culture or ethnicity, many descendants of the southern Labrador Inuit came to identify as Métis, though recently their political leadership in the NunatuKavut Community Council (NCC, formerly the Labrador Metis Association) has strongly emphasized their Inuit heritage. The Thule did not establish habitations beyond the coast and nearby islands. Forays into the interior were limited in distance and duration since, regardless of the resources available in the unfamiliar forests, these areas were mysterious and dangerous, particularly because of the "Indians," forebears of today's Innu, whose homeland it was.

The Moravians

The influence of the Moravian missionaries on Inuit society was as distinctive as it was profound. Moreover, it continues today in manifold ways, from the geographic definition of Nunatsiavut to various important elements of Inuit culture.[7]

The Moravians, a minor Protestant sect from southern Germany who had been ministering to the Inuit of Greenland since 1733, made a brief and unsuccessful excursion to Labrador in 1764. Undeterred, they approached the British authorities seeking massive land grants in northern Labrador. The British, less concerned with bringing Christianity to the Inuit than in limiting Inuit presence near the increasingly important fisheries to the south, agreed, setting the stage for the founding of Nain in 1771, followed by Hopedale in 1782. Over the next century, other missions were established; several were abandoned, some after only a few decades.

The Moravians had learned from their mistakes in Greenland, so that "many of those measures which have been most strongly criticized with regard to the Moravian mission in western Greenland, were never transferred to Labrador. Thus, some aspects of social was [*sic*] less interfered with."[8] The Moravians were unusual among missionaries not only in emphasizing literacy and supporting Inuttut, but also in their strategy of attracting Inuit to permanent settlements and their practice of melding religious with commercial goals. Encouraging Inuit to settle around the missions was largely a control mechanism: having Inuit nearby meant that the Moravians could readily preach and promote conversion to Christianity, as well as discourage what they saw as objectionable traditional social and religious customs. The missionaries further hoped to isolate Christian Inuit from other European influences and from contact with unconverted "heathen" Inuit.

Mission stores served as incentives for Inuit to remain in the settlements, especially in hard times when meagre charitable food donations could be had. Initially at least, "the Eskimos were attracted to the mission more by the European goods and services that were available than by the Christian message."[9] The stores were expected to generate enough income to keep the missions afloat financially. Over the entire Mission period until the Moravians gave over their trading posts to the Hudson's Bay Company in 1926, significant tensions were evident between their religious and economic goals. Inuit were directly affected by the Moravians' commercial interests; we see this, for example, in their push for Inuit to prioritize cod fishing and fox trapping, which produced saleable merchandise, over hunting of seal and caribou, which had limited monetary value but were crucial sources of food and clothing.

Over time, many Labrador Inuit adopted settlement life for long stretches of the year, though hunting excursions to the interior and elsewhere on the coast were essential for survival. As intended, this facilitated the Moravians' conversion efforts, which in turn extensively affected Inuit culture, though the Moravians never exercised anything like total control over Inuit behaviour or beliefs.

Conversion entailed far more than exposure to Christian beliefs, bringing about "comprehensive reforms in all aspects of life."[10] Historians have documented how the Moravians taught Christian values and Protestant ethics while retaining what they saw as acceptable elements of Inuit society, such as self-sufficiency. As one put it, "the missionaries followed a policy of preserving Inuit (albeit Moravian-tinged) culture and positively reinforced those Inuit practices that were compatible with Moravian Christianity."[11] Jenness went as far as suggesting that the Moravians recognized the "undesirability of disturbing the native way of life except where it was absolutely necessary."[12] Carol Brice-Bennett offered a more critical view, arguing that the missionaries "seriously misunderstood the

Inuit culture and economy … [leading to] slow disintegration of social cohesion."[13] For anthropologist Helge Kleivan, the Moravian view of cultural retention "aimed only at selective preservation of Labrador Eskimo culture."[14]

That Inuit conversion to Christianity entailed far-reaching consequences is beyond doubt. At the same time, salient congruences should not be overlooked, as Ailsa Henderson suggests:

In some ways, Christianity offered not so much a radical break from traditional Inuit beliefs as a different venue within which to practise them … The speed with which Inuit took to Christianity could be seen as an example of their reputed ability to adapt. Instead, the values present in Christianity – the universe is animate, one must atone for one's sins, one benefits from good behaviour – required remarkably little transformation on the part of Inuit. The two belief systems were sufficiently similar to ensure their easy cohabitation … [yet] that Inuit and Christian values were not particularly different from one another should not lead one to underestimate the profound effect of Christianity on Inuit culture.[15]

One central element of Inuit society that the Moravians, unlike other missionaries across Turtle Island, were keen on preserving was language, a reflection of their commitment to education and literacy. The Moravians understood the centrality of language for the Inuit, though their encouragement of Inuttut was also designed "to keep Inuit isolated and protect the Moravians' special status among them."[16] Facilitating the missionaries' acceptance and promotion of Inuttut was the fact that they spoke German; until at least the second half of the nineteenth century, few, if any, spoke English.[17] Indeed, for a long period, reaching well into the twentieth century, teachers at the mission schools punished students for speaking English.[18]

The Moravians not only strove to preserve Inuttut, they also strongly encouraged literacy in it, as part of their commitment to education. The education of children, for the missionaries, was "a powerful way to effect change" to Christianity and away from Inuit "spiritual beliefs and cultural practices [they deemed] immoral."[19] With literacy, and thus the ability to read the Bible and other spiritual material essential for "achieving Christian enlightenment," the Moravians advocated universal education regardless of race, class, gender, or intelligence.[20] According to Kleivan, as early as 1840, illiteracy was all but unknown among young (converted) Inuit;[21] by the 1880s, all coastal Inuit could read and write in Inuttut, with some able to speak English.[22] As Brice-Bennett argued, "the achievement of literacy added a new dimension to Inuit society and introduced a cultural revolution, as dramatic and important as the adoption of Christianity itself."[23]

The missionary-fostered primacy of Inuttut literacy came to a crashing halt after Confederation with Canada in 1949, when the Government of Newfoundland, which took over responsibility for education from the Moravians, imposed teaching in English as a condition for school funding.[24] Still, prominent anthropologist John C. Kennedy maintained in 1987 that, in large part because of the missionaries' commitment to education, the Moravian legacy "prepared the Settlers and Inuit for the challenges of the 1980s to a degree few other native Canadians can match."[25]

Inuit Pushback

The Moravians' "well-meaning but misguided paternalism," entailing, among other things, "suppression of pre-contact Eskimo intellectual culture," made the Mission, according to one anthropologist, "the dominant force in all aspects of the economic, social, and religious life of the people of northern Labrador."[26] Jenness was even more definitive on the domination of the Moravians over the Inuit, claiming that until the First World War, "for all practical purposes, they [the Moravians] were the undisputed rulers of the north coast," running what amounted to "a benevolent theocracy."[27]

No one disputes the wide-ranging, indeed profound, Moravian influence. Yet a very different picture of Inuit-Moravian relations emerges from more recent, more extensive research. In her exhaustive study of nineteenth-century Labrador Inuit society, Brice-Bennett documented significant Inuit distrust of and opposition to the Moravians, as well as the Mission's failure to win Inuit respect,[28] concluding that the Inuit pushed back significantly against Moravian demands and pressures. Supporting evidence for this interpretation comes from, among others, Kleivan, who pointed out that Inuit simply rejected the Moravians' prohibition of dancing and tobacco;[29] from Peter Evans, whose research found that "Inuit resisted the Mission's discourses on happiness, fraternization, and frugality – among other things – through non-compliance, withdrawal, avoidance, and direct challenge";[30] and from Andrea Procter, who documented Inuit resistance to the Moravians' boarding (i.e., residential) schools, including stories of former boarding school students showing that Inuit "could challenge the missionaries' control and assert their independence," significant parental refusal to send children south to the schools, and, in at least one instance, an organized boycott of a school.[31]

"Inuit," Brice-Bennett argues, "retained command over their society and preserved their identity."[32] A telling example was the behaviour of the "chapel servants" or "chapel helpers," respected members of the Inuit community who were active in the church and were appointed by the missionaries as assistants.[33] Over time, the chapel servants became "a powerful elite among the Inuit over which they [the Moravians] were beginning to have difficulty controlling."[34]

It wasn't just that Inuit were not as subservient to the Moravians as might appear and as certain scholars have suggested. Evans has convincingly demonstrated not only that Inuit resistance was substantial, but also that it was rooted in traditional Labrador Inuit political institutions and political culture and that it significantly affected the development of political institutions during and after the Moravian period:

> many Inuit institutions, from the middleman traders of the 18th century to the village Elders of the 20th Century should be seen as vehicles for gathering and expressing Inuit resistance, and not merely as examples of Inuit accommodation of European cultural forms … Historically, Inuit evidenced active resistance to outside meddling, passive resistance through non-cooperation and withdrawal from engagement with external agencies, and cultural resistance, through which they created a hybrid Inuit-Moravian community mode by incorporating aspects of Christianity and European culture into new institutions.[35]

While Inuit resistance and pushback against the Moravians was significant, overall, the Moravian influence over Labrador Inuit society was profound. "During the long period of Moravian tutelage," argues Robert Paine,

> the Mission determined to keep the Inuit in Labrador alive as a distinct ethnic group; and the Mission went to particular pains to protect their wards against all other European contact along the coast. The Mission influence destroyed (usually deliberately) a good deal of the pre-contact Inuit culture, but what was destroyed was systematically replaced and blended with the elements that were allowed to remain. In short, a new ethnicity emerged in which these wards of the Mission became Moravian Eskimos.[36]

A final noteworthy point about the Moravians and their influence: Brice-Bennett has argued that, whereas women were "used as pawns" in traditional Inuit society, the missionaries substantially enhanced women's position. Moravian rule, she wrote,

> enhanced women's position and gave them a security that was lacking in traditional Inuit society … By defending the position of their female converts and providing the option of not marrying, the missionaries enabled women to have more independence and status than they could have achieved in traditional Inuit society … The Moravian system for maintaining social order and control within the community enhanced the role of women and provided them with the opportunity to attain social and political influence.[37]

Settlers and Their Descendants

In recent years, the term "Settler" has entered common usage, in Canada and elsewhere, as a label for people of non-Indigenous origin. Ironically, the word is rarely encountered in Labrador today, yet for the better part of two centuries those explicitly called Settlers exerted an outsized social, economic, and political influence. This section looks at the history of Inuit-Settler relations and the place of the Settlers' descendants in present-day Nunatsiavut and its politics.

Tectonic shifts in Labrador's political landscape over the past few decades have profoundly affected central elements of Indigenous identity, with far-reaching social and political implications. Anthropologist John C. Kennedy has recently written that "the politics of Aboriginality has fundamentally changed Labrador. Labrador peoples are reconsidering who they are; openly discussing their social origin, and reflecting on how their culture, that tacit set of customary rules and behaviours, relates to their declared identity."[38] A thorough analysis of Indigenous identity politics in Nunatsiavut, let alone all of Labrador, is beyond the scope of this chapter, and indeed my competence. However, given the central importance of culture and identity throughout this book, underlined by the constant attention assembly members devote to such issues, a brief overview is warranted. Moreover, beyond the importance of the Settler element within Nunatsiavut, understanding Nunatsiavumiut and their government entails appreciating their relationships to their Indigenous neighbours, the Innu and the NunatuKavummiut, and their political organizations.

One element of Indigenous identity and politics in Labrador is straightforward and unchanging and has nothing to do with Settlers: the clear distinction, despite nomenclature that can prove misleading to outsiders, between Inuit and Innu. Quite simply, "Inuit and Innu were and remain distinct peoples. Their languages and cultures were and remain completely different."[39] Once known as Montagnais or Naskapi, the Innu are First Nations living throughout Labrador and eastern Quebec, with concentrations in the communities of Natuashish (between Hopedale and Nain) and Sheshatshiu on Lake Melville. The roughly 2,200 Innu are represented politically by the Innu Nation, which has been pursuing a land claims agreement for many years. The Innu are a good deal less willing to compromise than the Inuit in dealing with the federal government: witness their long-stalled land claims negotiations,[40] and their refusal to accept Prime Minister Justin Trudeau's apology regarding the legacy of boarding schools in Labrador.[41] Relations between the Nunatsiavut Government and the Innu Nation have often been difficult, especially around land and resource issues, such as caribou harvesting, though they have adopted similar stances towards NunatuKavut claims for recognition.

In initially seeking to isolate the Inuit gathered around their missions from outside, primarily European, influences, the Moravians were most concerned about those they called "Southlanders," traders and fishers and unconverted Inuit ("degenerate Esquimaux" to the missionaries[42]) to the south of the lands granted the Moravians. Later, as intermarriage between Inuit and Europeans produced offspring of mixed cultural background, the Moravians labelled them, as well as Europeans, "Settlers." Geographic patterns of Settler habitation meant that for several decades it was possible for the Moravians to keep "their" Inuit separate from Settlers, but by the 1850s Settlers' growing numbers and their increasingly frequent interaction with settlement Inuit forced the missionaries to accept Settlers into their communities and their church, though they continued to treat the two groups differently – for example, by teaching Inuit children in Inuttut and Settler children in English.[43]

Although in many ways the Settler lifestyle was similar to that of the Inuit, the two groups remained distinct. Kennedy maintains that from the mid-nineteenth century on, Settlers and Inuit "would increasingly see themselves as separate peoples."[44] Well into the twentieth century, according to Kleivan, the primary indicator of Settlers was their speaking English, and all, "whatever their ethnic background, identify themselves with the white man and his culture."[45]

Writing of a mixed community in the 1960s, Shmuel Ben-Dor emphasized that "the social structure of northern Labrador admits two groups only – the Inuit and the Settlers." According to Ben-Dor,

> the attitudes of the Inuit to the Settler and vice versa are an integral part of the world-views and practices of each group; they are completely different. The Inuit maintain a social organization which is based on kinship ties. All individuals, both Inuit or non-Inuit, who are situated outside one's own kin group are regarded with suspicion … the Settler attitude toward the Inuit derives from his confidence that the Settler way of life is superior to any other form. This ethnocentric view assumes a defensive note in discussions about city life, but it finds an aggressive expression in the attitude of Inuit. The Settlers link themselves with the rest of the "civilized world" which does not include the Inuit.[46]

For their part, Inuit generally regarded Settlers as culturally and biologically inferior to "real" Inuit and "real" whites.[47]

As late as the 1970s, Hugh Brody's contribution to the Labrador Inuit Association's exhaustive research on Inuit land use and occupancy, *Our Footprints Are Everywhere*, observed that "Labrador still maintains three streams of life – Indian, Inuit and Settler. These streams have merged a little – overflowing, so to speak, their traditional banks, and shifting their time-worn channels. Yet they remain distinct, real and vital to the well-being of those who have been raised within them."[48] Not only were these groupings distinct, but relations across them could become ugly, marked by social separation and distrust, even overt racism. When the provincial government closed the two northernmost Inuit communities, Nutak and Hebron, in the 1950s, Inuit were relocated to various North Coast communities. Many of the relocated, especially those who went to Makkovik, a predominantly Setter community, experienced undisguised discrimination and hostility, symbolized by the use of the derogatory epithet "skimo," as was sometimes the case in other communities, and by physical assaults.[49]

Especially notable are the long-term consequences of the Inuit-Settler divide and the Moravians' role in perpetuating it. Writing in 1978, Barrett Richling noted that "the structural cleavages which followed from the missionization process defined the areas of conflict which persist between these groups [Inuit and Settlers] in the contemporary setting."[50] The missionaries, Procter argued four decades later, "fostered the notion that the only 'real' Inuit were Moravian Inuit – a narrative that continues to impact the ways in which governments and fellow Labradorians regard descendants of non-Moravian Inuit in both Nunatsiavut and NunatuKavut today."[51]

The differential impact of the Moravian Mission, which was geographically limited to the North Coast and did not extend into southern Labrador, continues to have profound political consequences. Throughout Labrador, as Kennedy points out, Inuit had long mixed with Europeans, so that the northern Labrador Settlers and people who would subsequently become known as Métis and later as Inuit, in south-central Labrador, "were essentially one people who would be divided administratively."[52]

Perhaps the most notable aspect of this "administrative division" is the close correspondence between the geographic definition of the Labrador Inuit Settlement Area – Nunatsiavut – and the lands overseen by the Moravian missions. Although rooted in Moravian influence dating from the eighteenth and nineteenth centuries, the formal, "administrative" division emerged from the politics of Indigenous organizations, especially with regards to land claims negotiations, which began in the 1970s.

Modern Indigenous political mobilization came to Labrador in 1973 when the Labrador Inuit Association was established as a branch of the Inuit Tapirisat of Canada (ITC, now Inuit Tapiriit Kanatami), the national Inuit organization. The following year, the Native Association of Newfoundland and Labrador (NANL) was founded to pursue First Nations interests. At the outset of the land claims era, the federal government stipulated that it would deal with only one Labrador Indigenous group, leading to deterioration in the initially cooperative relations between LIA and NANL. "Both groups courted the Labrador Settlers ... In the end, federal pressures convinced Inuit to ignore ITC's recommendation that all LIA members speak Inuttitut and, in the face of vigorous competition from NANL, to offer Settlers of Northern Labrador, many with Inuit ancestors, full membership in October 1974."[53] This decision reflected not only a political calculus, but also elders' preference for a geographic rather than linguistic definition of Inuit identity, so as not to divide communities within the settlement area.[54] The term "Settler" fell out of general usage, replaced by *Kablunângajuit* (almost Inuit), the wording used in the land claim. As one sociologist noted, "I can recall no one referring to themselves as 'Settler' during my two years [1975–7] in Labrador."[55]

Acceptance of Settlers by the LIA almost certainly contributed to the successful negotiation of the Labrador Inuit Land Claims Agreement, but it had other consequences as well. "Once Settlers accepted the invitation to join the LIA," Kennedy writes, "the long-term demographic and linguistic trends made it obvious that they would dominate the LIA and, after settlement of the land claim, Nunatsiavut." He goes on to cite a comment made by the LIA president in a 1993 interview: "hindsight may show that the LIA made a terrible mistake, allowing in the Kablunângajuit. The real Inuit will have dug their own grave."[56] At least some Labrador Inuit accept this analysis; consider, for example, the interview comments of an unsuccessful candidate for ordinary member: "When you look at who is controlling things in the Nunatsiavut government, it's the Settlers mostly who control things and who have controlled things, because when the LIA formed in the 70s, the elders in the community voted to accept the Settlers into the organization ... Now there's so much inter-marriage between Inuit and Settlers that you can't really make that distinction now."

The upshot has been that, "under the Labrador Inuit Land Claims Agreement, Settlers/Kablunângajuit with or without Inuit ancestry, are legally Inuit and today constitute most of the population of Nunatsiavut."[57] Moreover, given the claim's provisions offering Nunatsiavut membership to those able to demonstrate a "connection" to the settlement area, it is possible for some of mixed ancestry to become Nunatsiavut beneficiaries. "Southeastern Labrador people," are said to "apply [to become Nunatsiavut beneficiaries] mainly because of the Inuit government's generous Non-Insured Health Benefits program,"[58] and are accepted because they can demonstrate a connection to Nunatsiavut (i.e., the settlement area). During recent fieldwork in the Sandwich Bay region of southern Labrador, Kennedy found that, "though legally Inuit under the land claim, none of these ... beneficiaries self-identified as Inuit ... [and] would not call themselves Inuit, especially in front of an Inuttitut-speaking Inuk."[59]

By 1986, a Labrador Metis Association (LMA) had emerged, formed by people of mixed Inuit-European ancestry around Lake Melville who "felt boxed in" by the LIA and Innu land claims.[60] In 1998, LMA changed its name to Labrador Métis Nation and in 2010 to the NunatuKavut Community Council (NunatuKavut is an Inuttut word meaning "our ancient land"). In the late 1990s, Lawrence Dunn wrote, "many Settlers in Labrador of mixed Euro-Aboriginal blood who are ineligible for membership in the Labrador Inuit Association (LIA) have rejected the 'Settler' label and have politically embraced the Métis identity."[61] Though formal political organization is a recent development, the essentials of Labrador Inuit-Métis identity are well established: "the blended culture patterns that emerged from the union of Inuit and European populations maintained strong ties to Inuit traditions, and it is the enduring legacy of Inuit of southern Labrador that has defined Inuit-Métis culture from the eighteenth to the twenty-first century."[62]

Although as recently as 2014, Kennedy observed that many NCC members were more comfortable calling themselves Métis than Inuit,[63] NCC president Todd Russell vociferously emphasizes, as does the NCC's website, *Inuit* culture, identity, and rights.[64]

Relations between the NCC and the Nunatsiavut Government (NG) have at times been decidedly antagonistic. As the Inuit claim was coming into effect, Métis Nation leaders described it as "legislated genocide."[65] In 2019, NCC signed a memorandum of agreement with the federal government preparatory to negotiations on Indigenous rights, self-determination, land, and other resources. In response, the Innu Nation launched a lawsuit stressing that "the Innu of Labrador do not, and have never, accepted that NCC or any of its predecessors represent an Aboriginal people of Canada within the meaning of s. 35 of the Constitution Act, 1982."[66] The NG, initially non-committal, has sought intervenor status in the suit in support of the Innu Nation position, and in September 2021 mounted an uncompromising attack on the legitimacy of the proposed NCC claim. Citing a need to respond to uncertainty and concerns among beneficiaries, the NG issued a statement asserting that "the NCC has not established that it is a collective that is entitled to Inuit rights." It did acknowledge "that while some members of the NCC may themselves have some Indigenous ancestry and backgrounds, the NCC has no viable claim to land in Labrador."[67] In an interview with CBC's *Labrador Morning*, Nunatsiavut president Johannes Lampe explained that the NG's action stemmed from a need to protect Labrador Inuit and their rights; "we'll do whatever we have to do to protect our land claim," he said. Asked about NCC members who might qualify to be Nunatsiavut beneficiaries, Lampe indicated that this was not about to happen in the immediate future.[68]

Long-time observers of and participants in Labrador Inuit society tend to agree with the literature that the claim negotiation process and the creation of Nunatsiavut profoundly affected identities and inter-group relations. One commented, "the Inuit/Settler divide that was openly discussed in the 1970s and 1980s is now not really politically correct … [though] the awareness of these social divisions still lingers." Indeed, while overt divisions and hostilities between Settlers and Inuit have largely disappeared, distrust and tension remain among older generations. Some older Inuit are said to be resentful of people who, thirty or forty years ago, saw themselves as Settlers or Métis and exhibited disdain for Inuit, but who now call themselves Inuit. "If you were from north of North West River," one Settler/Kablunângajuk from Hopedale recalled in 2011, "you were called Inuit, even though we weren't Inuit. But they didn't call us Inuit, they called us 'dirty skimos.' Now today, some of those very same people are trying to get into the Nunatsiavut Government. They're trying to be Inuit themselves now."[69] Such distinctions have generally lost their relevance for younger generations, who uniformly and proudly identify as Inuit regardless of their parents' and grandparents' backgrounds and views.[70]

Inuit Political Culture

Inuit traditionally conceived of human society and the natural environment holistically, so that the notion of distinguishing Inuit political culture from overall traditional Inuit culture entails a certain artificiality. Still, an assessment of Inuit cultural influences on an explicitly political modern-day institution such as the Nunatsiavut Assembly requires attention to Inuit political culture. Moreover, important cultural traits, such as adaptability, that may not be inherently political in nature may have substantial effects on political institutions and governmental operations. Accordingly, this section looks broadly at Inuit political culture, while the following section focuses on Labrador Inuit political culture and political institutions.

The starting point must be the recognition that nothing like a uniform Inuit political culture ever existed. Rather, significant regional and temporal variations are clearly evident. Marc Stevenson's study for the Royal Commission on Aboriginal Peoples, *Traditional Inuit Decision-Making Structures*,[71] for example, highlights very different authority patterns and decision-making processes among Inuit across various parts of what is now Nunavut. As well, as will be seen, political patterns and processes among the Labrador Inuit vary significantly from those found in Nunavut.

The literature does identify a number of common, if not necessarily universal, Inuit traits that may bear directly on matters political. These include "the pragmatic adaptability that characterizes much of Eskimo behavior";[72] responsiveness to others' needs and reciprocity;[73] emotional control;[74] egalitarianism;[75] self-reliance, resourcefulness, and perseverance;[76] the primacy of the group over the individual;[77] avoidance or mitigation of conflict;[78] cooperation ("the bedrock of Inuit society");[79] and a strong non-interference imperative (on occasion leading to discomfort in exercising authority),[80] linked to a distaste for inquisitiveness and for questions or interruption of a person speaking.[81]

Throughout Inuit Nunangat, including Labrador, an important, if infrequently employed, mechanism of social control entailed ostracism, potentially extending to outright expulsion, of those whose behaviour was deemed seriously unacceptable.[82] Significantly, the Moravians also resorted to expulsion of disruptive persons or those thought physically or morally dangerous from church services and, occasionally, from communities. Chapter 7 explores a possible connection between Inuit and Moravian proclivities for expelling those guilty of serious transgressions and a distinctive feature of the Nunatsiavut Assembly.

Save in Labrador (as discussed below), Inuit society, although marked by strong social control, lacked formal authority structures: "no institution of authority, no organization of power … no group of individuals constitutes an assembly or equivalent to government."[83] As Stevenson documented, in parts of the Eastern Arctic, decision making could be decidedly authoritarian, but overall, decisions were taken by consensus. This typically involved extensive discussion leading to an outcome that was generally acceptable, but certainly no voting.[84] According to Pauktuutit Inuit Women of Canada, "Inuit leaders at every level of political involvement are still bound by traditional values and can see their public support dwindle it they go against these values too often."[85]

Labrador Inuit Political Culture and Political Institutions

To be sure, the political culture of the Labrador Inuit entails important elements of Inuit political culture, as outlined above. Adaptability and flexibility, for example, are key Labrador Inuit traits: "The ability to adapt to changes, environmental and social, by maintaining a diversity of skills, as well as mental and social flexibility to adjust lifestyles, are the defining characteristics of the Labrador Inuit."[86] Still, as Richling has noted, compared to that of other regions of the Canadian North, the Labrador Inuit experience has been "unique."[87] Labrador Inuit had earlier and far more extensive interactions with Europeans than other Inuit and had been living in permanent settlements in substantial numbers for a century and a half before other Canadian Inuit. Whereas F.G. Vallee could write that "the fact the Eskimo had no codified law, no political structure, no specialized institution to exert authority is so well known as to make comment on it superfluous,"[88] throughout the Moravian period, and indeed prior to that, the Labrador Inuit did have political structures and authority-wielding institutions. Relatedly, the reticence among Inuit to push back against the ideas and directions of Europeans emphasized by Vallee was, in Labrador, tempered by significant opposition and resistance.[89] All told, "the Labrador Inuit political culture was an exceptionally unique historical and cultural development."[90]

These perhaps surprising observations about the distinctiveness and significance of Labrador Inuit political organization are supported by Peter Evans's thorough and convincing analysis of Labrador resistance and identity from 1771 to 1959. Other historians and anthropologists have drawn similar conclusions. Evans's central argument is that

> Labrador Inuit political history may be traced through the development of distinctive Inuit institutions that formed or were transformed in encounters with a succession of whalers, fishers, missionaries, traders, and finally, state agents, over the course of the late 18th to mid-20th centuries. These institutions and their different spatial registers were adept at gathering and expressing Inuit resistance, and were informed by a wider cultural system that stressed management of personal emotions, intellect, and avoidance of conflict.[91]

Notably, while new forms of political leadership and organization emerged among the Inuit during the Moravian period, they drew not only upon the precepts of camp life but also on long-standing institutions and processes:

> Inuit maintained … settings and occasions when opinions could be voiced more freely. Katimaks, "Men's meetings," often referred to as "Councils" in Moravian reports, were a pillar of Labrador Inuit culture from pre-contact … Men's meetings mediated disputes between parties in the absence of recognized authority in large gatherings by providing another setting where the prohibitions on speech that presided in camp life could be circumvented.[92]

Men's meetings were not simply amorphous gatherings but were characterized by considerable institutionalization: "they appear to have been the very height of formality, since their appearance over a 200-year period implies the existence of protocols, expectations, forms of political rhetoric, and social contracts. Their contents – speech-making, consensual decision-making, expectations of attendance, etc … – imply formality."[93] For Kleivan, the men's meetings exhibited an "almost institutional nature."[94]

For their part, the Moravians created two sets of institutions that took on considerable political import. From earliest days, as mentioned above, they appointed well-known, pious Inuit as chapel "helpers" or "servants," but it quickly became evident that these chapel helpers had retained Inuit norms, and could not be counted on to be subservient: "The selection and success of chapel helpers hinged on Inuit notions of leadership; otherwise their authority and presence, their ability to act as brokers between Inuit and Mission, would have been untenable." Moreover, "the chapel servants led all the serious protests in Inuit history."[95]

Early in the twentieth century, the missionaries established elected elders' councils in the North Coast communities. According to Richling, this development "followed directly from a pre-contact tradition of collective political authority exercised by older men within local bands." Initially, the elders' councils were subject to Moravian influence – for example, elections were held in church – but before long the elders came to serve "as local political leaders whose influence in many cases paralleled that of the missionaries in effecting social control."[96] Again, Inuit influence on the operation of the councils came to the fore: the missionaries "seem to have regarded the new elders institution as a derivative of the Herrnhut community model [a Moravian ideal]. However, it was also animated by traditional Inuit governance cultural values, especially in its emphasis on katimaat, or public meetings, as venues where opinions could be freely spoken and gathered. In this sense, it also represented an Inuit refusal to fully recognize Moravian claims to authority."[97] The missionaries

> established roles for community leaders, laying a foundation for Inuit empowerment while simultaneously introducing social hierarchies. In this realigned social

organization there were opportunities for Inuit to assume decision-making roles, to voice dissent (within limits determined by the missionaries), and to rise to leadership positions … Community leadership fell to the councils of Elders in each settlement. These councils exerted considerable social and political influence right up until the time of Newfoundland's confederation with Canada in 1949.[98]

The councils were important in another way as well, in that elders "played a critical role in ensuring that Inuit values were not lost in changing times and that consultation and collective decision making continued to guide new Inuit-led organizations."[99]

A noteworthy socio-political division marked the elders' councils. Reflecting their emphasis on their white, European origins, Settlers declined the opportunity to take on village elderships, seeing them as Inuit institutions, and thus did not feel bound by their advice or direction.[100]

Inuit Identity and Post-Confederation Politics

In his overview of recent Labrador Inuit politics, David Lough notes that "in less than a decade, the Labrador Inuit had gone from being 'Eskimos' with no organization or recognition as Aboriginal peoples to negotiating a thorough case for a land claim."[101] In an important sense, this was not surprising, given their experiences with political institutions, as set out above. As Evans argues,

> Labrador Inuit of the 1940s had already been negotiating self-determination for decades … The Elders, with their maligaksait, their written laws, and together with local white patrons and middlemen on town Committees, constituted a more advanced form of social governance than was found in much of rural Newfoundland. Men's meetings – enlivened with Inuit political rhetoric, consensual decision-making, and written issuances – were a highly developed Inuit institution by the time of Confederation, and constituted a sort of Inuit bureaucracy that was unique in the Canadian North.[102]

In another sense, however, the political advances of the Labrador Inuit in the 1970s and later were notable in that the post-Confederation period marked the nadir of their ability to control their own affairs. The Terms of Union by which Newfoundland was brought into Canadian Confederation in 1949 contained no reference whatsoever to Indigenous peoples.[103] Moreover, not only did Confederation bring state involvement into the lives of Labrador Inuit to an extent previously unknown, but the centres of state power were now far removed, in St. John's and Ottawa, and were neither knowledgeable about nor attentive to the needs and desires of the Labrador Inuit. "Confederation," Evans has written, "inaugurated a period of state-sponsored welfare administration that altered nearly every aspect of Inuit culture that arose out of the nineteenth century. This period's most devastating impact was felt within the political system that had animated Inuit community life prior to Confederation."[104] To take but one example, the decline of Inuttut dates to Confederation, with the switch from Inuttut to English for schooling mandated by the provincial government.

The landmark events of the post-Confederation period for the Labrador Inuit were the closing by the provincial government – without consultation – of the two northernmost communities, Nutak and Hebron, in 1956 and 1959, respectively. These closures led to serious social disruption, the effects of which are still felt today: "the forced relocations from Hebron and Nutak in the 1950s, as well as the more general social and economic impacts of centuries of colonialism, have caused lasting social divisions and inequalities among Inuit in Nunatsiavut. Some have benefitted from the land claim settlement and new economic opportunities, but others have felt further marginalized."[105]

Paradoxically, one of the most potentially unsettling developments of the new, post-Confederation governance regime turned out to play a significant role in Inuit political mobilization. One of the rationales for closing Nutak and Hebron had been to supply labour for a proposed uranium mine near Makkovik. The provincial government, without consulting the Inuit or the Innu, had given a British mining company a long-term lease on a large tract of land for exploration and development. For economic reasons, the project was abandoned in the late 1950s, only to be resurrected in the early 1970s. By then, Indigenous peoples across Canada had taken to actively articulating and defending their rights; in Labrador this meant significant opposition to the Brinex uranium project. The mine proposal became "a catalyst for Labradorians to organize politically and to articulate their concerns and their values about large-scale resource development and about their role as citizens and as Aboriginal Peoples. 'The Brinex hearings were an important social turning point,' argues John Kennedy. 'They pulled people together and let them see that their opinions were important.'"[106] Concern about the mine, which did not go ahead, contributed to the emergence of the LIA, which in turn used the issue "to foster a sense of collective identity and vision among people on the north coast."[107] And yet, deep-seated ambiguities about identity were evident among the LIA members cited in Dunn's research in the late 1970s, so that "some came to see the [LIA] eligibility criteria and the organization overseeing membership as suspect, even capricious."[108]

When Newfoundland joined Confederation in 1949, "the idea, let alone the reality, of a self-governing Inuit homeland in northern Labrador would have seemed unimaginable."[109] Of course, much the same could have been said about significant Indigenous self-determination anywhere in Canada at the time. Still, through their literacy, their experience of political institutions, and their dealings with the Moravians, "by the late arrival of the state on the scene, Inuit had amassed a storehouse of political know-how related to self-governance, oratory, tact, diplomacy, intrigue, resistance, and representation. This was an important body of knowledge, equal in importance to the practical environmental and ecological knowledge around which contemporary discourse about Inuit epistemologies are focused."[110]

The LIA first approached the federal government with its land claim in 1977,[111] but it took years of oftentimes difficult negotiations before an Agreement-in-Principle (AiP) was initialled in 1999. Over nearly three decades of negotiations, "the Inuit had to contend with reluctant governments, unclear jurisdictions, inflexible positions, and unrelenting mineral explorations and other developments on claimed lands."[112] Agreement was reached, and the AiP quickly transformed into a formal agreement, in no small measure because of eagerness on the part of both the federal government and the often recalcitrant provincial government to eliminate possible hurdles in the way of the development of the massive Voisey's Bay nickel-copper deposit between Nain and Hopedale, discovered in 1993. Following ratification by 76 per cent of eligible LIA members in May 2004 and the passage of enabling legislation in Parliament and in the Newfoundland and Labrador House of Assembly, the final agreement was signed in January 2005, and came into force the following December.[113] A detailed constitution for the NG had been approved in a referendum by claim beneficiaries in early 2002 (see chapter 4).

Labrador Inuit Exceptionalism

Henderson's summary of Inuit political culture in Nunavut includes the following observation:

> Inuit political culture identified ideal behaviours that governed the distribution of resources, collective decision making, and leadership. It developed mechanisms of social control to ensure compliance with those ideal behaviours. However widespread those practices, Inuit society lacked an institutional bedrock for its political culture. This is not a normative statement about the value of Inuit culture or its state of development; rather, it merely indicates that the absence of political institutions denied Inuit culture a buffer against the successive influences of missionaries and government officials.[114]

In contrast, the Labrador Inuit did have significant political institutions. While not nearly as extensive or powerful as those found in European societies, they did serve to some extent as a "buffer" against outside forces, thereby helping retain Inuit culture and granting a modicum of control over Inuit affairs. They also represented important precedents when serious negotiations with the state over Inuit rights and self-determination began late in the twentieth century.

As early as the mid-nineteenth century, while literacy among the Labrador Inuit "deepened Inuit pietism and the Inuit-Mission conversation," the widespread ability to read, and especially write, "created a new sphere for expressing personal or social grievances and goals."[115] Important implications of the widespread emphasis on education include the LIA's strong promotion, from its early days, of more extensive Inuit involvement in education, which in turn led to increased attention to self-government.[116]

In its quest for self-determination and self-government, the LIA, like many other Indigenous organizations, developed and promoted cultural constructs – what it meant to be a Labrador Inuk, especially but not exclusively with regard to Settlers – with a very political edge.[117] The NG, including the assembly, is very much affected by the Inuit identity that has emerged in the past few decades.

The theme of this chapter has been the distinctiveness of the Labrador Inuit experience, culturally, socially, and politically, by comparison with the experiences of other Indigenous peoples in Canada, especially those elsewhere in Inuit Nunangat. Important elements of the profound and extensive Moravian influence – the inculcation of Christian values and practices, the stress on education and literacy in Inuttut, the long-standing habitation in permanent settlements, the sharp demarcation between Inuit and Settlers, the recognition and acceptance of traditional political institutions – have powerfully shaped political developments in Labrador to this day. While such factors don't necessarily map directly onto the identity of present-day Nunatsiavumiut and their politics, including the structure and operation of the assembly, neither can they be relegated to the status of irrelevant historical relics. Indeed, a study of the Nunatsiavut Assembly must recognize that the Labrador Inuit "organized their society around values and practices that remain important today."[118] This is evident in chapter 4, which sets the immediate political context for the assembly through an account of governance in Nunatsiavut in terms of its constitution, organization, and politics. In the meantime, however, the next chapter examines the elements of comprehensive land claims and the nature of Indigenous self-government, with special attention to Nunatsiavut.

Chapter Three

Comprehensive Land Claims and Indigenous Self-Government

Concepts of Indigenous self-government vary widely, as do the real-life forms it takes. Accordingly, it is worth prefacing this account of one particular self-governing institution, the Nunatsiavut Assembly, with an examination of the nature of self-government more broadly, and a consideration of what is entailed in successful Indigenous self-governments. Such is the purpose of this chapter. While the focus of this book, the Nunatsiavut governance model, ranks among the strongest, most autonomous self-government regimes in Canada, the following discussion includes insights developed from across the entire range of self-government institutions.

Inuit self-government in Labrador – the powers, structure, operation, and legitimacy of the Nunatsiavut Government (NG) and the assembly – is rooted in a settled comprehensive land claim, the Labrador Inuit Land Claims Agreement (LILCA). It is difficult to overstate the importance of the claim, not just for the NG, but for all Nunatsiavumiut. The chapter thus begins with a brief overview of comprehensive land claims, interspersed with features of LILCA. The balance of the chapter is given over to Indigenous self-government, beginning with a brief discussion of the nature of self-government. This is followed by an overview of the various forms of self-government currently operating in Canada and a review of the insights offered by the wide-ranging literature on self-government. A final section looks at the vociferous, hard-line criticism of land claims and self-government processes and outcomes put forward by certain Indigenous scholars.

Comprehensive Land Claims

The federal government accepts two distinct types of land claims.[1] Specific claims are designed to rectify wrongs against First Nations relating to Canada's implementation, or often non-implementation, of historic treaties.[2] This could involve failure to provide promised financial and other benefits, inadequate protection of First Nations lands, or other failures of implementation. Hundreds of specific claims have been settled, with hundreds more under negotiation or pending. Typically, settlements entail financial compensation; rarely, if ever, do they involve governance matters. By contrast, comprehensive claims are far more wide-ranging, involving financial compensation, land ownership, governance provisions, and other elements.

Centuries of treaty-making between British and Canadian authorities and various Indigenous peoples ended in 1923. However, huge swathes of Canada, including northern Quebec and Labrador, had never been conquered militarily, nor had treaties been signed between the local Indigenous peoples and the British, later Canadian, Crown, rendering tenuous the Canadian state's assumption that it owned and controlled the land.[3] Following the Supreme Court of Canada's landmark *Calder* decision in 1973, the federal government began to negotiate what came to be called comprehensive land claims with Indigenous organizations.[4] "Comp claims," as they're sometimes called, were designed to address uncertainty about ownership and control of lands where no treaties existed. Thus claims were only entertained in areas not already subject to treaty, though an important exception was made in the Northwest Territories, where implementation of Treaties 8 and 11 was judged to have been so fundamentally flawed as to warrant negotiation of a claim. A central objective for the federal government in comprehensive claims was certainty and finality as to jurisdiction over lands; accordingly, extinguishment of Indigenous title became a central requirement for settling claims.

The first comprehensive land claim, the James Bay and Northern Quebec Agreement, was finalized in 1975 between the Inuit and Cree of northern Quebec and the federal and Quebec governments. By the 1980s and '90s, extensive claims negotiations were underway, primarily in the territorial North. While several came to fruition, others, including that of the Labrador Inuit, dragged on without resolution. Initially, the federal government refused to consider Indigenous demands for self-government in land claim negotiations, though in some instances separate, parallel claims and self-government processes were underway. In 1995, as part of its recognition that section 35 of the *Constitution Act, 1982*, included Indigenous peoples' inherent right to self-government, Ottawa agreed that self-government proposals could form part of land claims negotiations. Settlement of several claims with self-government provisions followed, including, in 2005, the LILCA, a central component of which was establishment of the NG.

Two essential facts about comprehensive claims agreements highlight their significance. First, the claims are – and are recognized as such by the Government of Canada – treaties. A treaty is no run-of-the-mill government agreement, but rather a solemn, binding covenant between sovereign entities. Not for nothing do Indigenous peoples refer to treaties as sacred. Second, section

35 proclaims that, along with other "Aboriginal and treaty rights," Indigenous rights under existing or future land claims agreements are "recognized and affirmed." Thus, once settled, comprehensive land claims become part of Canada's constitutional framework. As of 2022, twenty-six comprehensive claims have been finalized, mostly in the North – the territories, Labrador, and northern Quebec – but also in southern British Columbia. Others are in various stages of negotiation in southern Canada as well as in Labrador.

The Labrador Inuit experience in achieving LILCA was typical of the comprehensive claims process, not least in the extraordinary length of time it took. The process has varied somewhat over the years; currently, it unfolds as follows. Once Ottawa accepts a claim for negotiation – by no means a given – a framework agreement is established to guide and limit negotiations. Eventually, an Agreement-in-Principle (AiP), the basis for a formal agreement, is initialled. Getting to an AiP and from the AiP to the text of a proposed agreement tends to be a fraught, stop-and-start process. If and when a formal agreement has been reached, it must be ratified by a vote of the Indigenous people seeking the claim, and authorizing legislation must be passed by Parliament and by the relevant provincial or territorial legislature.

Each finalized comprehensive claim is unique but all share, with variations, common elements. Principal among these are acquisition of cash and formal legal title to lands, both held in common by their governments or organizations for the Indigenous people included in the claim; land access and harvesting rights; a suite of co-management boards engaged in wildlife management and environmental regulation; and governance provisions, often with far-reaching implications. In addition, each settled claim includes a wide range of miscellaneous items, such as commitments for the creation and administration of national parks, Indigenous priority in certain economic activities, such as hunting lodges, and commitments to expand Indigenous employment in government.

The LILCA included most of the usual elements found in land claim agreements.[5] Chapters 19 and 23 of the claim committed the federal government to general payments totalling $140 million over fifteen years, plus $151 million over ten years for a broad range of implementation costs. Payment of these monies, into two arms-length trusts, is now complete. The $140 million was subject to a clawback of some $51 million that Ottawa loaned to LIA during negotiation of the claim, but in 2019, the federal government announced that it would be forgiving (or refunding) all loans – including the LIA loan – made to Indigenous organizations in support of their claims work.

The Labrador Inuit Settlement Area (LISA), which was established by the claim, comprises 72,520 square kilometres of land, an area slightly larger than New Brunswick, with roughly 22 per cent designated as Labrador Inuit Lands (LIL), owned by the NG, plus 48,690 square kilometres of adjacent ocean extending to Canada's territorial limit (see the map in chapter 1). Other than that owned by the Inuit, land within LISA is owned by the Province. Although it is outside the settlement area, some important provisions of the claim apply to the Voisey's Bay area, and to the Inco (now Vale) nickel mine there. The claim also set in motion a process to create a national park in the Torngat Mountains near the northern tip of the Labrador Peninsula, with Inuit playing a significant role running what became Torngat Mountains National Park through a co-management board. Extensive Inuit access and harvesting rights across LISA are enshrined in the treaty, with provision for access and harvesting by non-beneficiaries. As well, the treaty establishes certain harvesting rights for Labrador Inuit in areas outside the settlement area but adjacent to Inuit communities (shown as Schedule 12E on the map in chapter 1).

The legal foundations, activities, and influence of claims-mandated co-management boards vary a good deal but usually include land use planning, wildlife management, and environmental regulation. The Nunatsiavut claim established two such boards, the Torngat Joint Fisheries Board and the Torngat Wildlife and Plants Co-Management Board, and set the framework for the Torngat Mountains National Park Co-Management Board. In contrast to other settled comprehensive claims, co-management boards were not created for land use planning or environmental regulation. In these fields, all three governments – Nunatsiavut, federal, and provincial – are involved, which can result, as it has thus far for land use planning, in conflict and stalemate.

Uniquely for an Inuit land claim, the treaty established a far-reaching self-government regime. In December 2005, when it came into effect, the LIA board morphed into the NG. A "Transitional Assembly" met during 2006, giving way to the Nunatsiavut Assembly following elections in October 2006.[6] A detailed constitution, discussed in the next chapter, had been approved in a referendum of claim beneficiaries in early 2002. Specifics of the treaty's self-government provisions are set out in more detail in that chapter; for now, it will suffice to note that they include culture and language, education, environmental protection, health, social services, housing, law enforcement, justice, and taxation. The NG has discretion as to when it "draws down" – takes on responsibility for – specific jurisdictional powers, most of which are shared with the federal and provincial governments. To this point, the NG has been measured in drawing down powers available to it in the claim. A notable exception to the suite of powers typically found in self-government agreements is control over membership. The NG's role with regard to membership is limited to strictly administrative matters; criteria for membership, appeal processes, and the like are set out in the claim, and may only be changed with the agreement of all three parties – an unlikely prospect.

The official coming into force of a settled claim is by no means the end of the process. Far from it. Any number of claim features, not least financial support from Ottawa, require constant attention and hold potential for ill-feeling and conflict among parties to the claim. Each claim is supplemented by a detailed implementation contract or plan setting out each party's responsibilities for implementation, but inevitably disagreements arise. Concerns over implementation failures and inadequacies, primarily on the part of the federal government, led in 2003 to the creation by a number of Indigenous governments and organizations of the Land Claims Agreements Coalition to increase public awareness of land claims and to push the federal government on a range of implementation issues. The NG is an active member of the coalition, though its complaints about implementation are more often directed against the provincial government rather than at Ottawa.

In almost all significant respects, comprehensive land claims agreements are exercises in compromise. All sides are required to give ground on their preferred positions to reach agreement, but typically, and unsurprisingly, it is the Indigenous negotiators who must offer the most substantial concessions. After all, the federal government determines the rules of the process and effectively holds a veto over the outcome. Indigenous leaders and negotiators who have settled claims acknowledge the often substantial compromises needed to secure agreement but aver that, overall, the benefits of their claims outweigh the downsides. One of the more significant compromises of the Labrador Inuit claim involved the land quantum that the provincial government was prepared to agree would be Inuit-owned. Many LIA members considered the amount unacceptably small, so that the LIA leadership had difficulty convincing members that the proposed trade-off in the claim of limited land ownership in return for land use planning provisions was worthwhile.[7] Since the provincial government has yet to agree to any land use plans, the members' scepticism seems to have been well placed.

In some instances, compromise cannot be reached. During the negotiations, LIA "demonstrated a strong interest in recognizing Inuit customary law as part of any land rights agreement in Northern Labrador," believing customary law to be "the primary means through which Inuit have traditionally exercised their rights of self-government."[8] In the end, no customary law provisions were included in the claim, though they figure prominently the Labrador Inuit Constitution. Not all Indigenous peoples are prepared to give way on what they see as important principles, so that negotiations may stall for long periods or be abandoned altogether. By way of illustration, the Labrador Innu and the federal and provincial governments initialled an AiP in 2011, but finalization of the claim has thus far not been achieved. On occasion, Indigenous communities have rejected agreements negotiated by their leaders.

Whereas Indigenous leaders and community members may balk at specific provisions demanded by the federal or provincial/territorial governments in claims negotiations, some Indigenous academics and activists reject the entire notion of land claims and related self-government agreements. Dene scholar

Glen Coulthard, for example, writes, "from the state's perspective, the land claims process constitutes a crucial vehicle for the domestication of Indigenous claims to nationhood."[9] The rejectionist critique of land claims and self-government made by Coulthard and others is examined later in this chapter.

Indigenous Self-Government

In the 1970s, Indigenous leaders began to deploy the term "self-government," even as they pointed out that for centuries, if not millennia, prior to the arrival of Europeans, Indigenous peoples across Turtle Island were self-governing. "Countless Aboriginal leaders equate self-government with self-determination,"[10] writes Yale Belanger, but as the Royal Commission on Aboriginal Peoples observed,

> Although closely related, the two concepts are distinct and involve different practical consequences. Self-determination refers to the right of an Aboriginal nation to choose how it will be governed – whether, for example, it should adopt separate governmental institutions or join in public governments that embrace Aboriginal and non-Aboriginal people alike. Self-government, by contrast, is one natural outcome of the exercise of the right of self-determination and refers to the right of peoples to exercise political autonomy. Self-determination refers to the collective power of choice; self-government is one possible result of that choice.[11]

Self-determination has usefully been defined by Stephen Cornell as "the right of Indigenous peoples ... to govern their own affairs according to their own values and designs to determine their own futures."[12] For Cornell, self-government is

> the enactment of self-determination through the exercise of governing power: Indigenous peoples making and implementing collective decisions according to their own rules, values, and, ideally, law ... the ability to assert their own rules, expand the reach of their own law, and place their own values at the center of decision-making: these are measures of the degree to which they can move toward self-government and away from self-administration or self-management, both of which may accord Indigenous peoples some decision-making power but do so within rules set by others – typically central governments – and in the service of goals those others have set for Indigenous peoples.[13]

As with any number of such definitions, however, this highly abstract formulation offers little direction as to what self-government actually looks like. Thus Belanger's 2008 observation continues to ring true: "despite the impressive attention paid to the concept of self-government, a clear-cut definition eludes us as does transparency concerning self-government's fit with Canada's varied political processes. Nor are we sure how Aboriginal political ideologies will continue to drive self-government's operations once implemented or facilitate its ongoing evolution."[14] The Royal Commission on Aboriginal Peoples put it more simply: "Self government means different things to different Aboriginal groups."[15]

What follows is a thumbnail sketch of the forms of self-government recognized under Canadian law. A fully inclusive list would include traditional Indigenous governance arrangements existing outside the formal Canadian constitutional order.

Forms of Self-Government

The difficulty in formulating a single, clear-cut definition reflects the wide range of institutional forms – in actual operation, let alone proposed – that self-government can assume in Canada. The following typology sets out the varieties of Indigenous self-government that have thus far been implemented in Canada. They are roughly aligned from least to most autonomous for the Indigenous peoples involved, though specific cases of one form may, for various reasons, enjoy more or less autonomy than is generally found in adjacent forms.

Indian Act band councils: Band councils established under the *Indian Act* exercise virtually no autonomy, though they may engage in a degree of self-administration. For many First Nations, the principal impetus for pursuing self-government lies in escaping the paternalistic and colonial *Indian Act*. Imperfect as they may be, all other forms of self-government outlined below offer more autonomy than is possible under the *Indian Act*. Since the act does not apply to them, no Métis or Inuit band councils have ever existed.

Legislated sectoral self-government: Individual pieces of federal legislation have delegated to specific Indigenous groups, at both community and regional levels, significant authority in particular policy sectors such as education, health, child welfare, and land management. Illustrations include the 1998 *Mi'kmaq Education Act* and the *First Nations Land Management Act* of 1999. Within the limits of the affected policy sector, this approach has generally been welcomed as an effective means for Indigenous peoples to influence issues of prime importance to them.

Legislated general self-government: Beginning in the 1980s with the *Cree-Naskapi Act* and the *Sechelt Indian Band Self-Government Act*, and continuing with more recent agreements such as the 2003 Westbank First Nation Self-Government Agreement, the federal government has enacted legislation removing particular First Nation bands from the *Indian Act* and granting them substantial self-governing authority. These agreements may include provisions limiting certain political rights or access to programs and services to Indigenous peoples.

Alberta Métis settlements: In a unique provincial variation of legislated general self-government, eight Métis settlements in central and northern Alberta enjoy significant self-governing autonomy by virtue of provincial legislation, initiated in the 1930s and substantially extended in 1989 and 1990. The powers exercised by these communities are delegated from the provincial government, with Ottawa having little to do with their status or operation. A significant downside in this arrangement is that, "as provincial statutory entities with delegated authorities, the institutions of Métis government are vulnerable to unilateral change."[16] Indeed, in July 2021, the Métis Settlements General Council launched a constitutional challenge against recent Alberta legislation that modifies significant elements of the settlements' governance structure and process.[17]

Limited "self-governance": In their recent book *Nested Federalism and Inuit Governance in the Canadian Arctic*, Gary Wilson, Christopher Alcantara, and Thierry Rodon develop the concept of "Inuit self-governance," which they distinguish from Inuit self-government such as in Nunatsiavut. The term "refers to a set of institutions, such as land claims organizations, that exist outside the scope of government but play an important political and economic role at the regional level."[18] These include, for example, Inuit-only institutions established by the 1984 Inuvialuit Final Agreement, such as the Inuvialuit Regional Council and the Inuvialuit Game Council, which exercise certain governmental or quasi-governmental powers under the treaty. The numerous co-management boards mandated by various settled comprehensive land claims could also be seen as examples of Inuit self-governance. These institutions are not intrinsically Inuit; the concept could easily be extended to First Nation and Métis organizations. It is, however, notable that Wilson and his colleagues are careful to include only organizations created by settled claims.

De facto Indigenous governments: A fundamental distinction exists between "public" governments, in which rights and services are available to all residents, and Indigenous self-governments, characterized by exclusionary provisions relating to rights and services. At the same time, "regions such as Nunavik have *de facto* ethnic government models, by virtue of the overwhelming demographic and political weight of their Inuit inhabitants."[19] Nunavut, where Inuit comprise roughly 85 per cent of the population and a substantially higher proportion of elected politicians, is another oft-cited example. Their size, jurisdictional scope, and status as emanations of settled claims accord these governments significant power. Other de facto Indigenous governments, however, such as municipal governments in small communities in Yukon and the Northwest Territories that are numerically dominated by First Nation peoples, face sharp constraints in what they can do by virtue of both restrictive legislation and inadequate resources.

Claims-based self-governments: The power and effectiveness of claims-based self-governments such as that of Nunatsiavut very much depend on resources, relations with federal and provincial/territorial governments, and other factors. Still, it is clear that self-government agreements rooted in treaties offer the greatest potential for Indigenous peoples to exercise authority over the policies and issues affecting them. That their existence and their powers are constitutionally protected conveys upon them a degree of autonomy exercised by none of the other forms of Indigenous government. In particular, the governance arrangements listed above, which flow out of legislation that is primarily but not exclusively federal, are significantly less secure. Quite simply, Parliament undoubtedly has the legal authority to drastically revise or even repeal legislation on which self-governments such as the Westbank government or sectoral institutions like Mi'kmaw Kina'matnewey, the Mi'kmaq education authority, rest. It might be thought unlikely that Ottawa would in effect renege on long-standing, successful Indigenous governance institutions. Yet that is precisely what, in the eyes of territorial Indigenous leaders, the federal government attempted not so long ago. Critically important claims-mandated co-management boards, such as the Mackenzie Valley Land and Water Board and the Yukon Environmental and Socio-Economic Assessment Board, may be emanations of settled claims, but their structure and operational procedures are largely set out in federal statutes. In 2013 and 2014, the Conservative government of Stephen Harper introduced legislation to amend the *Mackenzie Valley Resource Management Act* and the *Yukon Environmental and Socio-economic Assessment Act* in far-reaching ways that Indigenous peoples and their organizations saw as fundamentally contravening the spirit of the treaties. Before the legislation was passed, the Conservatives lost power to Justin Trudeau's Liberals, who subsequently withdrew the bills.[20] While legal challenges launched by Indigenous organizations might have achieved the same result, the significant point is that Indigenous governance arrangements resting on legislation are necessarily at least somewhat tenuous.

As of 2022, Nunatsiavut was one of twenty-three claims-based, and thus constitutionally protected, self-government regimes. All save Nunatsiavut are in Yukon, the Northwest Territories, and British Columbia. In terms of membership and staff, NG is the largest.

It is essential to recognize that these self-governments, regardless of their form, come into existence only with the forbearance of the federal government and, to a lesser extent, of provincial/territorial governments, except the Alberta Métis settlements, which rest entirely on provincial legislation. The processes and rules of negotiations are set by the federal government; the limitations of what self-government can achieve are subject to federal government policy; levels of funding to support self-governments are determined by the federal government; and the federal government ultimately decides whether a particular self-government process comes to fruition, though the Indigenous people seeking self-government can, and occasionally do, reject proposals that were close to completion. In order to attain any sort of self-governing status, Indigenous peoples must accept that autonomy can only be realized within the confines of the Canadian state. Of course, Ottawa has an interest in reaching agreements and therefore has to take Indigenous demands and negotiating principles seriously, but the federal government is clearly in the driver's seat. Still, the unhappy experience of the proposed 2002 *First Nations Governance Act*, which was roundly rejected by those it would have affected, demonstrates that Indigenous peoples retain substantial agency in deciding whether to go where Ottawa wants them to go.

Self-Government Literature

The literature on Indigenous self-government is extensive, encompassing academic publications, reports from governmental agencies such as royal commissions and parliamentary committees, as well as policy statements and political manifestos from Indigenous groups. Given the all-but-total lack of genuine self-government, it is not surprising that until recently the literature was either highly normative, arguing the need and justification for self-government, or speculative, proposing possible structural and cultural models for achieving self-government. Much of this literature was highly legalistic or dealt with mega-constitutional concerns, most notably the role of self-government in (re)structuring relations between Indigenous peoples and non-Indigenous peoples or between Indigenous nations and the Canadian state.[21] Unsurprisingly, this literature was heavily oriented to the experiences of First Nations under the *Indian Act* and was thus of limited relevance in Nunatsiavut in that Inuit are, and have long been, excluded from the ambit of the *Indian Act*, though a 1939 Supreme Court ruling declared Inuit equivalent to Indians in terms of federal government fiduciary responsibilities.[22]

In 2008, John Hylton, editor of important collections on self-government, wrote that "experience and expertise are accumulating at such a rapid pace that it is now possible, perhaps for the first time, to meaningfully discuss self-government best practices. Thus, in little more than a decade, scrutiny and commentary have moved from an emphasis on theory to an emphasis on practice to emphasis on best practices."[23] Especially with respect to general, as opposed to sectoral, self-government, this assessment was somewhat premature at the time, and indeed remains questionable still. Certainly, a literature created by both academics and practitioners has emerged detailing and evaluating functioning Canadian self-government regimes, but it remains limited in scope as well as volume, hence the rationale for this book. Valuable studies have chronicled and analysed the processes by which Indigenous groups achieved self-government.[24] Others set out the institutional frameworks of specific self-government regimes without much in the way of assessment of their actual operations.[25]

In the past few years, significant analysis of the real-life operations of various self-government regimes, some claims-based, others not, has become available. Important examples include the work of Kelly Saunders and Janique Dubois on the influence of the traditional rules of the buffalo hunt on present-day Métis self-government processes;[26] contributions of both academics and practitioners to a recent edited volume, *Reclaiming Indigenous Governance*;[27] and Wilson, Alcantara, and Rodon's study of housing, education, and natural resource policy and policymaking in three Inuit regions, including Nunatsiavut.[28]

A very different strain of analysis, much of it from Indigenous scholars, is sharply critical of the processes and outcomes of self-government and land claims, maintaining that what is touted as progress is little more than lost opportunities and regression. This critique is examined below.

Insights from the Literature

That much of the literature is abstract or speculative, and often legalistic, and that to date relatively little exists on operating self-governments, is by no means to suggest that it is bereft of insight into the nature of self-government and the prospects for successful self-government regimes. The following insights – or perhaps better, principles – are drawn from across the literature; several hold particular relevance for Nunatsiavut and the Nunatsiavut Assembly.

Self-government offers the way to a better Indigenous future: As long-time analyst John Hylton put it, "realizing a better future depends in no small part on supporting the development of self-governing Aboriginal programs and institutions that are effective, transparent and accountable. This is the kind of governance that Aboriginal people enjoyed for tens of thousands of years before settlers arrived."[29] Few scholars or practitioners, Indigenous or non-Indigenous, would disagree. Indeed, even the fiercest critics tend to concur, though they reject the notion that present-day land claims or state-controlled self-government processes can achieve true self-government.

The Canadian constitutional order does not recognize that Indigenous peoples can simply declare themselves self-governing: Some Indigenous peoples assert that they possess precisely this capacity, but as the array of existing self-government forms above demonstrates, Indigenous peoples must extricate themselves, to a greater or lesser degree, from the legal control of the Canadian state through formal, highly restrictive processes established and controlled by the federal government. The resulting constraints on self-governments can raise concerns about legitimacy. Critics rail against this fundamental restriction and seek ways to subvert it.

Self-government solutions must come from Indigenous peoples: The experiences, cultures, needs, and resources of Indigenous peoples vary enormously across Turtle Island. Thus, not only is a one-size-fits-all approach doomed to fail, but only the people themselves can determine what they need and can achieve by way of governance, though advice and support from outsiders, especially other Indigenous governments and organizations, can be invaluable.

Self-government will not solve problems by itself or solve them quickly: As one official of a self-government regime rooted in a comprehensive land claim notes, the treaty does not create the reality, but rather provides tools and resources for governance.[30] Self-government is best understood as a process rather than an event, a direction instead of an end point, so that "the task of governing and adapting institutions to successfully govern in an increasingly complex world is an ongoing project."[31]

Self-government cannot succeed without adequate financing: No government can operate effectively unless it has sufficient financial support; self-governments are hardly exempt from this primal reality. The Royal Commission on Aboriginal Peoples put it succinctly: "self-government without a significant economic base would be an exercise in illusion and futility."[32]

Self-government regimes may depart substantially from the familiar forms of contemporary liberal democracies: Self-government is characterized by institutional diversity, reflecting "Indigenous circumstances, experiences and political cultures."[33] This could entail inclusion in decision-making processes of hereditary chiefs, elders' councils, mass assemblies, and so on. Although the Nunatsiavut Assembly exhibits none of those features, its structure and operations are like no other in Canada. Distinctive, Indigenous-inspired political institutions may challenge Western norms and values, especially in the exclusionary provisions that characterize the strongest forms of self-government, but they can offer substantial promise of effective governance.[34] At the same time, substantial variation is evident in the balance Indigenous peoples have sought between, on the one hand, incorporating traditional principles into their governance and, on the other, emulating Eurocentric governance approaches.[35]

Self-government regimes must be rooted in Indigenous culture and traditions: This is an important corollary to the previous principle. A key finding of the Harvard Project on American Indian Development is the importance for effective Indigenous governance of what the project leaders termed "cultural match." "The formal institutions of governance," they write, have to have the support of the people. The community has to have a sense of ownership about the institutions themselves. This means those institutions cannot simply be imposed from outside according to someone else's model. They have to fit indigenous conceptions of how authority should be organized and exercised … Designing successful First Nation and tribal governance systems requires assiduous attention to questions of cultural match. It is clear that a "one size fits all" approach is neither necessary nor effective when it comes to governance forms and management systems.[36]

Indigenous people feel "a need to root contemporary governmental initiatives in traditional institutions."[37] This is by no means equivalent to simply duplicating the structures and processes of Indigenous governance of earlier eras. Belanger highlights the need for Indigenous peoples to examine "how traditional Aboriginal practices and customs can be adapted to address the contemporary realities in Aboriginal communities."[38] Key here is the emphasis on adaptation, necessitated by the challenges and opportunities currently facing Indigenous peoples and facilitated by the truism that Indigenous cultures are not static but are constantly evolving. The outcome, as William Nikolakis notes, may be "blended or modified liberal democratic institutions,"[39] as is very much the case in Nunatsiavut.

Self-governments must proceed in measured fashion in taking up their responsibilities: Experienced self-government officials emphasize that the task can be so overwhelming and the path so unclear that Indigenous governments must evaluate what they should and can do initially and pick a few key areas on which to spend time, energy, and resources.[40] Like the NG, few if any self-governments have drawn down the full range of powers to which they are entitled.[41]

The Critics

A prominent set of mostly Indigenous scholars and activists has mounted a tough-minded attack on land claims and self-government processes and outcomes, often explicitly linked to rejection of capitalism. This critique is rooted in profound dissatisfaction with state-initiated policies' lack of progress towards genuine social, cultural, and economic betterment of Indigenous peoples, opposition to the manifold compromises entailed in reaching land claims and self-government agreements, and emphasis on the restorative prospects of a return to traditional cultures and teachings.

For these critics, it is not simply that progress has been too slow. Rather, in the critics' eyes, what the state and many Indigenous leaders see as progress, hesitant and limited as it may be, is in reality negative and harmful. This position is set out in no uncertain terms. According to Coulthard, "much of our [Indigenous] efforts over the last four decades to attain settler-state recognition of our rights to land and self-government have in fact encouraged the opposite – the continued dispossession of our homelands and the ongoing usurpation of our self-determining authority."[42] In recent decades, argues Mohawk scholar Taiaiake Alfred, "our nations have been co-opted into movements of 'self-government' and 'land claims settlements,' which are goals defined by the colonial state and which are in stark opposition to our original objectives … Our people were promised that they would be recognized as nations and that their lands would be returned, but instead of realizing these goals we are left with a nasty case of metastasizing governmentalism."[43] Not all Indigenous scholars adopt such a hard line, though a significant and influential number, including Jeff Corntassel, Hayden King, Pamela Palmater, and Leanne Betasamosake Simpson, are of like mind, seeing land claims and state-sanctioned self-government as profoundly colonial processes incapable of realizing the fundamental political changes Indigenous peoples need.

The burgeoning literature on Indigenous "resurgence" is by no means uniform in its analysis of the prospects for Indigenous empowerment or the paths towards it, but generally emphasizes a return to traditional values and cultures, as opposed to formal structural processes, especially those acceptable to the state: "decolonization and regeneration are not at root collective and institutional processes. They are shifts in thinking and action that emanate from recommitments and reorientations at the level of the self that, over time and through proper organization, manifest as broad social and political movements to challenge state agendas and authorities."[44] Precisely what such shifts in thinking and action entail is not always clear, though they certainly do not occur at the negotiating table. Corntassel puts it this way: "decolonizing praxis comes from moving beyond political awareness and/or symbolic gestures to everyday practices of resurgence … Daily acts of renewal, whether through prayer, speaking your language, honoring your ancestors, etc., are the foundations of resurgence."[45]

Of what relevance for Nunatsiavut are the issues raised by the critics and the analysis and the proposals for action they offer? Their writings are not likely familiar to many Nunatsiavumiut, including those in government, but it is reasonable to suppose that their calls for a reinvigoration of the cultural basis of Labrador Inuit society through the sorts of actions Corntassel and others urge would find wide favour among both the political elite and the general population. At the same time, it is also probable that few, especially among the political class, would accept the critics' hard-line rejection of land claims and the Nunatsiavut form of self-government, not least because in order to settle their claim and achieve self-government, they have made precisely the difficult compromises decried by the critics. More speculatively, it could be argued that the vociferous, radical stance promoted by (primarily) First Nation scholars is incongruent with the pragmatic, non-ideological approach said to characterize Inuit. Still, engaging in the deep reflection the critics encourage would doubtless prove valuable, particularly for politicians and bureaucrats preoccupied with the everyday, mundane exigencies of governing.

Self-Government in Nunatsiavut

In order to provide context for the NG and its assembly, this chapter has touched on a wide range of Indigenous government regimes operating in Canada. All are described by some as self-government and all are characterized by opportunities for Indigenous peoples to shape and improve their futures as well as by substantial constraints, most notably those imposed by the Canadian state, on the extent to which they can develop political, social, and economic institutions and run their own affairs. However, Nunatsiavut is one of only a few that by virtue of their extensive autonomy and their exclusionary nature, whereby certain political rights and government services are restricted to Indigenous people, can be considered substantially self-governing. Relatedly, the character of self-government in Nunatsiavut and the assurance of its continuation reflects its origin in a finalized comprehensive land claim conveying constitutionally protected status. At the same time, some Indigenous scholars simply reject the land claims process and its state-sanctioned governance arrangements as offering anything like genuine self-government.

As is inherent in the federal government's approach, the LILCA is, for Nunatsiavumiut, very much a compromise, entailing important advances and guarantees as well as unfulfilled aspirations. So, too, self-government, as it unfolds in Nunatsiavut, offers great potential for the Labrador Inuit, though as the brief literature review above suggests, it is no sure thing that this potential will be reached. The success of self-government in Nunatsiavut is highly dependent on the design, operation, and effectiveness of the institutional framework of self-government. Hence this book's focus on the assembly.

The following chapter fleshes out the formal framework underpinning the structure and guiding principles of the NG and the assembly, as set out in the claim and the Nunatsiavut constitution, along with an overview of the NG's operation. Particularly notable are the distinctive aspects of the Nunatsiavut constitution and the organization of the NG, most obviously the adherence to the Westminster cabinet-parliamentary model, that place it clearly at the Western pole of a notional Western-Indigenous governmental continuum. Subsequent chapters examine the assembly and its operations in detail.

Chapter Four

Governance in Nunatsiavut: Constitution, Organization, and Politics

Central as it may be, the assembly is only one element of governance in Nunatsiavut. This chapter offers an overview of the institutional environment within which the assembly operates. It is principally concerned with Nunatsiavut's constitutional underpinnings as set in the two essential constitutional documents that establish governance in Nunatsiavut, the *Nunatsiavut Constitution Act*,[1] also referred to as the Labrador Inuit Constitution, and the Labrador Inuit Land Claims Agreement (LILCA).[2] Not only are these constitutional documents intrinsically important, but they are frequently referenced in the assembly both as guides to action and constraints on it. In particular, the Nunatsiavut constitution deserves close examination because of how prominently self-government and the primacy of Inuit culture figure in it. In addition to devoting particular attention to the many distinctive or unique features of Nunatsiavut's constitution, the chapter outlines the structure of government in Nunatsiavut and the legal framework of elections.

The Nunatsiavut Constitution I: Governance Provisions in the Claim

Indigenous constitutions,[3] according to Christopher Alcantara and Greg Whitfield, not only "establish and specify the internal political structures and practices of Aboriginal polities ... [but also] represent an important attempt to reconcile the separate legal traditions and constitutional orders of Indigenous and settler societies in Canada."[4] Thus, those creating, or recreating, Indigenous governments must find practical ways to manage the tensions and contradictions between Indigenous and Western modes of governance. None of the fourteen Indigenous self-government constitutions Alcantara and Whitfield analysed was "purely Western or traditional; all of them fall somewhere on a continuum between the two extremes," so that the challenge is "finding the right balance between Western and Indigenous traditions for achieving politically meaningful societies."[5] The Nunatsiavut constitution includes features designed to incorporate Inuit culture into the structures and processes of governance, but overall is clearly closer to the Western pole of the continuum than other Indigenous constitutions in Canada.

Just as the constitution of Canada is more than the *Constitution Act, 1982*, the "constitution" of Nunatsiavut entails more than the Labrador Inuit Constitution, which sets out principles as well as detailed provisions mandating structures and process of government. The treaty negotiated by the Labrador Inuit Association, the Government of Canada, and the Government of Newfoundland and Labrador is less detailed in terms of structures and operations but is no less fundamental. The importance of the treaty was underlined by President William Andersen III the first day the assembly met: "even though we have a constitution, one of the things that Assembly members must remember is that the real bible to this Assembly is going to be the Labrador Inuit Land Claims Agreement."[6]

LILCA not only establishes Nunatsiavut as a self-governing Inuit jurisdiction, it also prescribes with constitutional force many far-reaching governance provisions, for example, on citizenship, wildlife management, land use, water management, and taxation. Certain elements of the *Nunatsiavut Constitution Act* flesh out principles mandated or permitted by LILCA. By way of illustration, part 17.3.3 of the claim requires that the Nunatsiavut constitution ensure "the executive officers and the members of the legislative institutions of the Nunatsiavut Government be responsible to Inuit in accordance with principles of democracy"; that the Nunatsiavut Government (NG) be "financially accountable to Inuit"; and that a democratic process be developed for amending the constitution. A key distinction: whereas LILCA is very much a compromise between Inuit objectives and federal and provincial government policy, the Nunatsiavut constitution is essentially Inuit-made, albeit with provisions designed to secure approval from the federal and provincial governments.

In common with other settled comprehensive claims, much of LILCA relates, directly or indirectly, to governance. Significant governance provisions are found in chapters 9, 12, and 13, which establish co-management boards to advise government on wildlife, fisheries, and plants and on the operation of Torngat Mountains National Park; chapters 9 and 10, authorizing the NG to engage in land use planning and environmental assessment/regulation; and chapters 18–20, which set out how the NG is to be financed, including federal government obligations and the NG's ability to levy taxes on the same basis as the provincial government. Unquestionably, however, the most far-reaching provisions are found in chapter 3, on membership, and chapter 17, on self-government.

That the criteria for membership are specified in the claim rather than in the constitution matters a good deal, for it means that they cannot be modified solely by Inuit or by the NG, as would be the case were they set out in the constitution. Changes to the membership criteria require agreement of all three parties to the claim: the Inuit, as represented by the NG, the federal government, and the provincial government. Reopening settled land claims for other than minor concerns is notoriously difficult and rarely occurs.

Beneficiary status – membership – is important not simply in terms of political rights but also because it entails eligibility for significant government programs, such as the NG's generous post-secondary funding packages. Membership criteria are, to say the least, complex and confusing. Given the often ambiguous, occasionally quite arbitrary, character of Inuit identity and of Labrador Inuit Association (LIA) membership outlined in chapter 2, this is not surprising. The following is a simplified overview; additional qualifications and nuances apply in some circumstances.[7] For the most part, Inuit ancestry is key to membership eligibility, though Kablunângajuit (not quite white) are also eligible. A Kablunângajuk is described in the claim as "an individual who is given that designation according to Inuit customs and traditions" who either has Inuit ancestry or, lacking Inuit ancestry, settled permanently in Nunatsiavut before 1940 or who is a direct descendant of such a person, if born before 1990[8] (the 1940 cut-off date was chosen as it was then that substantial numbers of coastal Inuit moved to Goose Bay to work on the construction of the military airbase[9]). Other provisions convey membership eligibility in certain cases on persons "connected to" the settlement area, including persons whose grandparents were born or lived there. An important implication of these criteria is that it is possible to be a Nunatsiavut beneficiary without having any Inuit ancestry. The numbers of such beneficiaries are doubtless small, but the issue is symbolically important. One significant complication frequently gives rise to problems: members who were enrolled as children must reapply for membership upon reaching the age of majority (nineteen). Little wonder that misunderstanding and misinformation about membership, often leading to frustration and anger, are common.

Decisions on membership applications are made by local enrolment committees mandated in the claim, appointed and provided administrative support by the NG. Adverse decisions can be appealed to the Enrolment Appeal Commission, whose members are appointed by the NG and by the federal and provincial governments. Other than ensuring that enrolment committees have full membership and adequate administrative support, the NG has no involvement in enrolment. Assembly members frequently complain about errors and unpalatable decisions by enrolment committees. As responsibility for these committees falls within his portfolio, it is usually the first minister who responds. The response has consistently been that no one in the NG has the authority to intervene in the adjudication of membership applications.

The Nunatsiavut Constitution II: The Labrador Inuit Constitution[10]

The Nunatsiavut constitution stands out by virtue of its array of highly distinctive features. Especially notable are provisions that reflect Inuit values and incorporate Inuit approaches to governance, that establish self-government, and that recognize and enhance the position of women in Labrador Inuit politics and society. The Nunatsiavut constitution is also distinctive among the twenty-three Indigenous self-government constitutions across Canada for the extent of its Euro-Canadian influences.[11]

Origin and Overview

The Nunatsiavut constitution predates finalization of LILCA. LIA members approved the constitution by referendum in April 2002, two years before they ratified the final agreement and three years before passage of the requisite federal and provincial enabling legislation. LIA officials from that period explained that as negotiations proceeded through the 1990s, it became clear that the federal government would be changing its policy so as to permit inclusion of self-government in comprehensive claims. However, as in other self-government negotiations, Ottawa was concerned about how self-government would unfold and therefore insisted that the final agreement stipulate adoption of a constitution. Part 17.3 of LILCA thus required the Labrador Inuit to establish a constitution and set out a number of key elements that it either had to or might contain. Similar provisions are found in all other Canadian self-government agreements.

The LIA board had been thinking about possible self-government models for some time, and developed its ideas for the claim in tandem with plans for what would become the NG. In order to pre-empt possible post-finalization conflict with the federal or provincial governments based on objections to the constitution, LIA decided to formalize and ratify its constitution so that it could be sanctioned by the final agreement, which is what transpired. Developing and approving a constitution prior to finalizing the claim was not unusual; most other self-governing Indigenous groups have done likewise, though in many instances it was not required in their final agreements.

In working up its constitution, LIA was at pains to ensure that the document covered everything that Ottawa might possibly want in a constitution. This partially explains the length and detail of the Nunatsiavut constitution, which at one hundred and thirty text-heavy pages is by far the longest of the twenty-three written Indigenous constitutions currently in place across Canada. Most are roughly twenty to twenty-five pages, often with large font and generous margins. In places, the Nunatsiavut constitution goes into far more detail than is typically found in constitutions. For example, it specifies topics that the Standing Orders – the rules – of the assembly should cover, information that government financial documents such as the NG's financial plan and audit reports must contain, and administrative processes to be included in an *Election Act*. The unusual length and detail of the constitution also reflects the essentially blank legislative slate that would face the NG at start-up. Whereas the Government of Nunavut inherited all Northwest Territories legislation, and thus could take its time customizing its laws to fit the Nunavut situation, the NG would come into existence with no *Assembly Act*, no *Financial Administration Act*, no *Election Act*, and so on. Accordingly, the constitution included provisions that would normally appear in legislation. One observer described a "mad rush at the end [of the constitution process] to bring in laws that were absolutely necessary." Looking back, one LIA official, reflecting on the document's length and detail, recalled, "we were all a little worried that we were tying our hands with the constitution." Assembly members have commented that in certain instances this concern was justified.

The content of the constitution was discussed extensively both at the LIA board and at the community level. "We tried to have consensus on the process [for the constitution and the design of the NG]," said one LIA official, and "to do that we needed community involvement." Another LIA staff person described the public consultation/participation process as "a mixed bag." Two full rounds of community meetings were held in each Nunatsiavut community, with fewer meetings outside the settlement area. At some meetings, "it was LIA technocrats talking to themselves in an empty room," while at other times attendance was fulsome and debate vigorous. Some meetings were held on an invitation-only basis, while others were "wide open town halls." Formal meetings typically occurred in the evenings, but LIA staff were available through the day in an open house format in which individuals could speak one-on-one with LIA representatives. Draft versions of the Agreement-in-Principle and the constitution were widely circulated.

A broad range of issues arose within LIA and at community meetings, such as treatment of non-beneficiaries, the status of Inuttut, the possibility of guaranteed representation for women in the assembly, the status of the town councils, and the practicalities of operating the NG. Most were resolved without engendering significant opposition or discontent. Ideas about governance and the practical means for realizing them were almost entirely formulated in-house; few outside consultants were engaged.

What, then, did this process establish as the Nunatsiavut constitution? Mostly it consists of detailed nuts-and-bolts descriptions and requirements for governance structures and processes: the organization and membership of the Nunatsiavut Assembly, the powers and responsibilities of the president and the Executive Council, financial procedures, the organization and powers of the Inuit community governments and the Inuit community corporations, and so on. Many provisions relating to governance institutions are mundane and unexceptional, though some are distinctive and imaginative.

Perhaps the most noteworthy elements of the Nunatsiavut constitution are aspirational, expressing the culturally rooted principles, desires, and ambitions that the Labrador Inuit wish to underpin their government and their society. Few are justiciable, and indeed some might even appear unrealistically quixotic, but they stand as noteworthy statements of Inuit ideals that leaders and citizens alike should hold as their standards for political and social behaviour.

Following the preamble, which expresses the political and social goals of the Labrador Inuit in terms that are at once poetic and hard-nosed – a characteristic common in Indigenous constitutions – chapter 1 enumerates twenty-five "Founding Principles of the Labrador Inuit Constitution." These principles set out in broad language the characteristics, identity, and responsibilities of the Labrador Inuit, along with precepts to guide the policies and operations of Nunatsiavut's political, social, cultural, and economic institutions. Chapter 2 contains the *Labrador Inuit Charter of Rights and Responsibilities*. Many of its provisions are unexceptional, with some mirroring language in the *Canadian Charter of Rights and Freedoms*, and are clearly justiciable. Others, however, are more aspirational in nature: the rights of children, access to adequate housing, the responsibility of Labrador Inuit to share food and shelter with those in need and to speak Inuttut at home and teach it to their children, and the like. A number of the aspirational elements of the constitution are discussed below under the rubric of Inuit influences.

The essential objectives of the Nunatsiavut constitution are mirrored in the constitutions of other Indigenous self-government regimes, such as that of the Huu-ay-aht First Nations in British Columbia as articulated by Angela Wesley, a leading figure in the development of Huu-ay-aht governance:

> A constitution could articulate our own highest law based on our own idea of who we are and on our own view of the world. We could use it to teach and reestablish the governing roles of our Ha'wiih; to define not only the rights but the responsibilities of citizenship; to teach and reestablish our own principles and values; to take the best of the governance practices that worked for us for thousands of years and translate them into governance tools that could be effective in today's context.[12]

Self-Government

From its first pages, the Nunatsiavut constitution leaves no doubt as to the centrality of self-government. Institutional and procedural self-government provisions are far-reaching, bolstered by forthright statements, such as that in the preamble, as to the importance of self-government:

> [We] assert our inherent right to self-government and the right to continue, as we have always done, to determine our own political, social, cultural and economic institutions and our relationships with other peoples and their governments.

Public government in the fashion of Nunavut, as opposed to self-government, was never seriously considered by LIA as the design of the NG emerged. According to one key LIA figure, since the primary purpose of the NG would be realizing the objectives of the claim, and since only Inuit could be claim beneficiaries, self-government was clearly the route to be followed.

Far and away the most basic and significant practical expression of self-government in the constitution is the restriction of fundamental political rights – the right to vote and the right to stand for office – to beneficiaries. Only beneficiaries may serve as members of the assembly and only beneficiaries are entitled to vote for president and ordinary members and for chairs of community corporations.

At the same time, section 1.1.3(w) recognizes "that people other than Labrador Inuit live in Nunatsiavut … [so that] Labrador Inuit … must develop policies that embrace pluralism." This principle is given limited political effect at the community level. All community residents may vote in AngajukKâk elections, though only Inuit may stand as candidates. Non-beneficiaries may vote and run for a seat on the Inuit community councils. Certain non-beneficiaries may vote for councillors representing beneficiaries and can run for these offices. Depending on numbers, up to 25 per cent of council seats, but no more than two, are reserved for "new residents" – that is, non-beneficiaries who became residents of Inuit communities after 1999 (section 10.4.3).

As one former LIA official recalled, "we wanted to be inclusive, but it was to be a self-government, so there wouldn't be any non-Inuit in the government." However, the provincial government was adamant that the political rights of non-Inuit be formally protected at the community level. Thus, it was decided that non-beneficiaries should be represented in the local councils and that the AngajukKât should sit in the assembly to bring community concerns and perspectives into the governing process, reflecting the views of the entire community. A different official commented that the idea of including AngajukKât in the assembly was in part a realization of LIA's desire to give the government an Inuit flavour, in this instance reflecting the importance of certain family groupings in particular communities.

A number of constitutional rights or procedures are available only to Labrador Inuit. Examples include access to government-held information (section 2.4.31) and attendance at and participation in assembly proceedings not open to non-Inuit (section 4.14.6). Section 4.17.3 requires the assembly and its committees to meet "in places accessible to the Labrador Inuit public." The assembly is prohibited from excluding "the Labrador Inuit public, including media owned or controlled by Inuit," from committee meetings, unless such exclusion is deemed "reasonable and justifiable to do so in an open and democratic society" (section 4.17.5); no similar guarantee is offered to non-Inuit or non-Inuit media. It is important to add that in no instances have any of these provisions been employed to the disadvantage of non-beneficiaries.

The Inuit Court authorized in chapter 9 of the constitution has yet to be established. As recently as February 2018, First Minister Kate Mitchell indicated that the substantial costs associated with creating the court represent an impediment to its creation.[13] If and when the court comes to be, only beneficiaries may serve as judges (section 9.2.15).

Inuit Influences

Similar to other Indigenous constitutions, the Nunatsiavut constitution is replete with both hortatory and aspirational expressions of the importance of honouring and promoting Indigenous culture, as well as concrete provisions for imbuing governance in Nunatsiavut with Inuit principles. Many of the twenty-five founding Principles set out in part 1.1 speak directly to the centrality of Inuit culture and identity. The first affirms "the existence of the Inuit of Labrador as a distinct people whose identity is based on ties of kinship, a shared language, common customs, traditions, observances, practices and beliefs, a special relationship to and control over our ancestral territory, a common history, and our own political, social, cultural and economic institutions" (section 1.1.3(a)). Subsequent principles relate to the special relationship between Inuit and the land and animals and the need to steward natural resources; the importance of Inuit families and the responsibility of Inuit to look after children, elders, and the vulnerable; the right to use Inuttut in personal and public life as well as the responsibility to teach Inuttut and Inuit culture to children; the duty of leaders to be "respectful and considerate" of all and to "seek balance and agreement in their decisions [and] avoid conflict"; the admonition that Inuit institutions should consider and promote Inuit culture and "seek cooperation and consensus" in their operations; and the recognition that change and adaptation should occur in ways "appropriate to Labrador Inuit needs, values and aspirations" (sections 1.1.3(d), (e), (f), (g), (h), (n), (q), (r), and (x)).

Concrete procedures and requirements designed to instil Inuit culture into the NG and its operations primarily involve language, decision-making principles, and customary Inuit law. Inuttut is established as "the primary language" of Nunatsiavut in section 1.6.3, which includes firm rules setting out language rights. All elected officials, public servants, and members of community governments and community corporations are accorded the right to use Inuttut "to transact business and speak at meetings." Similarly, all beneficiaries are entitled to communicate with their governments, NG, community governments, and community corporations in Inuttut, both orally and in writing. All assembly bills and proposed community government by-laws, as well as all reports from the NG and the community governments, must be available in Inuttut. Paradoxically, should inconsistencies arise across different versions of the Nunatsiavut constitution, the English text is to prevail (section 13.2.7). According to a person familiar with the development of the constitution, this was not the result of any deference to colonial ways but was rather a matter of simple pragmatism: were a legal issue to arise, "no one could think of a lawyer or judge who would be able to read, understand and argue from the Inuktitut text."

Perhaps the most potentially far-reaching element of the Nunatsiavut constitution rooted in Inuit culture is the recognition of Inuit customary law in chapter 9. LIA negotiators had pushed hard to incorporate Inuit customary law into the claim, especially with respect to harvesting and sharing, but "they encountered great reluctance on the part of the province to accept non-codified laws, and more generally to relinquish any sort of real authority over resources to Inuit."[14] Inuit were, however, able to embed customary law in the constitution. In significant measure because the Inuit Court has yet to be established, customary law has not as yet been influential in Nunatsiavut governance. Proclaimed as "the underlying law of Labrador Inuit and of Nunatsiavut for all matters within the jurisdiction or authority of the Nunatsiavut Assembly" (section 9.1.2), which "may be recognized by any judicial or administrative authority" (section 9.1.6), customary law is defined as "the customs, traditions, observances, practices and beliefs of the Inuit of Labrador which, despite changes over time, continue to be accepted by Labrador Inuit as establishing standards or procedures that are to be respected by Labrador Inuit" (section 9.1.1).

In case of inconsistency, the Inuit Charter of Rights and Responsibilities is to prevail over customary law. However, customary law supersedes Inuit law passed by the assembly unless express provision is made in the Inuit law to the contrary (sections 9.1.3 and 9.1.4). Significantly, the claim sets out a range of areas, such as the management of Labrador Inuit Lands, language, and culture, where Inuit law, which includes customary law, prevails over federal and provincial law. Procedures are set out for proving "the existence and content" of customary law, in which oral traditions and the opinions of elders figure prominently (section 9.1.7). Although customary law has thus far not had significant influence in Nunatsiavut, its potential is substantial, especially should the Inuit Court be established.

The Inuit propensity for consensus decision making is explicitly affirmed in the constitution. Among the founding principles is "the belief that decision making by Labrador Inuit political, social, cultural and economic institutions should promote participation by Labrador Inuit individuals and organizations, seek cooperation and consensus" (section 1.1.3(q)). Section 5.15.2 requires of the assembly "reasonable efforts … to make all decisions, including decisions under section 5.4.1 [selection of the first minister], by consensus of the members." According to section 4.15.3, it is the president's "sole and exclusive discretion" to determine whether reasonable efforts have been made to reach consensus, and only the president may call for a vote in the assembly or ask the members whether consensus exists, with one negative response requiring a formal vote. In practice, it is usually the speaker who determines whether there is consensus on an item of business. With consensus in effect defined as the absence of objection, consensus decisions are deemed to have been unanimously passed (section 4.15.5).

Consensus and cooperation are to reign not only in assembly deliberations but in intergovernmental relations as well. The NG, the Inuit community governments, and the Inuit community corporations "must cooperate with one another in mutual trust and good faith." Precepts are laid out for ensuring harmonious relations, including the admonition to avoid legal proceedings against one another (section 12.2.2): disputes between or among governments "should be resolved by informal discussion and without necessity of invoking formal means of dispute resolution" (section 12.2.3), though provision is made for the assembly to refer disputes to "necessary or appropriate" means of resolution (section 12.2.4). The Inuit Court is to be the last resort for resolving disagreements; indeed, recourse to other courts is not mentioned (section 12.2.5).

Provisions Relating to Women

Among the nearly two dozen Canadian Indigenous self-government constitutions, the Nunatsiavut constitution is unique in the extent to which it emphasizes the aspirations and rights of women. It includes not only broad expressions of principles regarding the position of women in Labrador Inuit society and in the governance of Nunatsiavut, but also clear, explicit provisions for realizing these principles.

Other Indigenous constitutions affirm the equality of all citizens/beneficiaries, some explicitly mentioning men and women, but none go any significant distance beyond that; in some, the word "women" does not appear. At the level of principle, the Nunatsiavut constitution includes "the guarantee that Labrador Inuit men and women are equal in rights, freedoms and dignity" (section 1.1.3(k)), plus a further commitment to ensuring that the rights and freedoms in the *Labrador Inuit Charter* apply equally to men and women (section 2.4.1). Somewhat less abstract, though without explicit direction as to specific actions, is section 4.17.2, which reads as follows:

> Recognizing that Labrador Inuit women have historically been under-represented in many of the political, social, cultural and economic institutions of Labrador Inuit society, the Nunatsiavut Assembly and the Nunatsiavut Government, the Inuit Community Governments and the Inuit Community Corporations must take practical and positive measures, which may include the enactment of Inuit laws by the Nunatsiavut Assembly, to facilitate and promote the equal participation of Labrador Inuit women in the political, social, cultural and economic institutions of Labrador Inuit society.

Among specific provisions, particularly noteworthy is the proclamation that "every Labrador Inuk has the right to bodily and psychological integrity, which includes the right: (a) to make personal decisions concerning reproduction;

(b) to security within and control over his or her body" (section 2.4.7). This is an unusual and far-reaching constitutional declaration, to say the least.

The constitution includes several direct prescriptions designed to promote the active and effective involvement of women in the workings of the assembly, and in particular its committees. The assembly's Standing Orders are required by section 4.14.9 to ensure that committee membership be established with regard to "the balance of men and women." Relatedly, "if women are not represented in the Nunatsiavut Assembly or are under-represented [not defined] in the Nunatsiavut Assembly, the standing orders of the Assembly must include provision for appointing women who are not members of the Assembly to committees and subcommittees" (section 4.14.11). (Section 4.14.12 permits non-assembly persons to constitute up to one-quarter of committee members.) As well, the Standing Orders must ensure that proceedings of the assembly and its committees are held "at times that accommodate the needs of women members and the needs of members who are caregivers" (section 4.14.5).

What explains the unusual attention to women in the Nunatsiavut constitution? Knowledgeable observers, some of whom were close to the development of the constitution, offer various, interrelated explanations. Some see a reaffirmation of traditional Inuit culture, which had been characterized by equally important spheres of activity accorded to men and women and by mutual respect.[15] Colonization, this interpretation holds, eroded women's traditional roles in community governance. As an Inuit woman political leader observed, "it is only because we have become Westernized that we have forgotten that women helped to lead our communities."[16] This interpretation does not sit well with Carol Brice-Bennett's argument, noted in chapter 2, that women found themselves in subservient roles in traditional Labrador Inuit society and that their status improved because of the Moravian influence. The limited literature on Labrador Inuit women emphasizes their strength in leading families rather than in politics,[17] though Pauktuutit, the national Inuit women's association, maintains that their "traditional primary authority within the home has helped give Inuit women the confidence and tenacity necessary to take such an active and productive role in these [political and economic] organizations."[18] Another explanation focuses on the influence of strong women on the development of the constitution: LIA, as the NG today, had among its leadership a number of strong, assertive women with substantial organizational support. One participant recalled, "there were women's groups in the communities and an active regional Labrador Inuit women's organization, which took a strong position on the need to enshrine women's rights in the constitution ... with assistance from the national Inuit women's organizations and some of its women advisers." Another person identified a further factor, "the disdain some of the key women negotiators had toward the Moravian traditions, including the fact that elders were always men." It wasn't only Moravian traditions that privileged men in community decision making, as noted in the discussion of the long-standing Labrador Inuit tradition of men's meetings, discussed in chapter 2.

Participation

Decision making in traditional Inuit culture, as we saw in chapter 2, was usually premised on reaching consensus through broad participation. Accordingly, the Nunatsiavut constitution includes various provisions designed to facilitate and encourage public participation in governmental processes and public life. Taken together, the words "participate," "participation," and "participatory" occur twenty times with respect to the Inuit public or to individuals. Some provisions are primarily aspirational in nature. Section 6.2.1, for example, enjoins the public service to ensure that "Inuit … [are] encouraged to participate in policy-making," adding that Labrador Inuit are to be provided with "timely, accessible and accurate information" about the NG and its activities. Similarly, Inuit community governments are to make rules to "provide for representative and participatory democracy, accountability, transparency and public involvement" (section 10.3.2(a)), and to encourage participation by "new residents" (section 10.3.2). Specifics as to how these objectives are to be realized are not provided.

Other elements of the constitution do provide clear, specific guidelines and procedures relating to public involvement in governing processes. At the most basic level, as detailed in part 1.2 of the constitution, the public can be involved in – indeed, can initiate – constitutional amendments. A petition signed by five hundred Inuit voters proposing a constitutional amendment triggers a binding referendum on the proposed amendment. The president has discretion to reject the petition as "frivolous or vexatious" or to declare it "unclear or incomplete," and either disallow it or refer it to the assembly for "restatement and clarification." Certain elements of the constitution can be amended by a three-quarters majority in the assembly, but for the most part amendments require majority support in referenda in which all Inuit sixteen and older are eligible to vote. Fifty per cent is needed for government-initiated referenda; 60 per cent in petition-initiated referenda; in both instances, a majority of those voting, not of those eligible to vote, is required.

At the local level, the constitution sets out both aspirational goals and concrete measures to promote participation. An example of the former is the obligation of Inuit community governments to "provide for representative and participatory democracy, accountability, transparency and public involvement" (section 10.3.2(a)). Inuit community councils may only pass by-laws that have been published "for public comment" (section 10.3.8(b)) and a petition signed by 25 per cent of the members of an Inuit community corporation requires convening a special general meeting of the corporation membership (section 11.3.21).

All told, however, compared with the robust participatory elements in the constitutions of other Indigenous self-governments, those in the Nunatsiavut constitution are either weak, aspirational, or permissive. To take the most notable example, many self-government constitutions, such as those of the Kwanlin Dün, Toquaht, Tłı̨chǫ, Tla'amin, and Vuntut Gwitchin Nations, mandate, at least annually and often more frequently, general assemblies in which all adult citizens are entitled to speak, to discuss issues, and to hold their governments accountable. Citizens at such general assemblies or gatherings may be constitutionally empowered to, in the case of the Tłı̨chǫ, "ask questions, make recommendations and provide broad policy direction" to government.[19] Nothing in the Nunatsiavut constitution approaches that level of participation. Of course, the citizenries of many self-governing First Nations are both small and geographically concentrated, whereas, given the distances and the poor communications, a general assembly including only the beneficiaries in the five Nunatsiavut communities, let alone the majority of beneficiaries who live outside the Labrador Inuit Settlement Area (LISA), would be logistically and financially impossible. A recent background report on options for online voting prepared for the Fourth Assembly's Special Committee on Voting Alternatives for the Canadian Constituency suggested that electronic voting could serve as "an extension of governance capacity" by facilitating member participation in important political processes.[20] Ironically, in light of the disappointingly meagre response to the committee's request for public input, it declined to offer any recommendations with regard to online voting.[21]

Finally, two other institutions found in many Indigenous self-government constitutions for enhancing participation, elders' councils and youth councils, have no Nunatsiavut equivalents. This is noteworthy given that "historically, elders performed many of the roles of government, whether in dispute resolution or in responding to social crises."[22]

Euro-Canadian Influences

In many ways, the constitution is clearly a made-in-Nunatsiavut document, reflecting not just Inuit culture but also the extent of popular involvement in creating it. At the same time, it exhibits far-reaching Euro-Canadian influences. This was inevitable, given the compromises entailed in land claim and self-government negotiations, as well as the pervasive dominance of Euro-Canadian governance institutions and modes of thought not just in Labrador but throughout Canada. Specific provisions aside, that a detailed, legalistic document so centrally guides the governance regime of what was traditionally an oral Indigenous culture is a telling indication of the power of Euro-Canadian influences, bearing in mind the long-standing and extensive literacy among the Labrador Inuit.

The most prominent of the Euro-Canadian precepts and traditions is adherence to the principles of Westminster-style "responsible government," with the authority of the cabinet and individual ministers dependent on the retention of the assembly's "confidence," in the very particular Westminster meaning of the term (sections 3.2.7 and 5.3.3). The constitution explicitly requires the first minister, and by extension her ministers, to maintain the "confidence" of the assembly (section 3.2.7) – in other words, to follow the precepts of the Westminster cabinet-parliamentary system. Significantly, the choice to follow the Westminster model was made by Inuit. The claim includes no such provision and Ottawa has accepted decidedly non-Westminster arrangements in other Indigenous self-government agreements and constitutions.[23]

Those involved in designing the NG and in approving that design, recounted in interviews that, as they sought direction from the communities as to what the government should look like, it became evident that the people wanted something that would be familiar. Thus, the provincial government in St. John's and the federal government served as the primary models for the basic structure of the NG, which meant adopting a Westminster cabinet-parliamentary system. In turn, two related considerations underpinned the anomalous melding of presidential and parliamentary models. First, the LIA "acted on the basis of what they knew and were familiar with": the president and vice-president of the LIA were elected as at-large members, with other board members elected from geographic districts. Second, based on the decidedly uneven records of LIA presidents, concern existed about "inordinate power in the president's office." Hence it made sense to establish the NG along Westminster lines, requiring the executive to be responsible to the assembly, thereby providing significant checks and balances on the president's power. A former LIA official, asked about the decision to adopt the Westminster model, indicated that it was not that LIA was enthusiastic about the rather foreign Westminster system, but that the decision was made to go with it for the time being with the expectation that it would later be revised, perhaps fundamentally. He acknowledged that this approach may not have accounted for the possibility that the Westminster variation of the assembly might become entrenched and hard to change, a possibility that has indeed come to pass.

Such decisions are unsurprising, given the context in which the assembly's design – and, indeed, that of the government – emerged. According to one of LIA's key figures, during the negotiation of the claim, the association was primarily focussed on basic goals, such as control of land and resources and achievement of self-government, and hence devoted little thought to the nature and organization of what would become the NG. In those days, the same individual noted, "almost everything was geared to getting documentation to prove we were who we said we were as the basis of our claim negotiation." Asked about decisions on the basic structure of the government, a senior LIA board member indicated that staff presented options to the board, which then decided on them with little deliberation.

In keeping with the tenets of responsible government, all members save those of the Nunatsiavut Executive Council are constitutionally proscribed from even introducing to the assembly "money bills," which either raise revenues or directly allocate expenditures (section 4.18.10). And of course the terminology – speaker, president, minister, first minister, etc. – comes straight out of Euro-Canadian tradition. Other significant constitutional provisions have nothing to do with Inuit culture and everything to do with Euro-Canadian governmental norms, including the recourse to majority votes should consensus not be possible (section 4.15.6), the prominent written charter of rights (part 2) and provisions for recognized political parties and an "official opposition" (section 4.18.12(c)). To this point, no interest has emerged in political parties, and thus no official opposition exists in the assembly, but the constitution explicitly contemplates both. Finally, the absence of such institutions as general assemblies and elders and youth councils, common in other Indigenous self-governments but unknown in Euro-Canadian governance, is noteworthy.

The Nunatsiavut constitution figures prominently in the rhetoric, and guides the behaviour, of assembly members. President Andersen may have referred to the claim as "the real bible" for members, but they also clearly attach hallowed status to the constitution. In that the constitution was written and ratified in the abstract – that is, before the NG or the assembly came into being – reluctance to even consider revisiting its minor provisions is telling. The need to have the Inuit public on board doubtless figures into members' views on amending the constitution, but their unwillingness to review the document, let alone amend it in a major way, is striking. "What's the point of the Constitution," asked one member early on, "if when we're not happy about it we can loosely throw a motion on the table and just have changes made whenever we like?"[24] The only formal attempt in the assembly to amend the constitution, prior to the minor housekeeping amendment in 2021 (discussed below), sought to remove the requirement that candidates in presidential elections speak and understand Inuttut (brought forward, ironically, by the member just quoted). The debate not only addressed the substantive issue but also featured concern over the very propriety of changing the constitution.[25]

Not all in the NG regard the constitution as immutable. One of the members of the 2013 Special Committee to Review the Nunatsiavut Elections Officer's Report pointed out a frustration the committee experienced. Mentioning in particular the possibility of online voting in presidential elections, she said, "there were issues in the report that we hoped to get some resolution from, but it was a task that was beyond what we had expected. The Constitution … was something that we kept bumping into, and our recommendations kept getting squatted because of the actual Constitution."[26] Speaking for the committee, she said that at some point the assembly should "strike a committee to actually look at the Constitution as a whole to see what the errors are in the Constitution, if any, or if there are areas in the Constitution that we want to look at and tackle as a whole Assembly."[27] This idea seems not to have surfaced again, although a few years later, another member argued that the constitution can and should change if circumstances warrant:

> In conversations with my colleagues, whether formal or informal, when we talk about changes we'd like to make, laws we'd like to pass, it seems like there's always a roadblock, and that is a lot of details were included in our original Constitution … Constitutions are supposed to be overarching principles that guide laws. Our Constitution seems to have a lot of things that should be laws and trends … making change very hard for certain issues and details. Changing the Constitution, if deemed necessary, is a hard task. Hard does not mean impossible … If there is a consensus among Assembly in the future, amongst Inuit beneficiaries in the future that our Constitution could be better, could be made more flexible to benefit the Assembly and, most importantly, benefit our beneficiaries, I hope that we can start a discussion in the near future, the very beginnings of a long road.[28]

No formal moves to review, let alone amend, the constitution have occurred since the failed 2008 initiative, save a minor "emergency" provision enacted in 2021. The COVID-19 pandemic had brought home the need for flexibility, but the firm dates for elections set out in the constitution stood out as problematic. Accordingly, legislation was introduced and passed during the June 2021 session to amend the *Nunatsiavut Constitution Act* to permit the assembly in certain emergency cases to set alternate dates for presidential, ordinary member, and Inuit community government elections. A debate of sorts took place on the bill, consisting largely of technical questions from members and technical answers from the NG's director of legal services. No questions or comments arose about the propriety of the proposed amendment, though one member did enquire whether the bill might be amended since "we have discovered over the years looking at the Constitution, there might be more areas that may need to be changed, and if you're going to get a vote for the Inuit public, maybe we should look at other areas that may have confusion or controversy."[29] This was clearly out of order, being beyond the scope of the bill. No one followed up to support the proposal to consider other possible constitutional amendments.

In accordance with the amending process, a referendum was held on the proposed constitutional amendment. It was, unsurprisingly, a low-key affair with little debate or public interest. Ninety-five per cent of those casting a ballot supported the change. Fortunately for the proponents, ratification required 50 per cent of those voting, rather than 50 per cent of those eligible to vote, as turnout barely reached 13 per cent.[30]

The Structure of Government in Nunatsiavut

Under the claim, the NG is entitled to "draw down" jurisdiction in various areas currently controlled by the provincial government, most notably education, health, and social services. However, the NG has limited its take-up of jurisdiction. According to Toby Andersen, long-term chief negotiator on the claim and subsequently NG deputy minister, although the federal and provincial governments are prepared to pass over jurisdictional responsibility, "the reason we are not ready to take down certain programs and services is that we need to make them better, more applicable to our people not just to continue to implement them without first making changes to them … We are moving forward slowly, because the NG has a lack of human resources and expertise."[31] As well, based on their experiences in health, NG officials are wary of accepting responsibility without assurances that they will be given the financial resources needed to deliver programming.

Nunatsiavut is not alone among emerging Indigenous self-governments in following a phased approach to assuming the powers available to it in its treaty. One person involved in realizing the governance aspirations of the Huu-ay-aht First Nations in British Columbia has written that

> All five of the nations signing the Maa-nulth Treaty decided to assume their law-making authority in a slow, deliberate, and pragmatic way. Out of our lengthy experience in treaty negotiation and constitution building, our leadership in each community understood that returning to self-government was a big step. While citizens had high expectations of early benefits, change would not be easy, and it would take time. It would be important to lay careful foundations for a government that was accountable to citizens, was fiscally responsible, and could function as an effective steward of our lands, resources, and heritage.[32]

Although the comparison is necessarily tentative due to substantial differences in scale, resources, and the extent of pre-existing capacity, the Nunavut experience suggests the wisdom of a measured approach. The widespread disappointment and dissatisfaction among Nunavummiut with their government more than two decades after its creation may be at least partially a function of Nunavut's taking control of all jurisdictions to which it was entitled immediately at start-up. From the outset, this interpretation runs, the Government of Nunavut has quite simply been overwhelmed by too many responsibilities for its overstretched, inexperienced bureaucracy to manage, so that it would have been better to gradually take over jurisdictional responsibilities as it gained experience and built capacity.[33]

Although the Province remains predominant in health and education policy and administration, the NG is active in these fields, delivering the important

Non-Insured Health Benefits program as well as drug and alcohol programming and support for post-secondary students, fields the LIA had previously developed or taken over prior to finalization of the claim. A three-year transition is underway that will see NG taking responsibility for child welfare services.[34] In that considerable thought had already gone into this possibility, the fact that the NG opted for a three-year transition speaks to the prudence with which it is expanding its jurisdictional scope. The NG has substantial presence in the field of natural resources, both non-renewable resources, especially on Inuit-owned lands, and renewable resources such as fish and wildlife. Most decisions affecting wildlife are ultimately made by the Government of Newfoundland and Labrador, while fisheries decisions largely fall to the federal Department of Fisheries and Oceans, though the NG and the co-management boards established by the claim have significant influence in these areas. Housing is a critical issue throughout Nunatsiavut, especially in Hopedale and Nain; former president Sarah Leo once acknowledged that "housing is probably the number one priority of this government."[35] However, with its limited financial resources, the NG's ability to take an active role in housing is sharply constrained. Legislation establishing a Nunatsiavut Housing Commission, similar to the housing corporations in Nunavut and the Northwest Territories, which effectively operate as government departments, was passed in 2019. The commission is mandated to take over housing policy and administration from the Torngat Regional Housing Association (TRHA), a non-profit organization linked to the provincially controlled Newfoundland and Labrador Housing Association. The TRHA's mandate extends well beyond Nunatsiavut, and although the NG provides funding, it has no control over it. Other fields in which the NG is active include culture, economic development, tourism, and recreation. As noted, the constitution and the claim authorize creation of an Inuit Court, but no moves have been made in that direction; the administration of justice, including policing, remains under provincial control. The same is largely true of transportation, though Ottawa also plays a significant role.

The constitution covers the structure and operation of the NG's civil service, its revenue and taxation powers, and its financial procedures, but, save for the odd detail, in unexceptional ways. Administratively, the NG is very much built on the Euro-Canadian governance model found at the national as well as provincial and territorial levels, albeit on a much smaller scale. Six hierarchically organized sectoral departments have ministers as their political heads and apolitical deputy ministers as administrative heads: Education and Economic Development; Finance, Human Resources, and Information Technology; Health and Social Development; Lands and Natural Resources; Language, Culture, and Tourism; and Nunatsiavut Affairs, which is responsible for claim implementation, housing, justice, and the Office of Registry (for beneficiaries). A central agency, the Nunatsiavut Secretariat, is responsible for coordinating government activity as well as for intergovernmental relations and NG-wide communications. Like the Government of Nunavut, the NG was effectively forced to match its organizational design to the departmental structures of the provincial and federal governments.[36] The basic principles as well as the specific provisions of the *Civil Service Act* and the *Financial Administration Act*, which undergird the NG's day-to-day operations, would be familiar to public servants anywhere in Canada.

The position and powers of NG deputy ministers closely resemble those of their counterparts in other Canadian governments. At the same time, other Canadian public servants would find some the characteristics of these key NG figures unusual. In federal and provincial/territorial governments, deputy ministers are primarily appointed on the basis of their managerial ability and accordingly are routinely shuffled across departments. Deputies in Nunatsiavut, by contrast, are selected for their subject-area expertise. As well, they are hired through human resource processes that are similar to those used for lower-level positions, whereas deputies elsewhere (though they are not partisan appointees) are typically selected through processes outside the usual human resource procedures. Accordingly, movement of NG deputies across departments is unknown; no deputy minister has ever been moved from one department to another. One deputy explicitly stated that she would be unsuitable as a deputy minister in other departments.

NG deputies' subject-area expertise is likely related to another unusual characteristic: their remarkable longevity. As of the end of the Fourth Assembly in April 2022, two deputies had been in place since the NG came into being in 2006, and, even including three relatively recent appointments, as of April 2022 the average tenure of an NG deputy minister was over seven and a half years.[37] Of the sixteen persons who have held deputy minister positions, five served for eleven to sixteen years (the maximum possible), two for six to ten years, eight for two to five years (three of whom were still in place in 2022), and one for just over a year. This is a marked contrast with the experience of provincial/territorial and federal governments, where individuals may remain deputy ministers for extended periods but are typically shuffled among departments or ministries every two or three years.[38]

Beyond community liaison officers, wildlife officers, and the like posted to them, all LISA communities have at least a minimal NG presence. Notably, deputy ministers' offices are located in the smallest communities, Postville and Rigolet. The largest single contingent of NG staff works in Happy Valley–Goose Bay, which is not in the settlement area; however, plans are underway (and as assembly members point out, have been for some time) to relocate virtually all NG employees to Nunatsiavut communities. Significantly, the expectation is not that all staff will find themselves in the legislative or administrative capitals. According to section 1.5.3 of the Labrador Inuit Constitution, "the Nunatsiavut

Government must decentralize its offices to the extent that it considers reasonable and economically feasible with a view to placing at least one Nunatsiavut government administrative centre in each of the Inuit Communities other than Hopedale or Nain over time."

The NG has been remarkably successful in filling staff positions with beneficiaries, especially in the settlement area. As of March 2022, the NG employed 450 staff, roughly 80 per cent of whom were permanent employees, the balance casual or temporary,[39] with 61 per cent of all staff located in the settlement area and 39 per cent in Upper Lake Melville (two worked at the Voisey's Bay mine site; none were located in St. John's or in Montreal, as had been the case in previous years). In the five Nunatsiavut communities, 91 per cent of all employees were beneficiaries; in Upper Lake Melville, the corresponding figure was 53 per cent. Seventy-eight per cent of all staff were women. As of August 2020, a high proportion of senior bureaucratic positions was held by beneficiaries: 71 per cent of deputy ministers and 83 per cent of directors, the rank immediately below deputy minister.[40] Overall, the NG's record of employing Inuit has been much stronger than that of the Government of Nunavut, where overall rates of Inuit employment have hovered around 50 per cent since start-up, though it is fair to note that total staff numbers have increased substantially over that period.[41] Neither NG staff nor those of the community governments are unionized.

By fiscal year 2022–3, the NG budget had reached $264 million.[42] The lion's share of revenue, some $242 million, came from Ottawa in the form of an ongoing fiscal financing agreement. The NG does not levy taxes itself, though it has the same taxing authority as the Province. It receives 95 per cent of personal income tax levied in the LISA, provided residents tick the appropriate box on the tax form; this was the largest component of the NG's "own-source" revenue, some $8.7 million. The NG is entitled to roughly 85 per cent (determined by a complex formula) of GST, amounting to $1.3 million in 2022–3. The other significant revenue sources were $5.9 million in fisheries access fees, $3.3 million from the Labrador Inuit Land Claims Trust (a fund managing land claim money with 50 per cent of profits directed to the NG), and $1.8 million interest. The NG does not currently receive any royalties from the Voisey's Bay mine, but is hopeful that the legal proceedings it has launched against the provincial government for a share of royalties will be successful. The largest outlays went to the Nunatsiavut Affairs Department, $97.5 million, primarily for housing; the Department of Health and Social Services, $54.3 million; the Department of Finance, Human Resources, and Information Technology, $48.6 million, largely for transfer payments; and the Department of Education and Economic Development, $28 million. Inuit community governments were allocated $12.8 million, with a paltry $161,500 for the two community corporations. Projections were for a precise balance of revenue and expenditure, but the likelihood was that, as in previous years, a surplus of several million dollars would emerge at year's end.

At the community level, chapter 10 of the constitution, as required under parts 17.3.3(b) and 17.40 of LILCA, establishes the Inuit community governments and sets out how they are to be structured and operated, plus their powers and those of the AngajukKât. Whereas Canadian municipal governments are entirely subservient to the provincial/territorial governments, the Inuit community governments enjoy substantial autonomy, not least because their existence is recognized in both the constitution and the claim (parts 17.3.3(b), 17.38). Their budgets have to be approved by the NG, but this is the only aspect of their activity in which they are routinely answerable to it. The NG may only intervene in community government operations in cases of mismanagement, following a rigorous review process; to date, none have occurred. Chapter 17 of LILCA does set out a wide range of local community government matters in which the NG can legislate, and Inuit law passed by the assembly prevails over community by-laws. Thus far, the NG has exercised these authorities only minimally. That said, the community councils have very limited resources and little capacity to generate own-source revenue and thus are almost entirely dependent on block funding from the NG, operating grants from the Province, and project-specific grants from the federal and provincial governments. Their primary concerns are "hard" services such as water and sewage, road maintenance, and recreation, delivered by a small number of administrative and front-line staff.

Chapter 11 of the constitution deals with the Inuit community corporations, specifying the conditions under which they may be established. Whereas LILCA, in section 17.41, enumerates the powers and jurisdictions of the Inuit community governments, it is silent with respect to the powers of the community corporations. The constitution mandates the latter's structure, membership, and operating procedures. It also makes it clear that the assembly has the power to create, and to dissolve, community corporations, and that the corporations have no substantive powers other than those delegated to them by the assembly.

Elections[43]

Electoral processes in Nunatsiavut are highly formalized, as set out in lengthy, detailed legislation specifying, among other things, election machinery, candidate and voter eligibility, voting procedures, and election finance. An independent officer of the assembly, the Nunatsiavut elections officer, oversees elections and electoral processes.

Elections for the different classes of members of the Nunatsiavut Assembly normally follow fixed four-year terms held at staggered times. Presidential elections take place two years after/before ordinary member elections, which in turn occur several months before AngajukKât and community chair elections. With the recent constitutional amendment, the assembly has the authority to shift election dates in case of emergency. The Nunatsiavut constitution contemplates political parties in the assembly, but thus far no candidate for president, ordinary member, or AngajukKâk has run under a party label, though some have had publicly known affiliations with national parties.

Dissolution of the assembly, which would lead to a general election for ordinary members, can occur in two ways: First, on passage of a resolution supported by two-thirds of all members, not simply of those present in the assembly. Second, if the president removes the first minister but the assembly is unable to nominate a replacement candidate within twenty-eight days; as the December 2019 resignation of Kate Mitchell demonstrated, this provision does not apply should the first minister resign. Presidential and ordinary member elections are held on the first Tuesday of May, unless the assembly is dissolved for a general election, which would also alter the two-year separation between presidential and ordinary member elections.[44]

The winning candidate in a presidential election must garner a clear majority of votes; should no one win a majority in the initial vote, a run-off election is held between the top two candidates. If the president resigns, dies, or is removed from office, a special election is held, unless the next presidential election is less than a year away, with the successful candidate serving the remainder of the term. By-elections for ordinary members, AngajukKât, and community corporation chairs occur as needed. The voting age in all elections is sixteen.

To run in ordinary member elections, beneficiaries must be eighteen and live in the constituencies for which they are nominated. AngajukKât, community chairs, and those in the employ of the NG are ineligible, as are those who are "of unsound mind," are undischarged bankrupts, or are in arrears for their NG or community council taxes. Members of Parliament, senators, and members of the provincial House of Assembly are likewise ineligible; so, too, persons convicted of certain offences over a specified period.[45] Candidates in Inuit community council and Inuit community corporation elections must be nineteen but otherwise must meet qualifications similar to those for ordinary member.[46]

A unique feature of the *Nunatsiavut Elections Act* requires the president to step in should any constituency in a general election not have a woman candidate once nominations have closed and to "take reasonable steps" to find and nominate a woman.[47] On several occasions, the president has done just that, though no woman so nominated has won a seat.

Healthy numbers of candidates came forward in the first four general ordinary elections for ordinary members (2006, 2010, 2014, and 2018); the number of candidates ranged between twenty-two and thirty-one for the ten seats (nine from 2005 until 2010). In the May 2018 election, for the first time a candidate was acclaimed (by-elections in 2017 and 2020 were won by acclamation). This may have been a precursor to a notable decline in the number of candidates in the 2022 election, which saw only eighteen candidates, and, for the first time, the nomination period ended with no candidates having come forward in one riding, necessitating a subsequent by-election. In addition, three of the five AngajukKât elections that year were won by acclamation, as was one of the community corporation chair elections. It is too early to tell whether the 2022 elections mark a permanent change from what was previously a notable contrast to the experience of the other two prominent Canadian consensus governments, Nunavut and the Northwest Territories, whose legislatures are only slightly larger than that of Nunatsiavut and where in all recent general elections at least one candidate has been acclaimed, often two or three, and as many as five. The first two presidential elections, in 2008 and 2012, were both contested by three candidates, while two candidates ran in the 2020 election; in 2016, Johannes Lampe was acclaimed.

Candidates for the presidency face similar qualifications as those for ordinary members, though they must be twenty-five and may live anywhere in Canada. In addition, a controversial constitutional provision, discussed more fully in chapter 8, requires that the president "be able to understand and to speak Inuttut." For some time, the issue was complicated by uncertainty as to how presidential candidates' language abilities could and should be determined. One unsuccessful candidate for president was said by assembly members to have admitted on CBC to a lack of adequate Inuttut skills.[48] In 2014, after protracted debate and a discussion paper,[49] a procedure was developed whereby candidates who otherwise met the qualifications for president would be required to participate in a "debate" carried out entirely in Inuttut. An amendment to the *Nunatsiavut Elections Act* created a process overseen by an independent moderator, appointed by the assembly, empowered to report to the Nunatsiavut elections officer candidates who either refused to take part or declined to answer a question in Inuttut. In such cases, the elections officer would declare them ineligible; the moderator is not to comment on the quality of the Inuttut. President Sarah Leo's observation at the time, that this process entails not so much a debate as a test,[50] was confirmed in the 2016 presidential election when the sole candidate was required to "debate."

Election finances are strictly regulated, though only candidates running in the Canada Constituency or for president incur more than minor expenses.[51] Only Inuit or Inuit-owned businesses may contribute to candidates, with a limit of $200 a year per candidate.[52] Candidates may spend up to $1,000 of their own money on election expenses ($1,500 in the Canada Constituency and $2,000 for presidential candidates). Overall expenses are limited to $3.33 per eligible voter, with yearly inflation increases. Records of all contributions and expenses are available to the public. Candidates receiving 15 per cent of the vote are eligible for rebates of up to 25 per cent of their expenses. Candidates who fulfil the reporting requirements have their $100 deposit returned.

Turnout in Nunatsiavut elections varies a good deal. In the 2014 ordinary members election, overall turnout was 46.7 per cent, but this figure obscures the wide difference in turnout between the five communities within the settlement area (68.4 per cent, with little cross-community variation) and Upper Lake Melville (47.4 per cent) and the Canada Constituency (25.8 per cent).[53] The 2018 ordinary members election saw a substantially different pattern of turnout: overall, 39.8 per cent, with the Upper Lake Melville and Canada constituencies registering rates of 35.4 and 35.9 per cent, respectively; turnout was 49.5 per cent in the settlement area communities. The decline in settlement area turnout reflected a drop of nearly 12 percentage points in Hopedale and a remarkable change in Nain's turnout rate from 70.6 per cent in 2014 to 33.7 per cent in 2018. In contrast, turnout increased marginally in Postville and Rigolet (Makkovik saw an acclamation).[54]

In the 2012 presidential election, 2,132 votes were cast in the first round and 2,183 in the second round, which translates into turnout in the order of 37–38 per cent.[55] Poor turnout in the 2020 presidential race, 26 per cent,[56] prompted victorious incumbent Johannes Lampe to highlight in his post-election statement his deep concern "that less than 30 per cent of eligible voters actually went to the polls. While there may be many reasons for the low turnout, it is obvious that more needs to be done to encourage Beneficiaries to play a more active role in determining our future."[57] Data on community government elections are not readily available; according to an OK Society report on the 2014 AngajukKât and community chair elections, 1,554 of the 3,632 eligible to vote did so, for a turnout rate of 42.8 per cent.[58]

Although systematic data that might explain levels and volatility of turnout are not available, comments from the Nunatsiavut elections officer (NEO) point to possible informational and logistical barriers to voting. One potential barrier, mentioned repeatedly by the NEO, is the lack of sufficient information on voters' parts about candidates. Commenting on the 2012 presidential election, the NEO reported that "soon after the mail in ballots went out each day we were continually getting calls from members of the Canadian Constituency asking 'Who are these Candidates? Where can I find some information on them?'"[59] In her report on the 2016 presidential election, the NEO remarked, "I did receive a complaint that there was not enough publicity about the Presidential election. Maybe now is the time to look at better ways to get this information out to the electors."[60] Following the 2020 presidential election, NEO Nanette Blake said in an interview with *Labrador Morning*, "locally there wasn't much information out about the candidates and people were calling our office [looking for information] … [Beneficiaries] knew Johannes Lampe because he was the incumbent but they didn't know anything about the other candidate and they were sort of saying, you know, people really didn't know them enough to make a good decision."[61] That information about the candidates was lacking and turnout was low in 2020 is not surprising in light of the unique circumstances of the election. The COVID-19 pandemic, which had already caused a five-month postponement of the election, meant that candidates did not travel to communities to meet with voters as they normally would have. Nor did either candidate campaign very actively. Lampe, the incumbent, spent much of the campaign in hospital having undergone major surgery, while Andrea Webb/Tuglavina, his opponent, displayed a rather hit-and-miss approach to getting her message out, rejecting the use of Facebook and relying instead on telephone calls.[62]

While the NG provided sufficient material for beneficiaries to make an informed decision in the 2021 constitutional amendment referendum, the very low turnout – just over one-eighth of those eligible voted – doubtless reflects the low salience of what was essentially a technical matter.

It may be that polling stations, advance polling procedures, and mail-in ballots are inconvenient for some beneficiaries. As the NEO put it in 2010, "How come I can't vote by using my computer by phone or can I fax you my ballot? is a question that was very common for our electors to ask during this election."[63] Widespread dissatisfaction among beneficiaries in the Canada Constituency with mail-in voting prompted the creation in early 2021 of a special assembly committee to look into alternative voting methods for that constituency. A report commissioned by the committee recommended adopting online voting for the Canada Constituency, and possibly for all beneficiaries, as a way of overcoming the shortcomings of mail-in ballots.[64] The committee ran out of time before its mandate ended with the dissolution of the Fourth Assembly in April 2022 and had to abandon plans for public consultations about possible alternative to mail-in voting because of a resurgence of the COVID-19 pandemic. Accordingly, it was only prepared to recommend that the Nunatsiavut Executive Council consider possible legislative improvements to mail-in voting, suggesting that, should a subsequent committee be charged with a similar task, it be given adequate time for consultation, research, and reflection.[65] It did not address a constitutional complication. Under sections 3.3.3 and 4.10.3, the Labrador Inuit Constitution requires that mail-in ballots be sent to all beneficiaries in the Canada Constituency. Without a constitutional amendment – something of an uncertain prospect – electronic voting would be problematic in that anyone opting to vote online would also receive a mail-in ballot, requiring an administratively complicated process to ensure that no one voted twice. A final factor dampening turnout may be the voting age of sixteen, since low turnout rates for young people are common across a wide range of political systems.

Whereas informational and logistical barriers may partially explain low turnout in Nunatsiavut elections, federal and provincial elections should not be as subject to such barriers; moreover, they are contested by political parties, whose activities generally encourage turnout. And yet turnout in Nunatsiavut at federal and provincial elections is also volatile and often low. In the most recent federal elections, turnout in Nunatsiavut was 33.1 per cent (2021), 48.4 per cent (2019), 62.4 per cent (2015), and 51.8 per cent (2011), while in the most recent provincial elections it was 28.6 per cent (2021), 54.1 per cent (2019), 38.0 per cent (2015), and 72.7 per cent (2011).[66] All this suggests that basic behavioural factors significantly affect turnout in Nunatsiavut.[67]

Perhaps the most noteworthy feature of elections in Nunatsiavut is that despite the emphasis in the constitution on participation, for one reason or another substantial numbers of Nunatsiavumiut are not exercising their right to vote.

Hybrid Governance in Nunatsiavut

The NG, and the assembly within it, combines institutional features that underpin public governments throughout Canada with distinctive and unique governance structures and processes derived from Inuit culture. Euro-Canadian elements in institutional arrangements and operational principles are pervasive, from the overarching dominance of the Westminster cabinet-parliamentary system, otherwise unknown among Indigenous self-governments in Canada, to the basic organization of the NG, with its hierarchical departmental structure and its politically neutral public servants, to the design and conduct of elections. At the same time, as is manifest in the constitution, the essential purposes of the NG, and thus of the assembly, are the protection and enhancement of Inuit culture, the betterment of Inuit society, and the well-being of Nunatsiavumiut. This entails not simply legislation and policy to advance Inuit interests but also governance structures and practices drawn from, or at least congruent with, Inuit culture. The emphasis on consensual decision making is a prime example, as are the strong aspirational and operational precepts for Nunatsiavumiut – all beneficiaries not just political leaders – to follow embodied in the constitution's founding principles and the Inuit Charter of Rights and Responsibilities. The constitution, as indeed the overall approach to governance in Nunatsiavut, reflects a "balance between maintaining traditional practices and adapting to changing circumstances that has long been a part of Inuit life."[68]

With the overall context of Nunatsiavut politics in place, the analysis now turns to the structure, operation, and effectiveness of the assembly itself, beginning in the next chapter with an account of its setting, atmosphere, and membership.

Chapter Five

The Assembly: Setting, Atmosphere, and Membership

Introduction

As a constitutionally protected Indigenous self-government, the Nunatsiavut Government (NG) is unique among Canadian Inuit organizations and unusual among Canadian Indigenous organizations. It follows that the Nunatsiavut Assembly, as the central institution of the NG, exhibits unique and distinctive features. It does not, however, necessarily follow that such features arise from or contribute to the NG's self-government mandate. Nor can it be assumed that elements of the assembly's structure and operations rooted in Inuit values and culture serve to advance self-government or, conversely, that Euro-Canadian-influenced elements don't reflect or further self-government aspirations.

Accordingly, divining the relationship between the orientation and operation of the assembly and the realization of self-government in Nunatsiavut requires a close examination of the assembly's practices and activities. Such is the objective of this and the following two chapters. This one begins with a short account of the Transitional Assembly, then moves on to describe the basic structure of the assembly, as well as its setting and its atmosphere. A brief look at the characteristics of the members follows. Subsequent sections examine the speakership, the AngajukKât and community chairs, and, finally, interpersonal relations among members.

The Transitional Assembly

When the Labrador Inuit Land Claims Agreement came into effect on 1 December 2005, the Labrador Inuit Association (LIA) transformed into the Nunatsiavut Assembly and the Nunatsiavut Executive Council. This was accomplished through an appendix to the Nunatsiavut constitution, which had been approved prior to the finalization of the claim. A Transitional Assembly was authorized to govern until the first elections were held, within a year of the claim's coming into force. The Transitional Assembly consisted of twenty-one ordinary members, most of whom were LIA directors, with the LIA president as president and the LIA vice-president as first minister. The secretary and treasurer of LIA became ministers.[1] The AngajukKât and the one community chair were *ex officio* members but had no vote. Beneficiaries outside Nunatsiavut and Upper Lake Melville were not represented. The Transitional Assembly fleshed out its own structure and process through the *Transitional Assembly Act*, the first statute it passed.

The Transitional Assembly put in place the basic structure of the NG and passed several essential pieces of legislation, beginning with the *Nunatsiavut Constitution Act* and including the *Beneficiaries Enrolment Act*, the *Labrador Inuit Lands Act*, the *Civil Service Act*, the *Nunatsiavut Assembly Act*, the *Nunatsiavut Government Organization (Transitional) Act*, and the *Financial Administration Act*. Publicly available records of the Transitional Assembly are sparse.

Six members of the Transitional Assembly ran in the first ordinary member election in October 2006. Only two won: First Minister Anthony Andersen, who continued as first minister in the First Assembly, and Ben Ponniuk, minister of health, education, social, and economic development, who took on a similar portfolio in the First Assembly. Two of the four unsuccessful candidates had been ministers in the Transitional Assembly.

Some Basics

In governance terms, the word "parliament" carries greater weight and authority than "assembly." It is thus surely significant, particularly with respect to Nunatsiavut's self-governing status and aspirations, that while "assembly" is the day-to-day usage, the constitution stipulates in section 4.1.1 that "there shall be a Labrador Inuit *parliament* for Nunatsiavut to be known as the Nunatsiavut Assembly" (emphasis added). Other than in reference to the federal or provincial governments, neither "parliament" nor "assembly" appear in the claim, which speaks only of Nunatsiavut's "legislative institutions" or "legislative body."

The most basic feature of the assembly is its firm placement within the conventions of the Westminster cabinet-parliamentary system, also known as "responsible government." The central structural and operational Westminster principles entail a collective executive, the cabinet, typically dominated by its leader, the prime minister/premier/first minister. Cabinet gains and retains power by maintaining the support of the elected legislature – its "confidence" – by winning votes on key policies and decisions. Thus it is always possible, though unlikely, for the legislature to depose a government. Ministers, including the first minister, must be members of the legislature.[2] Proceedings are regulated by a non-partisan speaker. Power is concentrated in the cabinet, as symbolized by the prohibition against legislators who are not ministers from even introducing for debate so-called money bills, legislation that directly allocates public spending or that imposes taxes. The key principle of cabinet solidarity means that regardless of ministers' personal views on a government policy or decision, they must support it in public; if they cannot in conscience do so, they must resign from cabinet or be dismissed by the first minister.

In Ottawa, the provinces, and Yukon, as indeed in the vast majority of Westminster-style legislatures, all or virtually all elected members belong to political parties, whose hold over their members, through the political convention of party discipline, is very strong. It is widely, but incorrectly, believed that political parties are essential elements of Westminster parliaments. Hard as it may be to imagine a large legislature operating without political parties, none of the principles set out in the preceding paragraph necessarily entail parties. Indeed, the "consensus government" assemblies of Nunavut and the Northwest Territories, which clearly follow the tenets of Westminster-style responsible government, function without political parties, as does Tynwald, the parliament of the Isle of Man, and, in the past, some former British colonies in the South Seas, such as Fiji.

Even aside from the notable absence of parties, the Nunatsiavut Assembly is a decidedly unconventional Westminster parliament. Some might argue that the presence in the assembly of a popularly elected president constitutes a fundamental departure from Westminster principles. I contend, however, that the cabinet-centred organization of the assembly and the precepts by which it operates are very much within both the spirit and the letter of Westminster parliamentarism. This is the view of Veryan Haysom, one of the principal architects of the NG structure.[3] The Nunatsiavut constitution states explicitly that ministers may not hold office "if they no longer enjoy the confidence of the Assembly."[4] With its sometimes stuffy, arcane rituals, the Westminster system may appear an outdated colonial holdover, and certainly it is not without serious shortcomings, yet it is a remarkably adaptable governance model, capable, for example, of accommodating very different ways of electing members (first past the post, proportional representation, transferable ballot, and so on) and of functioning with or without parties. Thus, the inclusion of the AngajukKât and community chairs as assembly members is not at all problematic within a Westminster context, though the same cannot be said about their ineligibility to serve in cabinet.

That Nunatsiavut adopted the Westminster model entails far-reaching implications for the operation of the assembly, and indeed for that of the NG. On a practical, day-to-day level it mandates that the assembly follow such procedures as question period and the money bill rule. More significantly, like any system of governance, the Westminster model carries with it far-reaching, often implicit assumptions and imperatives about politics and decision making that can profoundly shape the attitudes and behaviours of elected members. In the case of Nunatsiavut, as in Nunavut, the concentration of power characteristic of the Westminster system and its adversarial nature run directly counter to central elements of Inuit political culture: namely, the consensual basis of decision making and the expectation of inclusive consultation on important issues. The nature of consensus government in Nunatsiavut and the influence of Inuit culture on the assembly are discussed in chapter 8.

Similar to declaring the assembly a parliament as an affirmation of self-government is the constitution's claim of privilege for assembly members. Parliamentary privilege is a technical term referring to the immunity enjoyed by parliamentarians, individually and collectively, from certain legal restrictions and procedures. As a classic authority on parliamentary procedure notes, these are protections and immunities "without which they [parliamentarians] could not discharge their functions, and which exceed those possessed by other bodies or individuals."[5] Section 4.16 asserts a freedom-of-speech privilege for all assembly members, exempting them from liability from "proceedings, penalties or damages under any Inuit law for anything that they have said in, produced before or submitted to the Nunatsiavut Assembly or any of its committees or subcommittees." It also contemplates additional privileges that "may be prescribed by Inuit law." These privileges are far more limited than those enjoyed by members of Parliament and members of provincial legislatures, which extend to exemption from various civil proceedings, such as jury duty. Moreover, the reach of assembly members' privileges is far from certain. Assembly legal adviser Haysom warned members in an orientation session that the immunity asserted by the constitution is "not clear or simple," and he voiced uncertainty when asked whether the Nunatsiavut constitution can "trump the law of defamation."[6] Cases where members have claimed privilege have yet to emerge.

The assembly currently consists of eighteen members, all of whom must be Inuit: a president, elected by all beneficiaries; ten ordinary members elected in first-past-the-post geographic constituencies; the AngajukKât of the five Nunatsiavut Inuit community governments; and the chairs of the two Inuit community corporations. The Nunatsiavut Executive Council (NEC) consists of the president, the first minister, and (usually) five ministers. Aside from the president, only ordinary members are eligible to serve in the NEC. The assembly meets in Hopedale four or five times a year, usually for two-day sessions. (Although the *Nunatsiavut Assembly Act* uses the terms somewhat differently, I use "sitting" to refer to a single day, whereas "session" entails all sittings in a given week – no session has ever extended into a second week.)[7] A politically neutral speaker, who also must be an ordinary member, presides.

All sittings are open to visitors, Inuit and non-Inuit, though on occasion the members do meet privately. Since 2015, a live audio feed of assembly proceedings has been broadcast via the internet. The value of the audio stream is somewhat undercut in that most Nunatsiavumiut, save those in Hopedale, are unlikely to know that the assembly is meeting since the NG does not usually announce sessions and the widely followed OK Society generally only mentions assembly sessions once they're finished. Hopes for a video feed came a cropper owing to the lamentable state of broadband capacity across Nunatsiavut, though it remains a long-term objective. During her brief time in office, Speaker Marlene Winters-Wheeler began a project to archive all assembly videos on a YouTube channel. In March 2021 and January 2022, during the COVID-19 pandemic, the assembly held completely virtual sessions that live-streamed via the video-conferencing app Zoom. The quality of the images varied a good deal, a few minor technical glitches occurred, and viewers could only see individual members at their computers (i.e., no group or "gallery" views), but, overall, the experience augured well for full video coverage of the assembly at some point.

Setting

All sessions of the Nunatsiavut Assembly take place in Hopedale (population 596 in 2021).[8] Long known by Inuit as Agvituk, "the place of whales," it served as an important whaling station between the sixteenth and eighteenth centuries. In 1782, the Moravian Church established a mission there called Hofenthal (Hopedale). The settlement developed around the mission, a large wooden building that still dominates the old part of the community and is a National Historic Site still used for services. Several hundred metres away is a newer section of town, closer to the ferry dock and the airstrip. The Assembly Building is on the shore road between the two sections of the community.

The Nunatsiavut Assembly Building exemplifies Charles Goodsell's contention that the architecture of a legislative building is often linked to central elements of a jurisdiction's culture and politics. Legislative buildings, he writes, "as self-consciously built stages for the performance of political rituals, may be assumed to reflect shared norms of governance and underlying patterns of political behaviour that constitute political culture."[9] Opened in 2012, the Assembly Building mimics both an igloo and the nearby Moravian mission. Combining the two traditions, the building sports an unconventional steeple featuring a large inukshuk. No one approaching it either by land or from the water – it sits towards the bottom of a substantial hill only a few metres from Hopedale Harbour – could miss either the Inuit or the religious influence (see figures 5.1a and 5.1b below).

From the welcoming, airy lobby, a right turn leads towards a large committee room. A left turn leads down a corridor to a smaller committee room where members congregate before sittings and during breaks, a small kitchen, a row of offices along the rear of the building, and the entrance to the chamber. Behind the reception desk are stairs to the gallery for visitors and NG staff. Roughly ten

Figures 5.1a and 5.1b. Two views of the Nunatsiavut Assembly Building in Hopedale, Nunatsiavut
Source: Courtesy of the Nunatsiavut Government

Figure 5.2. The Assembly Chamber
Source: France Rivet, CC BY-SA 4.0 <https://creativecommons.org/licenses/by-sa/4.0>,
via Wikimedia Commons

by twenty metres, the chamber is dominated by an oval table at which the members sit (round or oval seating arrangements are unusual in Westminster parliaments). A magnificent polar bear hide all but covers the floor inside the oval. The walls, trimmed with Labradorite, a local mineral known for its remarkable play of colour and its supposed healing properties, showcase photos of prominent Nunatsiavut Inuit leaders and displays of local art. Technical staff and translators occupy recessed booths along one wall. Two video cameras operated by staff of the OKâlaKatiget Society record the sittings. On an upper level, a broad walkway surrounds the chamber, with chairs for NG staff and visitors. The acoustics in the chamber and gallery are good, though members, staff, and visitors often use the translation devices available, not usually for translation, since little Inuttut is spoken, but to hear debates more clearly.

Slightly behind one of the long sides of the oval, the speaker and the clerk sit at a small table with a *kudlik*, the traditional symbolic Inuit soapstone lamp. Opposite them are the members of the Executive Council, with the president in the middle. Three non-NEC ordinary members sit to the speaker's left, with the community chairs and the AngajukKât to the right of the speaker. This seating arrangement, which dates from the assembly's first session, came at the direction of the deputy minister to the president.[10] Two youth, from different communities each session, serve as pages, distributing documents and water to members and delivering messages. Senior NG staff sit at one end of the gallery, as do others waiting to appear before the assembly, such as representatives of the various trusts. The rare visitors – during the sittings I observed, barely a handful wandered in, none staying for more than a few minutes – sit where they like in the gallery. No security is evident in the building; visitors are free to wander freely about. When I enquired about a water fountain, I was directed to the kitchen at the back of the building and told to help myself to anything in the fridge. I was subsequently encouraged to wander into the kitchen whenever I wanted coffee, cookies, char, or other snacks.

Standing Order 11(4) requires members to "dress in a manner appropriate to the dignity of the Assembly and to Inuit culture." Speaker, clerk, pages, and almost all members wear *silapâk*, traditional light jackets, featuring subtle but significant variations in striping and embroidery. During the times I was present, most were white, though black and wine *silapâk* were also in evidence. One member wore a sealskin vest, and a few others jackets and ties. In earlier times, *silapâk* were much less in evidence, with at best a handful of members sporting them, the balance dressing in standard Western garb.

By any standard, the assembly building is impressive. All the more so by comparison with the facilities available to the assembly prior to the building's opening in 2012. For the first years, members usually met in a narrow, cramped boardroom in the NG's Katingavik building in Hopedale. Judging by the bureaucratic notices and the children's artwork on the walls, the room had a multitude of uses. Members were jammed together and sat across from one another, their tables barely inches apart. Space was so limited that guests making presentations sometimes had to stand beside the speaker or in an adjacent doorway and the clerk had to sit in the small visitors' area at the end of the table (see figure 5.3 below).

Atmosphere

The atmosphere in the chamber is typically congenial and collegial, the tone of debate civil and respectful. Members, almost all of whom are in the chamber throughout each sitting, listen attentively when other members or witnesses are speaking and rarely interrupt or heckle. Not once in the sittings I observed, listened to, or watched over Zoom did the speaker have to call for order. Applause and desk-thumping are unusual but not unknown. Requests for unanimous consent to extend time for ministerial statements, to advance

Figure 5.3. Assembly meeting in boardroom, 2008
Source: Courtesy of the Nunatsiavut Government and the OKâlaKatiget Society

certain procedures in the order of business, to waive a standing order, and the like are virtually always granted. Mirroring the other consensus systems in Nunavut and the Northwest Territories, other than during breaks, members rarely leave the chamber, and even then only very briefly.

A recent amendment to the Standing Orders ensures that members' attention to assembly proceedings is not distracted by electronic devices. Unless authorized by the speaker, as occurred in the pandemic-constrained October 2020 session, members may not use cell phones, computers, or other electronic devices in the chamber.

A member who served in the First Assembly and who continues to follow Nunatsiavut politics closely told me that the assembly is "not as lively as it used to be," "lively" being something of a euphemism. The more sedate, convivial atmosphere of the present-day assembly, this person suggested, reflects a learning process among members as to what is and is not possible, noting, for example, that Upper Lake Melville members initially pressed hard to get the same benefits and services for their constituents as beneficiaries in the Labrador Inuit Settlement Area (LISA) receive, but some of these, such as hunting rights, just aren't possible. As well, personality factors have been at work: according to the former member, two of the First Assembly members had been let go by LIA, and their bitterness showed in their behaviour.

Assembly proceedings are an incongruous mixture of formality and informality. The procedure for the assembly to resolve itself into committee of the whole can be ponderously formal. Members will not speak until recognized by

Figure 5.4. Assembly meeting, 2014
Source: Courtesy of the Nunatsiavut Government and the OKâlaKatiget Society

the speaker, and they routinely thank her for recognizing them. A minister will almost always thank a member who asked a question for the question, while a member asking a supplementary question will often thank the minister for the initial answer. Members are addressed, by the speaker and their colleagues, as "the honourable member," yet members also frequently address one another by first name, as, on occasion, do witnesses: during one debate a deputy minister addressed her minister as "Danny."[11] It is not uncommon for senior bureaucrats in the gallery above the chamber to signal or even shout out comments to ministers during proceedings.

Harsh words are sometimes spoken but are usually directed beyond the NG, most often towards the provincial government when it is seen, as it often is, as uncooperative if not actually hostile to the land claim. On occasion, members are aggressive and critical of colleagues. Most often this takes the form of attacks by non-NEC members on the cabinet's failure to involve them in governance processes or the adequacy of its communications with them, a dynamic discussed in chapter 8. The motions to expel members from the assembly, discussed in chapter 7, generated decidedly unpleasant exchanges.

To some extent, the typically non-confrontational character of the assembly reflects both the absence of political parties and the Inuit preference for collaboration and consensus over conflict, and of course the two are related. "Inuit are not aggressive or demanding," was how one long-serving Inuk bureaucrat put it. The interpersonal dynamics of assembly members also play a role. One member, in referring to the death of another member's spouse, commented, "as the Assembly we are like an extended family. We spend so much time together, and care for each other."[12] Indeed, members do spend considerable time together. Although the assembly usually only meets for about ten days a year, members are together almost constantly during those days and most arrive in Hopedale at least one day before the session. While in Hopedale, almost all members stay at the only hotel, the twenty-two-room Amaguk Inn, and take their meals in its small dining room, save for when meals are brought into the assembly to save time. Even travelling to and from the assembly, members spend time together. Other than the two representing Hopedale, they must fly to sessions, and air travel in Nunatsiavut, either by "sked" (scheduled) or by charter, means Twin Otters, whose limited seating can charitably be described as cosy.

Given Nunatsiavut's population and in particular the size of the five settlement communities, it is hardly surprising that members of the political elite know each other well. In the first two assemblies (2006–14) most members had been deeply involved in LIA politics, and even today a good many members trace their political involvement back to LIA days. The cliché that everyone knows everyone is only a slight exaggeration. That many members have histories with many other members cuts two ways. Shared experiences can lead to friendship and mutual respect, but conflictual experiences can generate residues of ill-feeling. This was evident even the first time the assembly met. In explaining why he could not support one of the nominated candidates for first minister, the president effectively said that he didn't trust him based on his bitter departure from LIA less than a year earlier and the member's criticisms of LIA officials. "I need to know," he added, "when I go somewhere or if I'm here in a community or in any other community or constituency that someone isn't going to stab me in the back."[13]

Sittings, Weather, and Planes

It took a few years for the assembly to settle into a predictable schedule, meeting five times a year, typically in January, March, June, September, and November. Specific dates are set by the president a year or more in advance, though the information does not seem to be widely distributed: more than one journalist I spoke with had no idea as to the timing of the sessions. In the assembly's early years, a session might last one, two, or three days, but for some time two-day sessions have been the norm, though single-day sessions do occur. Early on, in August 2007, a one-day emergency session was called by the president to pass a bill authorizing an NG guarantee of a $600,000 loan to the Torngat Fish Producers Co-op. The session lasted only a few minutes, with the bill, the only item of business, generating virtually no debate. As described in the next chapter, the need to pass a budget led to a short, highly unusual one-day session in the early days of the COVID-19 pandemic in March 2020, with another one-day session in October to put in place procedures allowing the assembly to function during the pandemic.[14]

Table 5.1. Number and duration of sessions, 2006–22

	Number of Sessions	Total Days	Length of Session			
			1 Day	2 Days	3 Days	5 Days
First Assembly	15	32	6	6	3	1
Second Assembly	17	36	3	9	5	–
Third Assembly	18	35	1	17	–	–
Fourth Assembly	17	29	5	12	–	–
Total	67	132	15	44	8	1

Criticisms have occasionally been levied against the number and length of sessions as undercutting the assembly's effectiveness. The constitution requires only that the assembly sit once a year (section 3.2.14). Sections 32 and 33 of the *Nunatsiavut Assembly Act* require a spring session, between mid-January and the end of June, and a fall session, between early September and mid-December, and they give the president discretion to call for additional sessions. The only formal statement about the duration of sessions is in section 36 of the act, which authorizes one-day sessions as well as longer sessions.

Table 5.1 presents data on the length and number of sessions from 2006 to the end of the Fourth Assembly in April 2022. It shows that, save for the first session, which extended over five days, no session has lasted more than three days and almost two out of every three sessions (65 per cent) lasted two days. Two-day sessions have clearly become the norm, with the last three-day session having occurred in 2013. In interpreting the numbers for the Fourth Assembly, it should be noted that two of the three sessions in 2020 lasted only a day because of pandemic constraints.

The table confirms that the sessions are indeed short. A former public servant with extensive experience of the assembly suggests that three factors explain the penchant for short sessions: members' dislike of being away from home for extended periods, cost concerns, and NEC's preference that members have neither the time nor the inclination to delve deeply into NG affairs. Concern over cost may be a red herring, in that additional accommodation and meal expenses for (say) three four- or five-day sessions over those incurred over five two-day sessions would likely be largely offset by reduced transportation costs. It is fair to note that losing or curtailing a week-long session to the ever-present threat of bad flying weather would be more problematic than for a two-day session.

What, then, are the implications of the assembly's short sessions? The former public servant argues that short sessions mean members lack the opportunity to question and challenge NEC as effectively as they might because they are affected by pressure, some self-generated, to wrap sessions up expeditiously. Short sessions were targeted in a 2011 report from the Standing Committee on

Rules and Procedures. In the committee's view, the brief sessions, along with "short notice of some sittings combined with little advance notice of business to be discussed," created the need for many waivers of Standing Orders by unanimous consent, which the committee saw as undesirable. The original Standing Orders, the committee argued, did not anticipate short sessions and the resultant time pressures, either for proper consideration of proposed legislation or for review of the budget:

> Members of the Standing Committee have on occasions [*sic*] experienced a very rushed approach to the Assembly's consideration of the operation and maintenance, and capital estimates due again to the time constraints of a short sitting. Concerns have also been expressed from other Members as not having sufficient time to examine the estimates of the Government before voting on the appropriations. The Standing Committee was aware that the impact of short sittings and the appearance of rushing through the process to finish the sitting and leave have caused frustration among Members.[15]

The committee recommended amending the Standing Orders to provide for five-day sessions with day-long sittings Monday to Thursday plus a Friday morning sitting, with provision for flexibility.[16] This recommendation was accepted and incorporated into the revised Standing Orders. Thus, Standing Order 4 stipulates that "the Assembly shall meet on Mondays, Tuesdays, Wednesdays and Thursdays from 9:00 a.m. to 5:00 p.m. and on Fridays from 09:00 a.m. to 12:00 p.m., unless otherwise ordered by the Assembly." Despite the mandatory "shall," this rule is not observed, nor does the assembly issue an order superseding it.

Even if it is not possible to assess systematically the implications of the short sessions that have come to characterize the assembly, it is hard to argue that they are of no consequence. The analysis in chapter 9 suggests that the brevity of the sessions both constrains review of the budget and of proposed legislation and all but precludes the possibility of mounting wide-ranging debate on important issues not tied to legislative or budgetary processes, thereby rendering the assembly less effective than it might be in performing key functions.

Members usually arrive on Monday and may hold informal meetings that day. Sessions begin at 9:00 a.m. Tuesday and typically wrap up Wednesday afternoon, with occasional Tuesday evening sittings. Timing of the lunch break, usually about ninety minutes, is at the discretion of the speaker and depends on how business is unfolding.[17] Two or three times a day the speaker calls a ten or fifteen minute washroom/smoke/snack break.[18] These breaks may seem a poor use of time but in fact symbolize the seriousness with which members take their assembly duties, as they enable members to attend to personal needs without missing any proceedings. If a tricky procedural issue arises, the speaker may call a brief recess to consult with the clerk and sometimes with the NG director of legal services. Similarly, uncertainty as to how to resolve a substantive political issue may bring about a short hiatus, thereby allowing key players to huddle and scope out a way forward, through a motion, delay, or another solution.

All this is subject to omnipresent provisos about the weather and planes. Other than the few who live in Hopedale, members and NG staff travel to and from sessions by air. The shortcomings of Hopedale's airstrip and those in other Nunatsiavut communities, together with the limitations of the Twin Otter – for all intents and purposes the only commercial passenger aircraft flying in Nunatsiavut[19] – mean that air travel is highly susceptible to the notoriously difficult weather on Labrador's North Coast.

The weather literally influences the assembly's ability to both come and go. On several occasions, planned sessions have been cancelled altogether because too many members were "weathered out." Less far-reaching hitches also occur: the start of one sitting I attended was delayed for an hour because the plane bringing an essential IT support person to Hopedale was delayed by weather. Another time, a similar problem with one member's late flight led to a forty-five-minute delay in starting a sitting. At session's end, time pressures imposed by "the plane" can affect the pace and extent of debate. For those booked on "the sked" to Goose Bay via Makkovik, Postville, and Rigolet, departure is mid-afternoon. Assembly staff often arrange a charter to take members home at the end of session, and while charters can and do wait, the length of wait may be limited by worsening weather conditions or, in Winter, approaching darkness since the Nain airstrip cannot accommodate night landings. Speaking about the need to rejig the assembly's agenda to accommodate a presentation by the NG's auditors, Finance Minister Tyler Edmunds once observed, "as with many things we are somewhat prisoner to the schedules of our flights."[20] Accordingly, completing the agenda in time to make flights sometimes requires a short lunch break with food sent in from the hotel, and it is common for the speaker to remind members of the timing of flights and the associated need to check out of the hotel as proceedings unfold.[21] At the same time, speakers have not been shy in reminding members where their priorities should lie. "We are in this community in our Legislative Capital to carry out our business," proclaimed Speaker Danny Pottle in 2009, "so if that means that the charter must wait then so be it."[22] In a subsequent assembly, Speaker Edward Blake-Rudkowski cautioned that debates would take as much time as needed: "there was some thought or perception that perhaps we would rush through proceedings to accommodate flight lines [*sic*: times?], timelines, personal agendas – and I want to assure everybody here and everyone in the public, that that would never be allowed to occur."[23] Still, the reality is that time pressures arising from flight times and weather concerns can constrain assembly activities. Indeed, the same day that Speaker Blake-Rudkowski indicated that debates would unfold heedless of time pressures, he explained that two significant items of business had to be postponed until the next session, "given all the problems the weather created," and that the planned two-day session would have to be truncated into a single day.[24] At the one day-session in October 2020 during the COVID-19 pandemic, he cut debate short on both a presentation on one of the trusts and on the package of procedural changes designed to cope with pandemic conditions, in order to ensure that "the Nain crowd" would be able to make their flight home; the pilots had been asked to delay take-off but were reluctant to do so.[25]

The Members

Systematic data on assembly members' characteristics are not available, but some observations can be advanced. By definition, all members have been Inuit, though usually no more than two or three have been fluent in Inuttut, so that beyond symbolic uses of a few words or phrases such as *UKatti* (speaker) or *Nakummek* (thank you), virtually all proceedings unfold in English. Women have been moderately well represented in the assembly, at least compared to other Indigenous and non-Indigenous Canadian legislatures. To the end of the Fourth Assembly, 19 of the 52 assembly members (37 per cent) were women. Notably, however, women were substantially more likely to have served as AngajukKât or community chairs (11 of 20, or 55 per cent) than as ordinary members (10 of 31, or 32 per cent).[26] This is significant since only ordinary members may be appointed to the NEC; the proportion of women ministers (7 of 23, or 30 per cent) is effectively the same as the proportion of women who were ordinary members. Women have served as president, first minister, and speaker.

The *Nunatsiavut Elections Act* requires that candidates live in the constituencies they seek to represent, so that members are rooted in their communities or constituencies.[27] The vastness of the Canada Constituency makes for an important exception, though it is notable that until the 2017 by-election that brought Edward Blake-Rudkowski, who lived in Toronto, into the assembly, all ordinary members representing the Canada Constituency lived in St. John's, which has a substantial Nunatsiavumiut community. Going into the 2022 election, the Canada Constituency members were Roland Saunders and Susan Onalik, both St. John's residents, though when first elected, Saunders lived in Edmonton.

My inexpert observation suggests that most members are probably in their fifties, though the Fourth Assembly included members in their early thirties and mid-seventies. On the basis of fragmentary conversations and documentation, it would appear that a substantial proportion of the members have university degrees or other post-secondary credentials. Their occupational backgrounds vary widely, including, for example, fishing, journalism, finance, and social work. Many, perhaps most, have worked for government or for Inuit organizations. Indeed, as elsewhere across the Indigenous North, it is common for individuals to switch back and forth between elected political roles and appointed bureaucratic roles. By way of illustration, Darryl Shiwak, who served as first minister in the Second Assembly and held several ministerial portfolios in the First and Third Assemblies, became an NG deputy minister; First Assembly speaker and finance minister Todd Broomfield became director of renewable resources in the NG Department of Lands and Natural Resources; former first minister Kate Mitchell was an NG deputy minister before entering politics; and Johannes Lampe held a bureaucratic position in the Culture and Language Department after a stint as an ordinary member but prior to becoming president.

Some shifting occurs across member types: three ordinary members have also been AngajukKât and two others have been community chairs. Sarah Leo was briefly an AngajukKâk before running successfully for president; indeed, all three elected presidents have served as ordinary members or as AngajukKât before or after their presidential tenures. A good many Nunatsiavut politicians have run for more than one type of office. An AngajukKâk wishing to run for ordinary member must resign, but the reverse does not hold.

The most recent salary review of members' salaries, conducted in 2017, set the basic indemnity for all members at $75,000, with an annual inflation adjustment based on Statistics Canada's Consumer Price Index (CPI).[28] As of 2021, members earned $79,756. The first minister, speaker, deputy speaker, and ministers receive additional indemnities that are not subject to CPI increases, currently ranging from $27,500 for the first minister to $8,250 for the deputy speaker. The president's basic salary is established separately; in 2017, it was set at $115,000 with annual CPI adjustments, so that as of 2020 it was $121,082. Members are nominally entitled to receive payments when engaged in committee work but the assembly has not established rates or processes for such payments.

All members, save those from the Canada Constituency, receive a Northern Allowance, formerly termed a Labrador Allowance: $7,550 per annum for those in LISA, $5,350 for those from Upper Lake Melville. In each instance, members without dependents receive half of these amounts. A levy of 5 per cent of members' salaries, with a matching NG contribution, funds members' pensions; members are also eligible for a severance allowance. The assembly pays members' travel, accommodation, and living allowances while on assembly business. Members receive various other minor benefits, such as use of an assembly-owned computer while in office. Ordinary members, but only ordinary members, are entitled to constituency allowances for office rental, newsletters, and the like. Salaries and benefits for members and ministers are set every five years by the assembly on recommendation of the Members' Services Committee. Other than annual inflation increases, section 8.4.7 of the Nunatsiavut constitution requires the Inuit public be consulted on any changes to salary levels and benefits. This is done via media announcements and notices sent to Inuit community governments. These requests for public feedback have generated virtually no comments.

Members of most Canadian legislatures are not required to account for their time or what they do with it, on the assumption that their political masters, the voters and/or senior party officials, will judge their performance on the basis of accomplishments. Members of the Nunatsiavut Assembly must of course convince voters that they have been effective representatives come re-election time. In addition, however, members must report formally as to the time they've spent on the job – or, more accurately, time off the job. Members are required to submit forms on a biweekly basis attesting to leave entitlements they have used or travel they have undertaken, even if none occurred during the reporting period, a requirement that some have found needlessly and annoyingly bureaucratic.[29]

According to the *Members' Handbook*, assembly members "must report to the Speaker on their time, leave and constituency spending."[30] The same document specifies that "the normal work week is 35 hours," though the *Elected Officials Policy Manual* adds that this need not necessarily mean 8:30 a.m. to noon and 1:00 to 4:30 p.m.; if official duties or travel are required on a weekend, for example, the following week's hours may be adjusted.[31] Members are entitled to various annual leaves: six weeks for vacation; five days for bereavement; five days for family responsibilities; fourteen specific Nunatsiavut-wide statutory and religious holidays, including LIA Day (26 March) and Nunatsiavut Day (1 December), plus certain community-specific holidays such as Levi Pottle Day in Rigolet. In a distinctive reflection of Inuit priorities, members get five days a year for hunting, fishing, trapping, and gathering. Modest sick leave is available and members "who after making reasonable efforts to report to work, remain unable to work due to unsafe or impossible travelling conditions are entitled to two paid adverse weather days per year."[32] Leave days are not permitted, save for adverse weather, illness, or bereavement, when the assembly is sitting. Pay and benefits are docked for members who miss a sitting or a committee meeting without valid reason. Standing Order 11(11) requires the speaker's permission for members to be absent; ministers' absence requires permission of the president. On occasion, *Hansard* records the speaker noting a member absent without authorization.[33] Far more common is the speaker's announcement at the start of a session of members who have, for various reasons, been excused for missing the session.

Turnover

Turnover among assembly members is high, while change in the composition of NEC and in the assignment of portfolios within NEC is also substantial. Important implications ensue from these features of political life in

Table 5.2. Length of members' service, 2006–22 (years)

	0–1		1–2		2–4		5–8		9–12	
	M	W	M	W	M	W	M	W	M	W
Ordinary Members	1	2*	–	–	14****	4**	4*	3	3*	–
AngajukKât	–	1	1	–	7**	2	1*	3**	1	–
Community Chairs	–	1	1	1	2	3**	1	–	–	–
Total	1	4	2	1	23	9	6	6	4	–

*An asterisk indicates that one member in this cell was in office in April 2022

Nunatsiavut for the operation of the assembly and in particular for relations between NEC and non-NEC members. Table 5.2 presents data on members' length of service to April 2022 (four members appear twice in the table, having served, for example, as both ordinary members and AngajukKât). With four years constituting a full term for all three types of members, at the end of the Fourth Assembly nearly three-quarters of all members served only a single term (40 of 56, or 71 per cent). Relatedly, longevity is uncommon. No one served in all four assemblies; three ordinary members, all men and all ministers for most of their time in the assembly, and one AngajukKâk served all or part of three terms, but they constitute a mere 7 per cent of the total membership. One of the three long-serving ordinary members returned for the Fifth Assembly.

Roughly two-thirds of ordinary members (68 per cent) served a single term or less, while 10 did not complete the terms to which they were elected. Two ordinary members were expelled, and another lost his seat when his beneficiary status was revoked, with the balance leaving for various personal and political reasons. Of 16 AngajukKât, 11 (69 per cent) served in just one assembly, 2 of whom resigned early in their terms. If ordinary members and AngajukKât generally have fairly short stays in office, community chairs' assembly careers have been remarkably brief: 8 of 9 (89 per cent) were single-term members;[34] 3 left their posts early.

A different, and more telling, way of measuring turnover is to compare assembly membership at the beginning of consecutive assemblies. Of the 17 members at the start of the First Assembly, only 7 returned for the start of the Second Assembly, 2 of whom had been defeated in the 2010 ordinary members election but were successful in the subsequent AngajukKât elections,.[35] Only 5 of the initial 18 Second Assembly members (a second Canada constituency member had been added in 2010) were present at the start of the Third Assembly and only 3 of the 18 members from the start of the Third Assembly were among the those at the first meeting of the Fourth Assembly. The Fifth

Assembly began with 8 of the members present at the outset of the Fourth Assembly. In only one of the four comparisons was either of the community chairs from one assembly still in place at the start of the next assembly. This is a remarkable level of membership flux.

Systematic electoral data are not available for AngajukKât or community chairs, but it is possible to determine why, on twenty-nine occasions, ordinary members in one assembly were not serving in the following one. Three were removed from office, though 2 could presumably have contested the next election but did not, and 6 others resigned for one reason or another, 2 of whom were ministers who resigned immediately after being removed from NEC. In the other twenty cases, it was most often the voters who determined whether sitting members returned to the assembly: 7 members chose not to run, with 13 going down to defeat in re-election bids.[36]

No matter the cause, the high turnover among assembly members has significant implications. The most obvious is that at any given time, a substantial proportion of members face daunting learning curves due to inexperience. In turn, it would be reasonable to surmise that NEC finds it easier to deal with inexperienced, rather than veteran, members.

But is NEC any more stable than the general membership of the assembly? The data shown in tables 5.3 and 5.4 below provide an answer. Overall, and with significant exceptions and important nuances, members of NEC can draw on more extensive experience than non-NEC members. Table 5.3 shows the spans of time ministers have spent in cabinet (some on more than one occasion). Notably, 40 per cent of the twenty-five individuals who served in NEC were in cabinet for five to ten years; three have been presidents. In April 2022, two NEC members had more than eight years of ministerial experience and another had almost eight years.

Though variation in length of tenure on the part of both NEC and non-NEC members is evident, overall, the more extensive experience of some, but not all, ministers cannot help but work in favour of NEC. To be sure, relations between NEC members and non-NEC members are more than a simple zero-sum game, but to the extent that conflict does occur, experienced ministers enjoy a distinct advantage over non-NEC members, who are generally less experienced.

Ministers' total NEC experience is certainly significant, but it is also important to recognize that their experience is typically marked by shifts in portfolio responsibilities. This is so since even the most able and experienced ministers require time to get up to speed on their new remits. Table 5.4, which fleshes out the consequences of ministerial shuffles, resignations, and replacements, shows the length of time, in months, that ministers have spent at the helm of departments, as well as the total number of ministers for each department. The picture that emerges from the table is mixed. On the one hand, 10 ministers remained in their departments for at least forty months, more than enough

Table 5.3. Ministers' length of membership in NEC, 2006–22 (years)

Years in NEC	0–1	1–2	2–4	5–7	8–10
Total Time in NEC	4*	5	6	7****	3**

*An asterisk indicates one minister serving in NEC as of April 2022

Table 5.4. Ministerial tenure, 2006–22 (months)

Department	Total	1–3	5–11	12–24	25–36	40–68
First Minister	5	1	–	–	1*	3
Education and Economic Development	13	3	4*	3	2	1
Finance, HR, and IT	7	–	2	1	3*	1
Health and Social Development	7	–	3	–	2	2*
Lands and Natural Resources	12	1	5	4*	1	1
Language, Culture, and Tourism	7	1	–	3	1	2*
Total	51	6	14	11	10	10

*An asterisk indicates one minister in office as of April 2022

time to master files and to move them along. On the other hand, 14 ministers stayed less than a year in departments, 20 if the six stints that lasted only two or three months are included, and another 10 were, or had been, as of April 2022, in their portfolios for less than two years. All but one of the very brief tenures occurred when an acting minister was dispatched to fill in for a colleague who departed unexpectedly. Not least because the acting ministers retained responsibility for their primary departments, these short stints can represent significant instability for affected departments.

In short, NEC typically has ministers relatively new to their current portfolios as well as others with considerable experience in their departments. Internal NEC dynamics must surely be affected by the varying levels of familiarity ministers have with their assignments, and with NEC generally. One facet of these dynamics looms especially large: save the first (non-elected) president and first minister Tyler Edmunds, who was selected in January 2020 to replace Kate Mitchell who had been removed from office, all presidents and first ministers have served for at least four years. Thus, even aside from the power inherent in sitting atop the NEC hierarchy, they enjoy the advantage of having held their positions longer than most, if not all, of their ministers.

Looking at the data from a departmental perspective suggests further implications of frequent ministerial reassignments. Calling it revolving door departmental leadership may be an overstatement, but it is surely of moment that no department, other than that of the first minister, has experienced fewer than seven different ministers during the sixteen years of the NG's existence, an average of just more than two years per minister, and that two departments have known more than ten ministers, barely more than one year per minister on average. In a few cases, the same person has served more than once as minister of a particular department. Taken in concert with the longevity and subject expertise of NG's deputy ministers, the frequently short tenure of ministers has potentially significant implications for the interaction between elected and appointed officials. This is not to suggest that NG deputies behave as North Coast versions of Sir Humphrey Appleby,[37] but it cannot help but affect the minister-deputy relationship.

The Speaker

The speaker of the Nunatsiavut Assembly follows the standard non-partisan precepts for presiding officers in Westminster-style parliaments. At the same time, the assembly's openness to unconventional practices, together with its distinctive structural features, have made for unusually active, and indeed unusually powerful, speakers.

As is standard in Westminster parliaments, the speaker only votes to break a tie. Prior to the 2013 revisions to the Standing Orders, the speaker was required to vote on any matter requiring a two-thirds majority of the members. This provision was removed since the only situation specified in the constitution, the *Assembly Act*, or the Standing Orders turning on a two-thirds vote was the removal of the speaker.

Speakers are elected by the assembly on nomination of the president.[38] Thus, competitive elections for speaker are uncommon, though one did take place at the start of the Third Assembly. President Sarah Leo nominated Sean Lyall for the speakership, bypassing Patricia Ford, who had served as speaker for the entire Second Assembly. On asking for consensus for the nomination, Ford registered a "nay," whereupon the president called for a secret ballot, which Lyall carried. Through the first four assemblies, five men and three women have served as speaker, half of whom represented the Canada Constituency. Speakers select their own deputy speakers. On one occasion, all three eligible ordinary members declined the speaker's invitation to serve as her deputy, whereupon the president called an adjournment. On returning, he suggested that the assembly move on, saying that he would "lobby some of the people that she might be able to appoint."[39] The following day one of the three agreed to be deputy speaker.

In other Canadian legislatures, the once common practice of appointing speakers to cabinet has largely fallen into abeyance, but in Nunatsiavut it is the norm, with five of seven former speakers having moved from the speakership to the NEC. This is less concerning than it might be in a party-based system, for two reasons. First, with only ordinary members eligible to serve in the NEC, the talent pool is sharply limited. Second, the prospect of a speaker moving into cabinet in a party system raises fears that the speaker's rulings might tilt towards the government in order to curry favour; this is far less likely in Nunatsiavut's consensus system.

The Nunatsiavut speaker enjoys the usual range of powers held by Westminster speakers: regulating debate, resolving procedural issues without the prospect of having rulings challenged, and supervising assembly administration. For the first few years, should unanimous support for a bill or motion be absent, the president could call for a "Committee on Consensus" (essentially a committee of the whole) to resolve disagreements. The president could, and sometimes did, chair the Committee on Consensus, or he could ask the speaker to chair. This procedure was replaced in the 2011 revision of the Standing Orders with a more conventional committee-of-the-whole process. In other legislatures, committees of the whole are chaired by a deputy speaker, but in Nunatsiavut the speaker remains in the chair. Indeed, the deputy speaker is only rarely asked to fill in for the speaker. The speaker chairs two important internal committees, Members' Services and Rules and Procedures, taking the lead in recommending to the assembly who should serve on the latter.

The speaker wields some unusual powers, such as discretion to call for secret ballots on certain votes. Most notable is the speaker's role in disciplinary actions against members. Under the Code of Conduct, complaints about members' behaviour, be they from other members or from the Inuit public, go to the speaker for an initial adjudication. The speaker can dismiss them as trivial, groundless, or otherwise inappropriate. Depending on the circumstances, the speaker may, with the consent of the member and the complainant, attempt to mediate the issue. Alternatively, the speaker may determine that the matter warrants formal investigation, in which case she refers it to an ad hoc discipline committee. Not only does the speaker chair the committee, she also appoints the other two members of the committee, which has authority to issue reprimands or suspensions or to recommend that a member be removed from office. In all this, the speaker's decisions are not subject to appeal.[40] All told, these are formidable powers, which have been exercised on several occasions, including once against the speaker, with the deputy speaker performing the speaker's functions in the process.

At the end of his stint as the first speaker, Todd Broomfield spoke of the trials and joys of serving in that position in a newly created legislature: "being Speaker has been very difficult with no rules to sort of guide me other than the Assembly Act [which at that time included the Standing Orders] and the Constitution and trying to interpret that on the fly has been very difficult and yet at the same time rewarding."[41] The difficulties Broomfield mentioned were evident in the frequency with which, especially in the early years, the speaker would call a short recess when a tricky procedural issue or point of order arose in order to seek advice and formulate a response. As speakers, indeed all members, and assembly staff gained experience and confidence, such interruptions became much less frequent, though they still do occur from time to time.

From the outset, Nunatsiavut speakers have involved themselves in assembly business more extensively than is usual in more conventional Westminster parliaments. These interventions have taken three broad forms: participation in assembly proceedings on the same basis as other members, offering advice and direction in new or difficult situations, and actively shaping assembly processes. In the first category are such activities as leaving the chair to make a member's statement or participate in debate, questioning ministers or guests, answering questions from members, and moving motions. While such involvement by the speaker is certainly notable, it is also important to recognize that it is far from a daily occurrence; several sessions may pass without any such interventions from the speaker. Moreover, some of the more unusual – some would say inappropriate – actions engaged in by early speakers no longer occur: moving motions and entering the debate on them, making reports from speaker-chaired committees, and in one instance, levelling sharp criticism at the president.[42]

The propriety of the speaker making members' statements was debated recently in response to a speaker-commissioned report from the Rules and Procedures Committee. Unlike with the various other issues addressed by the committee, no recommendation was made one way or the other as to adding a provision to the Standing Orders sanctioning members' statements by the speaker. Rather, the committee sought the assembly's guidance on the matter.[43] Speaker Blake-Rudkowski explained his actions as follows:

When I was first elected, I came here as the Ordinary Member for Canada and was subsequently elected to the Speaker's role. Unfortunately, during the early part of my tenure, the other Ordinary Member for Canada was on extended sick leave, and that other person also happened to be the Deputy Speaker. I thought it was necessary for me to be able to give a Member's statement because of the fact that the Canadian Constituency represents almost one-third of our beneficiary population and being Speaker, there was no vehicle per se for me to be able to give a Member statement on behalf of the 2,000 members of the Canadian constituency. So what I did in those cases was ask permission from the Assembly to step aside from the Speaker's chair such that I can give a Member statement and, as soon as the Member statement was concluded, which we're talking a maximum of five minutes, regained the Speaker's chair. But, again, it was a bit of an ungainly procedure. It doesn't happen with frequency so we're seeking direction from the Assembly, if any, about how they would like to handle those circumstances going forward.[44]

During his tenure, Blake-Rudkowski made several member's statements about events and developments in his Canada Constituency, but only after seeking and receiving unanimous consent from the assembly before proceeding.[45] Subsequently, Speaker Susan Onalik, with agreement from the assembly, asked two questions in question period.[46]

In the debate on the report, Language and Culture Minister Jim Lyall, a former president, spoke strongly against the notion that the speaker should in any way engage in addressing the assembly: "the Speaker's supposed to be absolutely free of any political statements of any kind … bringing politics into the conversation. I think the Speaker's absolutely got to be free of anything like that. He's making decisions on what we're doing and what the politicians are doing. I absolutely disagree with this."[47] Several other members weighed in, some objecting to the prospect of regularizing members' statements by the speaker, others actively supporting it on the grounds that all members have a duty to represent their constituents. The NG director of legal services, who was a member of the committee, argued strongly against the speaker taking part in debate but acknowledged that participation in members' statements could be treated differently. In the end, no decision was taken.[48]

Less controversial have been various speakers' sometimes extended explanations of assembly processes, either for the benefit of newly elected members or in anticipation of new, unfamiliar procedures. Examples include Speaker Lyall's long explanation of the legislative process, from the definition of a bill through to second reading,[49] and Speaker Blake-Rudkowski's explanation of the role and the selection process for the moderator of the Inuttut presidential debate.[50]

Since the First Assembly, the speaker has taken an active role in a range of assembly and government business, with, for example, Speaker Broomfield urging the assembly to fill vacant trustee positions on the Inuit Capital Strategy Trust in order to avoid its being unable to function for lack of the requisite number of trustees.[51] More recently, Speaker Blake-Rudkowski was involved in a range of governance processes, suggesting a course of action when the assembly became bogged down in developing a response to the new, much-criticized provincial ferry service,[52] participating in the recruitment of the moderator of the presidential Inuttut debate,[53] and devising a process for the assembly to hold virtual meetings.

Nunatsiavut speakers have adopted an unusually activist role for a Westminster presiding officer, including by comparison with their counterparts in the consensus governments of Nunavut and the Northwest Territories, though they remain well within the bounds of non-partisanship. Overall, as is the case generally for the assembly, a fundamental adherence to the precepts of Westminster-style parliamentarism is evident. Still, if the distinctive features of the Nunatsiavut speakership have not arisen from deliberate design decisions, they nonetheless clearly illustrate a pragmatic willingness to adapt Euro-Canadian institutions to Nunatsiavut conditions.

AngajukKât and Community Chairs

According to section 4.14.4 of the constitution, the function of the AngajukKâk in the assembly is to "represent the Inuit Community Governments to ensure that issues affecting Inuit Communities and Inuit Community interests are considered in the Nunatsiavut Assembly." While it would be incorrect and unfair to suggest that AngajukKât care and speak only for their communities, their prime focus is indeed on their communities. In interviews, AngajukKât were explicit in stating that their primary job was running their community governments, though they also involve themselves in Nunatsiavut-wide issues. One commented that "we bring more local knowledge to the table … about what is actually going on." A former minister added that, because of their position, some AngajukKât have more extensive connections with their communities than is the case for ordinary members. One AngajukKâk spoke of operating "on a different level" than ordinary members, most of whose concerns are not community-specific, reflecting the fact that most are ministers. Support for this assessment came from a minister: "you have to be aware of your relations with your community colleague; as a minister you have to lean on your [AngajukKâk] colleague on local issues." At the same time, the AngajukKâk commented that "I try to handle everything that comes to me [from constituents] but the ordinary member [from the same community] can do things I can't." One person who served as both AngajukKâk and minister agreed, noting a "big gap" between what is possible for someone in NEC and what a non-NEC member can do.

One of those involved in designing the NG was asked about the anomaly of constitutionally barring AngajukKât from holding ministerial office. The explanation offered was that the strong community orientation among Inuit mandated the inclusion of AngajukKât in the assembly as a way of ensuring that all members understood community issues. However, since serving as an AngajukKâk was a full-time job, no one could properly cope with the workload that serving as both AngajukKâk and minister would entail. Recall from chapter 4 that other reasons cited for including AngajukKât as assembly members were the need to accommodate non-Inuit political interests in the assembly and the influence of prominent families at the community level.

According to one AngajukKâk, having both an AngajukKâk and an ordinary member representing a community in the assembly means "greater voice and more support for the community in government … We have a stronger voice when there are two." Whether this arrangement results in better representation than two ordinary members could deliver is difficult to say, not least because of the possibility that the ordinary members might be in competition for a cabinet post or votes come election time. The relation between the AngajukKâk and the community's ordinary member varies a good deal. Some work closely together; one ordinary member mentioned being in touch with the AngajukKâk daily through phone calls and emails, though in-person meetings might occur only every few weeks. Another ordinary member spoke of good relations with the AngajukKâk: no competition and extensive cooperation, with the AngajukKâk taking primary responsibility for matters relating to the municipal government, whereas the ordinary member adopted a more wide-ranging role. The two would routinely meet a week or two before sessions to coordinate their activities in the assembly, for example, by not asking the same questions yet supporting one another on various issues. In September 2019, Carlene Palliser, the ordinary member for Rigolet, teamed up with Charlotte Wolfrey, the AngajukKâk:

> [Palliser:] Charlotte and I … had gotten together to discuss who would present what issues today. So I'm just going to read what I have and she will present on [her] behalf …

> [Wolfrey:] Like Carlene said, she's talking on behalf of me and I'm talking on behalf of her, so not to be repetitive, we've combined our time.[54]

It is not unusual for one community representative to acknowledge and thank the other member for some accomplishment or for assistance in some way. Towards the end of her first year in the assembly, for example, Hopedale AngajukKâk Marjorie Flowers said about the ordinary member for her community, against whom she had run and lost in the 2014 ordinary member election, "I want to thank Minister Greg Flowers for all the help and expertise that he's given me over the year. He's a really big help and I think we work pretty good together, even though sometimes, I tell him what to do."[55] Other AngajukKâk–ordinary member pairings operate fairly independently, though no instances of hostility or significant reluctance to cooperate have come to light in the course of my research.

At the highly unusual October 2020 session, AngajukKât and community chairs refrained from attending out of health concerns. They were able to participate in proceedings by sending questions and comments to the assembly through the non-NEC ordinary members, to whom they were connected electronically. For the most part, this did not entail pairings of ordinary members and AngajukKât from the same communities, but it was a notable symbol of positive relations.

To an extent, the five AngajukKât are in competition for resources and support from the NG, but overall their relation is one of cooperation and mutual support, based on common interests. The analysis of "split votes" in chapter 8 shows that AngajukKât tend to vote together, even on issues not directly tied to their roles as heads of the community governments. On occasion, one AngajukKâk will ask a question on behalf of another who was unable to attend a sitting.[56] No caucus exists, but AngajukKât do meet informally. In response to a question about communication among AngajukKât, one had this to say:

> I'm not going to say daily, but certainly we do communicate … [On one issue] I started to touch base with the other mayors in the communities: 'Okay, what route did you go?' … [On another issue] I sought every mayor's support for my community in the way of writing up a letter to support the community … [On yet another issue] I've been in contact with each mayor this past winter quite frequently to inform them that this is happening … We communicate quite often and we get along well.

AngajukKât offer differing views on the extent to which they can be involved in the work of the assembly. For one, "it's exciting to have a say" as a full participant. By contrast, another complained of the secondary status of AngajukKât, expressing disappointment that a promised orientation to the policies and operations of the NG for AngajukKât never occurred; after several postponements the idea was simply abandoned. Early on, ordinary members were invited to a strategic planning session initiated by the president, but AngajukKât attendance was in doubt for financial and logistical reasons.[57] Whether in the end they were able to participate is unclear, but the fact that they might have been left out is surely significant in and of itself. Several years later, Nain AngajukKâk and former first minister Anthony Andersen voiced frustration at the limited involvement of AngajukKât in committee processes: "to me, democratic process is an inclusion of elected members and we [AngajukKât] sit over here. We can't be Ministers, of course, but we certainly do want to be part of the democratic process and we believe that we represent communities and we certainly do have a lot to offer."[58] More recently, an AngajukKâk's frustration that a new NG staff benefit would not be available to the community governments led her to ask "if we are actually a part of this Government or not as AngajukKâks; if not then why are we here at this table?"[59]

During a discussion of members' roles and salaries, a minister suggested that perhaps AngajukKât as well as community chairs and ministers should be members of the Members' Services Committee. This would require changing the Standing Orders or the *Nunatsiavut Assembly Act*,[60] which could easily be done but has not yet occurred. Conversely, Speaker Lyall, in his role as Rules and Procedures Committee chair noted, "the last Standing Committee on

Drugs and Alcohol was composed mainly of AngajukKâk [*sic*] because it was felt that these issues affect all areas but it does greatly impact the quality of life in our communities."[61]

Community chairs are, if anything, less involved than AngajukKât in NG governance, in that the community corporations have far fewer powers and resources than the Inuit community governments. In terms of their formal role, the wording of the constitution is similar to that specifying the function of AngajukKât: "to ensure that issues affecting Labrador Inuit Communities outside Nunatsiavut and Inuit Community Corporation interests are considered in the Nunatsiavut Assembly."[62] Whether the high rate of turnover among community chairs is a symptom or a cause of lack of involvement is unclear.

Members' workloads vary a good deal depending on position and the size and nature of their communities or constituencies. By way of illustration, Postville has fewer than a tenth of the number of beneficiaries in the Canada Constituency. The needs and concerns of beneficiaries in Postville and Canada also differ substantially, and they differ as well from those in Nain and Hopedale and those in the community corporations. In turn, the demands on members and thus both the nature and extent of their workloads can vary widely. From time to time, issues arise as to the services and facilities available to various kinds of members, for example, constituency allowances, which are only available to ordinary members. At one point, the possibility of establishing different rates of pay for different types of members to reflect their differing roles was raised. The largely unstated subtext was that AngajukKât and community chairs have less to do and thus warrant lower pay than ordinary members, notwithstanding the fact that most of them receive extra stipends as speaker or minister. The discussion was inconclusive but did stimulate one community chair, Gary Mitchell, a former ordinary member and minister, to mount a vigorous defence of the importance of community chairs in the assembly.[63]

Interpersonal Relations

Centrally important in any institution, interpersonal relations are especially critical in a small legislature designed to operate by consensus. Given human nature, the tenor of relations between and among members of the Nunatsiavut Assembly varies a good deal. Respect, mutual assistance, and accommodation are readily evident in assembly proceedings and are obvious to any observer. A particularly telling, and otherwise unrecorded, episode occurred during a sitting I observed. During a statement, a member became emotional while recounting a series of recent deaths in her community; as she struggled to maintain her composure, the member next to her wordlessly put his hand on hers in support. Yet a darker side can emerge as members interact, ranging from disagreement and distrust to bitter conflict. The often fraught relations between

NEC and non-NEC members, examined in chapter 8, exemplifies the conflictual dimension of the assembly, and the remarkable record of expulsions, near expulsions, and dismissals from cabinet, enumerated in chapter 7, illustrates the extremes that conflict can reach.

Both dimensions of the assembly, the amicable and the conflictual, were in evidence in its initial sitting. The first order of business was the selection of a speaker. After the president announced his choice to the assembly, Danny Pottle took him to task, voicing concern that such unilateral action contravened his promised teamwork-premised approach. The president replied with a call for members to work together and to avoid conflict. The next day, Pottle ran unsuccessfully for first minister, his loss doubtless at least partially a result of the president's harsh words about him. Tony Andersen, the successful candidate, subsequently told the assembly that Pottle was the first person to congratulate him.[64]

Some of what follows in this section highlights problematic relations among and between members, as does virtually everything in the accounts of expulsions and dismissals in chapter 7. This is not at all to suggest that ill feeling and conflict dominate the assembly; indeed, quite the opposite. Members' interpersonal relations are generally positive. The respectful, supportive atmosphere typically seen during assembly meetings is no charade, but an accurate reflection of its culture.

The cooperative, harmonious nature characteristic of most relations between AngajukKât and ordinary members representing the same communities is a good example. So, too, the constituencies with two ordinary members, Nain, Upper Lake Melville, and Canada, provide clear evidence that the members get along well personally and professionally and routinely work together in their constituents' interests. When asked about the frequency of communications with the constituency's other ordinary member, an interviewee responded,

> [X] is just down the hallway from me. We're in the same government office. I feel we have a really good relationship. We meet daily. It could be for a couple of minutes, or it could be planning upcoming open houses or community events that we're attending. We both work well together and we're highly involved in the community … If I'm away on vacation or [X] is away, we'll update each other on current events [and interactions with constituents].

When asked the same question, the second member agreed: "We try very hard to talk daily, sit down and have a chat, update each other on if beneficiaries have come in to chat with us. Yeah, we communicate pretty much daily." The ordinary members from Lake Melville and the two community chairs from the same area frequently cooperate on holding events and on other projects. Of course, members are elected politicians: one from a two-member constituency spoke of working closely with the other member, while understanding the politics of their situation and therefore striving to be the first to respond to constituents' concerns. Cooperation does have its limits, of course, as exemplified by the aggravation expressed by the NunaKâtiget community chair about the lack of assistance he received from other members during the time that both Upper Lake Melville ordinary members had resigned: "I have not had one call or email from anyone to offer any support or assistance if I needed it."[65]

The causes of conflict and ill-feeling are threefold. First, with strong personalities arises the prospect of personal antagonisms, based on past experiences, rivalry, or serious political differences. With the extensive web of personal, social, political, economic, and family links among members, many going back to LIA days, reflecting the limited size of the Labrador Inuit elite, it is hardly surprising that unpleasantry, if not outright conflict, characterizes the relations between particular members. Second, as in any political institution with a clear division between those with substantial power and those without, relations between the cabinet and the non-NEC members can be prone to friction, aspirations to operate by consensus notwithstanding. Chapter 8 examines the interplay between NEC and non-NEC members in some depth; for present purposes, the following episode is instructive. One evening at dinner in the hotel, I was sitting with a group of non-NEC members who were energetically slagging the cabinet in general, and certain ministers in particular, until several ministers and senior bureaucrats came into the small dining room. Nods and clipped greetings were exchanged. The ministers and staff sat at a different table and the conversation at my table shifted to hockey.

A third basis of division among members is less evident to observers – at least it was to me – but did emerge in interviews. A Canada Constituency member commented that some assembly members "have no time for the ordinary members for Canada." To some extent this reflects a natural competition for scarce resources. When asked whether conflict exists between the needs and interests of the Canada Constituency beneficiaries and those in Nunatsiavut, the answer was unequivocal: "every day; the conflict never leaves … there's only a limited pie." Another Canada Constituency member argued that more basic imperatives are at play: "you're considered [by members as well as by beneficiaries generally] less Inuit if you live outside the land claim area," even Upper Lake Melville, but especially outside Labrador. The same member added, "LIA and the Nunatsiavut Government perpetuated that divide." Roland Saunders, a Canada Constituency member, spoke recently of the discrimination felt by his constituents:

> We are isolated and disconnected from our homeland and culture. We want inclusion, equality and not to feel left out because of where we live … Just because we moved away for jobs, education and medical care and a better way of life for our

children, we should not be punished. Madam Speaker, the Canadian Constituents are able to feel less than other members because we are not on our land. Makes us feel like second-class citizens. We want to be treated and honoured for what we really are, Inuit from Labrador.[66]

Former Canada Constituency member Danny Pottle used less restrained language: "We feel that we're not valued, that Nunatsiavut government perpetuates the whole discourse that we often feel [that] because we don't live in the settlement area we're less Inuk than the people who live in our [LISA] communities … Nunatsiavut government is treating our membership in the same manner that colonial institutions treated us."[67] An ordinary member representing a LISA community offered credence to these perceptions in an interview, maintaining that the community corporations and the members and the people in the Canada Constituency "are not really involved in the land claim."

In terms of divisions – or perhaps better, conflicts – in what seems to have been a relatively isolated episode rather than a continuing problem, one member attributed a conflictual "incident" among members at a previous session to alcohol. "When we have been drinking when meetings are on the go," he said, "it is hard to focus on what we are supposed to be doing."[68] Significantly, this incident occurred shortly before the adoption of the Code of Conduct, with its uncompromising "zero tolerance" for consumption of alcohol or illegal drugs "while conducting or discussing" government business, and its harsh penalties for contravening the prohibition.[69]

A Pragmatically Unique Legislature

Every legislature is unique in various ways: structure, procedures, membership, and behavioural norms. At the risk of doing violence to the meaning of "unique," it is evident from this chapter that the Nunatsiavut Assembly is more unique than other Canadian legislatures, be they legislatures in self-governing Indigenous regimes or in public governments in Ottawa and the provinces and territories. To what extent are the unique or distinctive features outlined in this chapter a function of the Inuit culture so central to the governance aspirations of the claim and the constitution? Relatedly, to what extent do they reflect self-government principles?

Clearly, the assembly is very much a Euro-Canadian construct. At a fundamental level, its nature is defined by adherence to the tenets of the Westminster cabinet-parliamentary model, symbolized in the terminology: speaker, minister, clerk, confidence, and the like. Many of the trappings and procedures are unusual, if not unique, but anyone accustomed to Westminster parliaments would find the assembly's basic structure and operations familiar. Yet the very adoption of British-style "responsible government," as well as what one LIA figure called the "tweaks" to it, can be interpreted in terms of Inuit culture. Inuit are known for their pragmatism, so that adapting a familiar governance system that functions well, rather than experimenting with an original, untried system, stands as a very pragmatic choice. Similarly, the adaptations to the basic Westminster model, which are a good deal more substantial than tweaks, represent pragmatic Inuit responses to distinctive Nunatsiavut concerns. Especially notable are the emphasis on consensus decision making, the inclusion of AngajukKât and a popularly elected president as assembly members, and the activist, influential speaker.

For Nunatsiavumiut, self-government primarily means controlling their own affairs. With essential political rights, most significantly the right to vote and the right to hold office, restricted to Inuit, the structure of the assembly unquestionably advances their capacity for self-government. The structural and operational features Nunatsiavumiut have chosen for their assembly, as sketched out in this and other chapters, should be assessed with respect to their effectiveness in achieving control as well as in meeting specific objectives of their treaty rather than in terms of their correspondence with or variation from other governance models. Subsequent chapters pursue this line of enquiry. Finally, it is worth noting that as a self-governing regime, Nunatsiavut was clearly less constrained in building distinctive design features into the assembly than it would have been had it been a public government like that of Nunavut.

Chapter Six

The Assembly: Operations, Committees, and Services

Overview

Having set the stage and placed the actors on it in the previous chapter, I turn in this chapter to a description of the play, offering analysis – some highly detailed, some of a broader brush – of the assembly's organization and operation. The first section is an account of a "typical" assembly sitting, followed by a short account of some decidedly atypical days. Subsequent sections are devoted to committees and to the staff and services available to assembly members. As was the case in the previous chapter, the account of the assembly in this chapter reveals a mix of unremarkable features, common throughout Westminster parliaments, and unusual, oftentimes unique, attributes.

A Typical Day

Those familiar with legislatures would likely reject the notion that anything like a "typical" legislative day exists. What follows should be understood primarily as commentary on the various elements of the legislative day. Most days unfold with items of business ("Orders of the Day") taken up according to the listing set out in Standing Order 23, though on occasion, with assembly approval, always given, the timing of particular items of business can be adjusted, usually to accommodate the availability and travel imperatives of witnesses or guests. Orders of the Day are as follows:

1. Prayer
2. Opening address by the president (first day of session only)
3. Recognition of visitors in the gallery
4. Ministers' statements
5. Members' statements
6. Returns to oral questions

7. Oral questions
8. Written questions
9. Returns to written questions
10. Petitions
11. Responses to petitions
12. Reports of standing and special committees
13. Tabling of documents
14. Notices of motion
15. Notices of motion for first reading of bills
16. Motions
17. First reading of bills
18. Second reading of bills
19. Assent to bills
20. Adjournment

As the day proceeds, the speaker calls each Order of the Day in turn. Some, such as ministers' statements, consume substantial time virtually every day, while others, such as petitions, usually elicit no response and are over in seconds.

Sittings begin at 9:00 a.m., though occasional delays occur if key participants will be arriving late because of delayed flights. In this, as in many other aspects of assembly proceedings, the speaker exercises considerable discretion. The speaker will not commence or resume a sitting without quorum, which is not as simple as might be thought. Although the assembly consists of eighteen members, community chairs and AngajukKât do not count towards quorum, which requires the president and six ordinary members. With only ten ordinary members, if some are ill or otherwise absent, or if vacancies exist, little leeway exists if quorum is to be made.

To signal that a sitting is about to begin, a page is dispatched into the halls to ring an old-fashioned school bell. The speaker opens the sitting with brief introductory remarks, mentioning by name assembly staff such as interpreters, IT people, and pages, and indicating which members are absent and have been properly excused. Members and spouses or close relatives of members who are seriously ill or have passed away are noted. The first formal proceeding is a "prayer." In the early years, clergy were sometimes called upon to deliver a prayer, as was the clerk. Current practice is for the speaker to ask a member to say a prayer. Oftentimes it has an obvious Christian element, but at others, the "prayer" may be spiritual but not religious.[1] Prayers are not recorded in *Hansard*.

On the first day of a session, the president gives an opening address. This primarily involves updating members on developments in important files since the last session and an overview of current and future issues and plans. Meetings and dealings with the Province, with Ottawa, and with various Indigenous organizations often figure prominently in the president's report. Following this, or on subsequent days the prayer, the speaker recognizes visitors in the gallery. Senior staff of the Nunatsiavut Government (NG), who are present for virtually every sitting, are recognized each day, as is anyone else known to the speaker or to a member, which is to say almost everyone in the gallery (even Toronto academics). As the day progresses, the speaker recognizes and welcomes visitors as they come into the gallery.

Next come ministers' statements and members' statements. Ministers' statements are department-specific versions of the president's opening address, with updates on departmental activities and plans. A total of thirty-five minutes is allowed for ministers' statements, but unanimous consent is often sought and invariably given for ministers to complete their statements. During members' statements, all members, including ministers, may make two statements a day of up to five minutes each, though few members make second statements. Members' statements by ministers may not deal with departmental matters. Members often refer to their statements as "reports," and indeed most are just that, as opposed to policy commentary. The typical member's statement aims at bringing the assembly up to date on recent happenings in the member's community or constituency. This could include emerging, continuing, or resolved local problems, the passing of local residents, or the activities of sports teams: anything locally noteworthy is likely to be mentioned. Individual bureaucrats who are retiring or joining the NG or community governments are frequently mentioned by name and celebrated.

Before oral questions, responses ("returns") are given to oral questions that were not answered at an earlier session, or occasionally on the previous day. Ministers have seven calendar days to provide, through the Clerk's Office, a return to an oral question, which is forwarded to members. Typically during this proceeding, the speaker summarizes the question and the minister gives an oral response. Although Standing Order 32 would seem to allow for supplementary questions at this point, the speaker does not offer the member who asked the question an opportunity for a supplementary.

The assembly then moves on to oral questions. An extended analysis of the nature and effectiveness of question period, a term not often heard in the assembly, awaits in chapter 10. For now, it is sufficient to set out the main rules and some overall observations. Each day, a member may ask two questions, each with two supplementary questions. Whereas it is unusual in federal, provincial, and territorial legislatures for members to pass up opportunities to ask questions, members of the Nunatsiavut Assembly routinely do so. On any given day, barely a third of non-NEC (Nunatsiavut Executive Council) members ask two questions and more than a quarter ask no questions; only about a quarter of the time do members follow up their original questions with supplementaries. The Standing Orders limit question period to sixty minutes but most days it finishes in less time; it is unusual for members to seek unanimous consent to extend it. Given the non-partisan nature of the assembly and its non-confrontational Inuit character, it is unsurprising that question period does not assume anything like the central role in the legislative day that it does in party-based parliaments.

As in other Westminster-style parliaments, members seeking detailed information may do so via written questions. Thus, following oral questions, the next items of business are written questions and returns to written questions. Written questions are not common, though some speakers have insisted that oral questions requiring extensive detail be submitted as written questions. Ministers have ten days to file responses to written questions with the clerk. As with returns to oral questions, ministers routinely read responses to written questions to the assembly after the speaker reads or summarizes the questions. Speakers have been known to disallow written questions as being more appropriately asked as oral questions.[2]

The assembly also follows Westminster practice in allowing members to present petitions on behalf of their constituents, beneficiaries, or indeed, non-beneficiaries. Standing Order 35, on petitions, is silent as to who may submit or sign petitions. Ministers and the speaker, should the petition relate to the assembly, have sixty days to respond. The petition process is used sparingly. The Third and Fourth Assemblies saw, in total, only four presented, two of which proved problematic.[3]

At some point around this time, the speaker will call a smoke/snack/bathroom break that lasts fifteen or twenty minutes. Smokers congregate just outside the main door to the building and, after assuaging their nicotine craving, join their colleagues, staff, and even visiting academics in the small kitchen for healthy as well as not-so-healthy snacks, juice, coffee, and tea. A few members make phone calls or work on their laptops in the adjacent small committee room. In my limited experience, break-time conversations are less about politics than about local goings-on, hockey, news about hunting, and the like.

Committees play a relatively minor role at the assembly. Accordingly, many sessions transpire with no reports from standing and special committees. Most committee reports are short progress statements. Substantive reports are usually read into the record by the committee chairs, despite being available to members in written or electronic form.

The constitution, various Inuit laws, and the Standing Orders require the tabling of particular documents; this takes place during the next item of business, tabling of documents.[4] NG documents are often deposited in the Clerk's Office between sessions, constituting tabling for legal purposes. Non-NEC members may table documents, but few do so. No debate occurs, though the member tabling a document is permitted to make a brief statement about it.

The next two Orders of the Day, notices of motion and notices of motion for first reading of bills, are essentially pro forma rituals. The purpose of giving notice, which is required for most substantive motions, is to let members know that a certain piece of business will be coming before the House, giving them time to prepare. However, the requirement that the motion not be brought forward until the notice period has expired is routinely bypassed, with the mover of the motion typically seeking and receiving unanimous consent to waive the applicable standing order. Thus most motions, including those for first reading of bills, occur shortly after, sometimes minutes after, notice was given.

It is under the proceeding motions that the non-routine business of the assembly occurs, save debates on legislation. This includes presentations by the NG auditors, reports from the trustees of the various Nunatsiavut trusts, discussion and disposition of committee reports, and addresses from guests such as Inuit leader Mary Simon or provincial cabinet ministers. Motions may also relate to specific situations or issues; a recent example involved debate on a motion calling for an NG response to widespread concern over inadequacies of a newly launched ferry, providing essential transportation services to Nunatsiavut communities. With the budget taking the form of a bill, debate on it follows the procedures for consideration of legislation. Describing business considered under motions as "non-routine" simply means that it doesn't occur every sitting or session. Important matters, such as the auditors' report or trustee presentations, come before the assembly every year, though not necessarily at the same time of year.

When the assembly deals with such matters, the House usually reconstitutes itself as a committee of the whole, which is characterized by greater flexibility and less formality; for example, members remain seated when they speak. Unlike in House debates, members may speak more than once and witnesses may participate in the proceedings, including with PowerPoint presentations.

Following motions are first reading of bills and second reading of bills. The content and nature of assembly legislation are considered in chapter 9; here I set out only the legislative process. In a notable symbol of Nunatsiavut's status as an Inuit self-government, a bill passed by the assembly is not simply referred to as "a law" but rather "an Inuit law."

The Standing Orders contemplate private members' bills and, unlike most Canadian parliaments, do not give priority to government bills, stipulating that the same procedures apply to both government and private members' bills.[5] However, as of 2022 only three non-NEC member have introduced bills, and none was really a private member's bill. In 2008, the deputy speaker, in his capacity as chair of the Code of Conduct Committee, introduced and piloted through the assembly a bill to establish a code of conduct for members. A few years later, an AngajukKâk who had chaired a Rules and Procedures Committee review of the Standing Orders introduced and took charge of a bill to amend the Standing Orders and the *Assembly Act*. Similarly, the bill establishing the Inuttut debate for presidential candidates was brought forward by a non-NEC member. Thus the following account, as well as the analysis of the assembly's role in law-making in chapter 9, relates entirely to government legislation. Since by definition government bills are public bills, and since private members are only authorized to introduce public bills, the assembly has no capacity for private bills.[6] Section 4.18.12 specifies the order in which bills are to be taken up: money bills, bills introduced by the president, bills introduced by other members of NEC, and bills introduced by other assembly members. Non-NEC bills are to be considered in the order they were introduced, unless political parties have emerged in the assembly, in which case priority is given to bills from the official opposition, followed by those from "minority parties," independent members, and non-NEC members of the governing party.

Unlike all Canadian national, provincial, and territorial parliaments, which require three readings of bills, the passage of legislation in the Nunatsiavut Assembly entails only two readings. This is less of a deviation from standard Westminster practice than might appear. First reading in Ottawa, the provinces, and the territories is limited to the introduction of the bill and a brief statement about the bill from its sponsor. In contrast, in the Nunatsiavut Assembly substantive debate on the object of the bill is permitted at first reading, as are amendments. In short, the assembly combines in first reading what other legislatures do in first and second readings. Clause-by-clause review of bills occurs at second reading, whereas in other legislatures, this usually occurs at a committee stage once second reading, which is limited to the principle of the bill, has occurred. The Nunatsiavut Assembly has no equivalent to the third reading practised in Ottawa and the provinces and territories, which is usually perfunctory but can include substantive debate and amendments.

In other legislatures, substantial time typically elapses between first and second readings in order to give members and parties an opportunity to assess newly introduced legislation, which they will likely not have seen before. In the assembly, this delay is not as necessary since members will already have seen the proposed legislation. In the early days, members might only receive the text of proposed bills just before the start of a session. Standard practice now is that members are sent bills at least ten days before the assembly is to sit. Thus, the routine waiving of the standing order requiring one day's notice for first reading of bills is less problematic than it might initially appear, though some members and observers believe that the legislative process is overly rushed, to the detriment of effective scrutiny. In addition, thorough scrutiny is rendered more difficult in that only rarely are draft bills accompanied by explanatory material.

A member may speak to the principle of the bill for fifteen minutes and to each amendment for five minutes, though these limits rarely come into play.

By the end of the Fourth Assembly, only seventeen non-budget bills generated much more than perfunctory debate, whereas some thirty-eight bills passed with little or no debate, though ten of these were essentially the same, an annual bill authorizing a loan guarantee for the Torngat Fish Producers Co-operative Society. Whereas most Westminster-style parliaments authorize spending through review of what are known as "the estimates," the Nunatsiavut Assembly deals with the NG budget through the legislative process. At that, debate on the budget bill is not usually very extensive.

Once first reading has been secured, a bill may be referred to an assembly committee for study, which may include public consultations. Only four times has this option been exercised.[7] Instead, the standard practice is to send bills directly to second reading. Standing Order 54 stipulates that a bill "shall not be read a second time until the expiry of 10 business days during which Labrador Inuit may make submissions or representations to the Assembly about the Bill." This provision is routinely overridden by unanimous consent. Indeed, in only five instances has a bill not had second reading during the session, often the same day, it received first reading. One telling episode relating to the prescribed delay of second reading occurred over the budget bill in 2011. When the minister of finance sought unanimous consent to waive the ten-day-delay rule, three members refused, citing a desire to canvas their constituents' views on the budget. The speaker asked whether the dissenters would reconsider. They did not, whereupon the president called for a Committee on Consensus, which he chaired, pointing out the considerable expense involved should members have to stay in Hopedale for ten days or return after that time. Eventually, the hold-outs succumbed to the pressure and withdrew their opposition so that the bill could pass that day.[8]

During second reading, the assembly normally resolves itself into a committee of the whole for detailed, clause-by-clause review of the bill, or page-by-page review for budget bills. For the most part, individual clauses are approved with little or no discussion, with members' interventions usually taking the form of questions for clarification. Even contentious bills only elicit extensive debate on a few key provisions.

If any bills have received second reading, the president assents to them in the chamber under assent to bills. This is a necessary but purely pro forma step.[9] Adjournment follows, with the speaker either reminding the members of the next day's business or, on the final sitting day, wishing them safe travels.

Once the sitting finishes, members are offered rides back to the hotel, or to the airstrip, by assembly-owned vehicles, either a truck or a large, specially built komatik (a type of sled) pulled by a snowmobile. The same service is available for members at the lunch break, unless, as often occurs, lunch is sent into the building in order to save time.

Very Atypical Days

If the "typical" assembly day exists primarily as a heuristic device, two sittings in 2020, one in 2021, and another in 2022 were highly atypical. The annual March session ranks as the most important of the year since this is when the budget is presented and approved in anticipation of the start of the fiscal year, on 1 April. A session had been planned for the first week in March 2020 but was postponed until 12 March because the president, who must be present for the assembly to meet, was ill. On 11 March, the World Health Organization confirmed that the spread of COVID-19 constituted a global pandemic. Nunatsiavut, with its over-crowded housing and limited medical facilities, is highly vulnerable to serious contagious diseases. However, like other legislatures, the assembly lacked the authority to meet remotely. Nor does the NG have an equivalent mechanism to Governor General's Special Warrants, which can fund the federal government when Parliament is prorogued and, until 1997, during adjournments. Accordingly, the budget had to be passed or the NG would have to shut down on 31 March for lack of money.

Following extensive discussions, agreement was reached between the Speaker's Office and the President's Office to hold a one-day sitting on the seventeenth under unusual circumstances.[10] A chartered aircraft picked up assembly members, but no staff, from all Nunatsiavut communities and delivered them to Hopedale. Members drove themselves to the assembly on snowmobiles that had been left at the airstrip. The Assembly Building was closed to the public; the sole staff member present was the IT specialist.

Presentation and debate on the budget were the principal items of business. In normal times, the deputy minister of finance is present in the chamber to answer detailed or technical questions about the budget, but this was not possible under the circumstances. She did take part in the proceedings by phone from Goose Bay but the link into the assembly sound system broke down, so that her answers to questions went only to the speaker, who then relayed them to assembly members, a function few if any other Westminster speakers have been called on to perform. This jury-rigged process proved cumbersome but effective. The budget was passed and the members returned home later that day, having driven themselves back to the airstrip on borrowed snowmobiles.

With no let-up of the pandemic in sight, the assembly meeting of late October 2020 was, if anything, more unusual than that of March. As the need for the March sitting to proceed in extraordinary fashion had revealed, neither the constitution nor the *Nunatsiavut Assembly Act* contained provisions for the assembly to meet other than in person. NG staff and the Speaker's Office had been working up special procedures to allow the assembly to hold "hybrid" sittings or to meet completely virtually as "a safety valve, an escape hatch," as Speaker Edward Blake-Rudkowski put it, if "dire circumstances" made in-person meetings untenable.[11] With a case of COVID-19 identified in Happy Valley–Goose Bay at the end of September, some members were concerned about going ahead with a session planned for October, since the four members from the Upper Lake Melville area and the two from the Canada Constituency would have to travel through Goose Bay.

Speaker Blake-Rudkowski requested, since he had no authority to order it, that the AngajukKât and the community chairs not come to Hopedale for the sitting. He encountered no pushback on his request; if anything, the resistance was to holding the session at all. An unusually extensive consultation process was held on the proposed special standing orders and amendment to the act given that they entailed "pretty substantial changes to the way we do business." Changes drafted by NG legal staff to the Standing Orders and the act were reviewed by the Rules and Procedure Committee, chaired by the speaker. So that everyone understood the proposals and could have an opportunity to voice their views and concerns, they were thoroughly discussed during a conference call of all members. Members raised questions about the proposed process but satisfied themselves that the proposed special procedures were appropriate, would respect their opportunities to speak and to vote, and would only come into play if absolutely necessary.[12] Finally, the Rules and Procedure Committee prepared a formal report for the assembly. No substantial changes were made to the proposals during this process, though some minor tweaking occurred; for example, the original wording, which authorized "videoconferencing," was changed to "teleconferencing" out of concern that video meetings might not be feasible in light of the limited bandwidth available on the North Coast. A process was established to enable the AngajukKât and the community chairs to participate remotely in the session.

Speaker Blake-Rudkowski and the other Canada Constituency member, Roland Saunders, followed provincial travel guidelines, self-isolating for fourteen days on arrival in Labrador. They had COVID tests before flying to Hopedale for the sitting, which occurred on 26 October. Ironically, a few months earlier, a new standing order had been agreed, prohibiting all electronic devices in the chamber so as to ensure that members were giving their full attention to the proceedings. Thus the first order of business was to waive the standing order for the day. Laptops were set up on ordinary members' desks. Each AngajukKâk and community chair, who could listen to proceedings via the audio feed on the NG website, was paired with an ordinary member, mostly but not entirely non-NEC members, so that they could send in statements, questions, and comments to be relayed to ministers or to the assembly generally. Predictably, technical glitches occurred, but overall the AngajukKât and community chairs were accorded as extensive an opportunity to take part in the sitting as possible under the circumstances. Still, as one member commented at adjournment, "this was one of the strangest days ever."[13]

That day, following routine business, such as the president's opening address, as well as ministers' and members' statements, the assembly heard from representatives of one of the trusts, though the discussion had to be cut short to allow members and staff from Nain to make their plane. The main item of business was debate and approval of the temporary special provisions to allow the assembly to conduct meetings during the pandemic by way of electronic communications. Debate on the Rules and Procedures Committee report proposing special standing orders was folded in with debate on related amendments to the *Nunatsiavut Assembly Act*. The act was amended to permit the speaker to authorize members' participation in assembly or committee proceedings electronically. A further amendment restricted recourse to the special standing orders permitting members' electronic participation to situations "clearly established with respect to a specific public health emergency that is recognized by public health authorities in the province of Newfoundland and Labrador," with a maximum duration of eighteen months.[14] NG legal staff served by phone as witnesses during debate on the proposed special standing orders, and even though only one member asked a question, the process proved painfully slow, so that in the end the speaker expedited consideration of the requisite motion, enabling its unanimous passage.[15] The special standing orders were explicitly limited to necessary accommodations due to travel and other restrictions arising from the pandemic.

As it turned out, the special standing orders were not needed for the February 2021 session, which proceeded with all members present, though the gallery was closed, only essential staff were permitted in the building, and spacing out of members in the chamber meant that only some could sit at their normal places at the table. However, with a significant upsurge in new COVID cases in parts of the province, it was decided to hold a completely virtual session in March 2021 to deal with the budget and related matters. Assembly members and witnesses participated via Zoom. Some minor technical hitches occurred, and it was evident that not all members were comfortable with the technology. Overall, however, the process proved successful and the assembly completed its business in more or less a similar fashion as in normal sessions. A notice about the session, with a link to it, was posted on the NG website and on its Facebook page. Several members lauded the virtual session's side benefit of enabling beneficiaries all over Canada to watch the proceedings. Viewers were able to see individuals as they spoke and images of documents that witnesses posted. According to a counter on the screen indicating the number of viewers, as many as fifty people were watching at any given time.

The June, September, and November 2021 sessions unfolded in close to normal fashion, but a resurgence of COVID-19 necessitated another completely virtual session in January 2022.

Committees

With occasional important exceptions, committees play a limited role in the assembly. (Committee of the whole, essentially a variation of the assembly, is not considered in this section.) The Nunatsiavut constitution, the *Nunatsiavut Assembly Act*, the Code of Conduct, and the Standing Orders set the parameters of committee structure and powers, but these formal documents offer little guidance as to what actually transpires in committees or to their influence in Nunatsiavut governance.

The *Nunatsiavut Assembly Act* authorizes the creation of standing or special committees, which may meet either during a session or between sessions in locations they deem appropriate. Committees are empowered by the act "to compel witnesses and to require the production of documents," provided they fall under the jurisdiction of the NG and are subject to certain exceptions, notably judges and members of independent commissions and tribunals.[16] The only committee specifically mentioned in the act is the Members' Services Committee, comprised of all non-NEC ordinary members and chaired by the speaker. The act permits a different membership complement should the Standing Orders authorize it, but complaints that no AngajukKât or community chairs serve on the Members' Services Committee have had no effect. The committee is mandated, in consultation with the clerk, to prepare the assembly budget and present it to the assembly.[17]

The constitution requires that committee membership be balanced in terms of men and women and, should political parties come along, of party affiliation. Notably, if women are absent or under-represented in the assembly (though this isn't defined), women who are not members are to be appointed to committees. This is possible because another unusual constitutional provision permits up to one-quarter of committee membership to come from outside the ranks of assembly members. On the occasions when this provision has been employed, it has typically involved appointing to the committee an NG bureaucrat knowledgeable about a given topic. As in the assembly, members are to enjoy freedom of speech in committees.

The constitution contains two other potentially significant provisions relating to committees. Section 2.3.2 stipulates that any Labrador Inuk or group of Inuit who believe that their rights under the *Labrador Inuit Charter of Rights and Freedoms* have been infringed may apply to the assembly or a committee of the assembly for redress. An application of this nature has yet to occur. Section 2.4.35, reads, "The Nunatsiavut Assembly must enact an Inuit law, including reasonable limitation periods, to give effect to the rights in section 2.4.34 [fair treatment by the NG, the Inuit community governments, and the Inuit community corporations] by providing for the review of administrative action by a committee of the Assembly, a tribunal or forum and for an appeal of any decision by the committee, tribunal or forum to the Inuit Court." In that the court has yet to be established, it is not surprising that this constitutional requirement has not been met; no such committee has been established.

The Code of Conduct gives the speaker discretion to appoint and chair an ad hoc three-member discipline committee if allegations have been made that a member has contravened the code. Discipline committees have extensive authority to enquire into allegations of misconduct and to impose a reprimand or suspension from office without pay for a member found guilty of misconduct or to recommend that the assembly remove the member from office. Discipline committees are thus quite powerful, not least because their decisions are not subject to appeal. As evidenced in chapter 7, the power of discipline committees is more than theoretical in that they have dealt with several accusations against members and two members have been removed from office.

The Standing Orders repeat some of the provisions of the constitution and the act relating to committees, adding some details as to committee structure and mandate. Two standing committees are established: the Rules and Procedures Committee and the Members' Services Committee. The Rules and Procedures Committee is to have three to five members and is chaired by the speaker, who nominates its members for assembly approval. In addition to reviewing and proposing changes to the Standing Orders and assembly procedures, the committee serves as a striking committee, proposing to the assembly the membership of other committees, taking into account the need for a balance of men and women and for committees to be "representative of the various interests and functions within the membership of the Assembly."[18]

Other provisions of the Standing Orders relating to committees authorize committees to establish their own procedures and, save the two speaker-chaired committees, to elect their chairs. Standing committees, once established, exist for the life of an assembly. Membership of special committees is normally no more than five,[19] though the Language Committee in the First Assembly had eight members.[20] Table 6.1 below lists committees that have been established by the assembly. The precise names have varied somewhat, and some are truncated in the list; discipline committees are not included.

Simply listing committees offers little guidance as to their activity and effectiveness. An attempt to inventory the committees of the First Assembly concluded that "the Assembly's procedures and practices for the establishment and governance of committees has not been very consistent or very good," citing, for example, reference in the assembly budget of March 2007 to committees on health, transportation, and housing, none of which ever existed.[21] The Education and Language Committees of the First Assembly did meet and did hold consultations with various groups. Both produced brief oral progress reports, but *Hansard* does not record any substantive reports from

Table 6.1. Standing and special committees, 2006–22

Standing Committees

Rules and Procedures	(First, Second, Third, Fourth Assemblies)
Members' Services	(First, Second, Third, Fourth Assemblies)
Language	(First Assembly)
Education	(First Assembly)
Drug and Alcohol*	(First, Second, Third, Fourth Assemblies)

Special Committees**

Code of Conduct	(First Assembly)
Uranium Moratorium Bill***	(First Assembly)
Nunatsiavut Business Centre	(First and Second Assemblies)
Uranium Moratorium	(Second Assembly)
Environmental Assessment Bill	(Second Assembly)
NEO Report	(Second Assembly)
NEO Report on 2016 Presidential Election	(Third Assembly)
Housing Commission Bill	(Fourth Assembly)
Voting in Canada Constituency	(Fourth Assembly)

NEO = Nunatsiavut elections officer
* Originally established as a special committee.
** Among the last actions of the First Assembly was passage of a motion directing
the president to strike a special committee of the assembly at the start of the Second
Assembly, so as to look into a long-standing controversy relating to alleged irregularities
involving payments to beneficiaries following finalization of the claim (*Hansard*, March
2010, 175). No such committee was ever struck.
*** A committee of the whole

either committee.[22] The First Assembly's Drug and Alcohol Committee held public consultations that led to the passage of three motions in the assembly put forward by the committee chair, First Minister Tony Andersen, aiming at reducing alcohol use, in an attempt to deal with some of Nunatsiavut's most serious social problems. All three sectoral standing committees were chaired by ministers.

Since the First Assembly, beyond the two internal committees, Members' Services and Rules and Procedures, the only standing committee has been the Drug and Alcohol Committee. In September 2019, the committee chair, commenting on the committee's problems, declared that it "has been defunct since 2014."[23] Describing the committee as defunct was perhaps unduly harsh, as over the years it did meet from time to time, though its only concrete accomplishment since 2010 seems to have been a short written update in June 2015 as to its previous work and its future plans.

The checkered record of the standing policy committees, as distinguished from the two internal standing committees, contrasts markedly with that of the special committees. Some special committees, most notably the three on proposed legislation (see table 6.1), engaged in substantial public consultations; several produced written reports, some quite detailed, into their assigned topics. It is clear that the special committees on legislation influenced both policy and administrative elements of the bills they reviewed. Recommendations from other special committees with more limited mandates have been adopted and put into place – for example, the recommendation to dissolve the Nunatsiavut Business Centre. The Fourth Assembly's Special Committee on Voting Alternatives for the Canadian Constituency commissioned a detailed study on electronic voting and planned extensive public consultations, but it was unable to bring in a substantial report because of time constraints and limitations on its ability to consult because of COVID-19 restrictions.[24]

In her lament about the Drug and Alcohol Committee, the chair cited the need for staff support, asking that a senior NG official be assigned to assist the committee, with the acknowledgement that the deputy minister of health had been very helpful. Staff support made available to committees has almost always entailed the assignment of senior NG bureaucrats with relevant policy expertise. For certain undertakings, the NG's director of legal services has been appointed as a member of the Rules and Procedure Committee and the Special Committee on the Report of the Nunatsiavut Elections Officer to provide legal advice, as a complement to the procedural expertise of the clerk, who was assisting the committee.

The two internal committees have been continuously active, with a long list of accomplishments. The Rules and Procedure Committee, in addition to carrying out several reviews of the Standing Orders and related practices, has taken on such tasks as examining the process for recruiting and interviewing candidates for Nunatsiavut elections officer. In addition to preparing the assembly's annual budget, the Members' Services Committee deals with issues relating to members' indemnities and benefits and with administrative assembly matters, such as procurement of capital equipment. As well, it has been assigned additional responsibilities on an ad hoc basis, such as selection of the moderator of the presidential Inuttut debate.

As the Third Assembly was starting its work, Nain AngajukKâk Tony Andersen argued that the First Assembly had too many committees, perhaps explaining why the Second Assembly had so few.[25] During the Second Assembly, Andersen, a former first minister, warned that "there are too few Standing Committees and it takes away from the openness and transparency and trust when the Executive Council takes on responsibility of Standing Committees … We don't have in this government a Finance Standing Committee or a Health or an Education Standing Committee … Because the Executive Council doesn't have to report to the Assembly the way that Standing Committees is [*sic*] obligated to, it takes away something from [members'] trust."[26] Some important and effective assembly work does take place through committees, but overall, Andersen's negative assessment remains valid.

The issue, however, is not so much the number of committees as their mandates and resources, and thus their capacity for activity and effectiveness – plus, of course, members' openness to utilizing them to develop and review policy and to hold the government accountable. Should it not be evident from the foregoing discussion, it is worth making explicit that vast swathes of NG activity fall outside the purview of assembly committees. More generally, it is widely accepted among those who work in and study legislatures that well-resourced and active committee systems enable them to do their best work.[27] In this regard, assembly committees clearly fall short.

A final point about committees: the other principal Canadian "consensus" systems, Nunavut and the Northwest Territories, have an important institution called "caucus," consisting of all legislative members, including the speaker. In both, caucus meets on a regular basis, in closed session, to discuss issues, if not necessarily to resolve them. As discussed in chapter 8, no similar institution exists in the Nunatsiavut Assembly.

Services for Members

In 2022–3, the assembly budget amounted to $3.4 million, excluding the $138,000 for election expenses folded into the assembly allocation. The lion's share, 80 per cent, went for salaries and benefits for members and staff, with 8 per cent for travel, 3 per cent each for "operating expenses," constituency allowances, and committees, and 2 per cent for professional fees.[28]

Services and facilities available to members are limited. On the one hand, as with any legislature, members could perform their duties more effectively had they more extensive services, especially staff support. Yet on the other hand, additional staff and services can be expensive, and spending on the assembly already represents an unusually high proportion of overall spending. In 2022–3, the assembly accounted for nearly 2 per cent of the entire NG budget. With the many and varied demands on the NG, not least for more and better housing, justifying significant additional spending on the assembly would be difficult. Moreover, it is not at all clear that members perceive a need for substantially improved services. No one, either in formal interviews or in casual conversation, suggested to me that a lack of staff support or other services was of concern. Nor, except in a few minor instances, does *Hansard* record members' dissatisfaction with services.

The assembly has four full-time staff, bolstered by several casual staff during sessions, headed by the clerk. Mary Jane Sillett held that position from 2007 to 2022.[29] The speaker and the members came to depend heavily on Sillett, a prominent, experienced leader.[30] With one impermanent exception, members, including ministers, have no personal, political staff. The exception: for a period when both Canada Constituency members lived in St. John's, they shared a part-time staffer. The Canada Constituency members who resided in Toronto and Edmonton during the Fourth Assembly had no dedicated staff support. To a limited extent, AngajukKât can draw upon community government staff for matters of direct relevance to the community, though community-level staff are often overwhelmed with their regular duties, leaving little time for assembly concerns. The Inuit community corporations run on shoestring budgets, so that the community chairs cannot call on their sparse staff resources to deal with assembly matters. NG bureaucrats in Goose Bay provide modest administrative support to the Upper Lake Melville members, but of course nothing by way of research or political activity.

Citing the overall lack of staff support at the assembly is certainly not a criticism of current staff. Assembly staff perform procedural and administrative functions, whereas it is in the realm of research and political support that members could benefit from additional staff resources. Beyond the Clerk's Office, which serves as the repository of official assembly documents – some but not all of which are available online – no library exists for members. One person's non-facetious comment was that "the main research support for members is Google." When I raised the idea of independent research support for members in some interviews, it was clear that the concept was little understood. From time to time, the Members' Services Committee raises the possibility of hiring a law clerk, but no action has taken place on this front. In arguing the need for such a clerk, one member pointed out that the NG's director of legal services, whose prime responsibility is to the Executive Council, is de facto legal adviser to the speaker and the assembly, raising possible conflicts of interest.[31] Less measured was a question from a former minister: "Why is it that we have legal counsel and all the support in the world and all the lenience of this House for that side of the table [NEC] and not on this side of the table?"[32] Loretta Michelin, who retired as legal director in 2019, served on assembly committees and wrote committee reports. Members respected and trusted her, but also recognized that her prime responsibility was to NEC. Members' attitudes and perceptions of research and staff support are evident from the failed attempt in 2011 to establish a Nunatsiavut auditor general on the model found in Ottawa and the provinces, as outlined in chapter 10.

The first day the assembly met, one member plaintively noted, "I'm right honoured to be here … [but] I have no idea what I'm supposed to be doing."[33] Presumably, her understanding of her role improved later that day through a "training session" mounted by the Ottawa-based Institute on Governance. Since then, after each ordinary member election, orientation sessions have been organized for newly elected members, usually run by outside advisers such as lawyer Veryan Haysom, whose long involvement with the Labrador Inuit Association and with the assembly included a key role in drafting the constitution, and David Hamilton, former clerk of the Northwest Territories Assembly, on whose expertise the Nunatsiavut Assembly drew heavily in its formative years. As well, orientation is provided to newly elected AngajukKât and community chairs and to any member who has just won a by-election. As is evident from the experiences of other legislatures, while such orientation sessions have value, they typically provide new members with far more information and advice than they can assimilate just after they are elected. By the time members are in a position to take in and benefit from information sessions, they often see themselves as too busy to participate in ongoing training – which, in any event, is not usually on offer.

Although, other than in short phrases, Inuttut is only used sporadically, simultaneous Inuttut-English translation is available in the chamber and, more significantly, through the audio feed of assembly proceedings on the NG website. When two translators are working, they are able to spell one another off, but often only one translator is available. At an early sitting, the president noted that one interpreter had been weathered out and asked everyone to speak only in English.[34] Off and on, over the years, the Speaker's Office, in concert with the Department of Language, Culture and Tourism, organized Inuttut classes for members. These training sessions, held after sittings finished for the day, were popular with members but, being so episodic, made only a limited contribution towards improving members' language facility. With the retirement in 2019 of a key person who had been delivering the language training, the classes came to a halt, at least for the time being.

Ordinary members, but not AngajukKât or community chairs, are entitled to constituency allowances to pay for newsletters, events, and the like. Ministers receive the same allowance as non-NEC ordinary members. As of 2022, the allowance for members representing communities in the Labrador Inuit Settlement Area (LISA) was $4,000 annually. In recognition of the numbers and the geographic dispersion of their constituents, the allowance for Upper Lake Melville members was $7,500 and that for Canada Constituency members $37,000. In recent years, no member has spent close to the allocated amount. In 2020–1, five of the six LISA members charged nothing against their allowances, while one spent $365; the two Upper Lake Melville members spent just over $2,000 between them; the two Canada Constituency members together spent just over $9,000. All told, members spent just under $12,000 of a possible $109,000.[35] Beyond basic frugality and the fact that all LISA members represent small, or very small, communities and thus do not require much in the way of constituency resources, it is unclear why members spend so little of their allowances. Early on, several members indicated that they underspent their allowances or did not spend them at all because they did not know what expenses were allowed and what were not. One member indicated that he had wanted to use his allowance to purchase a TV and an overhead projector for use in his community hall but was not allowed to do so.[36]

AngajukKât and community chairs occasionally complain that they should be eligible for constituency allowances since they, too, encounter expenses in representing their constituents. Indeed, during the assembly's early years, all members received constituency allowances. The policy was changed in 2012 and subsequent requests that all members be given constituency allowances have been met with the response that the constitution stipulates that the term "constituency" refers only to districts that elect ordinary members.[37] While this is technically correct, it is significant that requests to provide AngajukKât and community chairs with a similar allocation – perhaps called, as one member suggested, "elected official allowance" to avoid a constitutional roadblock – have failed.[38]

In that this section has focussed more on what services are not available to members rather than on what is available, it is important to highlight one essential service: *Hansard*. Having a complete, permanent, widely available written record of proceedings is simply essential to the effectiveness of the assembly, for many purposes but most notably for accountability. That members only occasionally refer to comments and commitments made in *Hansard* does not diminish its importance. Searchable PDFs of all *Hansards* are posted to the NG website, though sometimes with substantial delays. Less helpful to members and to the public are the video recordings of assembly proceedings made by the OK Society under contract from the assembly; copies are given to all members and to the Clerk's Office. No recording is made of the simultaneous translation of proceedings.

A Procedurally Conventional Legislature

The conclusion to the previous chapter suggested that, while certain basic elements of the Nunatsiavut Assembly, such as adherence to the Westminster cabinet-parliamentary model, may be rooted in Euro-Canadian governance traditions, important elements of the NG and of the assembly were designed to facilitate the self-government aspiration of Nunatsiavumiut. It noted some features of the assembly directly linked to Inuit culture and others that could be interpreted as indirect manifestations of Inuit culture. Associating the account of the assembly in this chapter with self-government or with Inuit culture is more difficult.

It is evident that the assembly's procedures and key organizational features such as committees are highly conventional. Anyone watching from the gallery with rudimentary familiarity with Westminster-model parliaments would have little trouble understanding what was going on. The chapter did identify some deviations from conventional Westminster practice and from structures and norms of Euro-Canadian governance. Some, such as the requirement for bills to pass two rather than three readings on their way to becoming law, are essentially technical in nature. Others are both more substantial and more directly contrary to customary Euro-Canadian, especially Westminster, processes – for example, the requirement for adequate representation of women on assembly committees and the provision allowing non-members to be full participants on committees. At that, it is not at all clear that such anomalies are rooted in self-government imperatives or that they can be interpreted as manifestations of Inuit culture.

Successful self-government is less a matter of procedural form than of effectiveness in achieving political goals. Procedural effectiveness may of course conflict with cultural norms, and indeed a common complaint of assembly members is that the excessive formality of the assembly is foreign to Inuit culture. An obvious inference from this chapter is that the assembly's institutionalized routines facilitate its smooth operation and efficient dispatch of business. Yet the chapter also identifies shortcomings that could affect the assembly's capacity to fulfil its functions. The weak committee system, lack of research and political staff, frequent recourse to waivers of procedural requirements in order to expedite assembly business, among other deficiencies, are not conducive to effective (self-)governance. A full reckoning of the assembly's effectiveness awaits in chapters 9 and 10.

Chapter Seven

Distinctive Features of the Nunatsiavut Assembly

Previous chapters considered whether various structural and behavioural features of the constitution and the assembly could be interpreted as manifestations of self-government and/or of Inuit cultural influence. As such, particular attention was directed to certain distinctive or unique procedures and practices followed in the assembly, such as the requirement for only two, rather than three, readings of a bill, the capacity of the assembly to appoint non-members to committees, and the prohibition against AngajukKât and community chairs serving on the Nunatsiavut Executive Council or as speaker. Chapter 8 discusses in detail the most central of the assembly's distinctive features – namely the nature and operation of "consensus government" – and the closely related question of integration of Inuit culture into assembly practices. This chapter outlines other assembly procedures that vary substantially from the norm among Canadian legislatures. Again, a prime concern is the extent to which these practices derive from and further the imperatives of self-government and Inuit culture.

Every Canadian legislature, whether federal or provincial/territorial, is marked by practices and procedures found nowhere else, but almost invariably these are minor and politically immaterial. By contrast, the procedures and practices discussed here are, or at least can be, of considerable moment. The present chapter looks at the following distinctive features of the Nunatsiavut Assembly: procedures for the selection of the first minister, ministers, and the speaker; voting, with special attention to the use of secret ballots; provisions for "money bills"; and the expulsion of members and the dismissal of ministers.

Selection of the First Minister, Ministers, and Speaker

Among the Nunatsiavut Assembly's notable distinctive features is the anomaly, probably unique within Westminster systems, that its leader, the president, is elected not from an individual constituency but by all beneficiaries. In turn, this renders the first minister's position unusual. To be sure, it is a position of significant power, but given the president's Nunatsiavut-wide mandate and constitutional primacy, the first minister holds a secondary position, not least because ultimately it is the president who decides who holds it. The process by which the first minister is selected is unusual, potentially featuring presidential prerogative, a search for consensus, and a vote of the assembly.

The selection unfolds as follows.[1] The president, presiding over the assembly, adjourns and reconvenes it as the committee of the whole and calls for nominations. If only one ordinary member is nominated, the president accepts the "consensus" and appoints the first minister. Should more than one person be nominated, each is allowed to speak "for a reasonable amount of time," after which the president halts the proceedings "to allow the candidates to speak to each other and to the members of the Assembly to see if the candidates can, amongst themselves and their supporters, work out a consensus on who should be First Minister." If these conversations fail to narrow the field to one, a secret ballot is held. The president "at his discretion will make the appointment after considering the will of the Assembly as reflected in the ballots." In other words, the president does not have to choose the candidate with the most votes. This was the process followed at the start of the Fourth Assembly and in early 2020 to replace First Minister Kate Mitchell, who had resigned. In each of the first three assemblies, however, different processes were employed.

In the First Assembly, the president himself nominated a candidate. After a recess for members to think about the situation, a second candidate was nominated. After both had spoken briefly, and the president made it clear that he did not trust the second candidate, a member requested a secret ballot. Having sought advice from the government's legal counsel, the speaker announced, "it states in our Constitution that we have to have an open vote," and asked for a show of hands. The president's candidate won by a vote of 12–3.[2] As the constitution appears to be silent on voting procedure for first minister, subsequent first ministers have been chosen by secret ballot.

In 2010, at the start of the Second Assembly, two candidates were nominated. President Jim Lyall called a recess so that they could speak to one another and to other members in hopes of reaching consensus around a single candidate. When no consensus emerged, a secret ballot was held, producing an 8–8 tie. After speaking to both candidates and taking some time to reflect, he made his choice, indicating that he would have accepted either candidate and would have preferred that the assembly had picked one or the other.[3]

Yet another procedure was used to select the first minister at the beginning of the Third Assembly. The four candidates were given ten minutes apiece to address the assembly, following which all other members had an opportunity to question the candidates, though only four members did. This is effectively the model used in Nunavut and the Northwest Territories to select the premier and the ministers in what is termed the Territorial Leadership Committee. Three rounds of secret ballots were needed to produce a majority for one candidate, with the candidates garnering the fewest votes having been eliminated in the first two rounds.[4]

On the first day of the Fourth Assembly, in 2018, two candidates were nominated for first minister, including the incumbent, Kate Mitchell. Both spoke briefly but no questioning by members occurred. A secret ballot returned Mitchell to office.[5]

Selection of the speaker and ministers is set out in a "process sheet," which essentially codifies procedures used in the first three assemblies.[6] Unlike the prerogative he enjoys with the choice of first minister, the president must abide by the will of the assembly in appointing ministers and the speaker. With a solitary exception, no competition or dissension has marked these processes. Once the first minister is sworn in, she is given a short period to consider possible ministerial appointments before presenting her nominations to the assembly, having presumably thought about this beforehand and consulted the president. Should the assembly concur, the president appoints the ministers and swears them in. In no instance has the first minister's entire slate of proposed ministers failed to gain immediate assembly approval. Were consensus lacking and the committee of the whole unable to reach consensus, secret ballots would be held on individual ministerial candidates. Those receiving majority support of the members would be selected; should a candidate be rejected by the majority of members, a new nomination would be made and put to a vote.

The president nominates an ordinary member to serve as speaker and seeks the assembly's approval of the nominee. If unanimity is forthcoming, the president swears in the speaker. Failing unanimity, a secret ballot is held; if the nominee secures majority support, he or she becomes speaker. Only once has anything other than unanimity occurred (see chapter 5).

While the assembly's processes for selecting the speaker, the first minister, and ministers are distinctive, if not unique, it is difficult to discern a linkage between them and Inuit culture. The possibility of opposing candidates for office reaching consensus among themselves as to who will serve might seem congruent with Inuit decision-making processes, but the reality is that no such consensus has ever been realized. Nor is it evident that the selection processes serve to promote self-government, though, as a self-government, Nunatsiavut has more leeway to devise unusual processes than is possible in other, more constrained governance models.

Voting and Secret Ballots

The vast majority of assembly decisions on bills, motions, and other matters are unanimous. On occasion, disagreement leads to a vote, decided by a show of hands, with the speaker announcing the result but with no record in *Hansard* as to who voted each way or abstentions.[7] The Standing Orders permit any member to request a recorded vote in which members' stances are included in *Hansard*, but this has never happened. One member, commenting on the absence of this standard accountability mechanism, argued that voting results are captured on video by the OK Society.[8] This isn't entirely true since the different camera angles the OK Society crew choose means that it's not always possible to discern how all members voted. More significantly, as the videos are not readily available to the public – an interested person would have to request a video from the OK Society – they are of little help in informing the Inuit public as to where their representatives stand. That Nunatsiavumiut are interested in knowing how their members voted is suggested in an assembly document. An extensive report on the consultations held in 2011 by a special committee on the controversial moratorium on uranium mining and production enacted by the Nunatsiavut Assembly observed that "there was a strong recommendation from those attending the meeting [in Makkovik] that any vote in the NG Assembly, and specifically this vote on lifting the moratorium, ought to be transparent so that those elected members who vote for and against are identified by name."[9]

Even more unusual – and for some, problematic – is the assembly's occasional recourse to secret ballots. Whereas most Canadian parliaments only very rarely decide matters by secret ballot, the principal exception being the election of a speaker, the Nunatsiavut Assembly employs secret ballots in various situations involving individuals, including assembly members as well as candidates for a small number of governmental positions, such as Nunatsiavut elections officer.

The first secret ballot appears to have taken place at the start of the Second Assembly. In laying out the procedure for selecting the first minister, President Jim Lyall stipulated that if a vote were necessary, it would be by secret ballot.[10] At the next session, two secret ballots were held. One was on a motion to expel an ordinary member. Once the brief debate had wound down, the speaker announced that the decision would be made by secret ballot. One member objected, asking where in the assembly's rules secret ballots were authorized and arguing for an open and transparent vote by show of hands. The speaker did not answer the question about authority for conducting a secret ballot; instead, she asked the members if they were in favour of a secret ballot. By a count of 10–4, the speaker's proposal for a secret ballot was supported, the member was expelled by a 15–2 vote.[11] The following day, the mover of a motion to remove the speaker from office cited the precedent of the earlier motion to ask for a secret ballot. The president, who was chairing the session, declared, "If a Member calls for a secret ballot, the vote should be by secret poll."[12]

During the 2011 debate on proposed changes to the Standing Orders, former first minister Tony Andersen asked whether the committee that had reviewed the assembly's rules had considered the question of secret ballots, which he described as "very unparliamentary for Governments such as ours." The committee chair replied that sometimes flexibility was needed. Andersen agreed but suggested that some previous secret ballots hadn't been necessary, adding that the use of "secret ballots goes against the very spirit of the kind of Government we have in mind." Loretta Michelin, the NG counsel, who had been a member of the committee, commented, "if there was to be a secret ballot, I would see the only way it could be conducted is if somebody puts forward a motion for a secret ballot and it's voted upon by the Assembly."[13] Her admonition has not been followed.

In subsequent years, secret ballots have been held on a range of matters: on votes for a trustee for the Labrador Inuit Capital Strategy Trust, for speaker, for trustees for the Labrador Inuit Land Claims Settlement Trust, for the moderator of the presidential Inuttut debate, for first minster, and for the suspension of a member and subsequently for her expulsion. In none of these was a formal motion to hold a secret ballot put forward and voted upon. In one trustee vote, the speaker proposed a secret ballot and the members agreed without a formal motion. For one vote on the debate moderator, the speaker responded to a question about the decision to hold a secret ballot by stating, "it's a determination that would be made by the Speaker," but did ask for a show of hands in support, which he received.[14] In the other instances, either the president or the speaker simply declared that the matter would be decided by secret ballot and no one raised any questions or objections.[15]

In September 2019, the Rules and Procedures Committee proposed a number of procedural changes. Among them was a recommendation to amend the Standing Orders to confirm what had become accepted practice: that the speaker would decide the method of voting, in other words, call for a secret ballot, though that term was not in the committee's report. A vigorous debate ensued in which several members objected to the very idea of a secret ballot, with Tony Andersen again voicing the strongest dissent, arguing that the assembly should never resort to a secret ballot: "a ballot or other things should not be done in secret and this is a very Democratic form of government that we have, open and honest, and we should not hide things." Other members were accepting of secret ballots for "sensitive" issues but balked at giving the speaker carte blanche to impose secret ballots. Perhaps the most noteworthy comment came from Language and Culture Minister Jim Lyall: "a couple of times that during my Presidency we removed people from the Assembly, I've had Members come back at me before that actually came to the house saying if we're going to take a vote on this, I can't do it publicly. I'm scared of this person. He's already threatened me. I've been threatened." In the end, the matter was shelved.[16]

It is fair to raise one's procedural eyebrows at the Nunatsiavut Assembly's unusually frequent recourse to secret ballots. At the same time, comparative context is warranted. The only other major Canadian consensus legislatures, those of Nunavut and the Northwest Territories (NWT), select their premiers and cabinets by secret ballot. Elsewhere, the first minister is determined through election outcomes, both general jurisdiction-wide elections and internal party selection processes, and, once in power, he or she unilaterally decides on cabinet composition. As for other, now routine secret ballots in Nunatsiavut for important appointments, such as trustees for the critically important trusts and the Inuttut debate moderator, in other jurisdictions similar decisions are typically made behind closed cabinet doors. On occasion, their legislators may be asked to approve a nomination, but they are rarely given a choice of candidates. Nunatsiavut does diverge from the Nunavut and NWT assemblies on difficult decisions involving suspension or expulsion of MLAs (members of the Legislative Assembly). The only expulsions in the other consensus legislatures, of Nunavut MLA Samuel Nuqingaq in 2014 and NWT MLA Steve Norn in 2021, were done by recorded votes.

Assembly votes that are not unanimous are unusual; as documented in chapter 8, all told, over the entire life of the assembly only forty-nine non-unanimous votes have occurred, thirty-nine of them in the first two assemblies, with all but one such votes in the Third and Fourth Assemblies conducted in secret. Perhaps this partially explains why routine votes are not recorded. Whatever the explanation, it is important to recognize that this is a practice not rooted in a formal rule: a single member can require a recorded vote. Failing to record how members have voted seems inconsistent with the imperatives of transparency and accountability, which rank as central elements of self-government. As for secret ballots, in that they are limited to personnel decisions, it could be argued that they derive from the Inuit cultural trait of restraining conflict. Still, it is notable that some members have objected that they are incompatible with the democratic norms they see as underpinning self-government.

Money Bills

All Westminster parliaments restrict the introduction of "money bills," measures to raise taxes or directly allocate spending, to ministers, reflecting the long-standing principle of Crown control of key financial powers. Nunatsiavut has adopted an unusual variation of this stricture. The constitution, not the *Nunatsiavut Assembly Act* or the Standing Orders, limits the introduction of money bills to the first minister and the minister of finance.[17] Not only are other ministers not accorded this power, but even the president is excluded from this central governance function.[18] Standing Order 57.1 repeats this provision, partially following conventional Westminster practice, stating that "the Assembly may not adopt or pass any vote, resolution, address or Bill for the appropriation of public revenue except for a purpose recommended to the Assembly by the

President or Nunatsiavut Executive Council in the Session in which the vote, resolution, address or Bill is proposed. Only the First Minister or Nunatsiavut Treasurer may introduce a money Bill in the Assembly." Implied in this formulation is a potentially significant variation of standard Westminster precept: the absence of a prohibition against measures that would impose taxes, as is found in the Standing Orders of the Canadian House of Commons and elsewhere.

After some inconsistent speaker's rulings and questionable procedures in the early years,[19] the money bill rule has been consistently applied by speakers and accepted by members. More significant than technical interpretations of the rule, however, is its very existence. At root, the money bill rule in Westminster systems is a notable residue of Crown prerogative and a major contributor to the concentration of power in the executive. Otherwise put, Nunatsiavut has enshrined in its central financial processes a strong element of a colonial approach to governance.

Expulsions and Dismissals

Jim Morrison's warning, "the future's uncertain, the end is always near," is especially applicable to the political lives of elected officials. Members of the Nunatsiavut Assembly are especially prone to having their political careers abruptly ended, either by dismissal from cabinet or, in two – almost three – cases, by outright ouster from the assembly. These episodes warrant attention as they are so distinctive within the Canadian parliamentary context and accordingly offer significant insights into the mores of the assembly and the attitudes and behaviour of its members.

Expulsions

Two removals of members from office may not seem noteworthy until set in comparative context. The assembly's removal from office of two members in fifteen years, and the attempted removal of another, plus an attempt to remove the speaker from office, stands in remarkable contrast to the experience of the Canadian House of Commons. In over one hundred and fifty years, the much larger House of Commons has only expelled members on four occasions, most recently in 1947 (two of the expulsions were of Louis Riel). Removing members from office, an undoubted prerogative of elected legislatures, is also a rare occurrence in provincial and territorial legislatures, including in the two northern consensus systems: in more than twenty years, only one Nunavut MLA has been expelled, and in the NWT, in the almost half century since it became fully elected, one member has been expelled. Numbers of actual expulsions are misleading, however, in that on four occasions – twice each in Nunavut and the NWT – members convicted of criminal charges would likely have been expelled had they not resigned as MLAs. As will be seen, the events that led to expulsion proceedings in Nunatsiavut were of a far less serious nature.

The first member to face expulsion was William Barbour, a former president of the Labrador Inuit Association (LIA). In September 2008, Barbour, the ordinary member for Nain, had been dismissed as minister of lands and natural resources by President Jim Lyall because of problems with alcohol. Following an incident in Rigolet, three ministers sent a letter of complaint to the speaker, who subsequently formed a three-member discipline committee (it did not include the complaining ministers). After an investigation, the committee unanimously recommended that Barbour be removed from office, and a formal motion to that end was put to the assembly. In the thoughtful, anguished debate that ensued, all those who participated spoke of their respect for and friendship with Barbour. For some, the loss of his ministerial position and his public embarrassment were sufficient punishment; notably, the complaint launched by the ministers did not call for his ouster. Others argued that the need to send a clear message to the public confirming the assembly's commitment to high ethical and personal standards justified removal. Barbour acknowledged his problems but sought a reprieve to deal with them. By a show of hands, the members voted on the motion, the result being a 7–7 split. The speaker did not have to break the tie since section 4.3.7 of the constitution requires that 60 per cent of the members, not simply 60 per cent of those voting, must vote to remove a member. Barbour was re-elected in 2010 and was again appointed minister of lands and resources but was dismissed from cabinet by the president a few months later as a result of his drinking. He was defeated in the 2014 election and subsequently served as an interpreter in the assembly.

The next expulsion case, in October 2010, was quite different in both substance and tone. Four complaints were registered about the behaviour of the newly elected ordinary member for Upper Lake Melville, Max Blake. The ad hoc discipline committee established by the speaker reviewed the complaints and recommended that Blake be expelled because he "used language and displayed attitudes that are sexist and hurtful towards Inuit women on June 4th, 2010, while carrying out the functions as a Member of the Assembly."[20] No real debate took place; the mover of the motion spoke briefly and Blake responded; no other members spoke. Blake acknowledged that he was intoxicated, adding, "I have apologized to the Assembly and the public for that incident." However, he adamantly disputed the discipline committee's suggestion "that I may be prejudiced and disrespectful to women," maintaining, "I deserve a second chance, same as everybody else." A secret ballot produced a 15–2 majority in favour of expulsion, whereupon Blake, as he left the room, declared, "I no longer want to be part of an organization that has a double standard."[21] Apparently his views on the "organization" changed insofar as he ran, and lost, in the 2022 ordinary member election.

The final expulsion process proved the most rancorous as well as the most drawn-out. Rachel Saunders was elected ordinary member for Hopedale in May 2018 and shortly thereafter was appointed minister of education and economic development. That fall, at a meeting of the local housing authority involving her family's land, Saunders became angry and, according to the subsequent discipline committee report, "swore out loud [and] acted out in the Assembly building."[22] A CBC News story cited allegations not mentioned in *Hansard*: "the Nunatsiavut government [i.e., the assembly] … says Saunders used profane language in the Nunatsiavut Assembly building, 'stomped out of a meeting and chose to air her frustrations on Facebook' … [In that Facebook post she] used the term 'colonizers and oppressors' when referring to the committee, which included elders and residential school survivors."[23] In mid-November, Saunders was dismissed from cabinet by President Johannes Lampe following a report from an ad hoc discipline committee formed by the speaker. Based on interviews with several people involved, the committee imposed a week's loss of pay and directed Saunders to apologize in writing to "all offended parties." As per the Code of Conduct, these sanctions were not subject to appeal. Saunders refused to apologize, telling CBC Radio's *Labrador Morning*, "I'm not going to apologize for something I didn't do."[24]

A planned November session was cancelled because of bad weather. At the January 2019 session, a motion was brought forth by one of the discipline committee members, proclaiming that "by refusing to accept and follow the decision of the Disciplinary Committee, [Saunders] has failed to conduct herself in a manner that is respectful of the *Code of Conduct*, this Assembly, the Speaker and the Members of the Disciplinary Committee, and has acted in a manner that is detrimental to the order and decorum of this Assembly." The motion called for suspension of her rights and privileges as a member until the next assembly session. If she complied with the committee's directions before that, the suspension would be lifted, but if not she would face a motion to expel her from the assembly. Beyond explanations of the process from the speaker and the mover of the motion, and points of order reflecting members' uncertainty about the implications of the motion, no substantive debate occurred. Saunders only comment was, "I am still refusing to write those apology letters, and I will continue to refuse until you remove me from office." A secret ballot was held; the motion passed 12–1 and Saunders left the chamber.

To no one's surprise, Saunders had not apologized by the March 2019 session, so the motion to expel her went ahead. Again, virtually the entire discussion entailed procedural rather than substantive issues. One member asked whether the community had been consulted at any point. The speaker responded that the process laid out in the Code of Conduct makes no provision for such consultation and accordingly, none was held. In her brief speech, Saunders uncompromisingly defended her integrity and again refused to apologize for something she said she didn't do. She was expelled by a vote of 11–4; two members were absent and the speaker did not vote.[25]

A more serious situation, involving the first president of Nunatsiavut, might well have resulted in expulsion had the president not reached the end of his term before legal proceedings played out. William Andersen III, long-time LIA president, who became president in the transition from LIA to NG, took a leave of absence late in 2007 citing personal reasons. It turned out that the Royal Canadian Mounted Police were investigating allegations against Andersen for sexual assault. According to Acting President Tony Andersen, when assembly members became aware of the allegations, they approached the president: "an informal gathering of the members of the assembly felt that perhaps it would be in everyone's interest, including the president, that it would be more appropriate for him to take a leave of absence."[26] Andersen remained on leave until his term ran out in May 2008, and in 2010 he was convicted of sexual assault and given a conditional discharge.[27] Had events unfolded in a different time frame, given the vigour with which subsequent, far less serious transgressions were pursued, it is hard to imagine that he would not have been removed from office, a process requiring a fourth-fifths vote of the members.

Though not an attempt to expel her from the assembly, following a report from an ad hoc discipline committee recommendation, the assembly's debate on whether to remove Patricia Ford as speaker raised difficult questions. Ford admitted to smoking cannabis "while I was on my time off and not working, on holiday." Given this timing, the discipline committee did not find that she had contravened section 4.1 of the Code of Conduct, which prohibits alcohol and illegal drugs while on assembly business, and thus did not recommend her expulsion. Its motion to remove her as speaker reflected the view that her dalliance with (then) illegal drugs, even though on personal time, had destroyed her legitimacy and credibility, as speaker, to oversee any future discipline proceedings against other members. One of the committee members argued that such a harsh measure was justified because "the impact of drugs and alcohol on our youth and on our communities is too great to ignore ... Do we want a Speaker who admits to doing drugs?" Other members disagreed strongly that Ford's action warranted discipline of any sort, in that no transgression of the Code of Conduct had occurred and that pursuit of propriety had gone too far. As one put it, "none of us wanted to come into this job knowing that the details of our personal lives would be picked apart and scrutinized and brought before a kangaroo court of sorts, where people can just be open to all kinds of criticism and beat down for no reason that is a part of something that happened on the job." The removal motion was defeated 11–5 on a secret ballot.[28]

Although they did not lead to expulsion motions, other allegations about improper behaviour on members' parts went to the speaker and, in some cases, to ad hoc discipline committees. The number of such allegations and investigations is unclear, since official references tend to lack detail. In September 2014, for example, Patricia Ford, as deputy speaker, tabled a report of a disciplinary Code of Conduct Committee but with no explanation or elaboration as to its contents.[29] No further reference was made to it in *Hansard*, though an OK Society report revealed that Speaker Sean Lyall had been reprimanded for making inappropriate remarks to a constituent, reportedly while intoxicated.[30] Another report of a disciplinary committee was tabled in June 2017, with no indication of whether the committee believed misconduct had occurred or of the member's identity, though it appears that it involved AngajukKâk Herb Jacque.[31]

The bizarre removal from office of Speaker Edward Blake-Rudkowski, although it was not done at the behest of the assembly members, warrants mention. Blake-Rudkowski lost his seat as an ordinary member not for any wrongdoing, real or alleged, but because he had been found ineligible to serve as a result of having his status as a beneficiary revoked. According to Blake-Rudkowski, an LIA member since 1986, immediately after his victory in the 2018 ordinary member election, a losing candidate sought a review of his status by the Office of Registry, which oversees beneficiary status. The review determined that Blake-Rudkowski's Inuit blood quantum was 17.14 per cent, and that, with membership requiring a 25 per cent blood quantum, he had been removed from the register of beneficiaries.[32] The constitutional requirement that members of the assembly be beneficiaries left the president with no choice but to declare Blake-Rudkowski's seat vacant.[33] For his part, Blake-Rudkowski told *Labrador Morning*, "I feel no differently about myself this morning than I did this time last week. I don't feel any less Inuit, any less Indigenous ... I couldn't begin to hazard a guess at how someone comes up with a number of 17 per cent." He added that with all the serious issues facing Nunatsiavumiut, "people turning upon their own and people fighting among themselves ... is unimaginably counter-productive."[34]

Ministerial Dismissals

First ministers in Ottawa and the provinces remove ministers from office from time to time, but this almost always occurs in the context of a cabinet shuffle, either when the government team is rejigged to adjust to changing policy or political circumstances or when a senior minister resigns and a domino-effect shuffle ensues among senior and would-be senior ministers. In all political systems, ministers resign to "spend more time with my family" or to "pursue other career options." Doubtless these well-worn explanations are sometimes truthful, though some ministers resign to avoid the ignominy of being dismissed.

Since 2006, six Nunatsiavut ministers have been dismissed from cabinet, one twice; at least two others resigned, one as both minister and as ordinary member, rather than face certain dismissal from the Nunatsiavut Executive Council (NEC), while others left NEC for reasons that are unclear. The ministers who would have been sacked had they not resigned were Susan Nochasak and Kate Mitchell. Nochasak initially said she resigned as a minister in 2012 in order to run for president but was forced to admit that the real reason was inappropriate use of a government credit card. President Jim Lyall, who had cited "personal reasons" at the time, subsequently acknowledged that he would have dismissed her had she not resigned.[35] First Minister Mitchell resigned from cabinet in December 2019 after what President Johannes Lampe described as inappropriate actions "in discharging her duties as Minister responsible for housing by interfering in matters that are the sole responsibility of Torngat Regional Housing Association."[36] She resigned as ordinary member for Makkovik a week later. An attempted comeback in the 2022 election was unsuccessful.

The outright dismissals were those of William Barbour in 2008 and again in 2010, Keith Russell in 2011, Richard Pamak in 2015, Danny Pottle in 2016, Sean Lyall in 2017, and Rachel Saunders in 2019. The circumstances surrounding the Barbour and Saunders dismissals have already been outlined.

Ordinary Member Keith Russell was dismissed as minister of health and social services by President Jim Lyall in February 2011 for "not fulfilling his duties."[37] Several years later, Russell wrote a piece about his dismissal for *The Labradorian*. Disputing his version, President Sarah Leo, who was not in office when Russell was dismissed but had served briefly as AngajukKâk for Nain during Russell's time as minister, told the paper that Russell "claims he was dismissed from the Nunatsiavut Executive Council in February 2011 because he 'supported the elders and the low-income people of Hopedale by bringing a crisis situation to light with (the Nunatsiavut Government) and I guess there was some political splash back for that.' " Leo reiterated the explanation given at the time by President Lyall: "Mr. Russell was dismissed because he was not fulfilling his duties as the Minister of Health and Social Development … By his own admission, Mr. Russell agreed that he was not actively involved in the functions and operations of the Department of Health and Social Services, and had very little to no contact with senior officials."[38]

The dismissals of Pamak and Pottle were even more contested. Pamak had been minister of culture, recreation, and tourism for less than a year when he was removed from office early in 2015, ostensibly because of questions relating to his travel and expense claims. "As President," Sarah Leo stated in explaining Pamak's ouster, "I have to have confidence and faith that members of the Nunatsiavut Executive Council perform their duties with honor, integrity, and dignity … Ministers are in a position of public trust, and are expected to be truthful, trustworthy and to act without self interest in relation to issues such as travel and expense claims."[39] According to Pamak, his dismissal came as a "complete shock," and he maintained that all his travel and expense claims were approved by the first minister and any discrepancies were adjusted. He acknowledged that in his extensive travel as minister he made some small, inadvertent errors that warranted scrutiny and correction, but not removal from cabinet.[40]

Nearly two years later, Pamak told the assembly that he did not "gain financially from any travel while conducting Nunatsiavut Government business," pointing out that the NG's auditors had not raised any concerns about his expense claims and that no Code of Conduct complaint had been registered against him. As to why he was removed, "I truly believe that being relieved as a Minister was personal in nature. As a Member of the NEC, I did ask questions. I shared my opinions. I did not always agree with the direction NEC was heading on certain issues. Consensus was not always reached or achieved."[41]

In February 2016, Danny Pottle was dismissed from cabinet as minister of finance, human resources, and information technology by President Leo for missing an NEC meeting. "As Treasurer of Nunatsiavut, Mr. Pottle was required to attend an important meeting in Nain this week to present the government's annual financial plan to the Nunatsiavut Executive Council, but he decided not to attend in person … Mr. Pottle had no valid reason for his absence and, therefore, lost the confidence of the President and the First Minister in fulfilling his responsibilities as a member of Nunatsiavut Executive Council."[42] Pottle called his firing "harsh and very heavy-handed," and maintained that his actions were reasonable and in no way reflective of the insubordination Leo alleged. After having flown from Vancouver to Goose Bay, Pottle explained, his flight to Nain, with other ministers aboard, had to return to Goose Bay because of bad weather. The next day, with bad weather again forecast, Pottle, fighting exhaustion from travel, flew to his home in St. John's, and took part in the meeting by teleconference, a common practice at NEC meetings.[43] Leo was adamant that Pottle's failure to attend the meeting was sufficient cause for his dismissal, noting that the other ministers took the next day's plane and arrived in Nain for the meeting. According to CBC News, "Leo said above all, the principle of following the ministerial mandate to attend face-to-face meetings was at stake in this incident and hopes other ministers understand the message."[44]

Lyall was dismissed in March 2017 as minister of culture, recreation, and tourism for "abusing his position by charging significant amounts to his Nunatsiavut Government credit card for personal entertainment." He resigned the same day as ordinary member for Nain.[45]

Discussion

Writing about the recent expulsion from the NWT Legislative Assembly of an MLA for Code of Conduct transgressions relating to COVID-19 protocols and for threats against other MLAs, one political observer suggested that this demonstrated an important strength of consensus government. In party-based systems, he argued, decisions on disciplining members turn on partisan political considerations, whereas members in consensus legislatures are not shackled in this way and can vote according to their best judgment.[46] This interpretation could also be applied to the Nunatsiavut Assembly.

More interestingly, might the proclivity for expulsions and dismissals derive in part from Labrador Inuit culture? Such an interpretation, while highly speculative, is nonetheless worth exploring.[47] Certainly, it is well recognized that throughout Inuit culture, ostracism, or in extreme cases, outright expulsion from the group, was an important mechanism of social control.[48] An additional Labrador determinant is the Moravian influence. As recently as 1969, a manual of the Moravian Church in Labrador explicitly specified exclusion from the church community as a necessary response to unacceptable behaviour. A section on "discipline" included the following:

> No strict rule is set down for exclusion from membership, but adultery, carnal sin of a gross kind, continued drunkenness, gross theft, laying of violent hands on the person of others, etc. to [sic] lead to exclusion … An excluded person, if he is a communicant, loses the right to attend the Communion for a time, neither may he attend the Confirmation Service, and Choir Festivals. An excluded communicant member may not vote, or be eligible for election, at an election for the elders or attend congregation council meetings.[49]

In earlier times, the missionaries held to substantially more stringent standards of behaviour, and it was common for them to expel Inuit from the local congregation and occasionally from the community itself. In 1838, for example, Nain missionaries decreed that anyone using alcohol had to move from the village.[50] Carol Brice-Bennett's landmark study of Inuit-Moravian interaction in the nineteenth century is replete with examples of Inuit being expelled as communicants and as community residents.[51] In her study of the Labrador Inuit, Helge Kleivan commented, "the 'Church discipline', i.e. a temporary expulsion from the congregation, which is being imposed on the offender in more serious instances, also corresponds surprisingly with those [Inuit] taboo regulations after confession [to an angakok – shaman]."[52]

The frequency of attempted and successful expulsions from the assembly and ministerial dismissals is clearly congruent with Moravian Labrador Inuit traditions. Congruence, however, is not causation, so that this intriguing possibility remains speculative.

Leaving aside possible cultural explanations, what are we to make of these numerous ousters and dismissals? One conclusion that emerges with startling clarity is the remarkably high proportion of members and ministers who ran afoul of either the Code of Conduct or the president during their first few months in office. Of the eleven cases of expulsions, near expulsions, ministerial dismissals, and ministerial resignations in anticipation of expulsion, five occurred within eight months of the member's first election to the assembly and three others took place during the member's first term. In a detailed briefing of neophyte members, long-time assembly adviser Veryan Haysom observed that Code of Conduct problems tend to arise shortly after a new government takes power. His explanation: "members, newly elected officials, don't realize just how onerous and difficult the *Code of Conduct* is and how easy it is to go astray on it."[53]

Another factor at work is the president's unquestioned authority to retain or dismiss ministers. In view of what seem relatively minor transgressions, it is hard not to see the Pamak and Pottle sackings as the president (re)shaping her cabinet along her preferred lines. Still, the instances of members experiencing severe sanctions for inappropriate behaviour are both numerous and significant.

Is the Nunatsiavut Assembly populated by an abnormal number of immoral lawbreakers? Not at all. In one of the cases summarized above alleged illegality was a central issue, but in most it was entirely absent; two dismissals did involve alleged misuse of government credit cards but in neither instance were charges laid. Most involved allegations of inappropriate but far from illegal behaviour. Notably, this is very different from the members who resigned from the NWT and Nunavut assemblies before expulsion proceedings began, all of whom had been convicted of serious criminal offences; the Nunavut MLA who was expelled had been charged but not convicted of a criminal offence.

Early on, assembly members adopted a remarkably tough and legally binding Code of Conduct. Haysom once described it to newly elected members as "one of the toughest in this country."[54] His assessment betrays lawyerly caution: the Nunatsiavut code surely has no equal across Canadian legislatures. In addition to standard provisions relating to conflict of interest, it provides, among other things, that "an Elected Official shall not consume alcohol or illegal drugs or be under the influence of alcohol or illegal drugs while conducting or discussing Nunatsiavut Government business," and that "Elected Officials must treat colleagues, constituents, public servants and members of the public with the courtesy and respect that is their due."[55] The former has been interpreted to be operative not only when the assembly is in session but also during any meetings a member attends. Were such standards enforced in Ottawa and the provincial and territorial capitals, Canada's first prime minister, Sir John A. Macdonald, would have been only one of a massive number of elected members removed from office.

Why is the Code of Conduct so draconian? Unusually, the Nunatsiavut constitution requires establishment of an ethical code for members and, moreover, makes provision for members to be removed from office for "unethical or immoral behaviour."[56] According to the code's preamble, "the actions of Elected

Officials have a profound impact on the lives of all Beneficiaries of the Labrador Inuit Land Claims Agreement and must be carried out in accordance with the highest ethical standards." A more forthright explanation comes from a prominent former member, Danny Pottle:

> the actions of Elected Officials current and past has necessitated the need for a *Code of Conduct* … I, Mr. Speaker, took an oath of office as did other Members of this Assembly to upload [*sic*: uphold] the constitution; our founding principles and our provisions of the constitution state quite clearly that Elected Officials are role models. We set the example, it is up to us to help people come to terms with and deal with issues such as addictions.[57]

A senior LIA figure was more forthright in an interview, emphasizing that "we had to be seen as a working government; people had to trust the government," and that both the elected politicians and the bureaucrats could no longer permit the loose standards of behaviour that LIA had tolerated, which led to perceptions of it as "a bunch of drunks." According to this person, the approach, which proved successful, was to put in place strong, effective procedures, so that there would be "no more drunks."

Thus a key motivation for the toughness of the code: "if people don't think this is an organization that operates with integrity, if people don't think you are here for them, then self-government is a failure."[58] In light of the problems that bedevilled LIA, as noted by Pottle and by others in interviews, and the commitment to ensuring the success of Nunatsiavut's experiment in self-government, it is understandable, indeed, commendable, that the members of the assembly imposed such demanding ethical and behavioural standards on themselves. Ironically, however, the code's toughness and the uncompromising way in which it has been enforced may have contributed, perversely, to certain counterproductive consequences.

First, without for a moment downplaying or endorsing the sorts of behaviour that have brought members into contravention of the code – alcohol abuse, sexist outbursts, ill-treatment of constituents, and the like – it could be argued that the public may be taking the wrong message from how the assembly deals with its members' foibles. Save possibly the cases of credit card misuse and Speaker Ford's dalliance with cannabis, none of the offences that landed members in difficulty were illegal: improper behaviour, to be sure, at least in most cases, but hardly corruption or flagrant illegality, offences that in other jurisdictions would likely warrant a reprimand or a penalty, always assuming they weren't covered up or defended as trivial for partisan reasons. That members of the Nunatsiavut Assembly are so frequently called out in public for misbehaviour and dealt severe penalties could easily be interpreted by the public as demonstrating precisely the reverse of what the code aims at. Rather than being seen as operating with unimpeachable ethical standards, the assembly could appear as a nest of scoundrels and knaves.

Second, it is hard to imagine more conflict-ridden events than attempts to expel members, dismissals of ministers from their positions of power, and impositions of harsh penalties for alleged misbehaviour. Accordingly, whereas Inuit values, bolstered by explicit constitutional provisions, emphasize governance based on consensus and conflict avoidance, the inevitably fractious processes surrounding discipline of members and dismissal of ministers run directly counter to these principles. Any number of times during expulsion debates, members emphasized that there was "nothing personal" about their desire to remove a member from office, that it was simply a matter of respecting and enforcing standards. That may well have been true, but it's hard for members not to take personally efforts to expel them from the assembly.

Inuit Influence and Self-Government through Unusual Procedures?

Overall, neither self-government aspirations nor a desire to inculcate the assembly with Inuit culture are obviously or directly linked to the distinctive and unique procedures and practices examined in this chapter. An important exception lies in the rigorous enforcement of the tough Code of Conduct, which reflects, as Veryan Haysom argued, the view that success as a self-government requires public confidence in the integrity of its leaders, which in turn requires uncompromising standards of behaviour; "no more drunks," to put it in less elegant language. It may also be that expulsions and ministerial dismissals are partially rooted in Labrador Inuit culture. At the same time, the harsh disciplinary measures entailed in Code of Conduct, especially formal attempts to remove members from office, engenders conflict, in direct contrast to a prominent tenet of Inuit culture.

The occasional recourse to secret ballots, which is entirely restricted to what might be broadly termed personnel matters, could be seen as a way of muting conflict and disagreement, in keeping with Inuit culture. Conversely, concerns have been voiced that secret ballots undercut important democratic principles entailed in self-government. Little about the selection procedures for first minister, ministers, and speaker resonates with either self-government aspirations or Inuit culture, though it is fair to note that self-government status offers wide latitude to develop unconventional governance processes. The provision whereby contending candidates for first minister are encouraged to meet with one another and with other members to work out who should be appointed does have echoes of Inuit consensual decision making. Yet the reality is that it has yet to produce a consensus candidate, suggesting it is little more than a noble but impractical aspiration. Finally, even the most tortured imagination would be hard-pressed to discern any linkage between the assembly's curiously restrictive money bill rule and either self-government or Inuit culture. As Freud might have said, had he been interested in legislatures, sometimes an unusual procedure is just an unusual procedure.

The practices and procedures discussed in this chapter are all central features of the assembly, such that an appreciation of their operation is necessary in coming to as full an understanding of the assembly as possible. That they neither advance self-government nor derive from Inuit culture in more than limited ways is not of great significance. Not all facets of an institution as complex as the Nunatsiavut Assembly can be expected to reflect its fundamental purposes or values. What are of great significance, however, are the aspects of the assembly that are explicitly designed to realize the political aspirations of the Labrador Inuit through adherence to the consensus government model and the incorporation of Inuit culture into its operation. The following chapter turns to these subjects.

Chapter Eight

Consensus, Consensus Government, and Inuit Influence

In the fall of 1988, I ventured to Yellowknife – my first trip to the North – to investigate what struck me as the strange governance system of the Northwest Territories (NWT): "consensus government." Having served as a non-partisan clerk in the Ontario legislature before becoming an academic, I was familiar with the workings of Westminster parliaments and was thus intrigued as to how the NWT Legislative Assembly could operate without political parties. I was also curious about what influence Indigenous culture had on the legislature. Since then, I have observed many assembly sessions in NWT, Nunavut, and Nunatsiavut, and spoken formally and informally to a great many elected members, former members, legislative staff, journalists, and others about consensus government. I have written about consensus government in the territories,[1] yet three decades on, I'm still trying to figure out consensus government.

Conclusions about this strange governance beast in the territories? Perhaps the clearest, most important conclusion is negative. The highly romanticized notion, to which I initially subscribed, that consensus government represents a thoroughgoing Indigenous transformation of the Westminster model, built on northern Indigenous culture, while it does contain a kernel of truth, is nevertheless vastly overstated. Unquestionably, Indigenous culture influences the territorial assemblies, both in their formal trappings and, more substantively, in members' behaviour. As well, important elements of consensus government are congruent with traditional northern Indigenous decision-making processes. On balance, however, the territorial assemblies are first and foremost Westminster-model institutions, clearly exhibiting the principal features common to all Westminster parliaments, most notably a pronounced concentration of power in the first minister and cabinet, making for a stark division between members with power and those without it. Indigenous influences are definitely at work but are generally of secondary import.

Similar conclusions emerge from this chapter's analysis of the Nunatsiavut Assembly, though a close examination of the assembly's operations and mores offers significant insight into key elements of self-government in Nunatsiavut. The chapter assesses the Nunatsiavut variant of consensus government as well as the nature and extent of Inuit influence on the assembly. Special attention is devoted to relations between the Nunatsiavut Executive Council (NEC) and non-NEC members, in particular the vociferous and seemingly perennial criticism of NEC for failing to communicate adequately with non-NEC members or with beneficiaries. A final section looks at the relatively infrequent instances when consensus has not been achieved: issues marked by disagreement requiring a formal vote.

If Inuit culture, especially Labrador Inuit culture, does broadly influence the Nunatsiavut Assembly, what elements of it might we expect to encounter? First and foremost would be consensual decision making, marked by thorough, open, respectful discussion, and accommodation of differing viewpoints with final resolution reached not by voting but by acceptance on the part of all involved. Relatedly, a consensus assembly could be expected to exhibit behavioural norms to avoid or at least mitigate conflict, perhaps bolstered by formal processes as well as institutional arrangements reflecting an aversion to concentration of power. Cooperation would be emphasized, as would be recognition of the primacy of the group over the individual. Pragmatic adaptability would loom large in the design and operation of the institution, as would respect for and widespread use of Inuttut.

Consensus Government in Nunatsiavut

Institutional Factors Affecting Consensus Government

Consensus government in Nunatsiavut bears a family relationship with its namesakes in Nunavut and the NWT. However, the Nunatsiavut Assembly exhibits important differences from the territorial assemblies, which, unsurprisingly in that one devolved from the other, operate in quite similar fashion. To a significant degree these differences reflect institutional factors in which the Nunatsiavut governance model varies from its territorial forebears.

The most far-reaching differences stem from the degree to which power in the Nunatsiavut Assembly is concentrated. Several institutional provisions contribute to this concentration. First, the president, who has no analogue in Nunavut or the NWT, wields extensive powers by virtue of his legitimacy as the sole assembly member elected by all beneficiaries and also through explicit constitutional provisions, such as the power to select as first minister a member who is not the assembly's first choice. (The idea of territory-wide election of the government leader/premier has been mooted in both the NWT and Nunavut, but has not been adopted, in large measure because in both cases the members of the Legislative Assembly (MLAs) recognize that such a change would significantly reduce their power.[2]) In addition, although clearly second in command to the president, the Nunatsiavut first minister is more powerful than her territorial counterparts, principally because of the capacity, in concert with the president, to select ministers to serve in cabinet and also to remove them. Premiers in the NWT and Nunavut neither choose their ministers nor have they authority to sack them, though they are able to strip problematic ministers of their portfolios and may be able to exercise sufficient moral suasion over them to convince them to resign.

Another structural factor contributing to the concentration of power is the restriction that only ordinary members may serve in NEC. Thus, close to half the assembly members are, by constitutional fiat, excluded from the central decision-making body of the Nunatsiavut Government (NG). An AngajukKâk once pointed out that with the assembly quorum set at six ordinary members plus the president, NEC by itself could constitute quorum so that "we don't need an Assembly then,"[3] but no evidence exists to suggest that NEC has ever contemplated employing such a stratagem, other than during the unique circumstances of the COVID-19 pandemic. Yet if the exclusion of AngajukKât and the community chairs from NEC runs contrary to consensus government principles by facilitating the concentration of power, in another way it promotes consensus by dampening conflict. This is so for three reasons. First, in the NWT and Nunavut, all MLAs are eligible to serve as ministers, and since most are interested in cabinet posts, this can lead to serious and enduring conflict when ministerial positions are up for grabs, either when a newly elected assembly first meets or if a cabinet vacancy occurs.[4] In Nunatsiavut, AngajukKât and community chairs may feel aggrieved at being ineligible for NEC – or they may not, having accepted the roles they have taken on – but are unlikely to engage in overt or covert conflict over ministerial appointments. Second, the odds that any given ordinary member can secure a cabinet post or the speakership are very good, since typically, six ministers, including the first minister, and the speaker are chosen from ten ordinary members. Thus, the competition, and hence the prospect of conflict, is limited. Third, though ministerial nominations must be approved by the assembly, the real choice is made by the first minister and president rather than, as in Nunavut and the NWT, assembly members, further lessening conflict.

Yet another significant institutional difference that shapes how consensus government plays out in Nunatsiavut is the absence of a central component of governance in Nunavut and the NWT: a "caucus," consisting of MLAs, including the speaker. In both territorial assemblies, caucus meets on a regular basis, in closed session, to discuss issues, if not necessarily to resolve them. In the territorial legislatures, caucus stands as, in the words of NWT clerk Tim Mercer, "one of the most distinctive features of consensus government":

Caucus consists of all 19 members, including the Speaker. In addition to setting broad strategic direction, for each Assembly, the Caucus meets regularly when the Legislature is in session to discuss the scheduling of sittings, the timing of major debates, the appointment of independent officers of the House and administrative matters affecting all members equally. Disciplinary matters are also discussed in the Caucus and from time to time, politically sensitive issues concerning the NWT as a whole are added to the agenda. In theory, members are expected to participate in Caucus discussions free from cabinet solidarity or the expectations normally placed on those holding certain offices, such as Premier, Speaker, or committee chair. As Caucus meetings are held strictly *in camera*, they are not intended to be a forum for decision making or holding the government to account.[5]

By regularly bringing all MLAs together, caucus allows members to share views and concerns in a less politically pressurized environment than the assembly, encourages engagement by all members, and offers the prospect of more consensual, less conflictual behaviour on members' part. Caucus has been criticized for contributing to a lack of transparency as regards important government decisions, but whether caucus is seen positively or negatively, it unquestionably influences the operation of the territorial assemblies. As well, in both Nunavut and the NWT, caucuses of non-cabinet MLAs also meet to strategize and coordinate activities, though they should not be understood as anything like the "official opposition" in other Westminster parliaments.[6]

No similar, formally constituted institutions exist in the Nunatsiavut Assembly. From time to time all members have met outside of normal assembly hours, to discuss policy issues, such as the controversial uranium moratorium or the construction of the Illusuak Cultural Centre in Nain.[7] In reaching the extremely difficult decision to completely halt caribou hunting, several caucus meetings were held, with President Leo emphasizing that

> our beneficiaries need to understand that we made this as a decision as a whole and that we're all supporting this. Now I hope that there's nobody around this table that's intending on caribou hunting. We stood together in that caucus room and we made that decision as leaders in our communities, not as Minister of Land, not as President, not as AngajukKâk for Nain. We made it collectively, and I think we have to support each other collectively.[8]

Members have occasionally referred to these meetings as "caucus," though this is a loose usage of the term.[9] In an interview, one member indicated that non-NEC members meet regularly to strategize and act "almost like an opposition," but other members to whom I spoke said that such coordination is limited and of little importance; overall, I incline to the latter view. In contrast to Nunavut and the NWT, where assembly staff provide administrative support to caucus and regular members caucus, in Nunatsiavut, assembly staff are not involved in informal meetings of members. In May 2014, the newly elected speaker, Sean Lyall, together with the clerk and the clerk's assistant, visited the Nunavut Legislative Assembly in Iqaluit. Although it is likely that the Nunatsiavut delegation would have encountered mention of caucus and regular members caucus, no reference was made to either in the official report on the trip.[10]

According to one of the members of the First Assembly, in the early days a fair amount of caucusing occurred, but after a senior NG staff person advised against it, members accepted that they shouldn't meet that way. A more convincing explanation of the abandonment of caucus came from another First Assembly member, who recalled a number of caucus meetings that didn't work well: "they just became shouting matches … [some] came very close to fist-fights." It thus became clear that it made more sense to have difficult issues aired in the assembly, where discussions could be more reasonable.

While the assembly may lack a consensus-oriented caucus, the notion of an opposition has no place in assembly politics. A defining feature of consensus government in Nunatsiavut, as in the territories, is the absence of a formally constituted opposition. In party-based Westminster parliaments, the parties not forming the government comprise the opposition, with one party typically assuming the role of "official opposition," in effect a government in waiting. In many ways, the government-opposition dynamic is the defining feature of Westminster parliaments, save for those without parties.

At least a few members see assembly politics as at least partially structured along government-opposition lines. For one minister, "they [non-NEC members] feel they're the opposition; they don't want to work with us; it's not really a consensus government." The major problem with the assembly, this person added, is the opposition mentality: "they [non-NEC members] automatically take an opposition approach." Less dogmatically, one interviewee said that since Nunatsiavut does not have political parties, "the nearest we'll get to an opposition is us people. When I say "us," it's mayors, AngajukKât, the [non-minister] ordinary members that represent their constituencies in the house of assembly." Understanding that much of assembly politics occurs behind the scenes, as someone who has worked in a party-based legislature with a powerful opposition, I am hard-pressed to see anything like opposition behaviour in the assembly.

During an orientation session at the start of the Second Assembly, Keith Russell, who had been a vociferous critic of NEC in the First Assembly but had since become a minister, argued the need for an opposition, maintaining that it could function without parties. In order to deal with an unresponsive NEC, he said,

> people have notions of organizing … a structural opposition, for lack of a better word, in order to maximize … the level of accountability as shown by the executive

council … you have that level of organization on this [NEC] side of the table as opposed to this [non-NEC] side of the table because the executive council meets, strategizes, documents their efforts, documents their direction, and executes that, and yet for the remainder of the assembly it's left up to individuals or small alliances at times to then posture and strategize on their own, as opposed to it being a concentrated effort, and that's where I would see the role of opposition or whatever you want to call it … It's a level of organization of those members not inside cabinet that I think is lacking.

This "opposition," Russell proposed, should have the ability and the funds to meet outside normal assembly meeting times. Members who responded were not favourably inclined. "The whole notion of opposition," countered one, "is contrary to consensus government." "We're an Inuit government" said another, "we're not the Government of Canada; we're not the Government of Newfoundland; this government was built and based on Inuit values, not because they do it in St. John's."[11] Beyond Russell's abortive suggestions, no serious attempt to organize an opposition has ever been mounted in the assembly.

Two final points. First, for some members, the Westminster parliamentary system itself stands as an elemental impediment to achieving genuine consensus government. A former speaker captured the frustration expressed by several members about the formality of the assembly impeding consensual processes: "it's very difficult to govern by consensus if you're following parliamentary procedure," with its time constraints, formality, and decisions taken by voting. A more positive interpretation comes from long-time secretary to the NEC Isabella Pain, who attends almost all assembly sessions: "We do have rules and procedures in the assembly. Our challenge is how you incorporate Inuit culture into that. But when you sit there and observe, you can really see the traditional style of decision-making."[12] Second, a small but significant element of the assembly's rules may not contribute to consensus but symbolizes commitment to maintaining an atmosphere conducive to consensus. Whereas almost all Westminster parliaments have carefully crafted, and in many cases frequently deployed, procedures for ending or limiting debate through closure, time allocation, and other procedural devices, the assembly's Standing Orders have nothing of the kind. It is fair to add that to this point the assembly has never experienced anything like obstruction or filibustering, but the absence of any formal means of curtailing debate is surely favourable to consensual behaviour.

Constitutional Formalities and the Committee on Consensus

A veteran Inuit politician recently recalled the expectations during LIA days as to how Nunatsiavut would be governed: "I remember us talking about having a consensus government, and that was the Inuit way, and it was to have open discussions about everything … [Well before we were here in the assembly, we were] going to have a consensus government so we could have open discussions and, actually, come to an agreement that something we could all live with. In the end there wasn't going to be any voting, there was going to be discussions and talking and stuff like that until we all could live with some kind of a solution."[13] Indeed, the constitution emphasizes consensus, setting as a founding principle that those involved in decision making in all Labrador Inuit institutions should "seek cooperation and consensus" and mandating that the assembly must always make "reasonable efforts" to reach decisions by consensus, understood as unanimity.[14] The assembly's initial Standing Orders included provision for a "Committee on Consensus," a variation of the committee of the whole, in order "to come to a Decision based on unanimous agreement or consensus."[15] The constitution as well as the Standing Orders authorizes the president to determine whether consensus has been achieved and, in the initial Standing Orders, to call for a Committee on Consensus. Should the president conclude that consensus is absent, a vote must be held.

In the first two assemblies, the Committee on Consensus process was used a handful of times, including once for the selection of the first minister. In 2011, following a report from the Committee on Rules and Procedures, extensive revisions to the Standing Orders removed all but a passing reference to the committee. The debate in the assembly confirming the changes did not touch on the Committee on Consensus.[16] Since then, no recourse has been made to the committee. The implication is not that the assembly gave up on an important vehicle for developing consensus, but rather that it had become evident that the Committee on Consensus process didn't offer anything more than the assembly resolving itself into committee of the whole. A standard feature of Westminster parliaments, committee of the whole entails somewhat relaxed rules of debate. In Nunatsiavut it is used routinely for all manner of assembly activities. When asked whether the assembly actually operates by consensus, several interviewees commented that committee of the whole's informal atmosphere facilitates consensual discussion and decision making, thus fostering the realization of consensus government. Proceedings in committee of the whole, said one, "has more focus on getting the job done."

As exemplified in the abandonment of the Committee on Consensus, consensus government is less about formal structures than members' attitudes and behaviours, though of course rules and institutional design can facilitate or hamper attempts to operate consensually. Accordingly, the following subsection examines how assembly members view consensus government, with subsequent subsections focussing on issues of communications between NEC and non-NEC members.

Members' Views on Consensus Government

In briefing newly elected members of the Third Assembly, adviser Veryan Haysom explained consensus this way:

> Consensus is not simply agreement or simply unanimity. Consensus is grounded in equality between members. It's guided by respect among Members. It's based on informed decision making and it's based on the common objective of what is in the best interests of the Inuit. It's a process of walking together and working together in order to decide together, and all Members of the Assembly are expected, in their function and their roles, to work towards consensus and in that spirit.[17]

Members' views about consensus and consensus government are very much in the same vein. These views predominantly entail two related elements: full discussion and comfort among members as to the final outcome of a decision-making process. During the inaugural session of the First Assembly, a member had this to say: "my understanding of consensus government is that each and every one of us should be given an opportunity to be heard and to speak [honestly] like I've been speaking today."[18] For another member, consensus government means "an assumption that we're going to agree … we're going to come to consensus on things, we're going to talk things out until we're all okay and can accept whatever the decision is." In interviews, members emphasized the importance of full, respectful discussion, but made it clear that the value of such discussion went beyond the opportunity to put forward one's views; more importantly, consensus was tied to the decision that emerged from the discussion:

> [consensus means] we come to an agreement or everybody agrees with the final decision. Everybody's happy with the decision …
>
> [Question: Does the assembly live up to that ideal?] I think so. In my mind, consensus is talking through things until we all come to a united agreement. Not necessarily voting; I don't always consider that consensus. It's more like a discussion. And then you agree to something. There might be a little bit of change from the beginning, what was proposed in the beginning to what comes out in the end, but everybody agrees, and we are satisfied with what was the outcome … [Question: Does the assembly live up to that ideal?] Sometimes. Sometimes not … Sometimes it's better when it's committee of the whole, as opposed to the assembly itself, because there's more opportunity for discussion; consensus [government] pretty much is democracy within the assembly to ensure we are all on the same page within government.

Opinion as to whether consensus government in the assembly was similar to traditional Inuit decision making was less clear-cut. One member said, "Yes; it's about working together to find an acceptable solution. It's not about confrontation; it's about, 'Let's work together … to find a solution.' " For another, "it's our Inuit way of governing … It's like the [former] elders' councils, where there was lots of discussion but in the end everyone walked away happy." Conversely, another member responded, "No … it's a lot more structured [in the assembly]. It's just very structured like any other government, but it's more like it [consensus] when it's in committee of the whole." Overall, members were somewhat more inclined to the latter view, though one made the point that while consensus government in the assembly may look like what occurs in other Canadian legislatures, members keep in mind and are guided in their behaviour by the objectives of the elders whose work "got us here."

Not everyone is sanguine about whether the ideal of consensus government is realized in the assembly, as is evident from the bitter views of one former member: "In my view, consensus government is the president telling everybody, 'Now this is what we are, this is what we want, this is how we need to do this' … All [members are] going to support what he wants to do. That's not a consensus government anymore … I guess you could call it a type of authoritarianism … Consensus is the president saying, 'This is how we're going to do it.'" However, most members would likely agree with a colleague for whom consensus government "is great when it works," which is most of the time. Members suggest that consensus-affirming behaviour may occur in non-obvious ways. "Criticism has to be constructive for consensus government to work," said one, adding that this was typically how discussions unfolded. Another made the important point that "anybody can make things difficult in consensus government, but non-NEC members don't go that route." The assembly does work by consensus according to one veteran member, who acknowledged that while it's never going to be perfect, it's been successful with lots of disagreements, and "at the end of the day no one has walked away in disagreement … I'm fairly satisfied with how the place works." Perhaps the most notable comment came from a seasoned minister: "There is an inherent sense of conflict at the assembly table since resources are limited, but we are a consensus government and we are Inuit."

A recent, otherwise trivial, episode speaks to the high value assembly members place on consensus. After extensive discussion and public consultation, a major, and controversial, bill to establish a stand-alone Nunatsiavut Housing Commission was ready for first reading. Just before the vote was taken, it was realized that one member was out of the chamber on a bathroom break. Rather than proceed with the vote, which would have been unanimous, an adjournment was called so that the vote would not only be unanimous, but complete.[19]

Communications Woes I: Complaints about (Non)Communications

With open and fulsome discussion so central to consensus government, the endemic complaints from non-NEC members about poor or non-existent communications from the cabinet loom as highly problematic. One long-serving member maintained in an interview that key problems with the NG, such as poor communications, can be traced back to LIA days. According to this person, other than during the treaty-ratification period, little effort was made by LIA to involve people in the process and insufficient information was available on options about and implications of various policies. For as long as assembly members have been criticizing NG communications, ministers have been acknowledging the problem and promising to do better while disputing that the issue is as serious as some non-NEC members make it out to be. No government on the planet is immune to criticism that the information it provides to elected officials and to its populace is incomplete and inadequate. Still, since the nature and extent of communications are central to an assessment of Inuit influence on the assembly, in terms of the expectations of open and full discussion in consensus government, and since the criticisms are both serious and perennial, a detailed examination is warranted.

It would be easy to fill page after page with members' negative comments about communications from NEC, in *Hansard*, and in interviews, some bitterly harsh, others expressing mild disappointment. The following is a reasonably representative sample of statements in *Hansard*, covering the entire time the assembly has existed. Note that each quotation comes from a different member:

- Some members don't know how the government is operating ... some of us don't know how we have to work as of yet ... We really need to work on communications. At times I really can't get an answer to the questions I have. – Mina Campbell-Higgs, 2007[20]
- Communications, there's been no change. Time and again we've been promised that there's going to be increased efforts to communicate to every constituency, to every elected official in order to help them do their job and to serve the public in a better fashion. That simply hasn't happened ... Time and again requests for information were ... not delivered and I have made requests for time with ministers, [but] they simply do not have time. – Keith Russell, 2007[21]
- My responsibility ... is to be responsible to my constituents. If I'm asked a question and I can't answer I have to forward my question on. If I don't get an answer to my question asked how can I be responsible to my constituents? – Glen Sheppard, 2010[22]
- A few words about how overwhelmed I am Madam Speaker about the amount of information that we got from the Minister this afternoon, I suppose we asked for [it] because we keep saying that we don't know what they're doing and there's no information. They must of went away Madam Speaker, got all pissed off and come back and boy did they ever give it to us

this afternoon but that's a good thing, there was a lot of information and I know that the President was over there smiling, so proud of his Ministers. I must say though to only do it when we come to Assemblies there must be a better way to get information to us. –Tony Andersen, 2011[23]

- There is a need within NG to improve both internal and external communications. Our Members [i.e., beneficiaries] look for information but they have to find it for themselves … As an Ordinary Member I receive very little information outside of updates provided here at the Assembly, and also through press releases or statements of the Nunatsiavut Government … [Quotes George Bernard Shaw] "the single biggest problem in communication is the illusion that it has taken place." – Richard Pamak, 2016[24]

- Some of my past statements have dealt with communication or the lack of communication, and although I do not want to keep singing the same old song, I want to bring something to the floor of this Assembly to look for answers. Not just for my benefit, but for the benefit of all people who we represent and are interested in what we are doing with some of the partnerships and agreements that we sign [mentions two major agreements with the federal government] … Since these exciting announcements were made through the media, I have not seen anything come our way from NG on where we're going with this … I am requesting that more information on these agreements and partnerships be distributed to all Assembly Members and the public to inform beneficiaries of what projects we're all involved in and the impacts it will have on us and the benefits we can expect from it. Let's expand our circle of information to include the people that we represent. – Gary Mitchell, 2018[25]

- [The Canada Constituency] is very huge and we seem to be lacking in notifications … You [the President] have had two meetings in the Canadian constituency in the last year and I never knew of any of those meetings until the day they happened. – Roland Saunders, 2019[26]

- Can the NEC send out an email to those who are not in NEC when they make decisions that affect Nunatsiavut before it goes to social media or just keep everyone up to date on what is happening or planning for Nunatsiavut … I've been here a little over a year and all I hear from the ones who are not on the Executive Committee that they don't know what's going on most of the time. – John Andersen, 2021[27]

In interviews, members and former members were decidedly harsher. The following quotations and paraphrases, each from a different member, come, with only one exception, from different members than those cited above. Words in quotation marks are direct quotations; those without quotation marks are paraphrases.[28]

- "NG communications is utter rubbish … You're not in the know if you're not in Executive Council"; information provided to non-NEC members is "negligible." – ordinary member
- Non-NEC members are kept in the dark by NEC; constituents ask about NG developments that the member has only heard about at the same time as constituents; communications with NEC is a huge problem; they won't provide information to members and thus to the public; they just don't seem to want to share. – AngajukKâk
- Ministers' statements at the assembly are pretty much the only information members get beyond government press releases, which are few and far between and generally not very informative. – ordinary member
- People in the Upper Lake Melville area feel that the NG doesn't communicate with them enough because they are outside the claim area. – member from Upper Lake Melville
- "The Nunatsiavut Government is famous for not letting people know what's happening." – AngajukKâk
- "I find there isn't a lot of communication from … within the NEC to the other members. Usually you find out, kind of … things that may be happening at the assembly … As a person who is not a member of NEC, I don't know if they have a protocol [about communication] in place or anything like that. My understanding is that if somebody went to them and asked a question … I think they would just basically give a blanket statement … [saying] this issue is being discussed at the NEC." – ordinary member
- "Each minister and the president, they'll give an update [at the assembly]. And sometimes they send out emails of some things happening, but … [the emails] aren't very frequent … [Question: How does NEC communicate with beneficiaries?] They have community meetings where they travel once a month to a different community, and they have an open house and people can come and they can ask questions [Question: Is that effective?] Not really; it's really hard to communicate with people … There is a newsletter, but I don't know how well the newsletter is distributed in the community." – community chair
- "We don't hear a thing of what's going on there [NEC]. Why don't we, the members, know what's going on? [It's] bad communications, too much secrecy, too much self-centred authority … [The problem lies with] the cabinet, the inner circle … [There is] too much secrecy." – ordinary member

As this sampling makes clear, whether in public assembly statements or in private interviews, assembly members have long expressed serious dissatisfaction with communications from NEC. Moreover, the discontent persists unabated. It is fair to add that dissatisfaction has been widespread but not universal. One AngajukKâk commented in an interview, "mainly [I get information from NEC] at the Assembly and the open houses they have in communities. If I want to speak to the minister … if I want a question answered from the minister of finance, I email him and … I have to say, they're pretty fast responding and, other than the one issue with the president [where] they never responded for a couple of months, responses have been pretty good." Another Angajuk-Kâk's mostly positive assessment did note that getting adequate information on bills and estimates is a problem in that often information is not received on a timely basis, but that this has been discussed between members and cabinet and things are improving. This member was not of the view that NEC hides information or purposely delays getting it to members, but rather that communications problems are largely a consequence of lack of staff and of key people being very busy. Overall, the member was content with communications from NEC, noting that if members don't understand a bill or policy, they can contact the minister or the department staff: "the ministers are always there; if you have a question, ask them."

In September 2016, non-NEC members met to discuss problems they were experiencing in their communications with NEC. They drafted a letter to President Lampe seeking improvements in NEC's communications with both assembly members and beneficiaries. In January 2017, former speaker and finance minister Danny Pottle asked the president the following question:

> I think I'm speaking on behalf of all the non-executive members of this Assembly who were sorely disappointed that we didn't even get a recognition or acknowledgement to our request. Therefore, can you explain why after nearly six months we haven't had an answer to the letter that was written to you in September.[29]

The president responded as follows:

> The NEC is working at enhancing the communication that you are asking, and right now we have been looking at how we can better communicate, whether it's internal or externally, and so I believe that we are moving forward pretty well, but those details are still in the works with the Nunatsiavut Executive Council, but we will certainly need the help of the Assembly to work out those details that we need to enhance the communication that you are asking about.[30]

Over a year later, non-NEC members again voiced dissatisfaction with both the lack of response to their letter and to the continuing communications failings of the NG. Overall, President Lampe argued, the government was taking its responsibility to communicate seriously and things were improving:

> Communication certainly is very important to the Labrador Inuit, and certainly we are working on letting our people know in our communities through newsletters

and through the web and, most certainly, through the Assembly. And I know that we, as elected members, have that responsibility to communicate to our constituents and those who elect us. And certainly I go on CBC Radio or OkâlaKatiget to inform the Labrador Inuit of whatever it is that we are able to give to the Labrador Inuit and others. But still it's a challenge, but I do believe that we are doing more than we were before and we will continue to improve the communication as we go along.[31]

About this time, Speaker Edward Blake-Rudkowski convened a meeting of all assembly members to discuss communications issues. In interviews, non-NEC members alluded to this meeting, noting that nothing had come of it and emphasizing that NEC cannot have been unaware of the non-NEC members' discontent.

Communications Woes II: NEC Responses Regarding Communications

On occasion, especially in the early days, in responding to complaints about inadequate communications, the NEC has acknowledged that it, and the NG generally, have indeed not performed well in communicating with assembly members and with Nunatsiavut beneficiaries, committing to do better. At other times, especially in during one-on-one interviews, ministers and NG staff have disputed members' comments about poor communications, suggesting, sometimes not subtly, that a good deal of the "problem" lies with the non-NEC members themselves:

At the second sitting of the First Assembly, President William Andersen III admitted:

in the past year, the Transitional Government from all aspects have, in my view, done a relatively poor job of communicating the activities of the government in general and at our last Executive Council Meeting, Mr. Speaker, I made a commitment that we as a government must put more energy and resources into communications … I think it's important Mr. Speaker that everything we do not only be transparent but all the Beneficiaries have access to all the relevant information so that they too can voice their opinion, after all they're the ones that put us here and I look forward to developing a greater communications system in Nunatsiavut to address the problems that we've had in the past year.[32]

Two months later, the president closed off potential channels of communications, stipulating that only certain NG staff should deal with the media: "it came to my attention today that there were supposed to be a couple of media interviews by our employees. Some of the issues that are to be discussed are very difficult. I am asking from now on that only the appropriate people within the Government deal with the media."[33]

The first day of the Second Assembly, in response to a request from an Anga-jukKâk for better communications, President Jim Lyall pointed out that the NG website was now operative, adding, "I see absolutely no reason why Ministers cannot report regularly on what they're doing on a regular basis and certainly we will have this issue and it's one of the most important items I will have on the next Executive Meeting. We'll discuss the issue and we'll come forward and hopefully we'll have a really good plan for communicating what the Executive is doing."[34] A few months later, however, problems apparently remained, prompting the following admission from First Minister Darryl Shiwak:

> What we are doing and what we have done is that we requested that each of the Ministers of the Executive Council forward any relative [*sic*: relevant?] information from their department on to the Assembly Members. We will continue to do so because we believe communication is one of the things that we are lacking, that we need to do better and we will continue to make that commitment to forward that information on to the Assembly Members so that everybody's informed so that when we do come to this table that we are not out in the cold and I have to admit I've done a very poor job myself but I will do better in the future.[35]

A few years later, President Sarah Leo conceded that "we've been failing" at meeting the commitment to provide assembly members with information about NEC decisions, and she, too, promised to do better.[36] By the start of the Third Assembly a few months later, however, government responses to criticisms about communications had taken on a new tone. President Leo pointed to improvements:

> When I was elected as President, Mr. Speaker, I made a commitment to improving communications by ensuring the Nunatsiavut Government maintain a high level of openness and accountability, and I think we've been doing a good job, although there's some still communication issues, and we're trying to work through that because we keep saying our beneficiaries are not hearing enough from us, and we've talked about what we are doing, and we're trying to figure out other ways to do it. We have the media releases out. We have interviews on OK [Society], we have our Open Houses and our offices are very open. I like to think that any beneficiary feels comfortable going in and talking to any of their elected officials. But certainly there's room for improvement, and while I say that I want our beneficiaries to feel that they can come in and talk to each of the elected officials.[37]

Over time, the president and the first minister have become less willing to acknowledge communications shortcomings. Early in Johannes Lampe's presidency, after First Minister Kate Mitchell sloughed off a question about how NEC could improve communications, indicating that communications came under the Office of the President, and thus it's "not … in my department,"[38] he said,

> I really have not been given briefing wholly in terms of communication but, most certainly, the Nunatsiavut Executive Council, when we, you know, meet, we try our best to communicate to all Nunatsiavut elected members, and most certainly to try to make sure that everyone is knowledgeable of what is going on, but I have noticed since becoming President that lately that elected members have been taking some time off from their offices, and so maybe that way that communication is being missed.[39]

Not long after President Lampe's answer to the question about his lack of response to the non-NEC members' September 2016 letter about communications, he began to cite the need to maintain confidentiality in dealing with the federal and provincial governments as limiting the government's ability to pass on information to non-NEC members.[40]

In interviews, ministers and former ministers acknowledged the difficulties of communications with beneficiaries and with non-NEC members, one saying that this was the biggest challenge faced by any government. A former minister agreed that non-NEC members' criticisms about communications are often justified, explaining that with their inadequate staff support, ministers are easily overwhelmed by the tasks before them and are thus simply too busy to communicate as well and as often as they should. When asked about government communications, these interviewees cited the public sessions of the assembly, as well as the NEC's open houses and newsletters, though views as to the effectiveness of these channels were divided. For one minister, the open houses are good opportunities for genuine communications between NEC and community members. Another said they were "pretty useless," with ministers just talking about their departments, offering "the same rhetoric over and over and over again, rather than engagement with people." Even within NEC and across NG departments, more than one minister said that communication is sometimes problematic. Generally, according to one, ministers stay within their departmental silos during meetings, with "constant repetition [of inadequate communication] even on the inside."

"We try very hard" to communicate with non-NEC members, said one minister, adding that ministers don't purposely hold information back but are very busy and have no personal or political staff. One bright spot, mentioned by more than one minister, is the NG's relationship with the Inuit community governments. NEC, they suggest, does reasonably well in informing AngajukKât about proposed NG actions that could affect their communities. The Joint Management Committee, chaired by the minister of finance with AngajukKât as members, which deals with Inuit community governments' capital projects and funding, was cited as a useful communications channel. On occasion, ministers provide information to members outside normal assembly proceedings, as illustrated by a recent conference call involving all members, initiated by a minister who wanted to inform members about a policy issue on which misinformation had been widely circulating. In the same vein, when the session planned for June 2020 was cancelled because of the COVID-19 pandemic, each department prepared what would have been the ministers' statements to the House and circulated them to all members. Noting complaints from members about lack of information on certain issues even though the information had been contained in these statements, one NG official remarked that some non-NEC members "lash out without having read the documents." At the same time, when asked whether members' criticisms of inadequate communications were valid, this person replied, "Sometimes yes, sometimes no."

Overall, ministers tended to the view that while some criticisms are valid, communication, as one put it, "is a two-way street … The members know our phone numbers and our emails." Another minister, who emphasized his frequent offers to make himself available to all members, identified substantial variation among non-NEC members in terms of how often they contacted him. Some, he said, are regularly in touch, whereas some never call or email and wait to ask questions in the assembly. "I hear a lot less from non-NEC members than I'd like," added a third minister. According to yet another minister, although some aspects of government, such as intergovernmental negotiations, must be kept confidential, 95 per cent of government information could be shared with non-NEC members if they asked, but generally they don't ask. This minister described long-standing friendship with the local AngajukKâk, noting that they typically encounter each other at least every few days. And yet, the minister lamented, the AngajukKâk would come to the assembly saying, "it's been four months but now I can ask a question," rather than having raised the matter earlier. Another minister forthrightly maintained that "non-NEC members aren't following government closely enough to know what we [NEC] are doing; they wait until the assembly meets to find out." A different perspective was offered by an NG staffer who suggested that part of non-NEC members' discontent with communications stemmed from their unrealistic expectation that they should be deeply involved in all government decisions. This was not a view widely shared by members, either in interviews or in comments captured in *Hansard*.[41]

Inuit Influences

A central purpose, in some ways *the* central purpose, behind the land claim and the creation of Nunatsiavut was the revitalization and advancement of Labrador Inuit culture. It is therefore important to consider the extent and effect of Inuit influences on the assembly. The objectives and nature of consensus government, arguably the most far-reaching attempt at incorporating Inuit approaches to Nunatsiavut governance, have already been addressed. This section looks at language use in the assembly, at members' comments and actions that address or exemplify "the Inuit way" (or its absence), and, finally, at how the assembly has responded to the symbolic and controversial constitutional requirement that candidates for the presidency "understand and speak Inuttut."

The obverse of Inuit influence on the assembly, efforts at protecting and enhancing Inuit culture, is of at least equal importance. However, supporting Inuit culture is more a responsibility of the NG than of the assembly, and it is therefore largely outside the remit of this book. Moreover, a proper evaluation of the state of Inuit culture in Nunatsiavut would entail far-reaching research, not to mention greater familiarity with Nunatsiavut society than I possess. Accordingly, this undoubtedly crucial topic receives little attention here.

In his "Vision Statement" to the first sitting of the assembly in October 2006, President William Andersen III said, "I believe that the custom and tradition of learning out on the land can be transferred into the customs and traditions of this government."[42] In considering such optimistic, if nebulous, expectations about Inuit influences on the assembly and on Nunatsiavut governance generally, it is well to recognize that, as knowledgeable academics have argued, "because many aspects of Inuit governance have for centuries been undermined by a colonial presence in the name of religious conversion, commerce, and other justifications, many aspects unique to Inuit culture have been weakened and in some cases completely lost. As a result, one cannot reasonably expect traditional Inuit institutions of governance to resurface automatically in the wake of a land claims agreement."[43]

Inuttut in the Assembly

Virtually all debate in the assembly unfolds in English. Given the relatively low levels of Inuttut fluency across Nunatsiavut, this is not surprising. A review of the (highly incomplete) *Hansards* from the Transitional Assembly suggests that a fair amount of Inuttut was spoken. However, only two members of the First Assembly could speak it.[44] Sarah Leo, president from 2012 to 2016, was frank about her Inuttut facility: "the reality is that people are uncomfortable with me sitting here [as president]. I speak, I understand but I'm not fluent. I admit that and admitted that through my whole campaign."[45] In sessions that I observed or listened to, a few members made brief statements in Inuttut, but the only fluent speakers were President Johannes Lampe and former president Jim Lyall. Videos of sessions in the first three assemblies reveal a similar pattern. Members frequently express regret over their limited or non-existent Inuttut skills, often in discussions about the urgency of enhancing language capacity among

Nunatsiavumiut, especially youth. As mentioned in chapter 6, Inuttut training has been offered to members off and on over the years, depending on resources and on members' interest. Overall, however, it has been too limited to have made a noticeable difference to debate in the assembly.

Unlike in Nunavut, where unilingual Inuktitut speakers are occasionally elected to the legislature, no assembly member has been unilingual in Inuttut. Nevertheless, simultaneous interpretation is provided of all assembly proceedings for members and visitors in the gallery, but its prime audience is among the Nunatsiavut public, who can access it through the assembly's audio feed on the NG website. No data are available as to the extent of listenership.

Remarks delivered in Inuttut are usually translated into English in *Hansard*, prefaced by "(Speaks in Inuttitut.)." In recent years it has mainly been the president's opening address at the start of sessions and his answers to members' questions that have been in Inuttut. Unlike the Nunavut legislature, which publishes complete *Hansards* in Inuktitut and in English, the assembly does not produce an Inuttut *Hansard*. Considering the horrendous cost of translation, the pressure on NG's limited translation capacity, and the low potential readership, this seems reasonable.[46]

Language is a prime topic of assembly debate. Ministers, especially the culture minister, speak often about language policy and funding for language programs. Language issues are frequently raised by non-NEC members in questions and statements. Yet beyond statements and questions, the assembly's record of action on language is limited. The Language Committee in the First Assembly met infrequently and produced no substantive reports or recommendations.[47] Speaker Todd Broomfield, a committee member, did meet with various groups working on language issues and served on the NG's Language Strategy Committee (LSC) but the assembly committee itself was largely inactive. By contrast, the NG committee met frequently, held community consultations, and produced a language policy strategy. During the second half of the First Assembly, *Hansard* recorded several updates on the work of the LSC but made no reference to the assembly's Language Committee.[48] Early in the Second Assembly, Culture and Language Minister Johannes Lampe presented the NG's language strategy, as developed by the LSC, though it does not seem to have been subject to a dedicated debate in the assembly.[49] More than once, Lampe called for the assembly's Language Committee to be revived, indicating at one point that re-establishment was planned for the next assembly session; however, nothing appears to have happened along these lines.[50] Nor was a language committee struck in the Third or Fourth Assemblies. In August 2021, NG released a new five-year language strategy, but it was not debated in the assembly.

The NG has been active in promoting the learning and use of Inuttut, through language training programs, a "Language Nest" for very young children, a

"Rosetta Stone" language computer app, and other initiatives. Assembly members are enthusiastic and supportive of such measures, though often critical of their limited scope. One member lamented that barely 3 per cent of the NG budget was devoted to language concerns,[51] while another warned in an interview that "we're not treating it [the status of Inuttut] as the crisis that it is." Overall, members are vocal about the need for action and supportive of existing programs, but as evidenced by the absence of a committee mandated to deal with language, the assembly is only tangentially involved with language issues.

"The Inuit Way"

Assembly members may not speak much Inuttut, but they take seriously their responsibility to speak and act according to Inuit cultural precepts. An especially forceful appeal to follow Inuit principles came in Finance Minister Danny Pottle's comments about members' behaviour during a difficult session:

> The whole concept of Inuit Kaujummikatangit, looks at our belief, our world vision as Inuit, our value base, our traditions, our customs, everything that guides us and directs us in everything we do. I think we should all, Madame Speaker, do our best to strive to keep in memory, especially for those who have come before us and laid the foundation and gave us our value base, gave us our beliefs, gave us our traditions, that we honour those who came before us and we make sure that we move forward in keeping with those traditions so that our children and our grandchildren, our nephews, our nieces, our brothers, our sisters are educated and they are reminded of what our value base is, what our traditions are, what our beliefs are, and that each and everyone [sic] of us as Inuit have a right and an obligation, I believe, Madame Speaker, to uphold those traditions. Madame Speaker, the tenants [sic] of Inuit Kaujummikatangit, looks at the fact that we treat each other with respect, that we treat individuals with dignity. We share in a manner of cooperation what we have, not for the good of the individual, Madame Speaker, but for the collective, the good of the whole of Labrador Inuit Society. So I just ask that people keep that in mind, do a little bit of thinking about that and try to strive and do your utmost to integrate those concepts, those values and those beliefs in everything that we do.[52]

It is common for members to cite Inuit cultural precepts, sometimes rendered as "the Inuit way," when commenting on politics within the assembly or in responding to government policies or operations, in effect holding out the Inuit way as a standard of behaviour in judging the actions of members or of government. A few examples from *Hansard*:

- The debate is necessary, sometimes we get a little side tracked but I think it's important that we provide an opportunity for people to be heard; that is the

Inuit way and we are to stand by our laurels and our principles to support the Inuit way. – Ordinary Member Danny Pottle[53]

- The environmental protection Bill as amended still ensures that developments are consistent with Inuit values, culture and knowledge. – Minister Darryl Shiwak[54]
- We are no longer using the Inuit way of life; we are not working closely together. Full blooded Inuit will not do or go against another Inuk. – Minister Johannes Lampe[55]
- [Confronting a presidential candidate and challenging his or her Inuttut facility is] not really the Inuit way. – AngajukKâk Charlotte Wolfrey[56]
- [Commenting on poor communications from NEC] Before colonization the Inuit used to share everything, there was never secrecy by elders and leaders and the village when determining a course of action but this is what we practice from the Executive Council. – Ordinary Member Keith Russell[57]

In interviews, when asked directly, members stressed the importance of imbuing assembly processes with Inuit culture. Some suggested that the assembly does reflect such principles, though they were often vague as to specifics – as, for example, in the above-quoted statement from Danny Pottle. One member mentioned the atmosphere in the chamber: "there's no yelling; there's no name calling; there's respect." Others identified elements of the assembly that ran counter to Inuit values. Several commented that the proceedings were too formal and structured; one lamented the limited involvement of elders in assembly processes. Beyond concerns about formality, other instances of non-Inuit behaviour can be identified. While it is indisputable that members' comments in the assembly are indeed far more respectful of their colleagues than is the case in other Canadian legislatures, nasty, personal attacks do occur, albeit infrequently. Similarly, although he didn't frame it in terms of failure to bring Inuit principles to bear, the complaint from Community Chair Gary Mitchell cited in chapter 5 could certainly be interpreted in just that way. Mitchell, it will be recalled, took his colleagues to task for not offering help during a period when, owing to resignations, neither of the ordinary member positions for Upper Lake Melville were filled, leaving him with an onerous workload.

"Understand and Speak Inuttut"

The Labrador Inuit Constitution requires that candidates for the presidency understand and speak Inuttut. This controversial provision is unique across Indigenous self-government regimes in Canada. No other Indigenous self-government agreement or constitution contains any linguistic qualification for elected office, though facility in the local language would doubtless prove an electoral asset. The roots of this provision can be traced to the creation of the Labrador Inuit Association (LIA). Although the desire to enlist Settler support in the early days of the LIA entailed downplaying the importance of Inuttut facility as a criterion for membership, at the 1975 LIA annual general meeting a resolution was passed requiring that "the president must be able to speak Inuttitut fluently."[58]

From the outset, the "speak and understand" requirement generated passionate debate. In 2008, Ordinary Member Keith Russell put forward a motion proposing deletion of the section of the constitution prescribing Inuttut facility for presidential candidates. Debate on the motion was vigorous and polarized. Russell argued that his motion was not about the status or revitalization of the language, but about leadership, citing data from the Labrador Inuktitut language coordinator indicating that only 13 per cent of beneficiaries said that Inuttut was their first language, so that most could not qualify to run for president.[59] He portrayed the issue as one of widespread importance requiring public involvement through a referendum. Other members saw the matter as precisely one of language. They argued that the requirement not only sends a powerful symbolic message but also ensures that beneficiaries unilingual in Inuttut are able to communicate directly with Nunatsiavut's political leader. One member predicted that eliminating the language requirement for presidential candidates would greatly set back efforts to retain and promote Inuttut and would represent "a huge step into saying goodbye to Inuktitut in Labrador." Another said that such a move would mean "every bit of pride that we're bringing into our young people right now is going to be gone."[60] Supporters of the motion recognized these arguments yet emphasized that, given the low level of Inuttut fluency, including among assembly members, the requirement discriminates against the vast majority of beneficiaries excluded from consideration as potential presidents. Moreover, they added, it also sharply reduces the pool of good candidates for the top office. The motion was defeated 10–4, with several of those speaking against it acknowledging that their Inuttut skills were all but non-existent.[61]

Though no further attempts have been mounted to amend the constitution in this fashion, the debate, and the attendant polarization, have resurfaced from time to time, most notably when the assembly considered changes to the *Nunatsiavut Elections Act* to establish a process for enforcing the "understand and speak" qualification. For one member, doing away with this requirement would mean "we're going to lose the values that the people before us in LIA days were fighting for,"[62] whereas another claimed that "this colonistic standard severely erodes our government's potential to draw out those who may be best suited to lead our government forward ... [and raises the question of whether] our Constitution [is] discriminatory against unilingual English speakers."[63]

Consensus Lacking: Split Votes

Although the vast majority of matters requiring a formal decision are settled without a negative vote, consensus, understood as unanimity by members, is not always achieved. Even when they express reservations during debate, once the question is called, members usually agree to whatever is before the assembly, thus making for a unanimous decision. From time to time, however, "nays" are heard when the speaker asks if the assembly is in favour of a motion or a course of action. Formal votes in which unanimity is not achieved, few as they may be, are worth exploring. In the following analysis, they are inelegantly termed "split votes."

In analysing split voting, or indeed any form of voting, in the assembly, it is important to bear in mind that voting was unknown in traditional consensual Inuit decision making. That said, no one suggests that the assembly is anything like a pure analogue of how Labrador Inuit reached decisions in pre-contact times or in the elders' councils or men's meetings of the Moravian era.

All split votes, from the start of the First Assembly, are listed at the end of this chapter in appendix 8.1, while appendix 8.2 presents the results of votes for which individual members' choices can be discerned.[64] The most obvious, and perhaps the most important, finding from the admittedly incomplete data in the two appendices is how infrequent non-unanimous votes have become, not that they were ever common. Leaving aside the relatively few votes required to fill positions such as first minister and Nunatsiavut elections officer, the First and Second Assemblies saw a total of thirty-five split votes, whereas, all told, only three occurred during the Third and Fourth Assemblies.[65] To a limited degree, the higher rate of split voting in the First Assembly reflects the activities of a single ordinary member, Keith Russell. Russell was a constant and vociferous critic of the NG and on three occasions his disagreements with the government led to votes on motions in which Russell was the only member voting a particular way.

Yet the explanation for the dramatically higher rate of split voting in the assembly's early days entails far more than the actions of a single, at times obstreperous, member, not least because Russell resigned as an ordinary member early in the Second Assembly. The first two assemblies had to deal with a number of high-profile, contentious issues, such as the uranium moratorium, the fraught issue of $5,000 membership payments,[66] a proposal for an auditor general, and so on. These and other issues generated vigorous debates, some deeply dividing the assembly. Few far-reaching or controversial matters came before the Third and Fourth Assemblies, during which the assembly had to deal with only one major piece of legislation, the bill to create the Nunatsiavut Housing Commission, a bill that did generate extensive debate but in the end passed unanimously. Still, it is hard to avoid concluding that, having settled into established routines, and faced with fewer tough issues, the assembly and its members have taken on a more consensual approach. It may also be that NEC has become more adept at managing its relations with non-NEC members.

Appendix 8.2 below sets out, so far as can be determined, how individual assembly members voted in the specific split votes listed in appendix 8.1 (other than secret ballots). For example, entry number 1 shows who voted for and against second reading of the *Additional Revenue Act* in June 2007 while number 5 shows who voted for and against expulsion of William Barbour in November 2008. What does appendix 8.2 tell us about the cohesion of NEC, an important concern for a Westminster-model cabinet in a consensus government system? Bearing in mind that virtually all the relevant data come from the First and Second Assemblies and that the data encompass only a few votes, two tentative conclusions emerge. First, on issues that cannot be considered government initiatives, members of NEC are more frequently found on opposite sides of a question than not. Matters on which NEC voted together tended to be of greater moment – the motion to remove William Barbour from the assembly (entry number 5 in appendix 8.2) and the motion to increase constituency allowances (number 6) – than those on which it was split, such as minor administrative provisions relating to members' benefits (numbers 4, 6, 10, 11). Second, and more important in the Westminster context, NEC does vote as a bloc on some but not all matters that are or could be considered government measures. In several instances, such as the motions to create an auditor general and a special committee on the uranium moratorium, all NEC members voted the same way (numbers 9, 14, 15, 16, and 20). On other government measures, including financial motions, NEC members have split with their colleagues (numbers 17, 21, 22, 23, 24), apparently without consequence.[67] A particularly telling insight into NEC cohesion emerged from the passage of the bill to impose a three-year moratorium on any activity relating to uranium on Inuit-owned lands. This bill, considered in more detail in the following chapter, was by a wide margin the most far-reaching and controversial legislation ever to come before the assembly. At first reading, all six NEC members supported the bill, but a month later, after members had consulted their constituents, two ministers voted against the bill, which barely passed, 8–7. That cabinet split badly in a vote on a key government initiative is a strong indication of the limits of fundamental Westminster conventions in the assembly, at least in the early days: no similar split in NEC has occurred since the end of the Second Assembly. In interpreting these votes, it bears reiterating that all the votes referenced in this paragraph amount to only a very small proportion of the votes taken in the assembly, the vast majority of which are unanimous.

What of the cohesion of non-NEC members, both as a group and within the three categories of members, ordinary members, AngajukKât, and community chairs? To the extent that assembly dynamics are consensual rather

Table 8.1. Voting cohesion of non-NEC members

Vote	All Votes	Non-lopsided Votes
11–0/9–0	2	–
9–1/9–2	5	5
7–1/7–2	3	2
4–1	1	–
7–3	1	1
6–1/6–2	5	2
5–4	2	2
6–5	1	1
4–1	1	–
7–3	1	1
6–1/6–2	5	2
5–4	2	2
6–5	1	1

than adversarial and oppositional, non-NEC members would not be expected to manifest clear coherence in terms of voting. Tables 8.1 and 8.2 set out data on the extent to which these groups voted together. Again, it is important to recognize that, overall, in almost every instance, all members, NEC and non-NEC, were unanimous in their support of the matter voted upon. Both tables have two columns: the first includes all cases for which the votes of all members of the category could be discerned; the second excludes votes that were heavily lopsided, with only one or two members voting against the majority, on the grounds that such votes could be misleading as to members' cohesion.

Table 8.1 looks at the cohesiveness of the entire group of non-NEC members in split votes. It shows the number of votes that resulted in a specific tally; for example, the first row of the table shows that two votes of 11–0 and 9–0 occurred and that both of them were lopsided (since the cell in the second column is blank). In interpreting the data in this table, it should be recognized that, with a single exception (a proposed increase to constituency allowances), none of the split votes entailed matters that even tangentially related to common interests shared by non-NEC members. Whether one considers all split votes or only those that were not lopsided, it is clear that non-NEC members typically voted together, if not as a solid bloc (the two votes with all non-NEC members on the same side were on minor procedural motions that had lopsided outcomes). In all but four split votes, only one or two non-NEC members opposed their colleagues, one producing a strong 7–3 majority. The only instances of non-NEC members being split down the middle were on first and second reading of the uranium moratorium bill and on the motion to establish an independent auditor general.

Table 8.2. Voting cohesion of non-NEC members

Ordinary Members

Cohesion	All Votes	Non-lopsided Votes
4/4	1	–
3/3	2	1
2/3	5	2
3/5	4	4
2/4	1	1
1/2	7	5
1/1	1	–

AngajukKât

Cohesion	All Votes	Non-lopsided Votes
5/5	2	2
4/4	10	7
3/3	2	–
4/5	1	1
3/4	3	2
3/5	2	1

Community Corporation Chairs

Cohesion	All Votes	Non-lopsided Votes
2/2	10	8
1/2	6	5

As for the three categories of non-NEC members, two preliminary points. First, with the single exception noted in the previous paragraph, none of the split votes entailed matters that spoke at all to common interests within the three groupings. Second, the panel of the table presenting community chair voting has somewhat fewer cases than the other panels, reflecting resignations and one chair's protracted illness. As is evident from the table, both AngajukKât and community chairs were more cohesive in their voting than the ordinary members. Considering only the non-lopsided votes, the AngajukKât voted as a bloc 9 out of 13 times (69 per cent) and in 3 of the 4 other votes, only a single AngajukKâk strayed from the fold. The community chairs voted together in 8 of the 13 votes (62 per cent) in which both voted. In only 1 of 13 votes (8 per cent) were all ordinary members in agreement; in most of the remaining votes, they were badly split.

If voting by both NEC and non-NEC members usually produces near-solid blocs, are these blocs opposed or aligned? Table 8.3 provides an answer. It presents, for non-lopsided votes only, the tallies for each group; for example, the first row shows that on vote 2 in appendix 8.2, all 6 NEC members voted yes, whereas 5 non-NEC members voted yes and 4 voted no. Overall, the table demonstrates that just over half the time, 7 of 13 cases, NEC voted strongly one way and non-NEC members voted strongly the other way.

Table 8.3. Voting of NEC and non-NEC members (yes–no; non-lopsided votes only)

Vote #	NEC	Non-NEC
2	6–0	5–4
3	4–2	4–5
5	0–5	7–2
6	0–6	9–1
11	2–5	1–7
16	0–5	5–6
17	1–4	9–2
18	5–0	2–9
19	5–0	2–9
20	7–0	2–7
21	5–1	6–2
22	5–1	7–3
24	1–5	9–1

The number of split votes is very low and almost all the data come from the First and Second Assemblies, so that any conclusions from the review of the data on split votes must be viewed with caution. Still, useful findings have emerged. First, bearing in mind that from the outset the vast majority of formal decisions taken in the assembly have been unanimous, the assembly appears to have become more consensual over time. Second, at least in the early going, cabinet solidarity within NEC on important government initiatives, a key Westminster precept, was breached on several occasions. Third, as a group, the AngajukKât have been far more cohesive than either the ordinary members or the community chairs. Finally, a clear government/opposition dynamic (NEC/non-NEC) was evident in a substantial proportion of split votes.

Beyond the telling rarity of split votes – that is, votes indicating a lack of agreement among members – which is suggestive of the cultural imperatives to avoid conflict and to engage in consensual behaviour, it is hard to divine any clear or even tentative links to Labrador Inuit culture from the foregoing analysis. Interesting insights did emerge about the extent to which various types of members vote as a bloc, but none can be explained in cultural terms.

A Consensual, Inuit-Influenced Assembly?

The Nunatsiavut Assembly bills itself as a consensus government. Does this chapter support a judgment that the assembly indeed operates consensually? If the frequency of unanimous votes is a criterion, the assembly easily qualifies. In more than fifteen years, only about fifty votes were not unanimous; moreover, split votes have become increasingly rare in recent years.

Similarly, issues marked by deep disagreement and overt (verbal) conflict have been uncommon. Certainly, divisive issues have emerged from time to time, primarily during the First and Second Assemblies. Most were of short duration: the closing of the Health Department facility in Northwest River; potential NG support for a cruise ship project; errors in the distribution of the $5,000 payment to beneficiaries when the treaty was finalized; the proposed creation of an independent auditor general; the uranium moratorium; the cost of the Illusuak Cultural Centre in Nain; and formal proceedings to remove members from office. Recurring divisive issues have been very much the exception and, at that, are largely lacking in ideological underpinnings. The most notable have been dissatisfaction with membership processes, which are all but entirely out of the assembly's hands, since they are set by the treaty; non-NEC members' complaints about inadequate communications; and the requirement that the president "speak and understand Inuttut." The characteristically low levels of conflict raise a basic question: Do contentious issues only surface occasionally because assembly members consciously avoid conflict out of a commitment to consensus, or is consensus possible because widespread agreement exists among members on most political questions? Both processes are likely at work, but evidence is lacking to be able to say more.

In setting out their mostly positive assessments as to how consensus government is realized in the assembly, members stressed the importance of full, open, and honest discussion. Without raising doubts as to the sincerity of such views, it bears noting that to the extent that it entails the back-and-forth exchange of views, little discussion actually occurs. The vast majority of members' and ministers' statements are non-argumentative and are put forth in a respectful manner, but they rarely elicit responses. As detailed in chapters 9 and 10, most legislation is passed with little if any debate, while most opportunities for members to pursue – that is to say, discuss – issues via supplementary questions in question period are not taken up.

A member quoted earlier described assembly politics as "authoritarian." Another member's view, while less harsh, was nonetheless pointed: "NG is endangered by an overconcentration of power in a few individuals" – meaning bureaucrats as well as politicians. What is perhaps most noteworthy about these criticisms is how unusual they are. To be sure, members are not shy about complaining, in public and in private, about the (in)adequacy of NEC communications or about specific NG decisions and policies. Nor do members see the assembly consistently operating according to some consensual ideal. However, even in confidential interviews, with the exceptions cited above, members did not express serious concern about undue concentration of power or of bureaucrats wielding inappropriate influence. As a measure of the consensual nature of the assembly, this is of substantial moment.

On the closely related question of Inuit influence on the assembly, this chapter suggests a mixed but generally positive conclusion. With one glaring exception, the infrequent use of Inuttut in proceedings, the Nunatsiavut Assembly can be seen as imbued with Inuit culture. It is by no means an Inuit institution in all respects, but key features of the assembly, beyond the formal trappings of attire and decor, clearly manifest Inuit influence. At a macro level, the hallmark pragmatic adaptability of the Labrador Inuit is evident in the distinctive modifications to render serviceable for Inuit purposes a decidedly colonial governance model, the Westminster system.

In the expectation that members behave according to "the Inuit way," in the powerful commitment to the aspirations of the Labrador Inuit, as expressed in the treaty and the constitution, and of course in the entirely Inuit membership, the assembly unquestionably exhibits a strong Inuit character. The generally successful efforts at living up to the ideals of consensus government point in the same direction. Significant in this regard are the characteristically low-key, respectful debate, the behavioural norms and institutional mechanisms for mitigating conflict, and the avoidance of divisive votes. The assembly's aspirations for truly consensual politics are undercut by continuing shortcomings in communications from NEC to non-NEC members as well as by the substantial concentration of power in NEC. Overall, however, consensus government works tolerably well in Nunatsiavut and contributes to the assembly's Inuit character.

Symbolically and substantively, the Inuit character of the assembly is of signal importance. Yet the assembly is not just an Inuit institution; it is a legislature, charged with essential governance functions. The following two chapters examine how effectively the assembly fulfils its legislative functions.

Appendix 8.1. Split Votes

Does not include vote held 18 March 2009 on trustees for Inuit Capital Strategy Trust (eleven candidates)

Date	Subject	Outcome
FIRST ASSEMBLY		
Oct 2006	Vote on nominees for first minister: Andersen (A) and Pottle (P)	A: 12 P: 3 SB
June 2007	Second reading *Additional Revenue Act*	11–1*
March 2008	First reading of uranium moratorium bill	11–4*
March 2008	Proposed constitutional amendment on Presidential "speak and understand" criterion	4–10
April 2008	Motion to set salary for acting president	4–9
April 2008	Second reading of uranium moratorium bill	8–7*
June 2008	Proposed financial contribution to Makivik cruise ship	5–10
June 2008	Proposal to reallocate $902K in supplementary budget bill	3–12
Nov 2008	Motion to discuss process for amending trust deed	13–1*
Nov 2008	Motion to remove Ordinary Member Barbour from assembly	7–7*
March 2009	Proposed increase in constituency allowances	9–7*
March 2009	Proposal to increase assembly professional development budget	10–6
June 2009	Selection of trustee: Campbell (C) and Obed (O)	C: 2 O: 13**
June 2009	Selection of trustee: Andersen (A) and Turner (T)	A: 10 T: 5**
June 2009	First reading supplementary budget bill	13–2*
June 2009	Administration of members' benefits	12–2**
June 2009	Administration of members' benefits	3–12*
March 2010	Motion to establish special committee to review issues with $5K membership payment	3–10**
March 2010	Motion to delete section of bill regarding administration of land claim funds	12–2*
March 2010	Motion to delete section of bill regarding administration of land claim funds	12–1*
March 2010	Motion to delete section of bill regarding administration of land claim funds	12–1*
March 2010	Motion of defer resolution on Drug and Alcohol Committee report until next assembly	3–10
March 2010	Motion to create special committee on $5K membership payment	8–5
SECOND ASSEMBLY		
May 2010	Vote on nominees for first minister: Pottle (P) and Shiwak (S)	P: 8 S: 8 SB
Oct 2010	Whether to have secret ballot on motion to remove Ordinary Member Blake from assembly	10–4

(Continued)

Date	Subject	Outcome
Oct 2010	Motion to remove Ordinary Member Blake from assembly	15–2 SB
Oct 2010	Amendment to Code of Conduct re alcohol abuse	12–4
Oct 2010	Motion to remove Speaker Ford from speakership	5–11
March 2011	Motion to create auditor general	5–11*
March 2011	Bill to improve enrolment procedure	13–3
March 2011	Amendment to budget re civil servants' salaries	10–6*
March 2011	Motion to modify budget amendment re civil servants' salaries	7–9*
March 2011	Motion to rescind budget amendment re civil servants' salaries	7–9*
Sept 2011	Motion to establish special committee on uranium moratorium	9–7*
Dec 2011	Motion to adopt new Elected Officials Policy	12–5
Dec 2012	First reading of bill authorizing additional $2.1M for Torngasuk Cultural Centre	11–3*
Jan 2013	Second reading of bill authorizing additional $2.1M for Torngasuk Cultural Centre	12–4*
Jan 2014	Motion to proceed with a bill for a presidential debate	16–1*
March 2014	Section of bill to amend *Nunatsiavut Elections Act* authorizing presidential debate moderator to disqualify candidates	10–6*

THIRD ASSEMBLY

Date	Subject	Outcome
May 2014	Vote on four nominees for first minister	Unrecorded SB
May 2014	Vote on speaker: Ford and Lyall	Unrecorded SB
June 2015	Motion to appoint candidate as Nunatsiavut elections officer	7–8 SB
Nov 2015	Motion to clarify forms members must complete	11–4
Feb 2016	Vote on candidates for presidential debate moderator	13–1 SB

FOURTH ASSEMBLY

Date	Subject	Outcome
May 2018	Vote on nominees for first minister: Mitchell (M) and Blake-Rudkowski (BR)	M: 11 BR: 5 SB
Jan 2019	Motion to suspend Ordinary Member Saunders from assembly	12–1 SB
March 2019	Motion to remove Ordinary Member Saunders from assembly	11–4 SB
Jan 2019	Vote on nominees for first minister: Asivak (A) and Edmunds (E)	E: 13 A: 3 SB
Jan 2020	Vote on candidates for moderator of presidential debate: Hay (H) and Townley (T)	T: 12 H: 4 SB

SB Secret ballot
* Complete vote available (see appendix 8.2)
** Partial vote available (see appendix 8.2)

Appendix 8.2. Individual Members' Votes in Split Votes

1. **June 2007 second reading *Additional Revenue Act*: 11–1**
   Yes   Andersen (Pres), Andersen (NEC), Barbour (NEC), Flowers (NEC), Gear (NEC), Ponniuk (NEC), Shiwak (NEC), Decker (Ang), Dicker (Ang), Erickson (Ang), Jacque (Ang)
   No   Russell (OM)

2. **March 2008 first reading of uranium moratorium bill: 11–4**
   Yes   Andersen (Acting Pres), Barbour (NEC), Flowers (NEC), Gear (NEC), Ponniuk (NEC), Shiwak (NEC), Pottle (OM), Dicker (Ang), Erickson (Ang), Jacque (Ang), Winters (CC)
   No   Russell (OM), Decker (Ang), Michelin (Ang), Tuttauk (CC)

3. **April 2008 second reading of uranium moratorium bill: 8–7**
   Yes   Andersen (Acting Pres), Barbour (NEC), Flowers (NEC), Ponniuk (NEC), Broomfield (OM), Dicker (Ang), Jacque (Ang), Winters (CC)
   No   Gear (NEC), Shiwak (NEC), Russell (OM), Erickson (Ang), Decker (Ang), Michelin (Ang), Tuttauk (CC)

4. **November 2008 motion to discuss process for amending trust deed: 13–1**
   Yes   Andersen (NEC), Flowers (NEC), Gear (NEC), Ponniuk (NEC), Barbour (OM), Pottle (OM), Russell (OM), Decker (Ang), Dicker (Ang), Erickson (Ang), Jacque (Ang), Tuttauk (CC), Winters (CC)
   No   Lyall (Pres)

5. **November 2008 motion to remove Ordinary Member Barbour from assembly: 7–7**
   Yes   Pottle (OM), Russell (OM), Decker (Ang), Dicker (Ang), Erickson (Ang), Tuttauk (CC), Winters (CC)
   No   Lyall (Pres), Andersen (NEC), Flowers (NEC), Gear (NEC), Ponniuk (NEC), Barbour (OM), Jacque (Ang)

6. **March 2009 proposed increase in constituency allowances: 9–7**
   Yes   Barbour (OM), Pottle (OM), Russell (OM), Decker (Ang), Erickson (Ang), Jacque (Ang), Michelin (Ang), Tuttauk (CC), Winters (CC)
   No   Lyall (Pres), Andersen (NEC), Flowers (NEC), Gear (NEC), Ponniuk (NEC), Shiwak (NEC), Dicker (Ang)

7. **June 2009 selection of trustee: Campbell (C) and Obed (O): C: 2 O: 13**
   Campbell   Andersen (NEC)
   Obed   Gear (NEC), Shiwak (NEC), Russell (OM), Jacque (Ang), Tuttauk (CC)
   Unknown   Lyall (Pres), Broomfield (NEC), Flowers (NEC), Ponniuk (NEC), Barbour (OM), Decker (Ang), Dicker (Ang), Erickson (Ang), Winters (CC)

8. **June 2009 selection of trustee: Andersen (A) and Turner (O): A: 10 T: 5**

Andersen	Andersen (NEC), Shiwak (NEC), Russell (OM), Jacque (Ang), Tuttauk (CC)
Unknown	Lyall (Pres), Broomfield (NEC), Flowers (NEC), Ponniuk (NEC), Barbour (OM), Decker (Ang), Dicker (Ang), Erickson (Ang), Winters (CC)

9. **June 2009 first reading supplementary budget bill: 13–2**

Yes	Lyall (Pres), Andersen (NEC), Broomfield (NEC), Flowers (NEC), Gear (NEC), Ponniuk (NEC), Shiwak (NEC), Barbour (OM), Decker (Ang), Dicker (Ang), Erickson (Ang), Jacque (Ang) Winters (CC)
No	Russell (OM), Tuttauk (CC)

10. **June 2009 administration of members' benefits: 12–2**

Yes	Andersen (NEC), Gear (NEC), Shiwak (NEC), Russell (OM), Erickson (Ang), Jacque (Ang)
No	Broomfield (NEC)
Unknown	Lyall (Pres), Flowers (NEC), Ponniuk (NEC), Barbour (OM), Decker (Ang), Dicker (Ang), Tuttauk (CC)

11. **June 2009 administration of members' benefits: 3–12**

Yes	Andersen (NEC), Shiwak (NEC), Barbour (OM)
No	Lyall (Pres), Broomfield (NEC), Flowers (NEC), Gear (NEC), Ponniuk (NEC), Russell (OM), Decker (Ang), Dicker (Ang), Erickson (Ang), Jacque (Ang), Tuttauk (CC), Winters (CC)

12. **March 2010 motion to establish special committee to review issues with $5K membership payment: 3–10**

Yes	Russell (OM)
No	Lyall (Pres), Andersen (NEC), Broomfield (NEC), Flowers (NEC), Barbour (OM)
Unknown	Gear (NEC), Ponniuk (NEC), Decker (Ang), Dicker (Ang), Erickson (Ang), Jacque (Ang), Tuttauk (CC)

13. **March 2010 motion to delete section of bill regarding administration of land claim funds: 2–12**

Yes	Russell (OM), Erickson (Ang)
No	Lyall (Pres), Andersen (NEC), Broomfield (NEC), Gear (NEC), Ponniuk (NEC), Shiwak (NEC), Barbour (OM), Flowers (OM), Decker (Ang), Dicker (Ang), Jacque (Ang), Tuttauk (CC)

14. **March 2010 motion to delete section of bill regarding administration of land claim funds: 1–12**

Yes	Russell (OM)
No	Lyall (Pres), Andersen (NEC), Broomfield (NEC), Gear (NEC), Ponniuk (NEC), Shiwak (NEC), Barbour (OM),

Flowers (OM), Decker (Ang), Dicker (Ang), Jacque (Ang), Tuttauk (CC)

15. March 2010 motion to delete section of bill regarding administration of land claim funds: 1–12

Yes   Russell (OM)

No   Lyall (Pres), Andersen (NEC), Broomfield (NEC), Gear (NEC), Ponniuk (NEC), Shiwak (NEC), Barbour (OM), Flowers (OM), Decker (Ang), Dicker (Ang), Jacque (Ang), Tuttauk (CC)

16. March 2011 motion to establish independent auditor general: 5–11

Yes   Kemuksigak (OM), Russell (OM), Piercy (Ang), Hefler-Elson (CC), Tuttauk (CC)

No   Lyall (Pres), Lampe (NEC), Nochasak (NEC), Pottle (NEC), Shiwak (NEC), Barbour (OM), Lane (OM), Sheppard (OM), Andersen (Ang), Gear (Ang), Jacque (Ang)

17. March 2011 amendment to budget re civil servants' salaries: 10–6

Yes   Lampe (NEC), Kemuksigak (OM), Lane (OM), Russell (OM), Andersen (Ang), Gear (Ang), Jacque (Ang), Piercy (Ang), Hefler-Elson (CC), Tuttauk (CC)

No   Lyall (Pres), Nochasak (NEC), Pottle (NEC), Shiwak (NEC), Barbour (OM), Sheppard (OM)

18. March 2011 motion to modify budget amendment re civil servants' salaries: 7–9

Yes   Lyall (Pres), Lampe (NEC), Nochasak (NEC), Pottle (NEC), Shiwak (NEC), Barbour (OM), Sheppard (OM)

No   Kemuksigak (OM), Lane (OM), Russell (OM), Andersen (Ang), Gear (Ang), Jacque (Ang), Piercy (Ang), Hefler-Elson (CC), Tuttauk (CC)

19. March 2011 motion to rescind budget amendment re civil servants' salaries: 7–9

Yes   Lyall (Pres), Lampe (NEC), Nochasak (NEC), Pottle (NEC), Shiwak (NEC), Barbour (OM), Sheppard (OM)

No   Kemuksigak (OM), Lane (OM), Russell (OM), Andersen (Ang), Gear (Ang), Jacque (Ang), Piercy (Ang), Hefler-Elson (CC), Tuttauk (CC)

20. September 2011 motion to establish special committee on uranium moratorium: 9–7

Yes   Lyall (Pres), Kemuksigak (NEC), Lampe (NEC), Nochasak (NEC), Pottle (NEC), Sheppard (NEC), Shiwak (NEC), Barbour (OM), Winters (CC)

No   Lane (OM), Andersen (Ang), Gear (Ang), Jacque (Ang), Piercy (Ang), Wolfrey (Ang), Tuttauk (CC)

21. **December 2012 first reading of bill to authorize Torngasuk Cultural Centre funding: 11–3**

Yes — Leo (Pres), Lampe (NEC), Mitchell (NEC), Pottle (NEC), Shiwak (NEC), Nochasak (OM), Andersen (Ang), Gear (Ang), Piercy (Ang), Wolfrey (Ang), Winters (CC)

No — Kemuksigak (NEC), Sheppard (OM), Tuttauk (CC)

22. **January 2013 second reading of bill authorizing additional $2.1M for Torngasuk Cultural Centre: 12–4**

Yes — Leo (Pres), Lampe (NEC), Mitchell (NEC), Pottle (NEC), Shiwak (NEC), Nochasak (OM), Barbour (OM), Andersen (Ang), Gear (Ang), Piercy (Ang), Wolfrey (Ang), Winters (CC)

No — Kemuksigak (NEC), Lane (OM), Sheppard (OM), Tuttauk (CC)

23. **January 2014 motion to proceed with legislation for a presidential debate: 16–1**

Yes — Leo (Pres), Kemuksigak (NEC), Lampe (NEC), Mitchell (NEC), Shiwak (NEC), Barbour (OM), Lane (OM), Nochasak (OM), Sheppard (OM), Andersen (Ang), Gear (Ang), Jacque (Ang), Piercy (Ang), Wolfrey (Ang), Tuttauk (CC), Winters (CC)

No — Pottle (NEC)

24. **March 2014 section of bill to amend *Nunatsiavut Elections Act* authorizing presidential debate moderator to disqualify candidates: 10–6**

Yes — Lampe (NEC), Barbour (OM), Nochasak (OM), Andersen (Ang), Gear (Ang), Jacque (Ang), Piercy (Ang), Wolfrey (Ang), Tuttauk (CC), Winters (CC)

No — Leo (Pres), Kemuksigak (NEC), Mitchell (NEC), Pottle (NEC), Shiwak (NEC), Lane (OM)

Ang – AngajukKâk

OM – ordinary member

CC – community corporation chair

Pres – president

NEC – Nunatsiavut Executive Council

Chapter Nine

Assembly Effectiveness I: Representation and Policymaking

Beyond – or perhaps better, as a complement to – its mission of realizing self-government for Nunatsiavumiut, the assembly performs functions common to all legislatures. These include representing the people; policymaking, primarily through legislation and budgeting; holding the government to account; and informing and educating the people about the issues of the day.[1] No legislature performs all of these functions well. Westminster-style parliaments, for example, are typically strong on accountability but weak on policymaking. In Nunatsiavut, the constitution sets out the functions of the assembly in terms that closely resemble the enumeration of legislative functions above:

a represent the Labrador Inuit and … ensure government of Nunatsiavut by the Labrador Inuit under the Labrador Inuit Constitution;
b decide who should be appointed the First Minister of Nunatsiavut;
c provide the forum for consideration of issues affecting Labrador Inuit and Nunatsiavut or of importance to Labrador Inuit and Nunatsiavut;
d make laws for the government of Labrador Inuit, the Labrador Inuit Communities, Nunatsiavut and the Inuit Community Corporations; and
e oversee actions by the Nunatsiavut Executive Council.[2]

This chapter and the next consider the effectiveness of the Nunatsiavut Assembly in fulfilling the standard legislative functions. Little is said about its "educating the people" function since, beyond limited aspects of ministers' and members' statements, question period, and occasional legislative debates, the contribution of assembly proceedings to public understanding of issues is slight. The discussion in chapter 8 about the communications issues of the Nunatsiavut Government (NG) speaks to the assembly's shortcomings in informing and educating the people, and so need not be repeated here. Virtually everything that transpires in the assembly either takes the form of short interventions – statements, questions, and the like – or is directed to specific transactional outcomes such as passage of bills and approval of reports from the NG auditors or trust representatives. The assembly has never held a general, wide-ranging debate about a policy issue or the overall direction of the government that was not tied to processing legislation or reports. Any number of topics important to Nunatsiavumiut, including language revitalization, food insecurity, suicide, economic development, housing, and relations with the Innu Nation and the NunatuKavut Community Council, commend themselves as subjects for such debates, offering members the opportunity to put forward their ideas and proposals for government action, thereby informing the public. It is fair to note that "educational" debates are largely unknown in other Canadian legislatures. Still, with sessions typically lasting less than two full days, the assembly could well afford to devote a day now and then to debates on issues of broader concern.

The chapter looks first at representation before turning to consideration of policymaking, through analysis of the policy role of committees and the legislative and budgetary processes, with a brief account of how the assembly dealt with an especially difficult and controversial issue, a moratorium on uranium mining and production. Chapter 10 examines the assembly's effectiveness at ensuring accountability.

Representation

For democratically elected legislatures, representation surely ranks as the most fundamental of legislative functions, and so it is at the Nunatsiavut Assembly. Political scientists distinguish different forms of legislative representation, most notably descriptive representation and substantive representation.[3] Descriptive representation entails the extent to which the socio-economic characteristics of the members of a legislature mirror those of the general population, whereas substantive representation refers to members' activities on behalf of their constituents and the general population or segments of it. In terms of descriptive representation, all legislatures fall short when their members' social characteristics are measured against those of the population. Typically, women and minority cultural/ethnic groups are under-represented, as are the poor, the young, the elderly, and the disabled. In Nunatsiavut, since only Inuit may serve as members, the composition of the assembly is strongly representative of the most salient social characteristic of the population. By the same token, non-Inuit are completely shut out, save in a very limited way in that they can vote for AngajukKât. Women have been less numerous than men as members, though by comparison with other legislatures, they are moderately well represented in the assembly. Few members share the characteristics of other social groupings such as the poor and the disabled.

In terms of substantive representation, whereas in many legislatures, including all those in Canada, representation is primarily determined in relation to the geographic location of the population, with members elected in districts of relatively equal numbers of voters, the Nunatsiavut Assembly exhibits huge variation in the numbers of beneficiaries that members represent. The very small communities of Postville and Rigolet, for example, each elect the same number of assembly members, as does the Canada Constituency, with its more than two thousand beneficiaries. Little concern has been expressed, however, let alone explicit criticisms voiced, over the assembly's shortcomings in terms of descriptive representation. When members or beneficiaries think of representation in the assembly, they have substantive representation in mind.

By definition, given the different types of members, with differing electoral bases and mandates, their approaches and priorities as representatives vary. Most notably, AngajukKât and community chairs may not serve as ministers and are thus particularly focussed on the interests of their community governments or corporations, whereas half or more of the ordinary members are also ministers, and therefore must concern themselves with Nunatsiavut-wide issues to a greater extent. Among ordinary members, the dynamics of representation differ between those from communities in the settlement area and those representing Upper Lake Melville and the Canada Constituency.

Despite these key differences, however, members were remarkably consistent in articulating the primacy of representation. When asked how they viewed their roles as members of the assembly, to a person, their first response referenced serving as a representative or spokesperson for their community or constituency; "giving voice to people," as one put it. Some members referred to what has been termed the ombudsman function of elected officials: assisting constituents, individually or in groups, in their dealings with government. "My job," said one, "is to go to bat for them [constituents]." This could entail advice on how to access an NG or provincial program. Another member spoke of being a "clearinghouse for information" since the NG was so poor at communications. Representation could involve advocacy for a local need or project, such as travel for a sports team or improvements to local infrastructure. Asked about their motivation for running, electoral candidates, successful and unsuccessful, consistently emphasized the importance of representing the views and needs of their communities to the NG, often commenting adversely on the failings of incumbent or former members on this score.

Beyond the standard representational responsibilities, ordinary members from the Canada Constituency face quite distinctive representational challenges. "The Canadian Constituency," said one, "has different concerns than the rest of Labrador, but concerns all the same."[4] Shortly after his election, Canada Constituency ordinary member Edward Blake-Rudkowski set out the particular needs of his constituents and his plans for addressing them:

Many people in the Canadian Constituency find themselves there not by choice. Many of my constituents are there because of [the Sixties] Scoop. Many are there because of economic considerations. Some are there because they are fleeing violence or tragic, domestic situations. The one common thread that I've found when talking to many people is their hunger to reconnect with where they're from, their hunger to reconnect to their home and the hunger to reconnect with their heritage. I've talked to several constituents who have been away for decades, 20, 30, 40 years at times, again, they're away, not because of choice, but because their life circumstances have forced them to be that way. My intention is to do all that I can to reconnect those people to others of similar circumstance, and to reconnect people in my constituency with their heritage.[5]

None of this is to suggest that the attention to local concerns of members outside the Nunatsiavut Executive Council (NEC) meant lack of interest or involvement in broader, Nunatsiavut-wide matters, or, conversely, that ministers lose sight of their community representation responsibilities. Non-NEC members routinely devote considerable attention to such issues as language capacity among Nunatsiavumiut, violence against women, harvesting rights, and so on. Members' interventions on issues such as housing and access to health care may be framed in a specific local context while pointing to the need for government-wide responses. The discussion of question period in chapter 10 includes analysis of the extent to which members' questions have a local or Nunatsiavut-wide focus.

Those who have served as ministers acknowledge that appointment to NEC necessarily calls for a shift in role definition towards greater attention to Nunatsiavut-wide issues. One who spent time as a non-NEC member before being appointed to cabinet said "the [non-NEC] ordinary member's full focus is on the community … it's the only thing you prepare for in the Assembly … But the duty of being a minister is very important … [requiring] a lot more attention to regional [i.e., Nunatsiavut-wide] issues." Still, some maintain that they remain ordinary members first, giving priority to constituency concerns, and are ministers second. Not all ministers go that far; some speak instead of the need to balance local and regional elements of their role as representative. One put it this way in an interview: "being minister, you have to strike a real balance that you are not fixating on one community anymore, you are representing all five Inuit communities and you have to make sure you are not just favouring one. You defend what your community is … Like any government, once you are on Executive Council you have the opportunity to defend your community in different areas, but you have to remember that you are representing the region, not just one community." No suggestion emerged in the interviews that ministers unduly favoured their own communities. Indeed, one AngajukKâk expressed the view that once ordinary members become ministers, they lose sight of their constituencies, though representing them is their principal job.

The small scale of Nunatsiavut politics necessarily entails that all members, NEC and non-NEC, are in regular, close contact with their constituents. As one noted, "you are constantly in touch with your constituents; you go to the store and are questioned about what the government is doing." Moreover, he added, a strong expectation exists that as a member you are visible, that you attend community events and visit with people: "the people are watching."

Tensions can and do arise between members' duty to their constituents and their duty to act in the best overall interests of Nunatsiavut. One AngajukKâk explained that he had to take into account more than the interests and concerns of his community:

> When we're sitting in Hopedale, and not only when I'm sitting in Hopedale, I'm a member of the assembly and I have to support and, I guess, uphold the constitution, for one thing. There's a land claims agreement to take into consideration when decisions are being made. So, I have to make sure that my decision, what I vote for – I suppose I'm not the only person voting against or for – that I have to consider that, yes, it's in the best interest of the Inuit, what the land claim was settled for in 2005.

Another non-NEC ordinary member agreed: "it really depends on the issue, but I definitely think of the Nunatsiavut government as a whole… Okay, how will this benefit us as a government and the beneficiaries? You know, unless it's an issue that's very obviously detrimental to the beneficiaries in the community."

When community interests differ from Nunatsiavut-wide interests, a strong tendency is evident among members towards what has been termed the delegate approach to representation, requiring members to speak and act according to their constituents' preferences, so far as they can be determined. An alternative role conception, the representative as trustee, sees members taking their constituents' views into account but ultimately exercising their own best judgment on the issues of the day.[6] During the debates on the far-reaching bill imposing a moratorium on development of uranium mining in 2008, several members made it clear that they were casting their votes in accordance with what they saw as their constituents' wishes. "Representing my community here today," said one, "I don't think that really that I am in favor of that Bill."[7] An AngajukKâk was even more explicit: "I have been directed," he said, to support the bill.[8] Addressing the conflict between Nunatsiavut-wide interests and the concerns of his constituents, another member's delegate orientation was clear:

> [I recognize] the benefits to all beneficiaries everywhere that may come from such a development. I understand the need for additional legislation and Land Use Plan and other things but I have to represent my constituency and the majority of the

people just about 99.99% of all that I've talked to on the issue would not be in favor of a moratorium and therefore I also say that I cannot support this at this time.[9]

Some years later, an ordinary member offered an overarching perspective on how local-regional tensions play out in the assembly, commenting, "it's important that eighteen rather than two people represent you."

Evaluating the effectiveness of the assembly in terms of representation, either as a corporate whole or with respect to individual members, in any systematic way would entail far more extensive research than is reported here. One, albeit very partial, way to assess constituents' evaluations of their representatives is to look at the success of incumbent members when seeking re-election. Table 9.1 below presents data on how ordinary members have fared when facing their voters come election time at the general elections of 2010, 2014, 2018, and 2022 (data on AngajukKâk and community corporation chair elections are either unavailable or incomplete). The table shows, for both ministers and non-ministers (at the time of the election), how many incumbent members chose not to run, how many ran, and how many won. The numbers are small, but the basic conclusion is clear: sitting ordinary members are almost as likely to be defeated as to retain their seats. Only 55 per cent of all ordinary members have been successful in their re-election bids. Overall, the difference between the rate at which non-NEC members won re-election, 64 per cent, and that of ministers, 50 per cent, was relatively marginal.

It is intriguing to contemplate why in 2010 only 1 of the 5 ministers who ran for re-election was successful whereas all 3 non-NEC Ordinary Members held their seats, yet four years later only 1 of 5 non-NEC ordinary members seeking re-election won but 3 of 5 ministers did. However, with the very small numbers and the doubtless pervasive influence of individual personality and record, drawing conclusions about wide short-term variations is not possible. Similarly intriguing, but no more amenable to systematic analysis, is the question of how electoral success rates of Nunatsiavut incumbents compare to the rates in the other northern consensus systems. Incumbents in Nunavut have been only slightly more likely to win re-election than Nunatsiavut ordinary members, but incumbent members in the Northwest Territories (NWT) have been overwhelmingly successful in seeking re-election, especially since division in 1999, which saw the Inuit of the Eastern Arctic depart the NWT with the formation of Nunavut.[10]

Johannes Lampe, the only president to have sought re-election, won handily in the 2020 election. By contrast, Jim Lyall, president from 2008 to 2012, came in a distant fourth in a bid to become an ordinary member in 2014. Specifics aside, to the extent that their ability to secure re-election is a valid measure of how their constituents evaluate their effectiveness, ordinary members of the Nunatsiavut Assembly are, at least in the voters' eyes, falling short in providing representation.

Table 9.1. Ordinary members' incumbency

Election	Ministers			Non-ministers			Total		
	DNR	Ran	Won	DNR	Ran	Won	DNR	Ran	Won
2010	–	5	1	1	3	3	1	8	4
2014	–	5	3	–	5	1	–	10	4
2018*	1	4	3	2	1	1	3	5	4
2022**	2	4	2	1	2	2	3	6	4
Total	3	18	9	4	11	7	7	29	16

DNR Did not run
* Two seats were vacant when election called
** One seat was vacant when elected called

Limited but intriguing support for this interpretation comes from an unlikely source: an assembly committee report. In 2011, the assembly established a special committee to consult the Inuit public about the moratorium on mining and development of uranium on Inuit lands. The consultation report produced by the committee was primarily devoted to setting out beneficiaries' views on the moratorium, but along the way it cited pointed criticisms of assembly members' effectiveness as representatives that had come forward in public meetings. Some criticisms were included in the report at the express direction of beneficiaries at the meetings, even though they had nothing to do with the moratorium. Among the negative assessments of assembly representation, the Postville meeting summary noted that "there is frustration with the NG Assembly leadership not being as vocal or visible in communities as people would like," while at Makkovik "concerns were raised as to Community Representatives to the Assembly being representative of community views."[11] Though worth noting, like the tabulation of successful incumbents, this is at best fragmentary evidence of popular discontent over representation in the assembly. Indeed, the discontent seems to have had mixed electoral consequences: at the next elections, in 2014, the ordinary members for Postville and Makkovik both went down to defeat but the two AngajukKât were re-elected.

The distinctive nature of Nunatsiavut as a self-governing Inuit territory gives rise to another, rather less tangible form of representation. If often implicitly, members give voice to the political, social, and cultural aspirations of Nunatsiavumiut. This could entail comments about specific NG activities on issues such as language enhancement or food insecurity, or it could take more abstract form, reiterating the principles of the treaty and the constitution. That this facet of representation does not lend itself to systematic analysis does not reduce its importance.

Policymaking

Effective representation entails two quite separate components: giving voice to people's concerns and aspirations and taking action to assuage concerns and to realize aspirations. One non-NEC member pointed to a structural feature of consensus government that for those not in NEC presents an impediment to meeting beneficiaries' expectations about representation: people assume that once you're elected, you're in government, but "I'm not in government." "I'm not in opposition either," he added, noting that many people don't understand this. At the same time, consensus government does not, as do party-based parliaments, routinely exclude members outside the governing party from any semblance of policy influence. A long-serving member, with experience in NEC, maintained in an interview that assembly members are very good at bringing forward the views and concerns of their constituents but fall short in getting results because it's up to NEC to develop policies and to allocate resources, and that members lack both the power and the inclination to push NEC to take action. Tellingly, a long discussion of policy and policymaking in a recent study of self-government in Nunatsiavut, focussing on education, housing, and resource development, made only two passing references to the assembly.[12] In short, as is typical of Westminster-style legislatures, the assembly, as distinct from NEC, exerts little policymaking influence, which for this discussion includes not only policy development but also its implementation, administration, and funding.

Committees

Members of the assembly have a number of methods for influencing policy. A pointed statement or question in the chamber could encourage or embarrass a minister into taking action, as could a quiet, offline conversation. However, policy influence mostly occurs through the activities of assembly committees or during the review and passage of legislation. This is in keeping with the widely held view among those who study Westminster parliaments that committees stand as the most effective vehicles for members to exert policy influence.[13] As outlined in chapter 6, beyond the internal committees (Rules and Procedures, Members' Services, and ad hoc discipline committees), the assembly's recourse to committees has been limited. This is particularly evident when it comes to committee involvement in policy issues.

Some special committees have exerted substantial influence over major government policies. These include the committee tasked with advising on the proposed moratorium on uranium mining, the committee looking into creation of a housing agency, and the committee on the environmental protection bill. Notably, all entailed broad consultation with the Inuit public as well as with a range of organizations and businesses. By way of illustration, based on its consultations, the Special Committee on the Environmental Protection Bill proposed a number of amendments to the bill, all of which were accepted. The committee held consultation meetings in eight communities and met with over a hundred people; it also received submissions by email and teleconference.[14] Other committees have, within their confined mandates, achieved concrete results: the Code of Conduct Committee and the committee on the Nunatsiavut Business Centre are examples. Others, such as the committees of the First Assembly on education and on language made little if any impact; the effectiveness of the Drug and Alcohol Committee is unclear. Moreover, large swathes of NG activity are not normally subject to review by assembly committees. The lack of dedicated committee staff with policy expertise is doubtless a factor here, as is the reliance on NG staff for committees that do have access to advice and support. So, too, logistical and financial constraints limit committees' capacity to consult the Inuit public or to tap into the expertise of those outside government. In short, the assembly exerts occasional policy influence through its committees, but overall, assembly committees do not provide regular, substantial influence on government policy. This is characteristic of Westminster parliaments, which are typically dominated by their executives. What of the legislative process?

Legislation

Westminster-style parliaments rarely create or develop legislation; rather, they review, revise, and pass (or reject) legislation. So it is with the Nunatsiavut Assembly. In part because the NG has been measured in drawing down jurisdictional powers authorized in the claim, the assembly devotes relatively little time and energy to its legislative function. Since the assembly's creation in 2006, five stretches of a year or nearly a year have passed without any bills whatsoever coming forward, save the annual budget bill, which is only technically legislative in nature. The lion's share of proposed legislation coming before the assembly is of limited significance, passing perfunctorily. Almost all bills constitute minor corrections to existing legislation, fill legislative gaps, or else deal with highly localized situations, such as clarifying the status of a quarry in a community or authorizing a fur farm. The few bills of substantial import do receive close attention and generate extensive debate, if not always serious disagreement.

Appendix 9.1, at the end of this chapter, sets out the characteristics of all fifty-five non-budget bills considered by the assembly from its first sitting in 2006 to the end of the Fourth Assembly in April 2022. The annual budget bills and the occasional supplementary budget bill are excluded on the grounds that, important as budgets are, they are not really legislative in nature: they authorize government spending and revenue generation but do not in any way alter the basic legislative framework relating to finance or to any other element of NG activity. The appendix, and thus the analysis, also excludes several foundational Inuit laws passed by the Transitional Assembly: the *Constitution Act*, the *Labrador Inuit Lands Act*, the *Beneficiaries Enrolment Act*, the *Nunatsiavut Assembly Act*, the *Nunatsiavut Elections Act*, the *Financial Administration Act*, and others. Records are too fragmentary to permit analysis; moreover, the personnel and structure of the Transitional Assembly differed significantly from that of the assembly. Amendments to the foundational Inuit laws are included in the analysis. Finally, the data should be interpreted in light of the fact that ten separate bills did precisely the same thing – namely, provide a year-long loan guarantee for the Torngat Fish Producers Co-operative Society, a key economic institution.

The appendix shows the title of each bill, the session at which it was introduced, and, if it extended over more than one session, the session at which it was passed; an assessment of its significance; the extent of debate over the bill; the number of days the bill was considered in the assembly and whether the bill received consideration in committee other than the Committee on Consensus or in committee of the whole; and the result of the vote on second reading. A column was planned to indicate whether the sponsor of the bill sought and received unanimous consent after first reading to proceed immediately or almost immediately to second reading by waiving the standing order mandating a ten-day hiatus. However, in that barely a handful of bills were not expedited in this fashion, all of substantial import, this seemed pointless.

Assessment as to significance is highly subjective, based on the content of the bill, which I determined mostly from the debate on it. Five bills were judged to be very substantial in nature, 3 of which related to land, land use, and the environment. A similar number were classified as of substantial significance; 2 of these related to land issues. Another 5 were of moderate import; all had to do with government procedures, such as procurement processes and civil service operations. The balance, some 40 (31 if the Torngat loan bills are considered together) were of limited significance.

Categorization of debates on proposed Inuit laws was somewhat less subjective, taking into account the length of the debate and the number of members who participated in it. The routine and inevitably brief introductory statement by the minister introducing the bill for first reading was not included while assessing the extent of the debate. A debate was judged extensive if most members spoke in it more than briefly; for bills considered in committee of the whole, this often entailed multiple interventions by individual members. A short debate was one in which no more than three or four members spoke, none at length. In a minimal debate only one or two members briefly participated.

Instances deemed as having no debate were those in which no members spoke other than the sponsoring minister, who only made the requisite procedural motions and statements.[15] Not surprisingly, all the extensive debates were on bills judged to be of very substantial significance. Six of the 8 short debates were on bills of limited significance, which may seem odd until it is recalled that "short" is in this regard indeed short. Some 38 bills, 29 if the Torngat loan bills are not considered individually, generated only minimal debate (20) or no debate at all (18). This could be interpreted as a lack of diligence on the part of members, but a more likely explanation is that most of the bills that passed on the nod were of minor import and/or highly technical in nature. A strong correlation exists between bills judged of limited significance and those generating minimal or no debate.

Data in the appendix confirm that only infrequently is the assembly asked to consider legislation with far-reaching implications or that generates unusual controversy. Even more significantly, when bills come before the assembly, be they of minor or major significance, their passage intact seems all but guaranteed, though some do give rise to considerable debate. No bill has ever been defeated in the assembly. Save the bill in the First Assembly to establish a three-year moratorium on uranium development, which squeaked through second reading by a single vote, no bill has even come close to being defeated; indeed, only two other bills were not adopted unanimously at second reading. The land use plan implementation bill, introduced in December 2012, was abandoned, though not because of opposition in the assembly; at first reading the only intervention was strongly supportive and the bill passed unanimously. Rather, under the treaty both NG and the provincial government must approve any plan, which the Province has refused to do.[16]

Moreover, the assembly has made precious few amendments of any kind, let alone major, to legislation before it. The only significant amendment to proposed legislation occurred with respect to the uranium moratorium bill. A small number of minor amendments were made to various bills, but overall the assembly has proven remarkably accepting of legislation it has been asked to consider. Nor have assembly members made use of private members' bills to advance their legislative goals. As outlined in chapter 6, no private members' bill has ever been introduced in the assembly, though the Standing Orders clearly contemplate them, subject to the standard prohibition of money bills.

The Budget

Like other aspects of the assembly, the budgetary process is unusual. Over the years, procedures for reviewing and approving the NG budget have changed only slightly, so that the process typically unfolds as set out in the following paragraphs. Assembly consideration of the budget is often rushed and suffers from a lack of detailed information.

The Labrador Inuit Constitution sets some fundamental parameters for the budgetary process. Section 8.4.1 requires a balanced budget, though a 60 per cent vote of assembly members can authorize a deficit, provided the Inuit public has been consulted about the prospective deficit (section 8.4.2).[17] No deficits have been considered or authorized. Part 8.8 requires that an annual financial plan, containing the NG's spending plans for the upcoming year, be presented and approved by the assembly prior to the start of the fiscal year, 1 April.

Like Caesar's Gaul, the financial plan consists of three parts. An overview text sets out the basics of the NG's financial position, highlighting significant changes in the spending planned for the assembly, for each department and for capital infrastructure, and, on occasion, for significant changes to the funding of the Inuit community governments. The financial plan also includes the complete text of the budget bill, which lists revenue sources and specifies the total allocation to each department and to the assembly but offers no details. An annex to the bill outlines the government's consolidated financial plans for the upcoming fiscal year, five-year projections, and breakdowns of certain elements of the budget such as payments to the Inuit community governments. All elements of the plan are presented with limited detail. A table lists total planned spending across the entire NG broken down into nineteen categories, some very narrow (e.g., insurance; postage and shipping), some very broad (e.g., salary; programs).

In short, the financial plan provides assembly members with broad-brush expenditure information but few details. Members are welcome to ask for additional financial information and explanations before the assembly meets, but only rarely do so. Members can and do seek additional information during the consideration of the budget, but lacking anything like extensive detail on planned spending, they are limited in their ability to delve comprehensively into NG finances. In the early years, members didn't receive the financial plan until they arrived at the assembly, giving rise to complaints about the adequacy and timeliness of the information it contained. Members are now sent the plan ten days in advance of the assembly's March sitting.

In other Westminster parliaments the budget is presented, debated, and approved (or rejected) through motions. Specific budget measures, in most cases changes to the tax regime, may entail legislation, but the budget itself is not put forward as a bill. In Nunatsiavut, the budget takes the form of a bill, though to date no budget bill has included tax changes or similar measures. After tabling the financial plan, the minister of finance begins the process with the budget address, in effect the start of first reading debate of the budget bill. The address is usually short; most do not require the minister to seek unanimous consent to exceed the ten minutes allowed in the Standing Orders for speeches by members introducing bills. The budget address mostly offers a broad overview of the government's spending plans. With the lion's share of NG's revenue coming in the form of federal transfer payments, the address touches on revenue only briefly, if at all; some have said nothing about revenue. It would be open for any member to speak for up to fifteen minutes in the first reading debate, but in practice none do and the finance minister closes the debate on the bill, which invariably receives first reading with no dissenting voices.[18]

As with all legislation, the Standing Orders, echoing the constitution, require a ten-day pause between first reading and the start of the second reading debate, so that "Labrador Inuit may make submissions or representations to the Assembly about the bill." Ministers, however, routinely seek and receive unanimous consent to waive the ten-day rule on all legislation in order to proceed without delay to second reading. In the single instance of members refusing to accede to the finance minister's request so as to hear from constituents on the merits of the budget, recounted in chapter 6, sufficient pressure was exerted on the dissenting members that they withdrew their objection and the budget process resumed unimpeded.

Shortly after first reading, sometimes just a few minutes later, the assembly resolves itself into committee of the whole to consider the financial plan and the budget. The deputy minister of finance is called as a witness and leads the members through the financial plan page by page, including the budget bill and its annex. The dominant role played by the deputy minister is unusual and noteworthy. In other Canadian legislatures, senior staff frequently appear before committees, usually standing committees but occasionally committee of the whole, but are far less centre stage. The finance minister usually takes little part in this phase of the process. On more than one occasion, the minister had nothing at all to say, leaving all explanations to the deputy minister.[19] Members typically ask a good many questions, though the entire process is usually wrapped up in an hour or two. The vast majority of questions, some highly detailed, others broad in scope, simply seek clarification about specific expenditures. Some questions either explicitly or implicitly aim at securing funding for members' communities or for their policy priorities. An occasional question takes the form of a pointed challenge to government spending priorities or its effectiveness in running a program, though members rarely take such criticisms beyond the talking stage.

As the deputy finance minister goes through the financial plan, the assembly approves each page in turn. Amendments to the budget bill are permitted at both first and second readings, but these are few and far between. In common with legislators throughout Canada and beyond, assembly members are keener on increasing rather than decreasing expenditures, which, under the money bill rule is not permitted to non-ministers. In at least one instance, however, a non-NEC member successfully moved a motion to add $242,000 in enhanced wages for non-management NG staff; no one, the speaker included, objected that it was improper for a non-NEC member to move a "money" amendment that increased spending.[20]

Once all pages of the financial plan have been approved, the speaker puts each section of the budget bill to a vote. Since questioning and debate on the substance of the budget has already occurred, this is a purely pro forma exercise, though it would be open to any member to engage in further debate. This completes second reading of the budget bill. In short order the president assents to the bill.

A central question: How effective is assembly review of the NG budget? It is fair to observe that few Westminster-model parliaments are better than barely adequate in reviewing government budgets and spending plans. In Nunatsiavut, one long-time assembly observer bluntly asserts that "members have no idea where the money goes." This may be overly harsh, but it is clear that, with occasional exceptions, members do not delve deeply into NG finances, let alone challenge spending priorities. Members do not have access to the detailed information that would permit or encourage such enquiries; they have authority to require the NG provide them with more extensive financial data, but they do not exercise it.

Standing as both cause and effect here are the very short sessions, two days at most in recent years. Members expect and believe that they will – indeed, for some, must – be done all the business of the March session, of which the budget is only part, in no more than two days. Thus pressure to complete consideration of the budget expeditiously is substantial, if usually unstated. In turn, this discourages members from seeking the additional information that more thorough review of the budget would require, reinforcing the likelihood of quick passage. In short, assembly review of the budget is not very effective.

One exception to this discomforting judgment lies in the assembly budget. The *Nunatsiavut Assembly Act* requires the Members' Services Committee to prepare the assembly budget and present it to the assembly for approval and inclusion in the budget bill. Members typically take a lively interest in the assembly budget, so that from its development to its formal approval, members are meaningfully involved. Since the committee's budgetary recommendations do not take the form of actual legislation, it is open to members considering the proposed assembly budget to increase or decrease elements of it without running afoul of the money bill rule. Extrapolation of this process could see the creation of a standing budget committee, which could meet in advance of the session, review the proposed budget on the basis of more extensive information than is currently available, and make recommendations to the minister of finance and to the assembly about possible changes. Committees of this nature have been used in the NWT and Nunavut, and while they typically haven't suggested many significant changes to proposed budgets, they have enabled members' meaningful involvement in reviewing and approving government spending. It does not appear that such a process has ever been proposed, either by assembly members or by NG staff.

A Quiescent Assembly?

Why have assembly members been so willing to accept legislation, including budget bills, placed before them, typically without pushback or amendment? The prohibition against non-NEC members putting forward money amendments does constrain attempts to modify legislation. As well, a high proportion of bills have been of minor import, but by no means all. Overall, though, members' acquiescence when it comes to legislation is noteworthy. The explanation is unlikely to lie in extensive, responsive consultation by NEC on planned legislation. At best, members only see draft legislation a few days before it is introduced in the assembly, and they typically receive little if any explanation as to its content. Lack of dedicated staff support is doubtless a factor, with non-NEC members lacking access to independent research assistance or legal advice.

One long-time member, with experience both in NEC and as a non-NEC member, maintained in an interview that the explanation largely rests with members' disposition towards their role in the governance process. Assembly members, according to this person, "don't seem to recognize the power they have under the constitution; not that you should abuse it, but you should use it to achieve your goals." In this interpretation, members tend to be reactive to what is put before them and don't initiate new ideas; they are usually focussed on current policy or legislation rather than on new directions. They "take advice too readily," accepting what they are told. Thus, although non-NEC members don't get sufficient information about forthcoming budgets or legislation and what is provided doesn't always come in time to make proper use of it, they don't usually voice concerns. This is because members "have faith in other people … They take what they've been told at face value" and don't question deeply. As well, members often lack the confidence necessary to make changes.

While this interpretation rings true, some nuance may be needed. When it comes to policies and pronouncements from the provincial government, and to a lesser extent the federal government, assembly members clearly do not have faith in other governments. Nor do they take what they've been told at face value or refrain from questioning deeply. Sceptical and critical, they are not at all quiescent. Perhaps pride in having achieved significant self-governing capacity with the NG, as well as reluctance to engage in what might be perceived as un-Inuit confrontation, are factors in the assembly's highly accommodating reception of government legislative and financial initiatives.

In one memorable instance, the assembly did show itself willing to delve deeply into an important, divisive issue and to subject proposed legislation to a prolonged review, which led to significant change. The following subsection looks at this unusual but instructive episode.

The Uranium Moratorium

Bill 2008-03, *An Act to Amend the Inuit Lands Act*, otherwise known as the uranium moratorium bill, and the subsequent assembly review of the moratorium stand out not only as the most controversial legislation to come before the assembly but also as the most extensive consultative legislative process in Nunatsiavut history. As such, they warrant a close look, not only for what they say about the assembly's handling of legislation but also for important insights they offer into governance in Nunatsiavut.

The uranium-related issues faced by the NG and the assembly went back several decades. Significant uranium deposits were found near Postville and Makkovik in the early 1950s and the prospect of a major mine was a significant factor in the relocation of the residents of Nutak and Hebron later in the decade.[21] When uranium prices dropped, Brinex, the British company holding the mining rights, lost interest. By the 1970s, prospects for improved profitability led to revived mining plans, but whereas Inuit interests and perspectives were of no moment in the 1950s, Inuit were deeply involved in this second wave of interest in uranium. Concerns about possible mining contributed to the development of the recently formed Labrador Inuit Association (LIA), which "used the dispute about the potential uranium mine to try to foster a sense of collective identity and vision among people on the north coast."[22] "The high level of risk involved with a uranium mine," Andrea Procter has written, "created a sense of crisis around the project, which propelled all discussions and hearings into high-profile opportunities for the LIA to highlight its concerns and claims, and to gain support among both its members and the general public for the recognition of Inuit rights."[23]

A 1980 report from an environmental assessment board concluded that the company's mining proposal "did not prove that the project was environmentally, socially, and economically acceptable [and] that serious concerns about Aboriginal rights must be addressed."[24] By the time the report was released, however, the company had, for various reasons, abandoned the project. According to John Kennedy, the hearings that were held "were an important social turning point ... [as] they pulled people together and let them see that their opinions were important."[25]

Early on, the Nunatsiavut Government decided to prohibit uranium development on Labrador Inuit lands, but the policy lacked legal backing. The largest proven deposit was on Labrador Inuit land, giving the NG complete authority as to whether mining could occur, though exploration was proceeding elsewhere in Nunatsiavut on land not directly under NG control. When Aurora

Energy Resources, which had acquired the lease on the land with the uranium deposit, announced that it intended to seek an environmental assessment on a projected mine, the NG faced "one of its first major crises,"[26] though it is difficult to see any other earlier, or later, crisis of similar magnitude. At that point, Nunatsiavut had neither a land use plan nor environmental assessment legislation, though both were under development.

Thus at the October 2007 sitting of the assembly, Minister of Lands and Resources William Barbour put forward a resolution seeking the assembly's support in amending the *Labrador Inuit Lands Act* so as to prevent uranium mining. The resolution spelled out the details of the proposed amendments, but no bill was introduced. Barbour's intent was clear: "that the Assembly Members and all would have time to consider possible amendments at the next sitting and possibly a later sitting."[27] An important proviso in the resolution required

> that the proposed amendments to the *Labrador Inuit Lands Act* to prevent the working, production, mining, milling or development of uranium on Labrador Inuit Lands be referred to a committee of the whole for investigation and study and that the Committee hear from witnesses resident in Makkovik and Postville as well as any industry representatives and experts it may consider advisable and that the committee report to the Assembly at its first sitting in the new year.[28]

In the debate on the motion, which passed unanimously, several members referred to a long debate "in caucus" the day before that had thrashed out the motion's content. Two amendments were accepted, one extending to all residents of Nunatsiavut, not just those in Postville and Makkovik, the opportunity to be heard by the committee. The other moved the committee's reporting deadline forward to the December session.[29] A curious but ultimately irrelevant procedural wrinkle saw the motion given "first reading" (resolutions such as this require only a single vote). At the December session, Barbour sought and received agreement to delay "second reading" of the motion, putting the entire matter off until the March session.

The committee established by the October resolution, notably a committee of the whole including all members, consulted widely but does not appear to have made a formal report. The minister indicated that the committee had "technical support" but did not specify what this entailed.[30] In March, another lengthy caucus meeting on the issue appears to have been held the day before the formal assembly session began. When the session commenced, Barbour introduced a bill that followed the outlines of the resolution, with one major change reflecting the work of the committee. Rather than a blanket ban on uranium development, the bill sought a temporary moratorium with a requirement that the assembly review the moratorium in three years' time. The bill provided for assembly review "after March 31, 2011," without specifying when it had to take place. Several members noted this reassurance in declaring their support for the bill, though others cited the views of their communities in opposing it. In the end, the bill received first reading on a vote of 11–4, with all NEC members in support.

Especially noteworthy in the debate was First Minister Tony Andersen's forthright declaration on the importance of self-government for Nunatsiavut:

> For a number of years Mr. Speaker, exploration companies have come to Nunatsiavut and have tried to set the agenda for us. We were a brand new government and we're being told not only by exploration companies but governments as well "Get your act together, look progress is here any [*sic*: and?] you guys are unprepared."
>
> I think at least what this, what this Bill says Mr. Speaker is to send a message to exploration companies, mining companies and other governments is that look, we are in charge here in Nunatsiavut Mr. Speaker. We are the decision body, we will make the rules that apply to our land. It is our land and we will continue to protect it and we have newfound powers that we will use to ensure that development that takes place will be done so on our terms.[31]

Second reading of the bill was put off to the April session, according to the minister, to accommodate members "who wanted to get back to their constituencies to consult further with their constituents."[32] Their consultations clearly had an effect. Virtually every member spoke at least briefly in the second reading debate to put his or her position on record. Three members who had supported the bill at first reading voted against it at second reading, including two ministers. The bill passed by the narrowest of margins, 8–7. It does not appear that any members voted against the bill because they wanted a permanent ban.

The debate brought out strong but civilly expressed positions, with supporters and opponents acknowledging the legitimacy of one another's views. Those favouring the bill stressed the importance of protecting the land, while noting that a moratorium was not equivalent to a permanent ban. Those opposed emphasized that, especially with made-in-Nunatsiavut environmental assessment legislation on the way, allowing early phases of development did not necessarily imply acceptance of actual mining. They also pointed out the need for jobs as well as the possibility that imposing a moratorium would be interpreted by the mining industry as announcing that Nunatsiavut was not open to development. Procter points out that both sides were making "way of life" arguments. Whereas the proponents feared that uranium mining on the scale envisaged by Aurora could have serious, long-lasting adverse effects on the land and the animals so central to Inuit culture, opponents worried that without mining jobs, young people would move away in search of employment and lose touch with their homeland and culture.[33]

Just as Tony Andersen had highlighted self-government in the first reading debate, Speaker Todd Broomfield, who left the chair to participate in the debate as ordinary member for Makkovik, made an insightful point about the nature of governance in Nunatsiavut. In outlining why he supported the bill – even if, as speaker, he did not vote – he told the assembly, "one common virtue that Inuit culture is based on is patience. We are an Inuit Government."[34]

Over the next three years, the uranium issue was never far from assembly members' thoughts, though neither the assembly nor the NG were actively engaged with it. At the September 2011 session, Lands and Natural Resources Minister Glen Sheppard, the ordinary member for Postville, brought forward a resolution to establish a special committee, to be chaired by the lands minister and whose aim was holding "public consultations on the moratorium issue. The public consultations will include information on the uranium mining and the use cycle and are to be completed before the next session of the Assembly."[35] This was to be a standard, four-person special committee, not a committee of the whole, as in 2007–8. The Department of Lands was to "secure a qualified consultant" to assist the committee. Should the committee recommend lifting the moratorium, the minister was to draft the appropriate legislation, including a proviso that it would not come into effect until the recently passed *Nunatsiavut Environmental Protection Act* came into force.[36] All assembly members had taken part several weeks earlier in a three-day workshop on uranium mining put on by a well-known consulting firm.[37]

The resolution encountered stiff opposition led by Andersen, for whom the resolution had "too many unknowns," including membership of the committee, the process for their appointment, and the identity of the consultant. Moreover, in its silence as to what should occur if the committee recommended that the ban remain, the resolution appeared to privilege lifting the moratorium. Andersen did not hold back in his criticism of the process: "I think that, as well, [it's] getting a little late in the game for starting community consultations after almost four years having this moratorium in place … And you don't have to stall because work is slow. Tell us the truth."[38] The resolution passed by a 9–7 vote, with the entire NEC plus two non-NEC members, one of whom was former minister Barbour, in support and all AngajukKât plus Denise Lane, the ordinary member for Makkovik, and one community chair opposed. Once the resolution passed, Finance Minister Danny Pottle announced the committee membership: Sheppard, Barbour, Lane, and Lands Deputy Minister Carl McLean.

The committee consulted widely, holding public meetings in all five Labrador Inuit Settlement Area (LISA) communities as well as in Happy Valley–Goose Bay, Northwest River, and St. John's. Meetings took place in the evening, with technical presentations followed by questions and comments from attendees, and lasted until no one had any more questions or comments. Attendance at meetings ranged between 19 and 45 people, exclusive of the committee and its staff, 240 all told.[39] Local AngajukKât and ordinary members were present at most meetings, as were representatives of the mining industry. Committee members also offered individuals the opportunity to meet privately with them during the day. Submissions were accepted in hard copy as well as by email and Facebook. An online petition was received in favour of maintaining the moratorium, with 142 signatures, some anonymous. Those attending the consultation meetings registered satisfaction that their questions had been answered and their voices heard, though the committee did encounter complaints that the process was rushed and that Committee Chair Sheppard and the technical consultant advising the committee were biased towards the uranium industry.[40]

According to the committee report, a clear majority of those attending the meetings favoured lifting the moratorium or leaving any decisions to the environmental assessment process. The report also cited surveys conducted by the AngajukKât in Postville and Rigolet showing strong support for ending the moratorium.[41] In Makkovik, AngajukKâk Herb Jacque told the committee that he had personally interviewed sixty-one people and found a slight majority opposed to lifting the moratorium. Some at the meeting pushed back, questioning the validity of his survey; the committee's "reasonable estimate" was that three-quarters of those at the meeting favoured an end to the ban.[42]

The committee thus recommended ending the moratorium, though this did not imply, the report made clear, that mining would necessarily go ahead. At the December 2011 assembly session, Sheppard presented the committee's report on its consultations to the assembly. After a brief debate, members unanimously agreed to accept the report, a formal procedural move that did not entail an endorsement of its contents. The only noteworthy aspect of the debate was President Jim Lyall's vociferous rejection of the notion implied in the petition that outsiders should have a say in how Nunatsiavumiut run their affairs. Pronouncing himself "really bugged" that the anti-uranium petition was started by a non-beneficiary and that 64 per cent of the names on it were those of non-beneficiaries, Lyall echoed Tony Andersen's self-government panegyric during the original moratorium debates:

> We had a Land Claims Agreement, Madame Speaker, because we were governed from people from outside, or people that were Non-Inuit, or people that are non-beneficiaries ... That day has passed and long gone. We make our decisions on what we do. We'll make our own mistakes. We learn from our own mistakes. We don't need outside people from outside Nunatsiavut telling us how to run our region.[43]

The next day, Sheppard introduced the bill to lift the moratorium, which passed both first and second readings unanimously. Three main themes

emerged in the debate, in which several members participated. First, imposing the moratorium had been a good idea, in that it allowed for thoughtful
consideration of an important issue and for development of an environmental
assessment (EA) process and a land use plan. Second, with the EA process in
place, the moratorium was no longer needed. And third, that the people and
government of Nunatsiavut would decide when and if uranium mining took
place.[44] In 2015, Aurora Resources announced that, owing to low prices, it was
suspending exploration and other operations in Nunatsiavut.[45] No significant
uranium-related activity has since occurred.

What are we to conclude from this singular case study? Singular it may be,
but it is also instructive about the assembly's capacity to deal effectively with
difficult, controversial issues. If the process was at times less than sure-footed,
on the important points – broad public consultation; serious, reasoned debate;
willingness to confront a tough, divisive issue; and ultimately the achievement
of consensus – the assembly and its members acquitted themselves well. The
vast majority of bills may pass through the assembly readily, and none have ever
been rejected, but the assembly's handling of the uranium issue demonstrated
that, if need be, a determined assembly can perform effectively. It is hard to
judge how significant recourse to private caucus sessions may have been in the
process, but the conclusion must be that in such sessions the assembly has a
potentially valuable tool that might prove useful in different situations.

The debates also underlined members' recognition of the value of the treaty
and the self-government it provides as well as the strength of their commitment
to self-government. In dealing with the day-to-day governance matters that
come before the assembly, members rarely frame their comments in self-government terms. It is thus notable that on an issue of fundamental import, and,
significantly, one directly tied to protection of the land, members' resolve as to
the primacy of self-government came through so strongly.

Assembly Effectiveness in Representation and Policymaking

Is it appropriate to assess the effectiveness of an Inuit governance institution
by the standards – the functions a legislature should perform – developed to
analyse legislatures in the Western tradition? Certainly, traditional Inuit culture would not compartmentalize activities into discrete categories such as
representation, accountability, and policymaking. Whether traditional Inuit
culture would even recognize such concepts is a question beyond my competence. The constitutionally mandated assembly functions, outlined at the outset
of this chapter, show that Nunatsiavumiut have chosen to govern themselves
through institutions designed and operating very much according to the stric-
tures and values of Western, Euro-Canadian political culture. Accordingly, it
seems reasonable to evaluate the assembly in terms of those functions.

The assembly performs poorly when it comes to educating the public and debating the great issues of the day. Useful information and opinion does emerge in short, discrete bursts from ministers' statements, questions, and so on, but the absence of full-fledged, wide-ranging policy debates not directed to budgetary or legislative items is notable.

Assembly members think of themselves first and foremost as representatives, articulating the needs and aspirations of their constituents and of all Labrador Inuit as well as working to improve cultural, social, and economic conditions for Nunatsiavut. And while fragmentary evidence suggests some discontent with the performance of members individually and the assembly collectively, it is simply not possible to gauge popular views of the assembly's effectiveness in representation with any certainty. What this chapter does confirm, however, is the extent to which members' speaking and behaviour are motivated by representational imperatives. In turn, although no definitive calibration is possible, it would seem that the assembly is at least moderately effective in fulfilling its representation function.

As for policymaking, few ministers or non-NEC members made reference, either directly or indirectly, to their or other members' roles as legislators or policymakers. Doubtless to some extent members see this role as implicit in their involvement in Nunatsiavut-wide issues, but it is nevertheless noteworthy that it was so infrequently mentioned explicitly. This chapter shows that for the most part members of the assembly other than ministers were passive and reactive in terms of policy- and law-making. At times, proposed policies and laws were significantly modified or affirmed by thorough review and public consultation by special committees; the uranium issue stands out as just such an example of the assembly rising to the occasion. That the assembly's effectiveness in fulfilling its policy- and law-making function is limited is unsurprising; at best, Westminster-style parliaments typically have little policy influence. Still, the consensus-based legislatures in Nunavut and the NWT take a more active role in developing and adjusting policy, suggesting that the Nunatsiavut Assembly has significant capacity for heightening its policy influence.

The following chapter examines the assembly's effectiveness in fostering accountability.

Appendix 9.1. Characteristics of Legislation*

Title	Date	Significance	Debate	Days	2R Vote
FIRST ASSEMBLY					
Exploration and Quarrying Standards Act	March/07	Substantial	Minimal	1	Unan
Additional Revenue Act 2007	June/07	Limited	Short	1	11–1
Torngat Co-op Loan Guarantee Act 2007	Aug/07	Limited	Minimal	1	Unan
Labrador Inuit Lands Amendment Act	Oct/07–April/08	V substantial	Extensive	6 + c'ee	8–7
Code of Conduct	March/08	Substantial	Short	1	Unan
Torngat Co-op Loan Guarantees Act, 2008	June/08	Limited	None	1	Unan
Labrador Inuit Lands Amendment Act	June/08	Limited	None	1	Unan
Beneficiaries Enrolment Amendment Act	June/09	Limited	Minimal	2	Unan
Torngat Co-op Loan Guarantees Act, 2009	June/09	Limited	Minimal	1	Unan
LIDC Multi-use Bulk Fuel Storage Facility Act	June/09	Limited	None	1	Unan
Subordinate Legislation Rectification Act, 2009	Dec/09	Limited	None	2	Unan
Nunatsiavut Assembly Amendment Act	Dec/09	Limited	None	1	Unan
Nunatsiavut Elections Act	Dec/09	Moderate	None	1	Unan
Inuit Community Government Elections Act	March/10	Limited	Minimal	1	Unan
Inuit Community Corporations Chairpersons Elections Act	March/10	Limited	Minimal	1	Unan
Nunatsiavut Assembly Amendment Act	March/10	Limited	Minimal	1	Unan
Labrador Inuit Land Claims Agreement Funding Act	March/10	V substantial	Extensive	1	Unan
Torngat Co-op Loan Guarantees Act, 2010	March/10	Limited	Minimal	1	Unan

* See text for explanation of terms; 2R = second reading; c'ee = committee; Unan = unanimous

(continued)

Appendix 9.1. Characteristics of Legislation* (*continued*)

Title	Date	Significance	Debate	Days	2R Vote
SECOND ASSEMBLY					
Nunatsiavut Environmental Protection Act	Oct/10–Feb/11	V substantial	Extensive	3 + c'ee	Unan
Nain Health Building Act	Feb/11	Limited	Minimal	1	Unan
Torngat Co-op Loan Guarantees Act, 2011	March/11	Limited	None	1	Unan
Procurement Act	March/11	Moderate	None	1	Unan
Beneficiaries Enrolment Amendment Act	March/11	Limited	Short	1	Unan
Nunatsiavut Assembly Amendment Act	Dec/11	Limited	Minimal	1	Unan
Labrador Inuit Lands Amendment Act	Dec/11	Substantial	Extensive	1	Unan
Torngat Co-op Loan Guarantees Act, 2012	March/12	Limited	None	1	Unan
J.F. Fur Farms Act	Sept/12	Limited	None	1	Unan
Land Use Planning Act	Dec/12	V substantial	Minimal	1	Abandoned
Torngâsok Cultural Centre Act	Dec/12–Jan/13	Substantial	Extensive	3	12–4
Torngat Co-op Loan Guarantees Act, 2013	March/13	Limited	None	1	Unan
Torngat Co-op Loan Guarantees Act, 2014	Jan/14	Limited	None	1	Unan
Nunatsiavut Elections Amendment Act	March/14	Substantial	Extensive	2	Unan
THIRD ASSEMBLY					
Torngat Co-operative Loan Guarantee	June/15	Limited	Minimal	1	Unan
Financial Administration Amendment Act	Nov/15	Limited	None	1	Unan
Civil Service Amendments Act	Nov/15	Moderate	Extensive	1	Unan
Torngat Co-op Loan Guarantees Act, 2016	March/16	Limited	Minimal	1	Unan

Title	Date	Significance	Debate	Days	2R Vote
Commercial Fishing Camps Authorization Act, 2016	March/16	Limited	Minimal	1	Unan
Financial Administration Amendment Act	March/17	Limited	None	1	Unan
Nain Supportive Living Unit Loan Act	March/17	Limited	Minimal	1	Unan
Housing Initiatives (Hopedale and Nain) Act	March/17	Limited	Minimal	1	Unan
Nunatsiavut Laws Registration Amendment Act	June/17	Limited	Minimal	1	Unan
Nain Quarry Act (2017)	June/17	Limited	Minimal	1	Unan
Nunatsiavut Government Appointment Repeal Act	March/18	Moderate	Short	1	Unan
Financial Administration Amendment Act	March/18	Limited	Short	1	Unan
FOURTH ASSEMBLY					
Housing Act	Sept/18–March/19	V substantial	Extensive	3 + c'ee	Unan
Nunatsiavut Assembly Amendment Act	Sept/18	Moderate	Minimal	1	Unan
Communities Financial Administration Act	Sept/18	Limited	Short	1	Unan
Labrador Inuit Lands Amendment, 2019	Jan/19	Limited	Short	1	Unan
Housing Initiatives (Hopedale and Nain) Amendment Act	March/20	Limited	None	1	Unan
Nunatsiavut Assembly Amendment Act	Oct/20	Limited	None	1	Unan
Inuit Community Quarries Act, 2021	Feb/21March/21	Limited	None	2	Unan
Nunatsiavut Constitution (Amendment) Act, 2021	June/21	Limited	Short	2	Unan
Election Dates Amendment Act, 2021	Nov/21	Limited	Short	1	Unan
Housing Initiatives (Amendment) Act, 2022	March/22	Limited	None	1	Unan
Housing Act (Amendment) Act, 2022	March/22	Limited	Minimal	1	Unan

* See text for explanation of terms; 2R = second reading; c'ee = committee; Unan = unanimous

Chapter Ten

Assembly Effectiveness II: Accountability

In a study of Indigenous self-government accountability regimes, primarily concerned with institutional design, the Nunatsiavut Government (NG) fared well when compared with two smaller, non-claims-based British Columbia self-governments, the Westbank and Sechelt First Nations. The analysis was rather broad, focused on the design rather than the operation of government structures and processes – for example, emphasizing the significance of the Inuit Court, which has yet to be created. Specifics aside, however, a major takeaway from the study was the substantial range and potential of the NG's accountability mechanisms, in which the assembly features prominently.[1]

Westminster-style parliaments are frequently touted for their capacity to keep government accountable. Many activities of the Nunatsiavut Assembly are either explicitly directed to holding the NG to account or have that effect, even if not specifically intended as such. Yet overall, the assembly's record in fostering accountability is mixed. To some extent, this reflects the absence of accountability mechanisms found in other Westminster parliaments. As well, the low media environment in which the assembly operates is a factor. It may also be that the Inuit aversion to confrontation is at work.

Analyses of how well Westminster-style legislatures keep governments accountable typically focus on question period, financial procedures, and committees with explicit accountability mandates, such as public accounts committees. These elements are examined in this chapter but by no means do they tell the whole story of accountability – or more accurately, lack of accountability – in the assembly.

Accountability mechanisms operate on two levels. Within the assembly, members not belonging to the Nunatsiavut Executive Council (NEC) have a responsibility to hold the government – that is, NEC – to account for its policies and their implementation. Accountability also goes beyond the assembly, to the people. Ultimately, a legislature's effectiveness in terms of accountability must be judged on how well it provides information to the public as to the performance of their government and of their elected representatives. Here, the assembly's record is weak. Quite simply, the channels of information about the assembly and about the NG to beneficiaries are limited. To a significant degree, this is a reflection of the low media environment, which is largely, but not entirely, beyond the assembly's control. At the same time, the way the assembly operates contributes to the lack of public knowledge about it.

Accountability to Nunatsiavumiut

Unless they take it upon themselves to find out by contacting the assembly or their members, beneficiaries are unlikely to know when the assembly is in session because it does little to publicize sittings. With few exceptions, the NG website, including the section devoted to the assembly, does not post information about upcoming sessions. On occasion the OK Society runs brief notices or stories in advance of assembly meetings, but this is very hit-and-miss. Accordingly, the availability of the assembly audio feed during sessions is of limited significance since few beneficiaries are likely to be aware that the assembly is meeting. Once a session finishes, typically only limited information about it is available to the Nunatsiavut public. The audio feed is not retained and those interested in the video recordings must request them from the OK Society or from assembly members, who receive copies. It is unlikely that many people know about the videos. Indeed, an OK Society official told me that no one has ever asked to see a video of an assembly sitting. After some sessions, the OK Society posts short interviews, usually with the speaker, summarizing the proceedings. These provide useful information but, framed as they are in neutral, technical terms, it is difficult for listeners to gauge the significance of what transpired at the assembly or of the issues underlying its deliberations. *Hansard* is an invaluable accountability tool for both assembly members and beneficiaries, especially since all *Hansards* are posted on the NG website, though usually with delays of several months. *Hansard*'s value as a means of holding individual members to account for their stances on divisive issues is undercut in that, although the Standing Orders make provision for recorded divisions showing how all members voted, this option has never been employed throughout the assembly's history. Thus, while some members make their views and voting intentions clear in the debates on divisive issues, comprehensive tallies of members' votes do not exist.

The public's inability to access members' voting records is a special case of the limited availability of information about the activities of the assembly and of the NG generally. Until early 2022 and for several years previously, the assembly website was essentially devoid of content. Clicking on "Nunatsiavut Assembly" on the NG site brought up the following statement (and nothing more, not even a list of members): "Our Assembly consists of people from across Nunatsiavut, and they have a broad array of wisdom and experience that allows us to confidently provide leadership for the entire region."[2] No contact information was provided for members or staff. Most beneficiaries in the communities of the Labrador Inuit Settlement Area (LISA) likely know who their members are and how to contact them, though the extent to which this is the case for beneficiaries in Upper Lake Melville and the Canada Constituency is unclear. As of mid-2022, the assembly subsection of the revamped NG website includes pictures and contact information for all members as well as *Hansards* and text of legislation, regulations, and community government by-laws (all of which had previously been available elsewhere on the NG site), but no other information about the operation of the assembly.

The NG website is useful, though it, too, has significant limitations. For some matters – for example, procedures for applying for beneficiary status – the site has clear, extensive information, including contact information for key officials. For other areas, the site offers little more than broad-brush statements about departmental responsibilities, perhaps with a contact person or web page but no organization charts or staff lists. Few NG publications or reports are available online. The site also contains several years of NG and assembly media releases, though they provide at best spotty information about the policy and workings of government. Table 10.1 offers a glimpse into NG communications about public policies and government activities. Over the period 1 January 2017 to 31 April 2022, nearly five and a half years, NG put out 366 media releases.[3] As might be expected, a substantial number had little, if anything, to do with policy or politics: messages of condolence or congratulation to individuals or groups (8 per cent), notices that applications were available for various government programs or for hunting/fishing licences (4 per cent), and official statements on special days such as International Women's Day and National Indigenous Peoples Day (4 per cent). Thirteen per cent of the releases provided information about upcoming elections or election results and 5 per cent announced changes in the composition of NEC or the assembly, principally resignations and ministerial shuffles. The largest single category, NG policy statements and announcements (a broad category ranging from presidential statements about the Muskrat Falls power project, to statements about NG successes and disappointments in dealing with the federal and provincial governments, to reminders and updates on caribou hunting restrictions, and so on), comprises 51 per cent of the total, with another 5 per cent on NEC activities such as open houses and budget summaries. More than half of the policy statements/announcements (104 of 188, 55 per cent) provided information relating to the COVID-19 pandemic or NG responses to it, covering travel restrictions, vaccination schedules and NG programs for affected beneficiaries. Thus, excluding those on COVID-19 but including

Table 10.1. NG/Assembly news releases, 1 January 2017–31 April 2022

	Number	Percentage
NG policy statements/announcements	188 (104)	51 (28)
Election announcements	46	13
Condolences/congratulations	31	8
Local information/announcements	22	6
Changes in assembly/NEC membership	20	5
NEC activities	17	5
Availability of application forms	16	4
Statements on special days	14	4
Assembly activities	12	3

Figures in parentheses indicate statements relating to COVID-19

those categorized as NEC activities, NG was issuing media releases informing the Inuit public about policy developments or political stances less than twice a month. Unsurprisingly for a government rather than an assembly site, information about or notices of assembly activities, such as consultations by assembly committees or timing of sittings, comprised the smallest number of media releases, just twelve.

NG maintains a Facebook page, but beyond offering Inuttut "word of the day" and similar cultural postings, it primarily reproduces NG media releases and posts job ads.

In her first statement to the assembly in September 2012, newly elected president Sarah Leo acknowledged criticisms that the assembly was not meeting frequently enough "to deal with the issues that are important to the people in our communities … In the past sessions were held in crowded rooms and often sittings were rushed."[4] A few months later, she noted that her pledge to have more frequent assembly sessions had been met and also that NEC was not only meeting more often but also travelling to the communities more regularly. At that, she admitted, "we're still struggling with … [the] commitment that we are accountable to the people that we represent."[5] By the start of the Third Assembly, President Leo was reporting significant improvements to the NG's communications with beneficiaries, highlighting the open houses that NEC regularly held in LISA communities.

NEC is required by section 1.5.3 of the Labrador Inuit Constitution to meet "from time to time" in the LISA communities. When it does so, in addition to its own meeting, NEC holds an open house for local beneficiaries, a significant innovation in bringing the NG to the people. In interviews, members' views of the open houses' value varied a good deal, some praising them as effective information/accountability vehicles, others finding them pro forma and not all that useful. Each year, NEC schedules meetings in the five LISA communities and, most years, in the Upper Lake Melville region, though, as is the case for all Nunatsiavut activities, bad weather can disrupt travel plans, forcing cancellations and postponements.

A glimpse at the open houses is available through audio recordings of NEC open houses, both in Nain, in May 2017 and June 2018, posted to the OK Society website. The following account is based on these meetings.[6] Both beneficiary-only open houses took place in the evening. Lasting an hour and a half and just over an hour, respectively, they largely consisted of presentations by ministers, supplemented on occasion by comments from deputy ministers, much like the statements ministers make to the assembly. Most presentations were fairly brief, four to six minutes, though in the May 2017 meeting, President Lampe spoke for forty-five minutes, in Inuttut and in English. At both open houses, the president was the only minister to speak in Inuttut; simultaneous interpretation was available. At the first meeting, those attending (the recordings offer no indication of the number of people present) were offered the opportunity to ask questions, which several did, on a wide range of issues, including caribou management, the NG's plans regarding the pending legalization of cannabis, and seniors' housing. The second meeting wrapped up without beneficiaries' questions. At both meetings, ministers were at pains to encourage anyone who wanted to meet with them individually after the meeting to do so, or to contact their offices afterwards. On the basis of this very limited sample, it seems that substantial information was provided to beneficiaries, though almost all of it would have been available to someone listening to the assembly audio feed and most of the answers to the questions were of the "we'll look into it/we're working on it" variety. Perhaps more important was the simple fact that the leading governmental figures made themselves available to local residents to explain government policies and to respond to their questions and concerns, in private if not in public.

Assembly Accountability Mechanisms

Auditing the NG

Fostering government accountability entails a good deal more than close attention to finances, but ensuring proper management of public monies does rank highly as an accountability priority. Here the Nunatsiavut Assembly is seriously hamstrung, in that it lacks both a government auditor and a public accounts committee to review the auditor's reports and other financial matters. Section 8.11 of the Labrador Inuit Constitution stipulates that there be "an Auditor for Nunatsiavut," whose remit includes the Inuit community governments and the Inuit community corporations as well as the NG. The auditor is appointed for a five-year term by the president on nomination of the assembly. After early confusion, this requirement has consistently been met.[7] Thus far, however, auditing of the NG's finances has been done by Deloitte, a well-known private sector auditing firm. This stands in sharp contrast to the standard in Ottawa and all provinces and territories: independent officers of Parliament or the provincial/territorial legislatures – such as, in the former case, the auditor general of Canada – who audit government finances and review management practices.

The issue is not that private sector auditors lack competence but rather that their perspective is typically different from that of public auditors and, more significantly, that their mandates are narrower. Private sector auditors primarily perform "attest" audits, sometimes called "financial audits," in which financial records are scrutinized to ensure that funds have been spent with proper authorization, that financial transactions have been above board, and that records are complete and accurate. To be sure, these are essential functions that public auditors also perform. In addition, however, most public auditors perform what are termed "value for money audits," also called "performance audits," designed not just to ensure that government spending is on the up and up but also that government programs are run effectively and efficiently.[8] Such audits, which may directly challenge government management of policy, though not government decisions setting policy, are far more substantial than attest audits, offering far greater potential for promoting accountability.

Among many possible illustrations of the nature and value of performance audits, the 2015 report of the auditor general of Canada on the implementation of the Labrador Inuit Land Claims Agreement (LILCA) is especially apt.[9] One of a series of reports on the implementation of comprehensive land claims agreements, it looked in detail at how several federal government departments and agencies were fulfilling Canada's obligations under LILCA. The audit concluded that substantial progress had been registered but also identified shortcomings requiring action, most notably with respect to the Department of Fisheries and Oceans' policies for allocating fishing licences to Nunatsiavut beneficiaries, inadequate monitoring of implementation and tracking of contracts, and the lack of a federal program for funding Inuit housing "south of 60," which "affected the Nunatsiavut Government's ability to fulfil housing responsibilities it received" under the claim and the financing agreement for it.[10] The report made no mention whatsoever of financial statements or accounting practices, but focused, rather, on management. All affected federal departments and agencies agreed with the auditor general's recommendations for addressing the shortcomings it found. For present purposes, the specifics are less important than the scope and depth of the audit and, in turn, its contribution to holding the federal government accountable for its responsibilities under the treaty.

The constitution requires that the Nunatsiavut auditor report to the assembly annually and that the report "include the opinion of the Auditor" not only on standard accounting concerns such as the accuracy of the NG's financial statements, but also whether "the Nunatsiavut Government's programs were run economically and efficiently; and … [that] the Nunatsiavut Government's policies and programs were well implemented"[11] – obligations central to value-for-money audits. Reports from the NG's auditors, however, make no comments whatsoever about efficiency, economy, or managerial effectiveness.[12] Officials from Deloitte appear before the assembly annually, usually in September. Their presentations outline the nature of the audit and its central conclusions in a high-level, fairly technical manner, highlighting anomalies, which have never been serious, significant variances from previous years, the adequacy of internal controls, the overall financial position of the NG, and the like. These presentations consistently include comforting statements as to the cooperation of NG management in preparing the audit, the apparent absence of fraud or misrepresentation, and of serious financial errors or dubious practices. Typically, they elicit barely half a dozen questions from members, virtually all of which are requests for clarification. Occasionally, a member will ask a policy-related question – "Why couldn't the money in that line of the statement be used for housing?" for example – which the deputy minister of finance, or, less frequently, the minister of finance, answers. Similar presentations on the state of government finances are all but unknown in the provinces and territories, where legislators are concerned with the substance of spending rather than the accounting of it, though of course they have access to government financial statements.

The possibility of creating a conventional auditor general was broached during the Second Assembly, spearheaded by former minister Keith Russell, who had established himself during the First Assembly as an especially combative critic of the government. Early in 2011, Russell brought forward a motion to appoint an auditor general. The mandate to be accorded this government official was not specified with any precision. Nor did the term "value for money" appear, though it was clear that the rationale for creating an auditor general's office was a desire for financial and managerial information and advice that would be more useful in holding the government to account than barebones reports on the NG's financial statements. The Deloitte auditors had appeared before the assembly the day before the motion was introduced, and while members agreed that the auditors had answered questions adequately, some were disappointed that the auditors had no recommendations to offer on any of the programs or institutions they had reviewed.[13]

During the debate on Russell's motion, members repeatedly referred to the views they had solicited from constituents on the idea. All but one of the members present spoke in the debate, as did the speaker; most opposed the motion. Members' objections to the proposal were primarily based on the resistance they had encountered among constituents and on concern that creating a new, costly bureaucratic operation would mean less money for government programs, though no one mentioned the offset that would be realized with the end of the fees paid to private sector auditors. The minister of finance argued that such a move would be unconstitutional and the president objected strongly to the notion that any auditor should dictate or veto policy, a misunderstanding of the nature of public auditing. The motion's proponent claimed to have the support of hundreds of beneficiaries,[14] and another member noted that the constitutional requirement for the auditor to offer opinions on the effectiveness and efficiency of government spending was not being fulfilled. In the end, the motion was defeated 11–5.[15] Once the motion was disposed of, a motion to reappoint the private sector auditors passed unanimously. Attempts to establish an auditor general have not resurfaced since.

With the private sector auditors performing only attest audits, the constitutionally mandated auditing of government effectiveness and efficiency simply does not occur. Thus assembly members are without the penetrating, often highly critical value-for-money reports that members of other Canadian legislatures find so useful in fostering government accountability. Without such reports, little point would be served in creating a public accounts committee, elsewhere in Canada a staple of legislative oversight of government finances.

Reviewing the Trusts

A markedly more effective process for fostering government accountability than occurs when the auditors make their presentation involves four important trusts. Although the trusts operate at arm's length from the NG, they entail substantial amounts of public money and provide important funding streams for the NG and for Labrador Inuit generally. They are:

- The Implementation Trust, established to receive and invest the implementation funds from Ottawa specified in chapter 23 of the claim; the NG is the sole beneficiary. These payments are now complete. As of December 2020, the value of the trust was $333 million.[16]
- The Labrador Inuit Land Claims Settlement Trust, to which the capital transfers from Ottawa set out in chapter 19 of the claim were directed; they have now all been received. For its first eleven years, NG was the only beneficiary but in 2021, individual Inuit as well as charities and non-profits benefiting Inuit became eligible for payments.[17] Market value at the end of 2020 was $238 million,[18] with the recently forgiven $51 million lent to the Labrador Inuit Association (LIA) by Ottawa during claim negotiations earmarked for this trust. Ottawa's payments into the Implementation and Settlement Trusts were entirely separate from its annual fiscal financing transfers to NG.

- The Tasiujatsoak Trust, created in 2002 by LIA to invest and disburse funds received under the Voisey's Bay Impact and Benefit Agreement (IBA) with Inco (now Vale), is designed "to enable Nunatsiavut Government to meet its obligations under the IBA, to assist seven community volunteer centres to meet community needs, to reduce negative impacts of the Voisey's Bay project, [and] to promote social, cultural, educational, language and business initiatives."[19] The NG has been the principal beneficiary, though charities and Inuit community governments have received funds for various projects. Value as of December 2020: $347 million.[20]
- A fourth trust, the Labrador Inuit Capital Strategy Trust, has a very different structure and mandate. Created in 2006, it provides oversight of the Nunatsiavut Group of Companies, the holding company for corporations owned by NG, such as Air Borealis. Its overall objectives are to foster economic development, to provide training and employment opportunities for beneficiaries, and to provide services for Nunatsiavut beneficiaries and communities.[21]

Not only are the trusts important sources of revenue for NG and for Labrador Inuit, but the net worth of each substantially exceeds the annual NG budget. Day-to-day trust operations are handled by professional money managers, or in the case of the Capital Trust by experienced business leaders, under the direction of small boards of trustees appointed by the NG or the assembly. The trustees set overall investment policy and make decisions on disbursements. The composition of the boards varies somewhat, but overall they include senior NG officials (at the time of writing NEC Secretary Isabella Pain served on all four boards) and appointees from outside government, though non-government trustees often have governmental experience; former president Sarah Leo, for example, is a trustee on the Settlement Trust. Assembly members are well aware not only of the huge importance of the trusts to the NG, the Nunatsiavut economy, and beneficiaries generally, but also of their responsibility for preserving the achievements realized through the struggles and compromises in negotiating the claim and the Voisey's Bay IBA. They thus take a keen interest in the health and the activities of the trusts, manifested in vigorous questioning of trustees, typically the NG officials, when they appear before the assembly, as they do on an annual basis, to report on the performance of the trusts. Unsurprisingly, members are more engaged in presentations about the trusts than they are by the auditors' appearances, since the trusts together have assets in the range of a billion dollars and represent essential revenue sources for the NG and Nunatsiavut beneficiaries, with senior NG staff serving as trustees. Most questions, including a substantial number asked by ministers, seek clarification on specific statements or developments, but on occasion questioning takes on a tough, aggressive edge if members are concerned about specific trust investment decisions or about the trusts' overall records – for example, in the wake of serious market downturns resulting in significant short-term investment losses. For the most part, though, questions to trustees are neither confrontational nor critical. This appears to evidence general, though not universal, approval of how the trusts operate and are performing. As well, the lack of staff support for members, most of whom lack the expertise needed for deep analysis of complex financial documents, is likely a factor. Finally, it may reflect an overall culture of deference on the part of members towards ministers and senior bureaucrats, which may in turn partially be a function of Inuit distaste for confrontation.

(Non)Scrutiny of Regulations

An important area in which the assembly lacks a mechanism for holding the government to account is NEC's regulation-making power. Unlike the absence of an auditor general, this is a gap common in Canadian legislatures. A number of Inuit laws include the following provision: "the President-in-Council may make regulations required to achieve the purpose of this act." This provides the legal authority for NEC ("the President-in-Council") to create subordinate legislation or to issue executive orders without the need for assembly approval, since that power has already been delegated by the assembly to NEC through regulation-making clauses. Regulations are essential to the smooth running of modern governments, permitting them to quickly change details, but not the principles, of legislation, without having to seek passage of a bill in the assembly. By way of illustration, the process and the forms for approval of harvesting by non-beneficiaries can be changed by regulation. A regulation may not exceed the scope of the law under which it is made, nor can it override the law. For example, a 2017 regulation amended the rules of practice for membership committees, but it could not have changed the powers and responsibilities of the committees as set out in the *Beneficiaries Enrolment Act*. Without the ability to issue regulations, the wheels of government would grind to a halt in short order. A high proportion of Nunatsiavut regulations are executive orders appointing members to co-management boards and membership committees or appointing or dismissing ministers; others entail minor administrative matters. Some regulations, such as those affecting harvesting or setting out requirements for environmental reviews, carry significant policy import.

Perfectly legal and necessary for effective governing as regulations may be, they constitute a broad swathe of government activity that is for all intents and purposes exempt from legislative scrutiny. Regulations are public documents, available on the NG website, and only come into effect when formally registered by the registrar of Nunatsiavut laws, though relatively few people, possibly not all assembly members, understand the process or know where to find regulations. It would be entirely proper for a member to enquire about or challenge any regulation during members' statements, question period, or other proceedings, but this rarely if ever occurs. No mechanism exists – a dedicated committee on regulations, for example – to bring regulations to the assembly's attention. The black hole for accountability that regulations represent is by no means a failing limited to the Nunatsiavut Assembly. Inability to hold government accountable for its regulations is also evident in other Canadian parliaments in which regulations largely escape legislative scrutiny.[22] That it is a common problem does not, however, mean it is a minor one.

Question Period[23]

Question period stands as a key accountability mechanism in Westminster parliaments. At the Nunatsiavut Assembly, although a good deal of worthwhile information emerges from question period, its overall effectiveness in promoting accountability is limited. Non-NEC members ask far fewer questions than they might, and those they do pose are generally aimed at eliciting factual information rather than at questioning or criticizing government policy and administration. Acquiring information and understanding of government policies and practices is, to be sure, worthwhile, but in and of itself it does little to advance accountability.

The rules surrounding question period are unexceptional. The Labrador Inuit Constitution does not explicitly require a question period, though section 5.9.1 contains the following stipulation:

> Members of the Nunatsiavut Executive Council must respond to questions and requests for information made by members of the Nunatsiavut Assembly in relation to the performance of executive functions or the business of the Nunatsiavut Government but no member of the Nunatsiavut Executive Council is obliged to respond to a question or a request for information that is ruled by the presiding officer to be frivolous or vexatious.

The *Nunatsiavut Government Organization (Transitional) Act*, the Inuit law that establishes the basic structure of the NG and sets out the powers and responsibilities of NEC members, requires all ministers to attend at least three-quarters of question periods unless properly excused.[24] Perhaps symbolically important, this requirement is of little practical import since ministers rarely miss sessions.

Under the Standing Orders, question period may not exceed 60 minutes without a motion permitting a 30-minute extension. Tellingly, only once has a motion to extend question period been brought forward,[25] though apparently during the First Assembly, the then 30-minute limit was reached several times and at least once the speaker let question period run 10 minutes over.[26] A 2010 survey of members indicated widespread support for extending question period and for allowing members two original questions per day rather than the one then permitted. In response, the first minister acknowledged that on occasion, "sufficient time has not been provided [for questions] or allowed [members] to raise questions that they had received from constituents."[27] Accordingly, question period was expanded to 60 minutes, with members entitled to two original questions each day plus two supplementary questions for each question. As demonstrated below, this allotment is routinely undersubscribed.

Questions may be directed to the president or to ministers on matters "relating to public affairs," and they are to be "concisely and clearly put,"[28] though speakers exhibit considerable tolerance of rambling, verbose questions. The assembly's initial Standing Orders permitted "Members to ask questions of other Members or Ministers."[29] Only twice were questions put to non-NEC members, AngajukKât in both cases. However, until early in the Second Assembly, ministers occasionally asked oral questions of other ministers, including an instance when the first minister asked a surprisingly tough question of the president.[30] The 2010 amendment to the act extending question period to an hour kept in place the provision enabling "Members to ask questions of other Members and Ministers." In 2011, the wording was changed to read, "questions relating to public affairs may be put to the President or a Minister." Since then, with the solitary exception in 2017 of a newly appointed minister asking a question of an AngajukKâk, which was ruled out of order,[31] only non-NEC members have posed oral questions.

Although speakers rule questions out of order on occasion, they are accommodating in assisting members in their quest for information. By way of illustration, on a day when the first minister was absent, Speaker Blake-Rudkowski allowed members to pose questions that fell within her responsibilities, canvassing other ministers to see if any were prepared to answer. When none stepped forward, he directed that the questions be forwarded to the first minister's department. On another occasion, a wholesale cabinet shuffle having occurred during a sitting owing to the appointment of a new first minister, the speaker, recognizing that freshly reassigned ministers would not be able to answer questions about their new portfolios, offered the former ministers the opportunity to respond.[32]

It is common for ministers to take oral questions as notice, in which case written responses must be provided within seven calendar days. Written questions may be put to ministers, who must provide responses within ten calendar days,[33] but members resort to them sparingly. Only one written question was asked in each of 2017, 2018, and 2019; the upheaval caused by the pandemic led to nine written questions during 2020, 2021, and the first months of 2022, though six of them were subsequently ruled out of order for not meeting the criteria for written questions.[34]

Even a cursory review of assembly *Hansards* makes it evident that from the outset, a substantial proportion of queries posed in question period simply sought factual information from ministers, with others not so much seeking information as requesting funding or services. The 19 original questions asked in question period during the two-day session in November 2019, while not put forward as statistically representative, illustrate the dearth of aggressive, confrontational questioning. The questions were categorized as purely information seeking, as information seeking with a mild or implicit challenge or rebuke to government, as directly criticizing government, or as requesting government action or funding.[35] None of the questions directly attacked either government policy or its administration. Six were straightforward in simply asking for information. (Examples: Had the government been in touch with the federal Department of Fisheries and Oceans about turbot and crab stocks? Did the government have an update on gold exploration in a particular area?) Only one of these questions was followed up with a supplementary question. Five questions, none with supplementaries, were in the nature of requests. (Examples: Could the government provide funding for a community shed? Would the minister meet with the AngajukKâk to discuss obtaining firewood for her community? Could financial literacy workshops offered in LISA communities be made available in Upper Lake Melville?) Seven questions framed as information requests, 3 of which generated supplementaries, carried at worst mild or implied criticism of government but could hardly be categorized as direct attacks. (Examples: Had the NG consulted with Transport Canada about a new federal boating safety regulation with untoward effects on traditional Inuit culture? Does the minister have updated figures on the number of Inuit children who have left LISA through the activities of the provincial Department of Children, Seniors and Social Development and how many have been returned? What progress has the NG made in setting up the recently established Nunatsiavut Housing Commission and in hiring its director?)

In line with the largely non-confrontational, information-seeking nature of questions, one of the most noteworthy features of question period in the Nunatsiavut Assembly is the extent to which members do not avail themselves of the opportunities it provides. This was especially evident early on: in three of the first four sessions of the First Assembly and one subsequent session, no oral questions whatsoever were asked.[36] Other than the opening sessions of the Third and Fourth Assemblies, which were given over to formalities, no sitting day after 2013 was devoid of oral questions. This does not mean, however, that members came close to exhausting the possibilities offered by question period, as may be seen from table 10.2 below.

The table presents data on the frequency with which non-NEC members other than the speaker asked original, not supplementary, questions in question period during two three-year periods: 2010–12 and 2017–19 (more recent sessions were not examined since they were atypical due to pandemic-imposed constraints).[37] The few questions asked by ministers are not included. Only non-NEC members who were present are included in the tabulations. The first column shows the number of sitting days each year. The next three columns indicate on how many "member days" (a sitting day for one member) each year members asked no, one, or two questions. If a member was present on a particular day but asked no questions, that was recorded in the "None" column; members who asked one question or two questions on a given day were recorded in the following two columns. Thus, over the five sitting days in 2010, there were 13 occasions when a member was present on a given day but asked no questions, 21 occasions when a member asked one question, and 12 instances of members asking two questions on a single day. The final three columns show the number of questions members were entitled to ask, the number of actual questions asked, and the actual/possible ratio. Thus in 2010, if all non-NEC members present had asked the two questions to which they were entitled every day (one a day in March, prior to the revision of the Standing Orders), 76 questions would have been asked. With 45 questions asked, 59 per cent of potential questioning opportunities were taken up.

The clear message from the table is that during question period members did not come close to making use of all their opportunities to question members of NEC. Members consistently asked fewer than half the questions they could; 2010 was the only year in which more than half the opportunities to pose questions were taken up. Although the numbers varied somewhat from year to year, overall in both three-year stretches, members asked no questions on 43 per cent of member days.[38] Otherwise put, nearly half the time members were present during a sitting they did not avail themselves of the opportunity to ask questions.

It might be thought that the numbers in table 10.2 for potential original questions is artificially high in that, with members allowed two supplementary questions to each original question, the sixty-minute limit on question period could be reached before all members had the opportunity to pose two original questions. That only once has a member seen fit to move for an extension to question period suggests that this is not the case. The data in table 10.3 below offer confirmation. The table displays the percentage of original questions that were followed by supplementary questions. Entries vary widely by assembly and by type of member, with no clear patterns discernible as to the proclivity of different types of members for asking supplementaries. What is clear, however, is that members are not inclined to use supplementaries to pursue matters raised in their original questions, with barely a quarter (27 per cent) of original questions followed up with supplementaries. As with original questions, the data on supplementaries highlight questioning opportunities not taken up. This is in line with the tendency for members to use question period to obtain

Table 10.2. Frequency of members' questions in question period*

	Sitting days	Number of questions asked (member days)			Potential questions	Actual questions	Percentage
		None	One	Two			
2010**	5	13	21	12	76	45	59
2011	6	28	17	10	110	37	34
2012	5	29	18	14	122	46	38
Total 2010–12	16	70	56	36	308	128	42
2017	8	28	17	23	132	63	48
2018	5	16	16	12	88	40	45
2019	9	39	19	24	164	67	41
Total 2017–19	22	83	52	59	384	170	44

* Original questions only; supplementary questions not included; includes only non-NEC members, excluding the speaker, in attendance; excludes questions by ministers
** In the March 2010 session, members were allowed only one question a day

Table 10.3. Frequency of supplementary questions (percentages)

Assembly	Ordinary members	AngajukKât	Corporation chairs	Total	Number
First	45	27	56	36	92
Second	11	14	38	14	226
Third	44	30	40	38	234
Fourth	30	28	9	25	282
Total	30	24	27	27	834

information rather than to challenge government policy or to force it to defend its positions.

Are some types of members more likely than others to ask questions? According to table 10.4 below, some variation is evident over time, likely reflecting members' idiosyncrasies rather than systematic factors, but overall no dramatic differences are evident. From the beginning of the First Assembly to the end of the Fourth, ordinary members asked 33 per cent of original questions, AngajukKât 53 per cent, and community chairs 14 percent. Since, excluding the speaker, there are usually three non-NEC ordinary members, five AngajukKât. and two community chairs (30, 50, and 20 per cent, respectively)[39] these figures are reasonably in line with what would be expected if all types of members asked questions at the same rate. The most substantial deviation from expectations, the relatively low rate of questioning from community chairs, is partially explained by the disproportionate rate of community chair absences from the assembly, either for health reasons or because of resignations.

Table 10.4. Original questions asked by type of member* (percentages)

Assembly	Ordinary Member	AngajukKât	Community Chair	Number
First	34	57	10	92
Second	38	60	4	226
Third	38	41	21	234
Fourth	24	57	20	282
Total	33	53	14	834

* Excludes questions asked by ministers

Members ask more questions of some ministers and some departments than others. Table 10.5 below presents data on the distribution of original questions by portfolio over the four assemblies. Four of the five sectoral departments, Language and Culture being the exception, combine two or three distinct policy areas: Education and Economic Development; Finance, Human Resources and Information Technology; Health and Social Development; and Lands and Natural Resources. Questions directed to each sector of combined departments are shown in the table. In interpreting the data in the table, the NG's limited take-up of jurisdiction means that many issues of importance to members are beyond its control, though on occasion members do pose questions on such issues.

While we should not make too much of changes in rates of questioning from one assembly to the next, such as the decline in questions about economic development between the First and Second Assemblies, some patterns are evident. By substantial and consistent margins, outside of those to the first minister, the highest proportion of questions, 16 per cent, were directed to the natural resources side of the Department of Lands and Natural Resources, mostly in regard to fish and wildlife issues (questions relating to lands were primarily about environmental protection and land use planning). The importance, both cultural and economic, of hunting and fishing to the Inuit communities shows through clearly in the proclivity of members to ask questions about permits, quotas, and regulations relating to fish and wildlife. Save the human resources and IT components of the Department of Finance, Human Resources and Information Technology, which elicited relatively few questions, other departments or sections of departments generated roughly similar proportions of questions, between 4 and 10 per cent. A high proportion of the health questions, half or more in some assemblies, involved processes and funding for medical travel. A few of the finance questions asked about financial statements and documents, but most sought information or support for local capital and operational projects. During the First Assembly a distinct status of women remit existed within the department called Health, Social Development and Status of Women, but no questions were asked of the minister on women's

Table 10.5. Original questions by portfolio* (percentages)

Assembly	President	First minister	Culture/ Lang	Edu/Ec Dev		Finance/ HR/IT			Health/Soc Dev		Lands/Nat Res		Number
				Edu	Ec Dev	Fin	HR	IT	Health	Soc Dev	Lands	NR	
First	20	21	9	1	15	11	0	0	10	1	7	8	92
Second	5	26	5	7	4	11	4	0	9	5	7	17	226
Third	12	23	5	9	2	6	2	1	9	7	7	20	234
Fourth	13	22	6	6	2	7	5	4	11	4	4	16	282
Total	11	23	6	7	4	8	3	1	10	5	6	16	834

* Excludes questions by ministers
Rows may not add to 100 because of rounding

issues. At the start of the Second Assembly, responsibility for women's issues was folded into the social development side of the renamed Department of Health and Social Development. In the Second and Fourth Assemblies, questions were asked about the possible re-establishment of a dedicated status of women sub-department and about NG policies on women's issues, all by one member. In the table, these questions are included with social development questions; overall, they constituted just under 1 per cent of all questions.

Similar proportions of questions were asked of the first minister (23 per cent) as of the lands and natural resources minister (22 per cent). It is noteworthy that close to half of all questions were posed to just two ministers, but the reasons why these ministers attracted so many questions are quite different. As noted, Inuit concerns with fish and wildlife largely explain the questions to the lands and natural resources minister. Questions to the first minister ran the gamut of NG activities, with special attention to the first minister's responsibilities for housing, intergovernmental relations, and member enrolment issues;[40] members directed questions to him in recognition of his central role in NEC.

The table hints at the extent to which questions in the First Assembly were directed to either the president or the first minister. Closer inspection of the data proves revealing. During the first session at which questions were asked, February 2007, six of the eight questions went to either the president or the first minister, and as late as March 2009, fully half of all questions were directed to them. As well, during the first years, on more than a few occasions either the president or the first minister offered comments in addition to those from the ministers to whom the questions were addressed; this has rarely happened more recently. Although the proportion of questions to the president and first minister did not fall below 30 per cent in subsequent assemblies, their dominance of question period never returned to the extraordinary level of the first years of the assembly.

A review of the questions put to the president offers no single explanation as to why a fifth of all questions in the First Assembly but only a twentieth in the Second Assembly went to the president. In both cases, members asked a wide range of general policy questions and constituency-specific questions of the president, though in the First Assembly members also enquired of procedural-organizational matters, such as dates and frequency of meetings and the timing of the presidential elections, that did not arise in the Second Assembly. As well, for several sessions of the First Assembly, the first minister served as acting president, attracting questions as to his role and abilities. Finally, all told, only ninety-two questions were asked in the First Assembly, which may have artificially boosted the president's percentage.

A venerable bromide holds that all politics are local. However, as table 10.6 below demonstrates, this is only partially true of the Nunatsiavut Assembly, at least as far as question period is concerned. Questions were categorized as to their scope: either as local or regional – encompassing all of Nunatsiavut, general policy, or several communities. The vast majority of questions fit easily into these somewhat artificial categories. While all non-NEC members are elected by and represent individual communities or community corporations, it might be expected that their explicit role as representatives of Inuit community governments and Inuit community corporations would incline AngajukKât and community chairs to ask substantially more locally focused questions than ordinary members. The data in table 10.6 show that AngajukKât and community chairs did ask more questions concerned with local matters than ordinary members, but the differences were marginal. Overall, 44 per cent of ordinary members' questions were local, compared with 46 per cent for AngajukKât and 47 per cent for community chairs.

A more significant finding is evident from the table: despite the undoubted pressure to pursue local issues, all types of members asked somewhat more – 55 to 45 per cent – questions with Nunatsiavut-wide significance. To be sure, some "regional" questions were prompted by local situations, but their wide framing is nevertheless noteworthy.

With one exception, no substantial consistent patterns emerge from the local-regional data in terms of questions asked to specific ministers or departments/sub-departments. Unsurprisingly, given their broad mandates and elevated positions, the president and first minister were substantially more likely than other ministers to be asked Nunatsiavut-wide than local questions. All told, 65 per cent of questions to the two leading figures in the cabinet were regional in focus, compared to 49 per cent of questions to all other ministers.

Various factors might incline members to pass on opportunities to ask questions or to follow up original questions with supplementaries, and to avoid tough, confrontational questions. Overall, though, it is easy to conclude that fostering government accountability through frequent or aggressive questioning is

Table 10.6. Original questions with a local focus* (percentages)

Assembly	Ordinary Members	AngajukKât	Community Chairs	Total	Number
First	29	57	44	47	92
Second	44	42	62	43	226
Third	44	55	44	49	234
Fourth	50	40	47	44	282
Total	44	46	47	45	834

* Excludes questions from ministers

not a prime feature of the Nunatsiavut Assembly. That is not at all to suggest that question period and other assembly processes lack accountability value. By its very nature, question period has a salutary effect on government accountability in that ministers and the civil servants supporting them may be generally confident that members' questions will not give rise to undue difficulty, but they can never be certain that government activities, be they inappropriate, inadvisable, or simply controversial, won't be subject to grief-causing questions. Moreover, if most questions are posed in search of information or clarification rather than in an effort to foster NG accountability, over the years some members have been more than willing to ask tough, aggressive questions, explicitly seeking to hold NEC to account. In the First Assembly, for example, two ordinary members, Keith Russell and Danny Pottle, regularly attacked the government during question period on both policy and administrative issues, frequently bemoaning the lack of accountability. (By the start of the Second Assembly, both had been appointed to cabinet, though Russell lasted less than a year before being removed by President Lyall.) As well, members have other opportunities to ask questions and raise concerns, seeking information and/or accountability from NEC.

Low Media Environment

The assembly, like the NG generally, operates in what might be termed a low media environment. Assembly coverage of any kind by journalists is very limited, with critical and investigative journalism focusing on any aspect of the NG all but non-existent. Current and former journalists interviewed about coverage agree that the almost complete lack of media oversight significantly shapes Nunatsiavut government and politics, severely undercutting prospects for accountability. One went as far as to say, "they [NG officials] have all the benefits of government but none of the accountability."

Given the difficult logistics and the cost of travel to and around Nunatsiavut, it is hardly surprising that reporters rarely, if ever, attend assembly sessions.

One member said that he'd never seen a reporter at the assembly, though if "something big" happens, journalists call. According to a former journalist, the weekly *Labradorian* newspaper did attempt to find local stringers to cover Nunatsiavut, but it did not work out.

Mainstream media coverage is very limited. *The Labradorian* carries few stories about any aspect of Nunatsiavut, including politics. Over a two-year stretch (January 2018–December 2019) it published only a handful of articles about Nunatsiavut politics; those it did run mostly dealt with the lead-up to and results of the 2018 ordinary members election. At CBC, an official indicated that *Labrador Morning*, the daily radio program from Happy Valley–Goose Bay, has a policy of running at least one item a week relating to Nunatsiavut and that roughly half are of a political nature, with the balance dealing with "lifestyle." Another CBC staffer, not associated with *Labrador Morning*, commented that the show "is really treasured up and down the coast." Tight budgets and limited staff resources mean that CBC is only occasionally able to send reporters to the North Coast, though, according to front-line staff, management is eager to extend coverage of Nunatsiavut and its politics. A proposal to send a TV reporter to Hopedale for a session as an experiment in expanding coverage was said to have received serious attention, falling through not because of concerns about costs but because a key figure behind the idea left for another CBC posting.

CBC staff rely heavily on the NG's director of communications for information and updates; they are also in regular contact with the OK Society and use Facebook to stay in touch with political figures. During sessions, they may have the assembly audio feed on in the background but are usually too busy to pay close attention. From time to time, CBC Newfoundland and Labrador, both its radio and television services, carries items about Nunatsiavut, often political in nature, as does the CBC Newfoundland and Labrador website, but coverage is episodic at best. During the 2022 ordinary member election, no items about the election appeared on the CBC Newfoundland and Labrador website, and the only coverage on *Labrador Morning* was a short election-day interview with the Nunatsiavut elections officer, who listed candidates and location of polling places and explained required documentation.[41]

At first blush, the Nain-based OK Society, with its largely Nunatsiavut-focused interviews and daily newscasts, as well as its archives of past items, might appear an important mechanism for filling in the journalistic gaps in the coverage provided by *The Labradorian* and CBC. Widely considered very good at what it does – conveying information, especially at the community level, and promoting and enhancing Inuit culture – the OK Society simply does not engage in conventional journalism, but is, rather, a non-profit registered charity. According to the organization's website,

In English [OKâlaKatiget] means "People who talk or communicate with each other." It was incorporated in 1982. Stationed in Nain, Labrador the Society provides a regional, native communication service for the people on the North Coast and the Lake Melville region of Labrador. People have come to rely on the Society for information and entertainment via radio and television. A primary part of our mandate is to preserve and promote the language and culture of the Inuit within the region.[42]

For the most part, the OK Society broadcasts cultural programming, community service announcements, job ads, and news briefs, though it does run political items, including occasional interviews of politicians.[43] Items about the NG or the assembly typically entail verbatim repetition of NG media releases, especially on controversial matters, such as ministerial resignations. At election time, interviews with candidates are aired, but the interviews are little more than puffball questions – "What is your platform?" would be a typical example – with no follow-up or challenges from the interviewer. On occasion, a week or two after the session, the OK Society presents a brief report summarizing activities in the assembly, often by way of an interview with the speaker, who must necessarily be carefully neutral in her comments. Only rarely are the dates for upcoming assembly sessions mentioned.

Funding for the OK Society comes principally from the federal Department of Canadian Heritage, though on occasion it receives funding from NG earmarked for special projects or services, such as Inuttut programming; as well, it holds the contract for video recording of assembly sessions. That the OK Society sees its role as assisting the NG in getting information to beneficiaries, rather than in challenging government statements or questioning ministers, was confirmed in an interview with an OK Society official, who made it clear that the stories and interviews they do about government and politics and the information they provide are entirely contingent on "what we get from NG." OK Society staff do not seek out stories on their own; they take what NG provides. The response to a direct question as to whether they would give a non-NEC assembly member an opportunity to explain or promote a project or idea was an unequivocal "no": "we get everything from NG."

One former member's view was that the OK Society was more than just a passive conveyor of information from NG:

Nunatsiavut government controls what goes through the OKâlaKatiget Radio Society … [An interview I did at OK Society] was edited so much that my concerns and greatest issues were not addressed. And when I contacted the individual who did the interview, I was told by this individual that they were told by their supervisor to delete that because it was negative comments towards Nunatsiavut Government, and I asked who said it. They told me [senior officials], so when the state controls the media you become a dictatorship, and that's what's going on right now.

This is of course the perspective of a single individual, though it is worth pointing out that members were not asked directly for their views and experiences of the OK Society. What can be said with confidence is that whatever its successes as a champion of Inuit language and culture and its value as an information provider, its mandate does not include the essential journalistic function of keeping government accountable.

Each community in Nunatsiavut has a popular local radio station that broadcasts a few hours a day. Local radio offers information on community government activities, radio bingo, lost and found items, information about hunting possibilities, birthday greetings, and so on. NG has a limited presence on community radio, primarily through public service announcements.

What are the implications of having a low media environment for politics in the assembly and in Nunatsiavut generally? Current and former journalists believe that non-NEC members are reluctant to speak out in the media against the government for fear of repercussions against their communities. One argued that in consensus government, "you've got to cosy up to those in power to get what you want," and if you get on their wrong side you can be shut out, so that members are careful about their dealings with the media. This person mentioned being in regular contact with politicians, some of whom "would talk to you all day long but would shy away from doing an actual interview."

More generally, it could be argued that the lack of media attention devoted to NG has a potential dampening effect on conversations about important issues and on people's understanding of government policies. This was certainly the consensus among journalists. One commented that, while "news travels throughout Nunatsiavut whether there is a media presence or not … [as] there are no secrets in small communities … more robust communication with the people, partially through independent media, would be beneficial and enhance democracy." This person cited public anger and confusion around a controversial issue that arose during the summer of 2020 – the disposition of housing stock owned by the Torngat Regional Housing Association – as an example of a serious problem that might have been avoided or at least mitigated with better communication and more extensive media coverage.

Taking a comparative perspective, the overall lack of media attention to the activities of the assembly and of the NG stands in marked contrast to the substantial media attention focused on government and politics in Nunavut. The policies and practices of the Government of Nunavut, as well as the claims-based co-management boards and Inuit organizations such as Nunavut Tunngavik Incorporated, are subjected to vigorous oversight by the CBC as well as by the remarkably assiduous and perceptive weekly *Nunatsiaq News* (the weekly *Nunavut News/North* also carries political stories). However, this is not a fair comparison, for several reasons. For one, Nunavut's population is several times that of Nunatsiavut, especially if Canada Constituency beneficiaries are excluded, and, as a territory with a much broader range of responsibilities than Nunatsiavut, Nunavut is a player on the national stage. In addition, Iqaluit, Nunavut's capital, hosts a major CBC presence.

A more apt comparison would be with the extent of media attention to the other Indigenous self-governments of similar size, the Nisga'a Lisims Government in British Columbia and the Tłįchǫ Government in the Northwest Territories. Activities of the Nisga'a Lisims Government receive limited coverage in two weeklies, the *Terrace Standard* and Prince Rupert's the *Northern View*, both owned by Black Press Media. A search of the two papers' websites suggests that in the course of a decade the papers published roughly ten stories or commentaries a year about the Nisga'a, and that only a small proportion related to governance matters; most were about culture or tourism.[44] Notably, whereas travel from Goose Bay to anywhere in Nunatsiavut is difficult and expensive, Terrace is about a two-hour drive from the closest Nisga'a village. CBC and private radio pay only limited attention to Nisga'a politics. In the Northwest Territories, the Tłįchǫ Government receives roughly the same level of coverage in the Yellowknife weekly *NWT News/North* and the bi-weekly *Yellowknifer*, both owned by NNSL Media.[45] As well, CBC produces daily radio and television programming in Yellowknife that occasionally covers Tłįchǫ politics. Yellowknife is about a ninety-minute drive from Behchoko, the largest Tłįchǫ community.[46]

These broad-brush comparisons suggest that, even though coverage of Nisga'a and Tłįchǫ politics is much less constrained by logistical barriers than is the case in Nunatsiavut – though of course distance is but one factor – all three operate in low media environments. Though data are lacking, it is reasonable to speculate that the other Indigenous self-government regimes in Canada, which are much less populous than Nunatsiavut, also lack significant media coverage. Nor is this situation likely to change in any appreciable way. The upshot is that the assembly and its members have a special responsibility to hold the NG to account since the media presence is so limited.

Transparency

Transparency is a next-door neighbour of accountability. Indeed, without transparency – availability of information backed by a commitment to keep both assembly members and the public informed about public policies and practices as well as government decisions – accountability is scarcely possible. Though weak spots are evident, such as the lack of content on the NG website and the lack of advance notice of sessions, overall, the assembly itself scores reasonably well in terms of transparency. The NG, however, is often taken to task for its lack of transparency. As detailed in chapter 8, from the first sittings of the assembly to the present, members have bemoaned what they see as inadequate communications from the NG, with members frequently calling the NG secretive. Journalists were divided as to the NG's willingness to provide information. One said that getting routine information from the NG is difficult and that potentially sensitive information is simply unavailable. This person cited repeated unsuccessful attempts to interview a minister on what promised to be a "good-news story" for the government, adding that "as a journalist you have to pull your punches" because of the NG's reluctance to share information. Another, acknowledging that all governments can be hesitant in responding to information requests, indicated that, overall, NG officials were reasonably forthcoming with documents and that when the NG balked, assembly members were often willing to supply documents. My experience was very much along those lines, although the information and documents I requested were unlikely to prove embarrassing to the NG. Over several years, I asked for and received information on a wide range of assembly and NG activities and practices from assembly staff and from departmental officials. No request was denied or questioned.

The web page of the Nunatsiavut Secretariat proclaims the following: "Openness and accountability are vital principles of the Nunatsiavut Government. The Communications division is responsible for ensuring that all Beneficiaries of the Labrador Inuit Land Claims Agreement and the broader public are informed about the Nunatsiavut Government's affairs and programs in a timely and effective manner ... The Communications division of the Secretariat is responsible in ensuring that the Nunatsiavut Government is transparent and honest in everything we do."[47] It is difficult for a non-beneficiary to evaluate this claim. On the one hand, the NG website includes very few of the many annual and occasional reports that contain useful information about government operations and policies. Many of these reports are tabled in the assembly and thus are public documents, but they are not easily available to beneficiaries. On the other hand, the secretariat maintains a set of community liaison officers (CLOs) who, according to the website, "act as a bridge between Labrador Inuit and the Nunatsiavut Government. CLOs work at the community level, conveying information between the communications division and Beneficiaries, coordinating community meetings, organizing elections services, and assisting Beneficiaries with information requests." Judging the effectiveness of these staff, especially for beneficiaries in the Canada Constituency, is beyond the scope of this book.

Nunatsiavut has no freedom of information legislation, though section 2.4.31 of the constitution says, "Every Labrador Inuk has the right of access to any information held by an institution of Labrador Inuit government and that is required for the exercise or protection of any rights but this right is subject to reasonable restrictions which may be imposed under Inuit law including restrictions reasonably necessary to protect the privacy of individuals." A subsequent section (2.4.33) requires that "Inuit law must be enacted to give effect to the rights in section 2.4.31 and 2.4.32 [electronic communications] and Inuit law may provide for reasonable measures to alleviate the administrative and financial burden of implementing the right in section 2.4.31." As of 2022, this had yet to happen, though there were indications that action was being considered within the NG.

A telling episode, not least for the assembly's acceptance of what might have been seen as an NG move to reduce transparency, occurred in March 2018, with the repeal of the *Nunatsiavut Government Appointments Act*. Among the first Inuit laws passed by the assembly, the act set out a process for appointments to boards and committees established under the claim, such as the co-management boards and the community enrolment committees, including how pools of potential candidates were to be developed. The act required NG to place annual ads in newspapers, including a nationally published newspaper, soliciting candidates for appointment, and it established an advisory committee composed of ministers, public servants, and members of the Inuit public. After more than a decade's experience, NEC moved to reform a process the first minister described as "cumbersome and costly"[48] by repealing the entire act. Much of the limited debate in the assembly focused on the cost and apparent futility of the newspaper ads, especially since by this point, the print edition of the *Globe and Mail* was no longer available in Newfoundland and Labrador. As well, the ads, experience showed, attracted more interested non-beneficiaries than beneficiaries.

Top-ranking NG bureaucrat Isabella Pain explained that the government's plan was to repeal the act and replace it with an executive (i.e., NEC) order mandating a process. Citing positive results from social media campaigns and direct approaches to communities in turning up interested and qualified beneficiaries for board positions, she indicated that the new process would be far more effective in developing strong candidate pools. Only two members asked questions or made comments, either about the cost and effectiveness of newspaper advertising or about the need for fairness in attracting and appointing candidates. It is hard to argue with ending the mandatory newspaper ads and it is reasonable to expect that the new process will prove more successful than the old in bringing forward good candidates for appointment. At the same time, it is noteworthy that no assembly member mentioned, let alone voiced concern about, ending public involvement in the process resulting from the abolition of the advisory committee, or about the reduction of NEC transparency in making important appointments.

An Accounting of Accountability

As noted in the chapter's introduction, the assembly's effectiveness in terms of fulfilling its accountability function is mixed, which is significant in that advancing government accountability is generally considered a strength of Westminster-style parliaments. To some extent, assembly accountability shortcomings reflect the absence of institutional features common in other Canadian legislatures, such as an independent public sector auditor and committees with accountability mandates, such as public accounts committees. Members' approaches to their roles are also of moment. In interviews, comments from members about fostering government accountability were all but entirely absent. Members did mention concerns about improving government communications to the assembly and to beneficiaries, but this was mostly framed in terms of improving their ability to represent their constituents rather than as a means of enhancing accountability. The low media environment in which the assembly, like the NG, operates is unquestionably a factor here. Elsewhere, aggressive media raise issues about government policy and administration that legislators follow up, while legislators' interest in attracting media attention provides incentives to call governments to account for errors and shortcomings. These dynamics are far less in evidence in Nunatsiavut.

None of this is to suggest that accountability is of no concern to the assembly or its members. If not all accountability opportunities in question period are taken up, many are, and members take a lively interest in the performance of the trusts that loom so large both in terms of financing the NG and in enhancing Nunatsiavut's economy and society. Significant assembly activities contribute to accountability; overall, though, the assembly is at best moderately effective in holding government to account for its policies and administration.

A prominent theme in this chapter, especially evident in the analysis of question period, was members' reticence to use the tools available to them for enhancing government accountability. In question period, members frequently took a pass on asking questions, and when they did take the opportunity, they generally did not follow up with supplementaries and rarely framed their questions in aggressive or critical ways. It seems clear that to a substantial degree, this is less a reflection of any lack of concern with accountability as a commitment to consensual governance, which in turn may reflect traditional Inuit distaste for confrontation and discomfort asking questions.

Chapter Eleven

Change, Continuity, and Self-Government in the Nunatsiavut Assembly

All institutions, even those still in their first two decades, exhibit both change and continuity. Unsurprisingly for an institution defined by extensive formal constitutional-legal provisions, continuity rather than change has been the more pronounced feature in the Nunatsiavut Assembly. Changes can be identified, but for the most part they have been relatively minor, reflecting the institution's steady but gradual adaptation and maturation. In this concluding chapter, an examination of change and continuity in the assembly serves as a springboard to discussion of the overall significance of the assembly as the central governance institution in Canada's only Inuit self-government regime.

Change and Continuity at the Assembly

As befits a young institution, the assembly has experienced near constant changes, both formal and informal. Undoubtedly the most substantial change occurred with the 2011 opening of the fine, commodious new Assembly Building to replace the cramped, uncomfortable boardrooms of earlier meetings. The building's gravitas and permanence doubtless affected members' sense of themselves and their purpose, as well as public perception of the Nunatsiavut Government (NG) and the assembly. As well, the copious facilities of the Assembly Building allowed development of an internet audio feed of assembly proceedings, eventually slated to expand to video. Availability of the audio feed marks a notable change, even if lack of information as to timing of sessions limits its scope. Save the addition of the second Canada Constituency ordinary member in 2010, membership in the assembly has been stable in terms of numbers and composition, although high rates of turnover among members have characterized the assembly from the outset.

Continuity has been far more evident than change where the formal rules are concerned. The Standing Orders have been tweaked on several occasions: in 2010 in regard to question period, in 2013 and 2019 on various minor matters, and in 2020 to permit virtual sittings in emergency situations. Although whole-sale revision of the Standing Orders took place in 2011, virtually all the changes were minor, serving to clarify, streamline, and confirm existing practices. The most significant change at that time was the hiving off of the Standing Orders from the *Nunatsiavut Assembly Act* into a stand-alone document, so that the rules could be amended by an assembly motion rather than requiring legislation. Technical, housekeeping amendments to the act were made in 2009, 2018, and 2020. By a wide margin, the most far-reaching formal change to the operations of the assembly was the adoption in 2008 of the Code of Conduct and the disciplinary processes around it. One change of some moment occurred outside formal rules: the effective abandonment, after the first few years, of quasi-formal caucusing. The impact of this evolution is difficult to gauge, but it likely closed off certain potential lines of assembly development.

"Chaos, chaos, chaos" is how one member of the First Assembly characterized the early days. An overly harsh judgment perhaps, though certainly the First and Second Assemblies had more than their share of confusion (often occasioning recesses to determine how to proceed), strange procedures, dubious speaker's rulings, and the like. Such growing pains were only to be expected, given the lack of experience of both members and staff with the arcane mysteries of British parliamentary practice together with the need to address pressing issues while building a complex government, essentially from scratch. Before long, though, the assembly had largely overcome these initial uncertainties and inconsistencies. It helped that by the end of the Second Assembly, members had to contend with significantly fewer substantial, controversial pieces of legislation than in the early going.

As well, staff, observers, and former members agree that as members became more experienced, their comfort in their roles and with assembly processes increased markedly. The assembly's sharply reduced reliance on advice and direction from outside advisers Veryan Haysom and David Hamilton confirms this assessment. That is not to say that members have become immersed in parliamentary procedure; according to one observer, members "don't have a clue about the Standing Orders." This is likely true for some members, as it doubtless is for many other Canadian legislators, but it is also unquestionably the case that, over time, members have become more familiar with the assembly's rules and procedures and more adept at using them. Similarly, a veteran Nunatsiavut politician suggests that with more numerous and more experienced NG staff, "ministers are better prepared, more coached" than before. Still, as several of those interviewed pointed out, more comfortable and more confident are not necessarily equivalent to better. Assembly members, some suggest, especially those in the Nunatsiavut Executive Council (NEC), have become more polished and professional as politicians, but not necessarily more effective in governing, though of course this is a highly subjective judgment, impossible to evaluate at this remove. Whether the changes in members' behaviour that have rendered the assembly, in one former member's words, "less lively," is a function of different personalities or of more deeply rooted attitudinal maturation is unclear. What is beyond doubt is that the present-day assembly is patently more sedate and conventional than its early predecessors.

Minor as they generally have been, the near constant changes mean that the assembly has by no means been static or inert. Yet nothing leastways fundamental has changed. None of the principal procedures – members' and ministers' statements, question period, processes for review of legislation, the budget and the trusts, and so on – have changed more than marginally. Overall, the committee system remains much as it was when the assembly began work: largely inactive with limited impact save for occasional special committees on important, contentious issues and for the two internal committees, Members' Services and Rules and Procedures. The committee system is by no means a lost cause, as illustrated in the thorough and influential work of the two committees that dealt with the uranium moratorium. Subsequent special committees on creation of the housing commission and on voting in the Canada Constituency demonstrate that members recognize the potential of active committees, though the scope for expanding their use is substantial. Stasis in the committee system is evident in the continuing restriction of membership on the Members' Services Committee to ordinary members, despite the committee's remit to act on behalf of all members. To a substantial degree, committee inactivity is a function of the continuing unwillingness of the assembly to hire additional staff to take on research, as opposed to administrative, tasks, reflecting both concerns about cost and lack of appreciation of the potential benefits of research assistance. Beyond committees, two proposed changes that might have led to substantially enhancing the assembly's capacity to respond to NEC activities came to naught: the 2011 initiative to establish an auditor general and members' repeated interest in adding a law clerk to the assembly staff to offer independent legal advice not available from NG lawyers.

If formal structures and processes are essentially unchanged, so, too, are informal norms and patterns of behaviour. Most notably, although lapses and exceptions occur, members not only speak of their commitment to the ideal of consensus but to a substantial degree they act in accordance with consensus values. Members' reluctance to consider amending the constitution stands as further confirmation of acceptance of the status quo, regardless of whether it is rooted in a view that amending the constitution is inherently inappropriate or in an assessment that amendment would be difficult and conflictual. A key dynamic within the assembly, relations between NEC and non-NEC members, played out in similar fashion in 2022 as it did in 2006, evidenced by the continuing complaints from non-NEC members about inadequate communications from the NG and the cabinet. Two other significant continuities arise from factors beyond the assembly's control, yet they powerfully affect its operation: the minimal use of Inuttut and the low media environment.

In considering the predominance of continuity over change, it is worth recognizing that while interchanges with other legislative institutions can be an important catalyst of change, the Nunatsiavut Assembly is almost entirely isolated. It has little reason to seek information and advice from other self-government regimes since no other Indigenous self-government regime in Canada includes a Westminster-style legislature. Moreover, not only are the closest Indigenous self-governments thousands of kilometres away, but all involve First Nations, and relations between Inuit and First Nations organizations have never been strong. More promising would likely be contact with legislatures operating along Westminster lines, the federal and provincial legislatures, and especially the territorial assemblies. Even making allowance for the distinctive features of the Nunatsiavut Assembly, these institutions possess a wealth of experience in all manner of parliamentary concerns of potential value to the assembly, from procedure to staffing and services for members. Elected and appointed officials of these legislatures routinely share ideas and advice through private communications networks. As well, they meet in a host of annual conferences: elected members and senior staff gather in meetings of the Canadian Region of the Commonwealth Parliamentary Association, while speakers hold yearly get-togethers, as do clerks, sergeants-at-arms, and even chairs of public accounts committees. To be sure, these conferences involve a certain element of boondoggle, but they also facilitate exchange of information and ideas, both formally and informally.

Advice and support from other Canadian legislatures would likely be offered if requested. A long-time senior legislative official from another jurisdiction suggested as much when asked. Indeed, early on the Nunavut Legislative Assembly invited Nunatsiavut Assembly members and staff to come and observe consensus government there. For various reasons, the trip was repeatedly postponed, but in May 2014 a small Nunatsiavut delegation spent a few days in Iqaluit observing the administration and procedures of the Nunavut Legislative Assembly. Nunatsiavut speaker Sean Lyall subsequently described the visit as "a trip of a lifetime."[1] High-sounding rhetoric aside, the short official report of the visit displayed a certain envy about the prominence of Inuktitut in debate and about the legislative building's facilities, but proposed little in the way of change.[2] The "lessons" gleaned by the delegation were few in number, all relatively minor. Administratively, Nunavut's extensive page program drew attention, as did its practice of supplying members in the chamber with glasses of water rather than the expensive and wasteful bottled water provided Nunatsiavut members. The delegation also expressed interest in Nunavut's detailed *Hansard Production Guide* and its use of an Iqaluit-based firm to transcribe *Hansard*, as well as its "culturally designed Speaker's Chair."[3] In terms of procedure, save suggesting adoption of a method for reducing the formality of members' exits from the chamber, the report noted several points of divergence between the Nunavut and Nunatsiavut assemblies but made no recommendations arising from them. These included the strict time limits in Nunavut's question period as well as the extensive use by members of the Legislative Assembly (MLAs) of supplementary questions and Nunavut's practice of having members other than the speaker chair committees, including committee of the whole. The report mentioned, without comment, the research staff support available to Nunavut MLAs.[4] Few changes seem to have occurred because of the trip. Members now leave the assembly during sittings by bowing to the speaker rather than approaching her with a note, as before, and an elegant, custom-designed speaker's chair was built by a local craftsman. However, until 2021 members continued to go through large numbers of plastic water bottles during sessions. All told, this episode signals a significant reluctance to change.

The Assembly and Inuit Self-Government

Little of the foregoing speaks to the central preoccupation of this book: how the Nunatsiavut Assembly measures up as the central and most prominent component of an Inuit self-government. In approaching this question, while it is possible to analytically separate Inuit elements of the assembly from its self-governing features, their close intertwining requires that they be considered in tandem.

A recent overview of Inuit governance across the Arctic argues that the patient determination and pragmatism of the Inuit "have resulted in a variety of different institutional responses to the question of self-government and autonomy," adding that these institutions are "rooted in the grassroots and community traditions that have served Inuit peoples over thousands of years."[5] This is certainly the case in Nunatsiavut, where important elements of Labrador Inuit culture are evident in the assembly, including the legacy of the institutionalized men's meetings and the commitment to consensual decision making.

From their first encounters with Europeans, Labrador Inuit have consistently shown a marked degree of accommodation and a willingness to meld foreign institutions and ways with Inuit culture and world views. At first blush, the distinctive evolution of Labrador Inuit music may seem far removed from governance processes, but the similarities are striking and instructive. As musicologist Tom Gordon has documented, the Moravian missionaries brought with them rigidly stylized liturgical music that was vastly different from traditional Inuit music, yet the Labrador Inuit not only adopted it – they modified it in ways that rendered it thoroughly their own:

> Over time and with stalwart integrity to their identity, they transformed that imposed cultural product to something that reflected Inuit aesthetic and spiritual

values ... This music and the leadership exercised in its practice provided a vehicle for exercising Inuit agency over an imposed colonialism. The source of the original call upstairs [i.e., to the choir loft] may have been a call from the colonizer. But the answer was Inuit through and through ... Over the course of two centuries this music was gradually Indigenized, re-composed to focus on musical elements that resonated with historic Inuit expressive practices and performed in a voice that was far more Inuit than European ... The changes wrought by the imprint of the Inuit voice have transformed this once colonial music into an expression of Labrador Inuit identity.[6]

In similar fashion, while the structure and tenets of the Westminster cabinet-parliamentary system are decidedly foreign to traditional Inuit ways, the Labrador Inuit have placed their distinctive stamp on the organization and operation of their assembly. Adoption of the Westminster model with substantial and distinctive modifications is very much in line with an accommodative melding approach to governance. Both in everyday practical terms for Nunatsiavumiut and in theoretical terms for academics interested in Indigenous self-government, the NG and the assembly stand at the intersection of Western and Indigenous governance traditions. Especially considering the power of the Westminster model to shape politicians' behaviour to accord with its processes, the direction in which the interplay between Inuit and Western governance approaches leads is of serious concern. In identifying key challenges and opportunities facing the NG and the Labrador Inuit, three academics familiar with Nunatsiavut noted particularly "maintenance of traditional institutions of government and governance."[7]

The Westminster framework may lack ties to traditional Inuit culture, though the choice of a familiar, proven governance model is very much in keeping with a central element of Inuit culture, pragmatism. The far-reaching modifications to the Westminster system can be directly traced to a desire for self-government, and self-government with an Inuit character. Prime among the important deviations from standard Westminster structural forms are the grafting on to the assembly of a powerful, popularly elected president, the inclusion of the AngajukKât and community chairs as assembly members, and the extension of representation to beneficiaries living outside Nunatsiavut proper, in the Upper Lake Melville area and throughout Canada. All were designed to recognize and enhance distinctively Inuit self-government, as were lesser but nonetheless noteworthy structural features of the assembly, such as provisions for ensuring women's participation on assembly committees and for adding non-assembly members to committees as well as the remarkably tough Code of Conduct process.

It may not be evident in assembly debate, which is overwhelmingly carried out in English, but the institution's Inuit character is nevertheless fundamental to its structure and operation. First and foremost, of course, is the essential reality that only Inuit may vote for and serve as members of the assembly.[8] The requirement that the president speak and understand Inuttut is noteworthy but of far less moment than the thoroughgoing and widely honoured commitment to consensus in assembly proceedings and decision making. Anything as amorphous as consensual legislative behaviour may not be amenable to measurement, but it would appear that, rather than declining over time, as might be expected of a noble but perhaps impractical aspiration, the consensus imperative is stronger in the assembly currently than in the early days. The dramatic decline in the (always low) number of "split votes" detailed in chapter 8 suggests as much. Various factors are at play, including changes in assembly membership and the infrequency of big, contentious issues. Several members and observers suggested that greater recourse to the informal committee of the whole encourages consensual behaviour. One NG official who has dealt extensively with the assembly believes that maturation born of experience has contributed to members' greater willingness to strive for consensus, especially with respect to legislation. In a way that wasn't as true in the early days, this interpretation runs, members now recognize and accept that while they may not agree with all elements of a bill, if overall it is worthwhile, it warrants support. This, the official suggests, is consensus decision making in operation. Just as government by consensus defies anything like precise measurement, so, too, members' adherence to what they term "the Inuit way" cannot be systematically analysed, but it unquestionably affects members' behaviour both in the assembly and in their wider roles as representatives.

Assessing its individual features in order to determine the extent to which the assembly is characterized by and contributes to Inuit culture and self-government is a necessary exercise but it overlooks an elemental yet fundamentally important reality: the very existence of a substantial government speaks directly to Inuit self-government. No one expects the NG to function flawlessly in resolving the problems facing Nunatsiavumiut or in meeting their social, cultural, and political aspirations, and neither do politicians. Nor have members of the Inuit public been shy in calling out the NG for various deficiencies. Nevertheless, whatever its shortcomings, the NG stands as an avowedly Inuit self-government that figures prominently in the lives of all beneficiaries in the Labrador Inuit Settlement Area, if less so for others living outside Nunatsiavut proper. NG's success as an Inuit self-government depends on its effectiveness in delivering programs and services and on the assembly's effectiveness in fulfilling its legislative functions.

Also key, however, is symbolism, with the Nunatsiavut Assembly Building itself the most prominent symbol. Politicians are often given to overblown rhetoric when opening major capital projects, but the words of President Jim Lyall at the start of the first session in the new Assembly Building ring true:

The Nunatsiavut Assembly building, Madame Speaker, serves as a symbol of our strength as a people, and a resolve to control our own destiny, and a reflection of the great changes that we are making as a Government, not only here in Hopedale, but throughout the whole of Nunatsiavut. This is a very impressive building, Madame Speaker, something all Labrador Inuit should be proud to call their own.[9]

A leading figure from the Labrador Inuit Association days maintains that having an impressive, dedicated Assembly Building has made a substantial difference not only in how the NG is perceived, but also in the attitudes and behaviour of the members. The Assembly Building, in this view, provides a sense of formality and an impression of "a real government" that wasn't possible when the assembly met in cramped boardrooms lacking facilities.

Final Words

The shortcomings of the Nunatsiavut Assembly are many and substantial. To name a few: an underdeveloped committee system; a lack of research staff; ponderous, overly formal proceedings; unsatisfactory communications between NEC and non-NEC members; needlessly short sessions that limit members' opportunities to carry out their duties; and lack of involvement by elders and youth. The two previous chapters, which examined the assembly's effectiveness in fulfilling basic legislative functions, found its performance uneven in terms of representation, policymaking, and accountability, and seriously lacking in informing and educating the Inuit public on the issues of the day. Legislatures worldwide fall short, often far short, in discharging these responsibilities, so it comes as no surprise that the assembly is found wanting, though of course this is not to say that it shouldn't strive to do better, as indeed it could with respect to the shortcomings identified above.

Is it reasonable to criticize the assembly on the basis of standards, some implicit, established for legislatures with far more resources and far more experience to draw upon? I didn't pose that question to assembly members or NG staff, but I suspect that, had I done so, they would have been – quite properly – offended and insulted. While the assembly may be short on resources and experience, a prime rationale for self-government entails providing beneficiaries with the best possible government, including not just tangible policy outcomes but also modes of operation. That they cannot always achieve the best does not mean that members do not strive for it or that they would accept the idea of setting lower standards for themselves (witness the Code of Conduct). The key is that the assembly sets the standards, based on Inuit culture and traditions.

That any governmental institution falls short of the ideal is hardly unexpected. More importantly, enumeration of weaknesses must be counterbalanced with acknowledgment of strengths. Aside from the specific procedural and operational strengths discussed throughout the book, one elemental strength warrants highlighting – the assembly's very existence and raison d'être. That a small group of resource-strapped Indigenous people living far from mainstream Canada could design and operate a sophisticated parliamentary institution, adapting it to their particular needs and circumstances, is nothing less than remarkable.

Furthermore, a particular aspect mentioned only briefly in chapter 9's discussion of the assembly's effectiveness in representation bears emphasis. The distinctive nature of Nunatsiavut as a self-governing Inuit territory comes to the fore in the manifold ways in which assembly members, albeit often implicitly, give voice to the political, social, and cultural aspirations of Nunatsiavumiut. This may entail comments about specific NG activities on issues such as language enhancement or food insecurity, or it may take more abstract form, reiterating the principles of the treaty and the constitution. Indeed, it is noteworthy how often and how passionately members emphasize the centrality to their roles as legislators of their commitment to the values and the objectives, and in turn to specific provisions, of the claim and the constitution.

The importance to the Labrador Inuit of having their own government, a government operating to a substantial degree in accordance with Inuit culture, is a constant theme of assembly debate. The resolve to respect consensus and to abide by "the Inuit way" in conducting assembly business is a reflection of members' commitment to making Inuit self-government work in Nunatsiavut. So, too, in its own way, is the draconian Code of Conduct. Just as the Assembly Building symbolizes the strength and indeed the very existence of the Nunatsiavut Government, an important measure of the success of the NG and the Nunatsiavut Assembly is the confidence it bespeaks among both politicians and Nunatsiavumiut generally of their capacity to govern themselves. Various prominent political figures have been quoted in this book regarding the significance of Nunatsiavut's status as a self-governing Inuit region. The final word goes to a minister, who acknowledged in an interview the NG's shortcomings but asserted a key element of its success: "we're really strong on running our own show; this comes from the strength of our culture and our traditional knowledge."

Notes

Preface and Acknowledgments

1 UN General Assembly, Resolution 61/295, United Nations Declaration on the Rights of Indigenous Peoples, A/RES/61/295 (13 September 2007), articles 3 and 4.

2 See, for example, Nicole McMahon and Christopher Alcantara, "Running for Elected Office: Indigenous Candidates, Ambition and Self-Government," *Politics, Groups and Identities* 9, no. 2 (2021): 280–99; Michelle Caplan, Nicole McMahon, and Christopher Alcantara, "Representing the Constituency: Institutional Design and Legislative Behaviour," *Representation* 57, no. 4 (October 2021): 459–74.

1 Inuit Self-Government and the Nunatsiavut Assembly

1 On the difference between public and self-government, see Frances Abele and Michael Prince, "Four Pathways to Aboriginal Self-Government in Canada," *American Review of Canadian Studies* 36, no. 4 (December 2006), 568–95.

2 See Crown-Indigenous Relations and Northern Affairs Canada, "Self-Government," Government of Canada, last modified 25 August 2020, https://www.rcaanc-cirnac.gc.ca/eng/1100100032275/1529354547314.

3 Gary Wilson, Christopher Alcantara, and Thierry Rodon, *Nested Federalism and Inuit Governance in the Canadian Arctic* (Vancouver: UBC Press, 2020), 43.

4 The next largest self-government, the Nisga'a Lisims Government, has roughly 6,000 members and about 120 full-time staff. Adam Perry, *NLG – MAEST Labour Market Study Final Report* (New Aiyansh, BC: Nisga'a Lisims Government, March 2020), 9, http://www.nisgaanation.ca/sites/default/files/Final%20NLG%20LMI%20Report%281%29_0.pdf; personal communication from Nisga'a Lisims Government official, 18 March 2021. Nunatsiavut, by contrast, has over 7,000 beneficiaries and over 400 staff.

5 The word is often rendered as "Nunatsiavummiut" (i.e., with a double *m*). Consultation with interpreters at the assembly and with linguists suggest that "Nunatsiavumiut" is more correct.

6 Nunatsiavut Government, *Parliamentary Report* (henceforth, *Hansard*), 20 November 2019, 119–20.

7 Wilson, Alcantara, and Rodon describe the NG as "quasi-presidential": *Nested Federalism*, 138. Reviewing the book in manuscript form, one reader objected to my characterization of the assembly as a Westminster institution, on the grounds that having as a member of the assembly a powerful, popularly elected president is simply incompatible with Westminster principles. This is a valid point, but my view is that the assembly operates very much along Westminster rather than presidential lines, such as in the quasi-presidential French system, and thus warrants description as quasi-Westminster. In his review of self-government regimes, Nikolakis uses the term "blended Westminster models" to describe legislatures combining Westminster principles and traditional Indigenous elements such as inclusion of hereditary chiefs: William Nikolakis, "The Evolution of Indigenous Self-Governance in Canada," in *Reclaiming Indigenous Governance: Reflections and Insights from Australia, Canada, New Zealand and the United States*, ed. William Nikolakis, Stephen Cornell, and Harry W. Nelson (Tucson: University of Arizona Press, 2019), 63. In the end, the label matters less than the reality of how the institution functions.

8 Lisa K. Rankin, *An Archeological View of the Thule/Inuit Occupation of Labrador* (St. John's: Memorial University of Newfoundland, May 2009), https://www.mun.ca/labmetis/pdf/thule_inuit%20final%20report.pdf, and William W. Fitzhugh, "Indian and Eskimo/Inuit Settlement History in Labrador: An Archeological View," in *Our Footprints Are Everywhere: Inuit Land Use and Occupancy*, ed. Carol Brice-Bennett (Nain: Labrador Inuit Association, 1977), 1–41.

9 Veryan Haysom, "The Struggle for Recognition: Labrador Inuit Negotiations for Land Rights and Self-Government," *Études/Inuit/Studies* 16, nos. 1–2 (1992): 181.

10 These are data from the 2021 census: Statistics Canada, "Census Profile, 2021 Census of Population," Government of Canada, last modified 17 May 2022, https://www12.statcan.gc.ca/census-recensement/2021/dp-pd/prof/search-recherche/lst/results-resultats.cfm?Lang=E&GEOCODE=10. The NG strongly disputes the 2021 figure for Nain (847) and has sought a review from Statistics Canada; accordingly for Nain, the 2016 figure is used.

11 John C. Kennedy, "Identity Politics," in *History and Renewal of Labrador's Inuit-Métis*, ed. John C. Kennedy (St. John's: ISER Books, 2014), 245.

12 My thanks to Sheila Angnatok, NG registrar of beneficiaries, for providing data on numbers of beneficiaries. Owing to the complex membership requirements, discussed in chapter 4, some Nunatsiavumiut who would be eligible for membership are not enrolled.

13 Statistics Canada, "Inuit: Fact Sheet for Nunatsiavut," Government of Canada, 29 March 2016, https://www150.statcan.gc.ca/n1/pub/89-656-x/89-656-x2016015-eng.htm.

14 Paula Arrigada and Amanda Bleakney, "Inuit Participation in the Wage and Land-Based Economies in Inuit Nunangat," Statistics Canada Catalogue 89–653–2019002, 2019, 5.

15 Labrador Inuit Capital Strategy Trust, *Nunatsiavut Group of Companies, 2020 Annual Report* (Happy Valley–Goose Bay: Nunatsiavut Group of Companies, 2021), 12.
16 Methodological note: although the *Hansard* text is invaluable and fully searchable electronically, watching video recordings of sessions offers insights not possible through reading transcripts. Intonation, body language (of both speakers and listeners), and overall ambiance of discussion are evident in ways not apparent on the printed page. As well, *Hansard* only records vote totals, not individual members' votes, whereas the videos can reveal which members supported or opposed particular motions (see the analysis of "split" votes in chapter 8).
17 *Hansard*, 11 June 2013, 79.

2 The Labrador Inuit: History, Society, Culture, and Political Institutions

1 Andrea Procter and Keith Chaulk, "Our Beautiful Land: Current Debates in Land Use Planning in Nunatsiavut," in *Settlement, Subsistence, and Change among the Labrador Inuit: The Nunatsiavummiut Experience*, ed. David C. Natcher, Lawrence Felt, and Andrea Procter (Winnipeg: University of Manitoba Press, 2012), 439, 438.
2 William W. Fitzhugh, "Indian and Eskimo/Inuit Settlement History in Labrador: An Archeological View," in *Our Footprints Are Everywhere: Inuit Land Use and Occupancy*, ed. Carol Brice-Bennett (Nain: Labrador Inuit Association, 1977), 21.
3 Lisa K. Rankin, *An Archeological View of the Thule/Inuit Occupation of Labrador* (St. John's: Memorial University of Newfoundland, May 2009), 26, https://www.mun.ca/labmetis/pdf/thule_inuit%20final%20report.pdf.
4 Ibid.
5 Diamond Jenness, *Eskimo Administration: III, Labrador* (Montreal: Arctic Institute of North America, 1965), 9.
6 Lisa Rankin, Matthew Beaudoin, and Natalie Brewster, "Southern Exposure: The Inuit of Sandwich Bay, Labrador," in Natcher, Felt, and Procter, eds., *Settlement, Subsistence and Change*, 61.
7 This and subsequent sections particularly draw on, among others, Jenness, *Eskimo Administration*; Helge Kleivan, *The Eskimos of Northeast Labrador: A History of Eskimo-White Relations 1771–1955* (Oslo: Norsk Polarinstitutt, 1966); Barrett Richling, "Hard Times, Them Times: An Interpretive Ethnohistory of Inuit and Settlers in the Hopedale District of Northern Labrador, 1752–1977" (PhD diss., McGill University, 1978); Carol Brice-Bennett, "Two Opinions: Inuit and Moravian Missionaries in Labrador, 1804–1860" (master's thesis, Memorial University of Newfoundland, 1981); Lawrence A. Dunn, "Negotiating Cultural Identities: Conflict Transformation in Labrador" (PhD diss., University of Syracuse, 2002); Peter Evans, "Transformations of Inuit Resistance and Identity in Northern Labrador, 1771–1959" (PhD diss., Cambridge University, 2013); Andrea Procter, *A Long Journey: Residential Schools in Labrador and Newfoundland* (St. John's: ISER Books, 2020).
8 Kleivan, *The Eskimos of Northeast Labrador*, 79.

9 James Hiller, "Early Patrons of the Labrador Eskimos: The Moravian Mission in Labrador, 1764–1805," in *Patrons and Brokers in the Eastern Arctic*, ed. Robert Paine (St. John's: Memorial University of Newfoundland, Institute of Social and Economic Research, 1971), 84.

10 Brice-Bennett, "Two Opinions," 15.

11 Anne Brantenberg, "The Marginal School and the Children of Nain," in *The White Arctic: Anthropological Essays on Tutelage and Ethnicity*, ed. Robert Paine (St. John's: Memorial University of Newfoundland, Institute of Social and Economic Research, 1977), 345; see also Carol Brice-Bennett, "Missionaries as Traders: Moravians and Labrador Inuit, 1771–1860," in *Merchant Credit and Labour Strategies in Historical Perspective*, ed. Rosemary Ommer (Fredericton, NB: Acadiensis Press, 1990), 225.

12 Jenness, *Eskimo Administration*, 38.

13 Ibid., 245–6.

14 Kleivan, *Eskimos of Northeast Labrador*, 123.

15 Ailsa Henderson, *Nunavut: Rethinking Political Culture* (Vancouver: UBC Press, 2007), 51, 52, 54.

16 Procter, *Long Journey*, 51–2.

17 Kleivan, *Eskimos of Northeast Labrador*, 101.

18 Brantenberg, "Marginal School," 345; Procter quotes a 2010 interview with a former boarding school student about students being strapped for speaking English: Procter, *Long Journey*, 137.

19 Procter, *Long Journey*, 8.

20 Ibid., 45.

21 Kleivan, *Eskimos of Northeast Labrador*, 80.

22 Jenness, *Eskimo Administration*, 39.

23 Brice-Bennett, "Two Opinions," 199.

24 Kleivan, *Eskimos of Northeast Labrador*, 88.

25 John C. Kennedy, "Aboriginal Organizations and Their Claims: The Case of Newfoundland and Labrador," *Canadian Ethnic Studies* 19, no. 2 (1987): 22.

26 H. Anthony Williamson, "The Moravian Mission and Its Impact on the Labrador Eskimo," *Arctic Anthropology* 2, no. 2 (1964): 35, 32.

27 Jenness, *Eskimo Administration*, 20.

28 Brice-Bennett, "Two Opinions," 471, iii.

29 Kleivan, *Eskimos of Northeast Labrador*, 71.

30 Evans, "Transformations," 150.

31 Procter, *Long Journey*, 137, 367.

32 Brice-Bennett, "Two Opinions," iv.

33 On the chapel servants, see Hans J. Rollman, " 'So that in this part you should not lag behind other missionary congregations … ' The Introduction of National Helpers in the Moravian Mission among the Labrador Inuit," *Journal of Moravian History* 17, no. 2 (2017): 138–59.

34 Brice-Bennett, "Two Opinions," 355.

35 Evans, "Transformations," 8, 20. Evans's important analysis of Labrador Inuit political institutions is laid out later in the chapter.

36 Robert Paine, "Tutelage and Ethnicity, a Variable Relationship," in Paine, ed., *White Arctic*, 252.

37 Brice-Bennett, "Two Opinions," 96, 100, 105, 107.

38 John C. Kennedy, *Encounters: An Anthropological History of Southeastern Labrador* (Montreal: McGill-Queen's University Press, 2015), 323.

39 Ibid., 4.

40 Christopher Alcantara, *Negotiating the Deal: Comprehensive Land Claims Agreements in Canada* (Toronto: University of Toronto Press, 2013), 51–72.

41 Procter, *Long Journey*, 401.

42 Brice-Bennett, "Two Opinions," 442–3.

43 Procter, *Long Journey*, 57.

44 John C. Kennedy, ed., *History and Renewal of Labrador's Inuit-Métis* (St. Johns: ISER Books, 2014), 6.

45 Kleivan, *Eskimos of Northeast Labrador*, 90.

46 Shmuel Ben-Dor, "Inuit-Settler Relations in Makkovik, 1962," in Paine, ed., *White Arctic*, 310, 312, 314.

47 John C. Kennedy, "Northern Labrador: An Ethnocultural Account," in Paine, ed., *White Arctic*, 275

48 Hugh Brody, "Permanence and Change among the Inuit and Settlers of Labrador," in Brice-Bennett, ed., *Our Footprints Are Everywhere*, 317.

49 Procter, *Long Journey*, 346–54; see also Dunn, "Negotiating Cultural Identities," 153–4, and Kennedy, *Encounters*, 325.

50 Richling, "Hard Times," 7.

51 Procter, *Long Journey*, 57.

52 John C. Kennedy, "Introduction," in Kennedy, ed., *History and Renewal*, 17.

53 Ibid., 11. NANL changed its name to the Indian and Métis Association of Newfoundland and Labrador; after the Innu left IMANL, it "eventually returned to Newfoundland [i.e., the island]," changing its name to the Federation of Newfoundland Indians and later the Qalipu Mi'kmaq First Nation: John C. Kennedy, "Being and Becoming Inuit in Labrador," *Études/Inuit/Studies* 39, no 1 (2015): 230. At its founding, full LIA members had to be residents of Labrador and fluent in Inuttut; those lacking either qualification could only be non-voting associate members: comments from Sean Lyall, ordinary member for Nain, Nunatsiavut Government, *Hansard*, 3 February 2016, 104–5.

54 Kennedy, "Being and Becoming," 231n10. This approach followed the policy of the federal government, which reluctantly accepted responsibility for Inuit in the 1950s. In determining who was Inuit, and thus eligible for government benefits, Ottawa bureaucrats opted to identify specific communities, rather than

individuals, as Inuit: Andrea Procter, "Uranium and the Boundaries of Indigeneity in Nunatsiavut, Labrador," *Extractive Industries and Society* 3, no. 2 (2016): 289.

55 Dunn, "Negotiating Cultural Identities," 12–3, 90.

56 Ibid., 236.

57 Kennedy, "Being and Becoming Inuit," 231.

58 Kennedy, "Identity Politics," 255.

59 Kennedy, "Being and Becoming Inuit," 237.

60 Ibid., 232.

61 Dunn, "Negotiating Cultural Identities," 13. Unsurprisingly, the Métis of Western Canada did not consider the Labrador Métis to be true Métis, for "while the ethnicity of Labrador Metis resembles Canadian Metis structurally in that both are mixed peoples, it is also objectively different – other Canadian Metis are descendants of European-Indian rather than European-Inuit unions": John C. Kennedy, "The Changing Significance of Labrador Settler Ethnicity," *Canadian Ethnic Studies* 20, no. 3 (1988), 105.

62 Rankin, Beaudoin, and Brewster, "Southern Exposure," 61.

63 Kennedy, "Introduction," 2.

64 CBC, *Labrador Morning*, podcast, September 17, 2021, https://www.cbc.ca/listen/live-radio/1-31-labrador-morning/clip/d20210917-friday-sep.-17-2021; NunatuKavut Community Council, "Who We Are," Nunatukavut.ca, accessed 27 July 2022, https://nunatukavut.ca/about/who-we-are/.

65 Cited in Andrea Procter, "The Prospects of Culture: Resource Management and the Production of Difference in Nunatsiavut, Labrador" (PhD diss., Memorial University of Newfoundland, 2012), 196.

66 Jim Bell, "Despite the Naysayers, Southern Labrador Inuit Rise Up to Claim Their Rights," *Nunatsiaq News*, 5 March 2020.

67 Nunatsiavut Government, "Nunatsiavut Government Responds to NunatuKavut Community Council Land Claim," media release, 16 September 2021, https://nunatsiavut.com/media-release-nunatsiavut-government-responds-to-nunatukavut-community-council-land-claim/. See also Nunatsiavut Government, "Statement from President Lampe Regarding the NunatuKavut Community Council Land Claim," media release, 16 September 2021, https://nunatsiavut.com/statement-from-president-lampe-regarding-the-nunatsiavut-governments-response-to-nunatukavut-community-council-land-claim/.

68 CBC, *Labrador Morning*, podcast, September 17, 2021, https://www.cbc.ca/listen/live-radio/1-31-labrador-morning/clip/d20210917-friday-sep.-17-2021.

69 Procter, *Long Journey*, 347.

70 This observation reflects my discussions with several knowledgeable long-time participants in and observers of Labrador Inuit politics.

71 Marc G. Stevenson, *Traditional Inuit Decision-Making Structures and the Administration of Nunavut* (Ottawa: Royal Commission on Aboriginal Peoples, 1993), especially 43 and 65.

72 Jean L. Briggs, *Never in Anger: Portrait of an Eskimo Family* (Cambridge, MA: Harvard University Press, 1970), 49.

73 Ibid., 67.

74 Ibid., 4.

75 Pauktuutit Inuit Women of Canada, *The Inuit Way: A Guide to Inuit Culture* (Ottawa: Pauktuutit, 2006), 30; see also Hugh Brody, *Living Arctic: Hunters of the Canadian North* (Vancouver: Douglas and McIntyre, 1987), 11, 229.

76 Pauktuutit, *Inuit Way*, 32.

77 Henderson, *Nunavut*, 55.

78 Pauktuutit, *Inuit Way*, 10–13.

79 Henderson, *Nunavut*, 42.

80 Pauktuutit, *Inuit Way*, 34.

81 Hugh Body, *The People's Land: Inuit, Whites and the Eastern Arctic* (Vancouver: Douglas and McIntyre, 1975), 157; Brody, *Living Arctic*, 123, 125.

82 Pauktuutit, *Inuit Way*, 11–12; F.G. Vallee, *Kabloona and Eskimo in the Central Keewatin* (Ottawa: Canadian Research Centre for Anthropology, 1967), 192; Evans, "Transformations," 84.

83 See Pauktuutit, *Inuit Way*, 9. The quotation comes from Brody, *Living Arctic*, 121, 123. Here, as in much of the book, Brody is referring to the Dene of the Western Arctic as well as the Inuit.

84 Pauktuutit, *Inuit Way*, 30; Stevenson, "Traditional Inuit Decision-Making Structures"; Gurston Dacks, *The Adaptation of Public Governing Institutions in the Territorial North* (Ottawa: Royal Commission on Aboriginal Peoples, 1973), 7–11.

85 Pauktuutit, *Inuit Way*, 34.

86 Susan A. Kaplan, "Labrador Inuit Ingenuity and Resourcefulness: Adapting to a Complex Environmental, Social and Spiritual Environment" in Natcher, Felt, and Procter, eds., *Settlement, Subsistence, and Change*, 28; see also Procter, *Long Journey*, 22: "as they still do today, Inuit understood the need to adapt to changing situations and the importance of remaining flexible."

87 Richling, "Hard Times," 10.

88 Vallee, *Kabloona and Eskimo*, 187.

89 Ibid., ch. 9.

90 Evans, "Transformations," 217.

91 Ibid., abstract.

92 Ibid., 57.

93 Ibid., 58.

94 Kleivan, *Eskimos of Northeast Labrador*, 73.

95 Evans, "Transformations," 118, 124.

96 Richling, "Hard Times," 126, 128, 127.

97 Evans, "Transformation," 159.

98 Tom Gordon, *Called Upstairs: Moravian Inuit Music in Labrador* (Montreal: McGill-Queen's University Press, 2023), 228, 231.

99 David Lough, "Labrador Inuit Leadership – 1970s to 2005," in *Voices of Inuit Leadership and Self-determination in Canada*, ed. David Lough (St. John's: ISER Books, 2020), 97.

100 Richling, "Hard Times," 335.

101 Lough, "Labrador Inuit Leadership," 98.

102 Evans, "Transformations," 213.

103 Adrian Tanner, John C. Kennedy, Susan McCorquodale, and Gordon Inglis, *Aboriginal Peoples and Governance in Newfoundland and Labrador* (Ottawa: Royal Commission on Aboriginal Peoples, 1974), 26.

104 Peter Evans, "Abandoned and Ousted by the State: The Relocations from Nutak and Hebron, 1956–1959," in Natcher, Felt, and Procter, eds., *Settlement, Subsistence and Change*, 85.

105 Andrea Procter, "Uranium, Inuit Rights, and Emergent Neoliberalism in Labrador, 1956–2012," in *Mining and Communities in Northern Canada: History, Politics, and Memory*, ed. Arn Keeling and John Sandlos (Calgary: University of Calgary Press, 2015), 250–1.

106 Procter, "The Prospects of Culture," 135.

107 Procter, "Uranium and the Boundaries," 290.

108 Dunn, "Negotiating Cultural Identities," 106–7.

109 Andrea Procter, Lawrence Felt, and David C. Natcher, "Introduction," in Natcher, Felt, and Procter, eds., *Settlement, Subsistence, and Change*, 4.

110 Evans, "Transformations," 153.

111 Labrador Inuit Association, *A Statement of a Claim to Certain Rights in the Land and Sea-Ice in Northern Labrador by the Inuit and Native People: Presented to the Government of Canada*, 1976.

112 Procter, Felt and Natcher, "Introduction," 4.

113 For an account of the negotiation of the LIA claim, see Alcantara, *Negotiating the Deal*, 41–51; Veryan Haysom, "Labrador Inuit Land Claims: Aboriginal Rights and Interests v. Federal and Provincial Responsibilities and Authorities," *Northern Perspectives* 18, no. 2 (1990): 6–10; and Gary Wilson, Christopher Alcantara, and Thierry Rodon, *Nested Federalism and Inuit Governance in the Canadian Arctic* (Vancouver: UBC Press, 2020), 74–9.

114 Henderson, *Nunavut*, 217.

115 Evans, "Transformations," 136.

116 Procter, *Long Journey*, 378.

117 On the construction and emergence and political uses of Inuit identity, see Procter, "Prospects of Culture," especially 71–9 and 90.

118 Procter, *Long Journey*, 20.

3 Comprehensive Land Claims and Indigenous Self-Government

1 This section draws upon Graham White, "Shaping the Northern Political Landscape: Comprehensive Land Claims Agreements," *Northern Public Affairs* 6, Special Issue 2 (December 2019): 23–6.

2 For the federal government's perspective on specific claims and an outline of the specific claim process, see Crown-Indigenous Relations and Northern Affairs Canada, "Specific Claims," Government of Canada, last modified 1 December 2021, https://www.rcaanc-cirnac.gc.ca/eng/1100100030291/1539617582343.

3 A potentially important exception was the 1765 friendship treaty between Governor Hugh Palliser and the Inuit of southern Labrador. Although the brief treaty makes no reference either to governance or to control of land, the NunatuKavut Community Council bases its claim to self-government on the treaty: NunatuKavut Community Council, "British-Inuit Treaty of 1765," Nunatukavut.ca, accessed 27 July 2022, https://nunatukavut.ca/about/treaty-of-1765/. For specifics of the treaty, see Greg Mitchell, "The Palliser Friendship Treaty: The Esquimeaux-British Treaty of Southern Labrador (August 21, 1765)," *Labrador Quarterly* 98, no. 1 (2005): 48–50.

4 It is often incorrectly asserted that the *Calder* decision, which the Nisga'a Nation lost on a technicality but which nonetheless showed the fragility of the government position on ownership of land on which "Aboriginal title" had never been extinguished, forced Ottawa to develop a land claims policy. As Christa Scholtz has demonstrated through analysis of cabinet documents, while *Calder* doubtless hastened the process, the federal government was already close to implementing a comprehensive claims policy. See her *Negotiating Claims: The Emergence of Indigenous Land Claim Negotiation Policies in Australia, Canada, New Zealand, and the United States* (New York: Routledge, 2006), ch. 3.

5 See Minister of Indian Affairs and Northern Development, *Land Claims Agreement between the Inuit of Labrador and her Majesty the Queen in Right of Newfoundland and Labrador and her Majesty the Queen in Right of Canada*, 2004. For a plain-language summary of the treaty, see Labrador Inuit Association, *Understanding the Labrador Inuit Land Claims Agreement* (Nain: LIA, 2005).

6 The LIA still exists, at least on paper. Members of the assembly are the board members, but LIA has no funds and is not engaged in providing programs or services. According to one NG official, "it does not function other than [to] maintain its legal existence."

7 Andrea Procter and Keith Chaulk, "Our Beautiful Land: Current Debates in Land Use Planning in Nunatsiavut," in *Settlement, Subsistence, and Change among the Labrador Inuit: The Nunatsiavummiut Experience*, ed. David C. Natcher, Lawrence Felt, and Andrea Procter (Winnipeg: University of Manitoba Press, 2012), 232, 248.

8 Wendy Moss, "Inuit Perspectives on Treaty Rights and Governance," in *Aboriginal Self-Government: Legal and Constitutional Issues*, ed. Patrick Macklem (Ottawa: Royal Commission on Aboriginal Peoples, 1995), 97.

9 Glen Coulthard, *Red Skin, White Masks: Rejecting the Colonial Politics of Recognition* (Minneapolis: University of Minnesota Press, 2014), 67.

10 Yale D. Belanger, "Introduction," in *Aboriginal Self-Government in Canada: Current Trends and Issues*, ed Yale D. Belanger, 3rd ed. (Saskatoon: Purich Publishing, 2008), ix.

11 Royal Commission on Aboriginal Peoples (RCAP), *Report of the Royal Commission on Aboriginal Peoples*, vol. 2, *Restructuring the Relationship* (Ottawa: Supply and Services Canada, 1996), 169.

12 Stephen Cornell, "From Rights to Governance and Back: Indigenous Political Transformation in the CANZUS States," in *Reclaiming Indigenous Governance: Reflections and Insights from Australia, Canada, New Zealand and the United States*, ed. William Nikolakis, Stephen Cornell, and Harry W. Nelson (Tucson: University of Arizona Press, 2019), 16.

13 Ibid., 17.

14 Belanger, "Introduction," vii.

15 RCAP, *Partners in Confederation: Aboriginal Peoples, Self-Government, and the Constitution* (Ottawa: Supply and Services Canada, 1993), 41.

16 Catherine Bell and Harold Robinson, "Government on the Métis Settlements: Foundations and Future Directions," in Belanger, ed., *Aboriginal Self-Government*, 261.

17 Janet French, "Alberta Métis Settlements Challenging Provincial Legislation in Court," CBC News, 28 July 2021, https://www.cbc.ca/news/canada/edmonton/alberta-m%C3%A9tis-settlements-challenging-provincial-legislation-in-court-1.6120299.

18 Gary Wilson, Christopher Alcantara, and Thierry Rodon, *Nested Federalism and Inuit Governance in the Canadian Arctic* (Vancouver: UBC Press, 2020), 4.

19 Gary N. Wilson, "Nunavik and the Multiple Dimensions of Inuit Governance," *American Review of Canadian Studies* 47 (2017): 154.

20 Graham White, *Indigenous Empowerment through Co-management: Land Claims Boards, Wildlife Management and Environmental Regulation* (Vancouver: UBC Press, 2020), ch. 6 and 262–4.

21 This literature is far too extensive to list here. Good overviews are available in RCAP, *Report*, 2:ch. 3; Yale D. Belanger and David Newhouse, "Emerging from the Shadows: The Pursuit of Aboriginal Self-Government to Promote Aboriginal Well-being," *Canadian Journal of Native Studies* 24, no. 1 (2004): 129–222, and Belanger, ed., *Aboriginal Self-Government*.

22 See Richard J. Diubaldo, "The Absurd Little Mouse: When Eskimos Became Indians," *Journal of Canadian Studies* 16, no. 2 (Summer 1981): 34–40.

23 John H. Hylton, "Foreword: From Theory to Practice to Best Practices," in Belanger, ed., *Aboriginal Self-Government*, iv. Hylton had edited earlier editions of the book.

24 See, for example, Gurston Dacks, "Implementing First Nations Self Government in Yukon: Lessons for Canada," *Canadian Journal of Political Science* 37, no. 3 (September 2004): 671–94; Thierry Rodon and Minnie Grey, "The Long and Winding Road to Self-Government: Nunavik and Nunatsiavut Experiences," in *Northern Exposure: Peoples, Powers and Prospects in Canada's North*, ed. Frances Abele, Thomas J. Courchene, F. Leslie Seidle, and France St-Hilaire (Montreal: Institute for Research on Public Policy, 2007), 317–43; and chapters in Belanger, ed., *Aboriginal Self-Government*.

25 See, for example, Ross Hoffman and Andrew Robinson, "Nisga'a Self-Government: A New Journey Has Begun," *Canadian Journal of Native Studies* 30, no. 2 (2010): 387–415; chapters in Belanger, ed., *Aboriginal Self-Government in Canada*; Tracie Lea Scott, *Postcolonial Sovereignty? The Nisga'a Final Agreement* (Vancouver: UBC Press; Saskatoon: Purich Publishing, 2012).

26 Kelly Saunders and Janique Dubois, *Métis Politics and Governance* (Vancouver: UBC Press, 2019). See also Larry Chartrand, "'We Rise Again: Métis Traditional Governance and the Claim to Métis Self-Government," in Belanger, ed., *Aboriginal Self Government*, 145–57.

27 Nikolakis, Cornell, and Nelson, eds., *Reclaiming Indigenous Governance*.

28 Wilson, Alcantara, and Rodon, *Nested Federalism*.

29 Hylton, "Foreward," iii.

30 Angela Wesley, "Ancient Spirit, Modern Mind: The Huu-ay-aht Journey Back to Self-Determination and Self- Reliance," in Nikoladis, Cornell, and Nelson, eds., *Reclaiming Indigenous Governance*, 108. See also Garry Merkel in the same volume, "Conclusion: Building Yourself and Your Community," 306–19.

31 Ken S. Coates and W.R. Morrison, "From Panacea to Reality: The Practicalities of Canadian Self-Government Agreements," in Belanger, ed., *Aboriginal Self-Government*, 120; William Nikolakis, "The Evolution of Indigenous Self-Governance in Canada," in Nikoladis, Cornell, and Nelson, eds., *Reclaiming Indigenous Governance*, 55.

32 RCAP, *Report*, 2:775.

33 Cornell, "From Rights to Governance," 27.

34 Nikolakis, "Evolution of Indigenous Self-Governance," 55.

35 Coates and Morrison, "From Panacea to Reality," 117.

36 Stephen Cornell, Miriam Jorgensen, Joseph P. Kalt, and Katherine A. Spilde, *Seizing the Future: Why Some Native Nations Do and Others Don't* (Tucson: Native Nations Institute for Leadership, Management and Policy, University of Arizona; Cambridge, MA: Harvard Project on American Indian Economic Development, John F. Kennedy School of Government, 2003), 4, 24.

37 James Frideres, "A Critical Analysis of the Royal Commission on Aboriginal Peoples Self-government Model," in Belanger, ed., *Aboriginal Self-Government*, 128.

38 "Introduction," in Belanger, ed., *Aboriginal Self-Government*, xii.

39 Nikolakis, "Evolution of Indigenous Self-Governance," 67.

40 Merkel, "Conclusion," 312.

41 See Angela Wesley, "Ancient Spirit, Modern Mind," 123.

42 Coulthard, *Red Skin, White Masks*, 24.

43 Taiaiake Alfred, *Wasáse: Indigenous Pathways of Action and Freedom* (Toronto: University of Toronto Press, 2005), 255.

44 Taiaiake Alfred and Jeff Corntassel, "Being Indigenous: Resurgences against Contemporary Colonialism," *Government and Opposition* 40 (Autumn 2005): 611.

45 Jeff Corntassel, "Re-envisioning Resurgence: Indigenous Pathways to Decolonization and Sustainable Self-Determination," *Decolonization: Indigeneity, Education &*
Society 1, no. 1 (2012): 89, 98.

4 Governance in Nunatsiavut: Constitution, Organization, and Politics

1 Nunatsiavut Government, *Nunatsiavut Constitution Act*, CIL N-3, 2012.

2 Minister of Indian Affairs and Northern Development, *Land Claims Agreement*
between the Inuit of Labrador and her Majesty the Queen in Right of Newfound-
land and Labrador and her Majesty the Queen in Right of Canada, 2004 (hereafter,
LILCA).

3 This and the subsequent section draw heavily on Graham White, " 'We, the Inuit
of Labrador': Balancing Inuit and Western Traditions in the Nunatsiavut Constitution," *Journal of Canadian Studies* 55, no. 1 (Winter 2021): 84–113.

4 Christopher Alcantara and Greg Whitfield, "Aboriginal Self-Government through
Constitutional Design: A Survey of Fourteen Aboriginal Constitutions in Canada,"
Journal of Canadian Studies 44, no. 2 (Spring 2010): 123–4.

5 Ibid., 139.

6 Nunatsiavut Government, "Parliamentary Report," 16 October 2006, 32 (henceforth, *Hansard*).

7 For detailed specifications of eligibility criteria, see LILCA, ch. 3, and Nunatsiavut
Government, *Guide to Completing an Application to Be Enrolled as a Beneficiary*
of the Labrador Inuit Land Claims Agreement, Department of Nunatsiavut Affairs,
Office of the Registrar of Beneficiaries, accessed 22 August 2022, https://
nunatsiavut.com/wp-content/uploads/2021/06/Guide-to-Completing
-Beneficiary-Application-Form.pdf.

8 See LILCA, 3.1.1.

9 Andrea Procter, "The Prospects of Culture: Resource Management and the Production of Difference in Nunatsiavut, Labrador" (PhD diss., Memorial University of
Newfoundland, 2012), 194.

10 For the balance of this chapter, "the Nunatsiavut Constitution" or "the constitution"
refer only to the *Nunatsiavut Constitution Act*.

11 The 23 include the 13 Indigenous constitutions (the 14th was that of Nunatsiavut)
analysed by Alcantara and Whitfield plus 9 others that either they did not examine
or that came into being after their study was completed. Framing the contrasts as
1 versus 22 may be misleading in that all but 2 of the self-governing First Nations,
the Tłı̨chǫ and the Deline First Nations in the Northwest Territories, are either in
British Columbia or Yukon, and exhibit a good deal of sharing of institutions and
practices in their constitutions.

12 Angela Wesley, "Ancient Spirit, Modern Mind: The Huu-ay-aht Journey Back to
Self-Determination and Self- Reliance," in *Reclaiming Indigenous Governance:*

Reflections and Insights from Australia, Canada, New Zealand and the United States, ed. Nikolakis, Stephen Cornell, and Harry W. Nelson (Tucson: University of Arizona Press, 2019), 116.

13 *Hansard*, 7 March 2018, 67–8.

14 Andrea Procter, "Nunatsiavut Land Claims and the Politics of Inuit Wildlife Harvesting," in *Settlement, Subsistence, and Change among the Labrador Inuit: The Nunatsiavummiut Experience*, ed. David C. Natcher, Lawrence Felt, and Andrea Procter (Winnipeg: University of Manitoba Press, 2012), 195.

15 Pauktuutit Inuit Women of Canada, *The Inuit Way: A Guide to Inuit Culture* (Ottawa: Pauktuutit, 2006), 22–4.

16 Elisapee Sheutiapik, "The Art of Connecting People," in *Arnait Nipingit: Voices of Inuit Women in Leadership and Governance*, ed. Louis McComber and Shannon Partridge (Iqaluit: Nunavut Arctic College, 2011), 125.

17 Andrea Procter, Beverly Hunter, and Charlotte Wolfrey, "Inuit Women's Leadership: A Nunatsiavut-Based Narrative," in *Voices of Inuit Leadership and Self-Determination in Canada*, ed. David Lough (St. John's: ISER Books, 2020), 61–89.

18 Pauktuutit, *The Inuit Way*, 28.

19 Tłı̨chǫ Government, *Tłı̨chǫ Constitution* (2005), section 7.1.

20 Brian Budd, Nicole Goodman, and Michael McGregor, "Electronic Voting Alternatives to Support the Canadian Constituency," Tabled Document 05–4 (11) (November 2021), 19. All NG or assembly documents cited but lacking URLs are in the author's possession.

21 The committee's plans to hold public meetings in various Canada Constituency communities had to be abandoned because of a resurgence of COVID-19; Nunatsiavut Assembly, *Final Report of the Special Committee on Voting Alternatives for the Canadian Constituency*, Tabled Document 04–4 (10) (March 2022).

22 Lawrence Felt, David C. Natcher, and Andrea Procter, "Going Forward: Challenges and Opportunities for Nunatsiavut Self-Governance," in Natcher, Felt and Procter, eds., *Settlement, Subsistence, and Change*, 257.

23 The claim says only "the executive officers and the members of the legislative institutions of the Nunatsiavut Government be responsible to Inuit in accordance with principles of democracy," LILCA, 17.3.3(d).

24 *Hansard*, 8 April 2008, 11.

25 Ibid., 6 March 2008, 20–30.

26 Ibid., 11 June 2013, 54.

27 Ibid., 58.

28 Ibid., 7 March 2018, 160.

29 Ibid., June 9, 2021, 166–7.

30 On the basis of the 772 votes cast (personal communication from Bert Pomeroy 21 September 2021) and the 5,972 beneficiaries eligible to vote in the October 2020 presidential election (see note 55 below) turnout was 12.9 per cent.

31 Toby Andersen, "What Is Self-Government?," in Land Claims Agreements Coalition, *Modern Treaties 101: A Crash Course*, 30–31 October 2012, 15, available at https://landclaimscoalition.ca/modern-treaties-101/.

32 Angela Wesley, "Ancient Spirit, Modern Mind," 123. See also Garry Merkel, "Conclusion: Building Yourself and Your Community," in Nikolakis, Cornell, and Nelson, eds., *Reclaiming Indigenous Governance*, 312.

33 Although no formal decisions had been taken, it was initially expected by many involved that jurisdictional take-up in Nunavut would be phased in over several years. The first report from the Nunavut Implementation Commission argued strongly against a phased approach and effectively shifted the consensus towards complete jurisdictional take-up on day one: Nunavut Implementation Commission, *Footprints in New Snow: A Comprehensive Report from the Nunavut Implementation Commission to the Department of Indian Affairs and Northern Development, Government of the Northwest Territories and Nunavut Tunngavik Incorporated Concerning the Establishment of the Nunavut Government* (Iqaluit: Nunavut Implementation Commission, 1995), 36–41. Initially, the Government of Nunavut relied on the Government of the Northwest Territories to deliver certain services and programs, but within a year or less it had assumed all elements of most of these activities. See Jack Hicks and Graham White, *Made in Nunavut: An Experiment in Decentralized Government* (Vancouver: UBC Press, 2015), 230–1.

34 Nunatsiavut Government, "Process Underway to Take Over Child Welfare Services," media release, 17 June 2021, https://www.nunatsiavut.com/wp-content /uploads/2021/06/NEWS-RELEASE-Process-under-way-to-take-over-child -welfare-services.pdf.

35 Quoted in Gary N. Wilson, Christopher Alcantara, and Thierry Rodon, *Nested Federalism and Inuit Governance in the Canadian Arctic* (Vancouver: UBC Press, 2020, 145.

36 Felt, Natcher, and Procter, "Going Forward," 256.

37 Deputies' tenure was determined from the lists of persons attending (or absent from) assembly sittings, as recorded in *Hansard*. The clerk of the assembly was considered to hold a deputy minister–level appointment; Mary Sillett nominally retired as clerk late in 2020 but returned to serve as acting clerk until March 2022 since no replacement had been found.

38 A wide-ranging survey found that 45.7 per cent of Canadian federal, provincial, and territorial deputy ministers had been in the same position for two years or less, with only 7.3 per cent having spent five years or more in the same position. Bryan M. Evans, Janet M. Lum, and John Shields, "A Canada-Wide Survey of Deputy and Assistant Deputy Ministers: A Descriptive Analysis," in *Deputy Ministers in Canada: Comparative and Jurisdictional Perspectives*, ed. Jacques Bourgault and Christopher Dunn (Toronto: University of Toronto Press, 2014), 332.

39 All employment figures in this paragraph, save those relating to senior management, were taken or calculated from Nunatsiavut Government, Department of

Finance, Human Resources and Information Technology, "Composition of the Nunatsiavut Civil Service," 31 March 2022. Data do not include vacant positions.

40 Data provided by the Department of Finance, Information Technology and Human Resources.

41 The Government of Nunavut's Human Relations Department produces a quarterly report, *Towards a Representative Public Service*. The most recent report, dated November 2021, with data as of 30 September 2021, showed an overall Inuit participation rate of 50 per cent, with Inuit holding 42 per cent of executive positions and 23 per cent of senior management positions. See Government of Nunavut, *Toward a Representative Public Service: Statistics of the Public Service within the Government of Nunavut as of September 30, 2021* (Iqaluit: Department of Human Resources, 2021), 5, https://gov.nu.ca/sites/default/files/master_trps_eng_q2revised.pdf.

42 All figures from *Budget Act 2022*, Inuit Law 2022–01. See also Nunatsiavut Government, "Budget 2022–23 Focused on Continued Progress," media release, 8 March 2022, https://nunatsiavut.com/budget-2022-23-focused-on-continued-progress/.

43 Statistical material in this section is partially drawn from Graham White and Christopher Alcantara, "Institutional Design and Inuit Governance: Nunatsiavut and Nunavut Compared," in *Voices of Inuit Leadership and Self-Determination in Canada*, ed. David Lough (St. John's: ISER Books, 2020), 125–58.

44 The 2020 presidential election, initially scheduled for May, was postponed until October due to the COVID-19 pandemic.

45 Nunatsiavut Government, *Nunatsiavut Elections Act*, CIL N-4, s 28.

46 Nunatsiavut Government, *Inuit Community Government Elections Act*, CIL I-2, ss 15–16; *Inuit Community Corporations Chairpersons Elections Act*, CIL I-1, ss 12–13.

47 *Nunatsiavut Elections Act*, s 33.

48 *Hansard*, 5 November 2013, 63.

49 Ibid., 13 June 2013, 53–78; 11 September 2013, 130–62; 5 November 2013, 48–91; 21 January 2014, 57–104; Nunatsiavut Assembly, "Options Related to Language Requirements for Candidates for President under the Nunatsiavut Elections Act," Tabled Document 03–2 (9) (2013).

50 *Hansard*, 21 January 2014, 88.

51 See *Nunatsiavut Elections Act*, ss 169–97, for details of the election finance regime.

52 Transportation companies are permitted to donate services to Canada Constituency and presidential candidates provided that they offer such services to all candidates.

53 Figures calculated from data in "NG Election Results (Unofficial)," OKalaKatiget Society, 6 May 2014, www.oksociety.com/?p=10336. Turnout rates in this paragraph are calculated on the basis of official Elections Nunatsiavut figures for numbers of electors on the voters' lists and numbers of people who voted. Curiously, the number of names on the voters' lists are consistently higher – sometimes substantially higher – than the numbers of beneficiaries over sixteen for the LISA communities, as shown in spreadsheets provided by the registrar of beneficiaries. The

variation is widest for Postville: 104 beneficiaries but 142 on the voters' list in 2006; the comparable figures were 124 and 150 in 2014 and 134 and 151 in 2018 (data on voters' lists are not available).

54 Figures calculated from data in Nunatsiavut Government, "Official Election Results Released," Media release, 7 May 2018, https://www.nunatsiavut.com/wp-content /uploads/2018/05/Official-Election-Results.pdf.

55 Official results do not include data on number of eligible voters or of turnout. Based on the NG media release on the 2018 ordinary members election, it is possible to calculate that some 5,892 beneficiaries were eligible to vote (this includes an estimate of 180 for Makkovik, where the sole candidate was acclaimed, so that no data on eligible electors were available). A reasonable, though clearly imprecise, estimate that in 2012 roughly 5,700 beneficiaries would have been able to vote produces figures of 37.4 and 38.4 per cent.

56 Johannes Lampe received 1,015 votes, Andrea Webb/Tuglavina 533; with 5,972 eligible voters (personal communication from Bert Pomeroy, 15 December 2020) this produces a turnout rate of 25.9 per cent.

57 Nunatsiavut Government, "President-Elect Lampe Looks Forward to Continuing to Serve Labrador Inuit," media release, 7 October 2020, https://nunatsiavut.jac.digital /wp-content/uploads/2020/10/STATEMENT-from-President-Elect-Lampe.pdf.

58 "AngajukKât/Chairperson Elections," OKalaKatiget Society, 14 September 2014, http://www.oksociety.com/angajukkatchairperson-elections-audio-2/.

59 Nunatsiavut elections officer, "Report to the Nunatsiavut Assembly: The Presidential Elections of May 1, 2012 and the Run Off Election of June 11, 2012," 2012, 4.

60 Nunatsiavut elections officer, Letter to Kate Mitchell, First Minister re 2016 Presidential Election, 4 May 2016, 2.

61 CBC, *Labrador Morning* [interview with Nanette Blake, 7 October 2020], accessed 14 October 2020, www/cbc.ca/listen/live-radio/1–31-labrador-morning/clip /15802895-innu-nation-taking-hydro-quebec-court-nunatsiavut-government.

62 OK Society interview, 9 September 2020, available at www.oksociety.com/wp -content/uploads/2020/10/ON-AIR-Andrea-Webb-Campaign-09.20.20.mp3. She told the interviewer that she had not spoken with anyone in Postville because no one had returned her calls and that she intended to send her platform to Speaker and Canada Constituency Ordinary Member Edward Blake-Rudkowski and "ask him to distribute it because I don't know any email addresses and phone numbers. I just know that I can contact him and he can do that for me along with [NEO] Nanette Blake." Both were inappropriate requests of neutral officials, and were therefore disregarded.

63 Nunatsiavut elections officer, "Report to the Speaker Nunatsiavut Assembly: Ordinary Members Election May 4, 2010," 5.

64 Budd, Goodman, and McGregor, "Electronic Voting Alternatives."

65 Nunatsiavut Assembly, *Final Report of the Special Committee on Voting Alternatives for the Canadian Constituency*, Tabled Document 04–4(10) (March 2022), 8–9.

66 Data sources are as follows: federal: https://www.elections.ca/res/rep/off
/ovr2021app/53/11641e.html; https://www.elections.ca/res/rep/off/ovr2019app
/51/10932e.html; http://www.elections.ca/res/rep/off/ovr2015app/41/9691e.html;
http://www.elections.ca/scripts/ovr2011/default.html; provincial: https://www
.elections.gov.nl.ca/elections/; http://www.assembly.nl.ca/business
/electronicdocuments/GeneralElection2011-Report.pdf; http://www.elections.gov
.nl.ca/elections/. Note that federal and provincial turnout figures reflect all voters,
not just Nunatsiavut beneficiaries, in the five communities within LISA. Note also
that because of the COVID-19 pandemic, the 2021 provincial election was conducted almost entirely by "special" (i.e., mail) ballots, and that mail service can
prove problematic for the North Coast.

67 For an analysis of factors affecting turnout in LISA, see David Armstrong, Christopher Alcantara, and John Kennedy, "Exploring the Effects of Electorate Size on
Indigenous Voter Turnout," *Politics, Groups, and Identities*, 24 May 2021. https://
doi.org/10.1080/21565503.2021.1926297.

68 Felt, Natcher, and Procter, "Going Forward," 255.

5 The Assembly: Setting, Atmosphere, and Membership

1 Unlike as stipulated in the constitution, the president was considered an ordinary
member under the act. The terms of all ordinary members ended with the first
election in October 2006. The president remained in office until the first presidential election in May 2008.

2 This broad-brush description glosses over various nuances; for example, the fact
that in some jurisdictions, including Canada's Parliament, ministers may be appointed who are not sitting members (or, in Ottawa, senators), subject to the convention that they become members in short order.

3 See his orientation for newly elected members of the Third Assembly, *Hansard*, 13
May 2014, especially 37–8.

4 Nunatsiavut Government, *Nunatsiavut Constitution Act*, CIL N-3, 2012, 5.5.3(c).

5 *Erskine May's Treatise on the Law, Privileges, Proceedings and Usage of Parliament*,
cited by the standard text on Canadian parliamentary procedure, Robert Marleau
and Camille Montpetit, eds., *House of Commons Procedure and Practice* (Ottawa:
House of Commons/Chenelière/McGraw-Hill, 2000), ch. 3.

6 Video recording of assembly orientation session, May 2010.

7 In the act, "session" is used in reference to the yearly set of assembly meetings,
which are termed "sittings." No specific term is specified for individual sitting days;
Nunatsiavut Assembly Act, part 5.

8 Statistics Canada, "Census Profile, 2021 Census of Population," Government of
Canada, last modified 17 May 2022, https://www12.statcan.gc.ca/census
-recensement/2021/dp-pd/prof/search-recherche/lst/results-resultats.cfm?Lang
=E&GEOCODE=10.

9 Charles T. Goodsell, "The Architecture of Parliaments: Legislative Houses and Political Culture," *British Journal of Political Science* 18, no. 3 (July 1988): 287.

10 *Hansard*, 19 October 2006, 69.

11 Ibid., 13 September 2012, 103.

12 Ibid., 19 November 2019, 37.

13 Ibid., 17 October 2006, 42.

14 According to President Andersen the session was not held in Hopedale in order to avoid significant travel costs given how brief the meeting would be, but he did not specify where it did take place (likely Goose Bay). "Transcriptions to Emergency Meeting of the Assembly, 24 August, 2007," 4.

15 Nunatsiavut Assembly (Second Assembly), Standing Committee on Rules and Procedures, *Report on the Review of the Standing Orders, Rules and Procedures of the Nunatsiavut Assembly*, 7 September 2011, 15. Recall that I use the term "session" where the assembly says "sitting."

16 In order to deal with the problems arising because members had inadequate notice of session dates and of business to be conducted, the committee further recommended that the president and first minister annually list planned Assembly sessions and that the NG develop a four-year legislative agenda: ibid., 15–16. The former has occurred; the latter has not.

17 During a recent sitting, the speaker called the lunch recess midway through members' statements, on the premise that "a further continuation risks a cold lunch," which had been brought into the Assembly Building to save time: *Hansard*, 6 June 2019, 45.

18 As members' votes were being tallied on appointments to one of the trust boards, the president, doubtless speaking for other members, asked the speaker, "I haven't had a smoke break since nine o'clock this morning, I'm getting a little antsy. Are we going to have a smoke break while they're counting?" *Hansard*, 4 March 2015, 126. The president's request was accommodated.

19 This is by no means a slur on the indispensable Twin Otter or its pilots, who are skilled, hard-working, and intrepid. However, the high winds, sleet, and fog common in Nunatsiavut can make flying in a small plane like the Twin Otter unsafe, leading to delays that can last for a few hours or for days (in summer 2019, for example, persistent fog prevented all air travel to Nain and Hopedale for over a week).

20 *Hansard*, 19 November 2019, 46.

21 Fortunately, with the airstrip less than a kilometre from the Assembly Building, the trip by truck or snow machine takes only minutes. At one point during a debate on a bill on community government, the speaker told the House that a "resource person" who could assist the assembly's consideration of the bill was in the building but "has to be on a plane in about 13 minutes" (*Hansard*, 19 September 2018, 270). The "resource person," the deputy minister of finance, came into the chamber, answered questions, and departed … and made the plane.

22 Ibid., 9 June 2009, 92.

23 Ibid., 6 June 2019, 3–4.

24 Ibid., 70–1.

25 Ibid., 26 October 2020, 145.

26 One woman served as both an ordinary member and as an AngajukKâk, and another served as an ordinary member and as a community chair; they are only counted once in the overall totals.

27 The *Nunatsiavut Assembly Act* and the constitution are silent as to the implications of members moving away from their constituencies, though the act recognizes the possibility of a minister moving to Nain. Beyond that, even if technically legal, such a move is hard to imagine politically.

28 A review of elected officials' salaries was commissioned by the NG in early 2022, but any action on its findings would not occur until the Fifth Assembly.

29 *Hansard*, 24 November 2015, 53–61.

30 *Nunatsiavut Assembly Members' Handbook* (Amherst, NS: Burma Cove Consulting, 2012), 14.

31 Ibid., 20; *Elected Officials Policy Manual* (Hopedale: Nunatsiavut Assembly, 2015), 9.

32 *Elected Officials Policy Manual*, 7.

33 See, for example, *Hansard*, 24 June 2009, 92.

34 One community chair served in both the First and Second Assemblies, but for a total of just over three years.

35 The comparison is between the first September sessions of the assemblies, to allow for change among AngajukKât, whose elections occur a few months after the ordinary member elections.

36 One member was defeated in one election and chose to sit out another.

37 Sir Humphrey Appleby was a stereotypical obstructionist, empire-building bureaucrat in the wonderful British satirical television series *Yes Minister* and *Yes Prime Minister*.

38 *Nunatsiavut Constitution Act*, 4.14.2(a)(i).

39 *Hansard*, 12 May 2010, 38–9.

40 *Code of Conduct*, IL 2008–02, part 5.

41 *Hansard*, 19 March 2009, 112–13.

42 Speaker Todd Broomfield moved a motion about dental care and spoke in the debate on it: *Hansard*, 12 February 2007, 12–13. Speaker Danny Pottle spoke in a debate about alcohol policy and moved an amendment to a motion: ibid., 11 March 2010, 167–9. Pottle commented on a document brought forward by the president: "I have very grave concerns with respect to this Strategic Plan as presented … [The president] should produce something more professional to what's in here": ibid., 11 March 2010, 139.

43 Standing Order 8(2) states: "The Speaker shall not take part in any debate before the Assembly." A member's statement would not normally be considered "debate."

44 *Hansard*, 18 September 2019, 205. It may be worth noting that the situation described by the speaker could arise for any member.

45 *Hansard*, 19 September 2017, 49–52; 7 February 2018, 61–4; 6 March 2018, 77–9; 6 March 2019, 26–8. He also sought and received unanimous consent to respond to a question about the assembly budget: ibid., 6 March 2018, 77–9. He did not seek consent to ask questions from the chair about trust investment policy and the budget: ibid., 6 March 2018, 111, 220–1.

46 Ibid., 8 March 2022, 50–3.

47 Ibid., 6 March 2018, 207.

48 Ibid., 207–14.

49 Ibid., 4 March 2015, 131–3.

50 Ibid., 21 January 2020, 112–13.

51 Ibid., 18 March 2009, 89–91. The speaker's urging was prompted by the requirement that successful candidates required the support of 75 per cent of the members.

52 Ibid., 18 September 2018, 172–4.

53 Ibid., 21 January 2020, 111.

54 Ibid., 17 September 2019, 27–9.

55 Ibid., 20 September 2017, 113. The AngajukKâk and the minister were related.

56 See, for example, ibid., 6 March 2019, 67.

57 Ibid., 19 March 2009, 110.

58 Ibid., 14 May 2014, 120.

59 Ibid., 8 June 2021, 70.

60 Ibid., 7 March 2017, 68.

61 Ibid., 10 June 2014.

62 *Nunatsiavut Constitution Act*, 4.14.5.

63 *Hansard*, 7 March 2017, 63–9, 93–5.

64 Ibid., 16 October 2006, 27–9; 17 October 2006, 48.

65 Ibid., 6 March 2017, 39.

66 Ibid., 9 March 2021, 87–8.

67 Quoted in Regan Burden, "Some Nunatsiavut Beneficiaries Living Outside of Labrador Feel 'Abandoned.' Here's Why," CBC News, 26 April 2021, https://www .cbc.ca/news/canada/newfoundland-labrador/nunatsiavut-beneficiaries-left -out-1.5987096.

68 *Hansard*, 12 February 2007, 8.

69 *Code of Conduct*, s 4.1.

6 The Assembly: Operations, Committees, and Services

1 At one point, the question arose as to what would happen if someone objected to the prayer; the ensuing discussion was inconclusive. *Hansard*, 13 September 2011, 52.

2 Speaker Marlene Winters-Wheeler disallowed a written question she herself had submitted prior to becoming speaker: *Hansard*, 8 March 2021, 58.

3 In June 2015, Ordinary Member Richard Pamak presented a petition from constituents concerned that not enough was being done to combat a tuberculosis outbreak in Nain. While acknowledging his responsibility to represent his constituents by presenting their petition, Pamak commented that he had access to more comprehensive information than some of his constituents and stated that he was satisfied with the response to the outbreak: *Hansard*, 2 June 2015, 77–84. In March 2019, AngajukKâk Joe Dicker presented a petition from beneficiaries requesting that second reading of a pending far-reaching housing bill be delayed until the NG consulted with the Torngat Regional Housing Authority. First Minister Kate Mitchell objected that the petition was improper in that after it was instigated the NG had consulted the housing authority. The speaker agreed with Mitchell and ruled the petition out of order: *Hansard*, 5 March 2019, 44–5.

4 "Tabling" has a fundamentally different meaning in parliamentary settings than in the widely known *Roberts Rules of Order*. In the latter, to table a motion or item of business is to suspend discussion of it, perhaps permanently, whereas tabling a document in a Westminster parliament entails presenting it to the assembly, thereby rendering it public.

5 Standing Order 58 permits non-NEC members to introduce private members' public bills, with the standard Westminster proviso that they may neither direct the spending of public money nor impose taxes.

6 Private bills are uncommon but not unknown in Canadian parliaments. Whereas public bills, be they government bills or private members' bills, apply broadly, private bills apply only to individual institutions, such as companies, charities, or individual persons.

7 This includes the *Labrador Inuit Lands Amendment Act* of 2008, which imposed a moratorium on uranium exploration. Technically, the bill passed with limited debate and no committee reference, but as outlined in chapter 9, extensive debate did take place via a somewhat unconventional procedure.

8 *Hansard*, 16 March 2011, 120–34.

9 The president, under sections 3.2.4 and 3.2.5 of the constitution, may refuse assent to a bill he considers unconstitutional. Should this occur – to date it has not – she must either refer it back to the assembly for reconsideration or refer it to the Inuit Court, which as yet does not exist, for a decision on its constitutionality.

10 Nunatsiavut Government, "Nunatsiavut Assembly to Sit under Strict Conditions Amid Concerns over COVID-19," media release, 16 March 2020, https://www .nunatsiavut.com/wp-content/uploads/2020/03/Statement-Assembly-to-sit -under-under-strict-conditions.pdf.

11 Personal communication, 12 November 2020; quoted with permission.

12 See Nunatsiavut Assembly, "Assembly Discusses Special Standing Orders October 19, 2020." According to the notes in this document, the call took place on 20 October.

13 This comment came across on the audio feed, but, as it was made immediately after formal adjournment, the speaker was not identified.

14 *An Act to Amend the Nunatsiavut Assembly Act 2020*, IL 2020–03, s 4.

15 Nunatsiavut Assembly, "Special Standing Orders for the Conduct of Proceedings of the Nunatsiavut Assembly in the Exceptional Circumstances of the COVID-19 Pandemic (Schedule to the *Standing Orders of the Nunatsiavut Assembly*), adopted 26 October 2020."

16 Provisions relating to assembly committees are found in section 4.14 of the constitution: Nunatsiavut Government, *Nunatsiavut Constitution Act*, CIL N-3, 2012.

17 *Assembly Act*, ss 76 and 51.

18 Standing Order 65(5)(a)

19 Standing Orders 67 and 68.

20 *Hansard*, 12 February 2007, 14–15.

21 Veryan Haysom, "Notes on Committees of the Nunatsiavut Assembly," 17 May 2010, 2.

22 Occasional reports were also made from a Language Strategy Committee established by the minister of culture, language and recreation. This was a government rather than assembly committee, which seems to have been more active than the assembly's Language Committee.

23 *Hansard*, 17 September 2019, 56.

24 Brian Budd, Nicole Goodman, and Michael McGregor, "Electronic Voting Alternatives to Support the Canadian Constituency," Tabled Document 05–4 (11) (November 2021); Nunatsiavut Assembly, *Final Report of the Special Committee on Voting Alternatives for the Canadian Constituency*, Tabled Document 04–4 (10) (March 2022).

25 *Hansard*, 14 May 2014, 120.

26 Ibid., 16 March 2011, 152.

27 David C. Docherty, *Legislatures* (Vancouver: UBC Press, 2005), 165–72.

28 *Budget Act 2022*, IL 2022–01, 14.

29 Sillett retired in October 2020, but with the assembly unable to find a replacement, she served as acting clerk for the balance of the Fourth Assembly, to April 2022.

30 Sillett was president of Pauktuutit, the National Inuit Women's Association, and commissioner on the Royal Commission on Aboriginal Peoples. See also David Lough, "Labrador Inuit Leadership – 1970s to 2005," in *Voices of Inuit Leadership and Self-Determination in Canada*, ed. David Lough (St. John's: ISER Books, 2020), 91–113.

31 *Hansard*, 17 March 2009, 36–7.

32 Ibid., 15 March 2011, 62.

33 Ibid., 16 October 2006, 31.

34 Ibid., 12 December 2006, 2.

35 Nunatsiavut Government, *Report to the Legislative Assembly: Section 111 of the Nunatsiavut Assembly Act*, Tabled Document 01–4 (10) (18 June 2021), 3.

36 *Hansard*, 17 March 2009, 24–30.
37 Ibid., 13 December 2011, 37–8, 50–9; 6 June 2019, 153.
38 Ibid., 6 June 2019.

7 Distinctive Features of the Nunatsiavut Assembly

1 As outlined in a "process sheet" developed by David Hamilton, the former clerk of the NWT Legislative Assembly and long-time Nunatsiavut Assembly adviser: Nunatsiavut Assembly, "4th Assembly Process Sheet for Appointment of First Minister, Ministers and Speaker," n.d. (2018?). Direct quotations in this paragraph are taken from pages 1 and 2 of this document.
2 *Hansard*, 16 October 2006, 38–45.
3 Ibid., 12 May 2010, 22–5.
4 Ibid, 13 May 2014, 46–85.
5 Ibid., 16 May 2018, 12–19.
6 Nunatsiavut Assembly, "4th Assembly Process Sheet," 2–4.
7 An early speaker's ruling held that members could not abstain when a vote was called: *Hansard*, 24 June 2009, 86. The Standing Orders, the act, and the constitution are, and were then, silent on this matter; on at least one occasion, a member asked that his abstention be recorded in *Hansard*: 3 February 2016, 128.
8 AngajukKâk Charlotte Wolfrey: "if I put up my hand to vote, they [constituents] can see on the TV how I voted": ibid., 18 September 2019, 195.
9 Sikumiut Environmental Management, *Public Consultations Regarding a Moratorium on the Working, Production, Mining and Development of Uranium on Labrador Inuit Lands 2011* (Report for the Special Committee, 28 November 2011), 21.
10 *Hansard*, 12 May 2010, 21.
11 Ibid., 5 October 2010, 24.
12 Ibid., 6 October 2010, 120.
13 Ibid., 13 September 2011, 60.
14 Ibid., 2 February 2016, 78.
15 Ibid., 13 May 2014, 102; 4 March 2015, 123; 16 May 2018, 18; 19 September 2018, 208, 265; 22 January 2019, 18; 5 March 2019, 23.
16 Ibid., 18 September 2019, 191–204.
17 Nunatsiavut Government, *Nunatsiavut Constitution Act*, CIL N-3, 4.18.10.
18 Like all members, the president is entitled to introduce legislation: ibid., 4.18.11.
19 On 12 June 2008 (*Hansard*, 41–2), the speaker ruled out of order a motion from a non-NEC member to add money for a drum-dancing project to the budget on the grounds that something of equivalent value would have to be deleted, not because it offended the money bill rule. The next day (see ibid., 102, 104) an AngajukKâk and a non-NEC ordinary member moved different motions to reallocate money in the budget; one was withdrawn when the finance minister committed to funding the project; the second went to a vote and was defeated. In neither case did the

speaker or any member mention the money bill rule. On 25 November 2008 (ibid., 55), the speaker ruled out of order, as contravening the money bill rule, a motion moved by a non-NEC ordinary member to pay $5,000 to certain beneficiaries. On 16 March 2011 (ibid., 173) a motion brought forward by a non-NEC ordinary member to increase public servants' salaries was passed after a long debate about its merits; no one raised the money bill rule.

20 Ibid., 5 October 2010, 21.

21 Ibid., 21–5. Two members did raise points of order unrelated to the substance of the issue.

22 Save those from the CBC story, all quotations in this and the subsequent paragraph are from *Hansard*, 22 January 2019, 4–19.

23 "Nunatsiavut Government Member Suspended Indefinitely for Profane Language and Behaviour," CBC News, 24 January 2019, https://www.cbc.ca/news/canada /newfoundland-labrador/nunatsiavut-member-for-hopedale-suspended-1.4991170.

24 Ibid.

25 *Hansard*, 5 March 2019, 6–23.

26 Quoted in "Sex Complaint Linked to Nunatsiavut President's Leave," CBC News, 9 January 2008, https://www.cbc.ca/news/canada/newfoundland-labrador /sex-complaint-linked-to-nunatsiavut-president-s-leave-1.711758.

27 "Andersen Evades Jail for Sex Assault," CBC News, 22 October 2010, https://www .cbc.ca/news/canada/newfoundland-labrador/andersen-evades-jail-for-sex -assault-1.866731.

28 *Hansard*, 6 October 2010, 115–21.

29 Ibid., 16 September 2014, 89.

30 "NG Speaker Sean Lyall Reprimanded," OKalaKatiget Society, 18 September 2014, http://www.oksociety.com/ng-speaker-sean-lyall-reprimanded/.

31 *Hansard*, 6 June 2017, 57. See also Nunatsiavut Government, "Makkovik Inuit Community AngajukKâk Suspended for Making Inappropriate and Harassing Comments," media release, 2 May 2017, https://www.nunatsiavut.com/article /makkovik-inuit-community-government-angajukkak-suspended-for-making -inappropriate-and-harassing-comments/.

32 "Speaker for Nunatsiavut Assembly Removed from Government after Inuit Status Questioned," CBC News, 27 November 2020, https://www.cbc.ca/news/canada /newfoundland-labrador/blake-rudkowksi-membership-revoked-1.5817894.

33 Nunatsiavut Government, "Blake Rudkowski No Longer Ordinary Member for Canada after Having Membership Revoked," Statement, 23 November 2020, https://www.nunatsiavut.com/wp-content/uploads/2020/11/STATEMENT-Blake -Rudkowski-no-longer-Ordinary-Member-for-Canada-after-having -membership-revoked.pdf.

34 CBC News, "Speaker for Nunatsiavut."

35 "Nunatsiavut Candidate Left Cabinet over Credit Card Use," CBC News, 3 April 2012, https://www.cbc.ca/news/canada/newfoundland-labrador/nunatsiavut -candidate-left-cabinet-over-credit-card-use-1.1241253.

36 Nunatsiavut Government, "Mitchell Resigns as First Minister," media release, 3 December 2019, https://www.nunatsiavut.com/article/mitchell-tenders-resignation -as-first-minister/.

37 Nunatsiavut Government, "Russell Relieved of Duties as Minister of Health and Social Development," media release, 16 February 2011, reposted on *NationTalk*, http://nationtalk.ca/story/russell-relieved-of-duties-as-minister-of-health -and-social-development.

38 "NG President Responds to Keith Russell's Comments In Labradorian," OKalaKa- tiget Society, 18 August 2015, http://www.oksociety.com/ng-president-responds -to-keith-russells-comments-in-labradorian.

39 Nunatsiavut Government, "NG Relieves Pamak of Minister Duties," media release, 21 April 2015, reposted on OKalaKatiget Society, http://www.oksociety.com/ng -relieves-pamak-of-minister-duties/.

40 "Pamak Responds to NG Removal of Ministerial Duties," OKalaKatiget Society, 22 April 2015, http://www.oksociety.com/pamak-responds-to-ng-removal-of -ministerial-duties/. See also "Richard Pamak 'at a Loss' over Why He Was Fired from Nunatsiavut Cabinet," CBC News, 23 April 2015, https://www.cbc.ca/news /canada/newfoundland-labrador/richard-pamak-at-a-loss-over-why-he-was-fired -from-nunatsiavut-cabinet-1.3045286.

41 *Hansard*, 25 January 2017, 103–6.

42 Nunatsiavut Government, "Pottle Removed from Nunatsiavut Executive Council," media release, 18 February 2016, https://www.nunatsiavut.com/article/pottle -removed-from-nunatsiavut-executive-council/.

43 "Former Nunatsiavut Minister Daniel Pottle Speaks about Dismissal, Calls Move 'Harsh,'" CBC News, 19 February 2016, https://www.cbc.ca/news/canada /newfoundland-labrador/daniel-pottle-speaks-out-about-dismissal-1.3455482.

44 "Nunatsiavut President Sarah Leo Defends Decision to Fire Minister over Missed Meeting," CBC News, 23 February 2016, https://www.cbc.ca/news/canada /newfoundland-labrador/nunatsiavut-president-sarah-leo-defends-firing -minister-1.3458698.

45 Nunatsiavut Government, "Lyall Tenders Resignation as Ordinary Member for Nain Following Wrongful Personal Use of Nunatsiavut Government Credit Card," media release, 1 March 2017, https://www.nunatsiavut.com/article/lyall -tenders-resignation-as-ordinary-member-for-nain-following-wrongful -personal-use-of-nunatsiavut-government-credit-card/.

46 David Wasylciw, "Consensus Works, and the Last Thing the N.W.T. Needs Is Party Politics," CBC News, 27 November 2021, https://www.cbc.ca/news/canada/north /david-wasylciw-consensus-government-op-ed-1.6264930.

47 My thanks to the anonymous reviewer who suggested this connection.

48 Pauktuutit Inuit Women of Canada, *The Inuit Way: A Guide to Inuit Culture* (Ottawa: Pauktuutit, 2006), 11–12.

49 The Moravian Church in Newfoundland and Labrador, *The Labrador Church Book: The Book of Order of the Labrador Province of the Moravian Church* (Happy

Valley–Goose Bay: Labrador Province of the Moravian Church, 1969), 32–3. My thanks to Hans Rollmann for providing this document.

50 Peter Evans, "Transformations of Inuit Resistance and Identity in Northern Labrador, 1771–1959" (PhD diss., Cambridge University, 2013), 143.

51 Carol Brice-Bennett, "Two Opinions: Inuit and Moravian Missionaries in Labrador, 1804–1860" (master's thesis, Memorial University of Newfoundland, 1981), 337, 351, 388, 391, 398, 399, 400, 412, 474, 475, 477.

52 Helge Kleivan, *The Eskimos of Northeast Labrador: A History of Eskimo-White Relations 1771–1955* (Oslo: Norsk Polarinstitutt, 1966), 69.

53 *Hansard*, 18 November 2014, 83. He also suggested that sore losers are at their most vindictive soon after elections and, less convincingly, that the public has higher expectations of new governments and is thus horrified and stirred to action when things go wrong.

54 Ibid., 13 May 2014, 36.

55 *Code of Conduct*, ss 4.1 and 2.6. The code also applies to elected members of Inuit community governments and officers of Inuit community corporations. Similar provisions apply to public servants under the *Civil Service Act*.

56 *Constitution Act*, 4.3.7(c).

57 *Hansard*, 25 November 2008, 77–8.

58 Veryan Haysom, ibid., 18 November 2014, 62.

8 Consensus, Consensus Government, and Inuit Influence

1 See, for example, "Westminster in the Arctic: The Adaptation of British Parliamentarism in the Legislative Assembly of the Northwest Territories," *Canadian Journal of Political Science* 24, no. 3 (September 1991): 499–523; "Structure and Culture in a Non-partisan Westminster Parliament: Canada's Northwest Territories," *Australian Journal of Political Science* 28, no. 2 (July 1993): 322–39; "Aboriginal Influences on Governmental Institutions in the Northwest Territories," research study prepared for the Royal Commission on Aboriginal Peoples, in *For Seven Generations*, the Royal Commission's CD-ROM (Ottawa: Libraxus, 1997); "Traditional Aboriginal Values in a Westminster Parliament: the Legislative Assembly of Nunavut," *Journal of Legislative Studies* 12, no. 1 (March 2006): 8–31; "Size Matters, But so Does Culture: The Legislative Assembly of Nunavut," in *Legislatures of Small States: A Comparative Study*, ed. Nicholas Baldwin (London: Routledge, 2013), 148–57.

2 The possibility that direct election of the premier could lead to the advent and domination of political parties has also been a consideration. See Graham White, "Consequences of Electing the Government Leader of the Northwest Territories," paper prepared for the Strategic Planning Session of the Legislative Assembly of the Northwest Territories, Cambridge Bay, NWT, October 1993; Nunavut Implementation Commission, *Election of a Premier in Nunavut and Related Issues* (Iqaluit: Nunavut Implementation Commission, 1996), and *Direct Election of the Nunavut*

Premier: Schemes for Legislative Enactment (Iqaluit: Nunavut Implementation Commission, 1998).

3 *Hansard*, 13 September 2011, 49.

4 In NWT, the prospects for conflict are heightened by the convention apportioning cabinet seats by region, so that it is not a competition among 17 members (the speaker and the premier having already been chosen), for six cabinet posts but among three sets of five or six members for two regional cabinet positions.

5 Tim Mercer, *Consensus Government in the Northwest Territories: Westminster with a Northern "Twist"* (Ottawa: Canadian Study of Parliament Group, 2015), 2–3; http://cspg-gcep.ca/pdf/CSPG_NWT_Legislature-e.pdf.

6 See, for example, White, "Traditional Aboriginal Values." In the NWT, a policy and planning committee of the assembly acts as "a caucus of sorts for those members who do not serve in cabinet" (Mercer, *Consensus Government*, 4); in Nunavut, both caucus and the "Regular Members' Caucus," consisting of all non-cabinet MLAs, are defined in the *Legislative Assembly and Executive Council Act*.

7 *Hansard*, 5 March 2008, 14; 21 January 2014, 121. It was initially called the Torngasuk Cultural Centre.

8 Ibid., 23 January 2013, 99. See also ibid., 11 September 2012, 50, 88, and 22 January 2013, 26.

9 See, for example, ibid., 11 October 2007, 6; 12 September 2012, 50; 10 January 2013, 26, 96,

10 Nunatsiavut Assembly, "Nunavut Legislative Assembly Visit to Iqaluit May 25–28, 2014," May 2014.

11 Video recording of assembly orientation session, May 2010.

12 Quoted in Matthew Halliday, "Could Nunatsiavut Be a Model for Reconciliation?," *The Deep*, 12 December 2018.

13 *Hansard*, 18 September 2019, 199.

14 *Nunatsiavut Constitution Act*, 1.1.3(q); 4.15.2 and 4.15.5.

15 *Nunatsiavut Assembly Act*, IL 2005–09, Appendix A (Standing Orders), SO 130.

16 *Hansard*, 13 September 2011, 41–62.

17 Ibid., 13 May 2014, 32–3.

18 Ibid., 16 October 2006, 39.

19 Ibid., 18 September 2018, 129.

20 Ibid., 12 February 2007, 8.

21 Ibid., 11 October 2007, 15–16.

22 Ibid., 6 October 2010, 64.

23 Ibid., 2 February 2011, 18. Note the implication that normally non-NEC members are not provided with adequate information.

24 Ibid., 20 September 2016, 78–9.

25 Ibid., 7 March 2018, 150–3.

26 Ibid., 6 March 2019, 41.

27 Ibid., 9 June 2021, 152–3.

28 Readers are reminded that attributing a statement to "an ordinary member" does not necessarily mean that the member was serving in the assembly at the time of the interview, since a number of former members were interviewed.

29 *Hansard*, 24 January 2017, 65.

30 Ibid., 25 January 2017, 56–6.

31 Ibid., 7 March 2018, 181–2.

32 Ibid., 12 December 2006, 6.

33 Ibid., 12 February 2007, 15.

34 Ibid., 14 May 2010, 44.

35 Ibid., 6 October 2010, 64.

36 Ibid., 21 January 2014, 57.

37 Ibid., 10 June 2014, 6.

38 Ibid., 7 June 2016, 40.

39 Ibid.

40 Ibid., 7 March 2017, 42; 8 March 2017, 103–4.

41 Comments along those lines were occasionally voiced in the early days, and indeed still surface from time to time; a neophyte ordinary member recently asked, "Can there be more effort to get everybody involved in decisions that Executive Council makes concerning Nunatsiavut Government?" Ibid., 9 June 2021, 153.

42 Ibid., 18 October 2006, 61.

43 Lawrence Felt, David C. Natcher, and Andrea Procter, "Going Forward: Challenges and Opportunities for Nunatsiavut Self-Governance," in *Settlement, Subsistence, and Change among the Labrador Inuit: The Nunatsiavummiut Experience*, ed. Lawrence Felt, David C. Natcher, and Andrea Procter (Winnipeg: University of Manitoba Press, 2012), 260.

44 William Barbour (a fluent Inuttut speaker), *Hansard*, 16 October 2006, 36.

45 Ibid., 5 November 2013, 89.

46 It might be thought that the assembly could simply have the simultaneous Inuttut interpretation of proceedings transcribed into an Inuttut *Hansard*. Aside from the significant expense this would entail, it conflates simultaneous interpretation with translation. Although individuals may do both, experienced interpreters/translators stress that the difficulty of instantaneously rendering one language into another means that the quality of interpretation cannot match that of formal translation.

47 *Hansard*, which is spotty in the very early years, does not record the creation of the Language Committee; according to the *Hansard* of 12 February 2007 (p. 14), additional members were put on the Language Committee.

48 *Hansard*, 25 November 2008, 39, 53; 17 March 2009, 17, 48; 23 June 2009, 18.

49 Ibid., 13 December 2011, 24–6.

50 Ibid., 11 December 2012, 82; 22 January 2013, 19, 72.

51 Ibid., 9 March 2016, 144.

52 Ibid., 17 March 2011, 222.

53 Ibid., 23 June 2009, 58.

54 Ibid., 2 February 2011, 32.
55 Ibid., 195. At that point, Lampe was culture minister.
56 Ibid., 5 November 2013, 62.
57 Ibid., 11 March 2010, 142.
58 Terje Brantenberg, "Ethnic and Local Government in Nain, 1969–76," in *The White Arctic: Anthropological Essays on Tutelage and Ethnicity*, ed. Robert Paine (St. John's: Memorial University of Newfoundland, Institute of Social and Economic Research, 1977), 400.
59 *Hansard*, 6 March 2008, 21. Having Inuttut as a first language is not, however, equivalent to fluency since those with other first languages may have acquired facility in Inuttut.
60 Ibid., 23, 26.
61 Ibid., 6 March 2008, 20–30.
62 Ibid., 11 September 2013, 156.
63 Ibid., 2 February 2016, 43.
64 Some members' votes could be determined by their statements in *Hansard*, others by taking into account the overall outcome of the vote (for example, in an 11–1 vote if the one member's vote was known, this established the others' votes). In many instances, votes were determined by careful examination of the OK Society videotapes of sittings. Depending on the camera angle the operator chose, it was sometimes possible to ascertain how all members voted, but at other times only some members could be seen in the frame; their votes are recorded in appendix 8.2 as unknown.
65 The difference cannot be attributed to the number of motions to sanction or remove members from office: four in the first two assemblies, two in the following two assemblies.
66 Finalization of the treaty involved a $5,000 payment to beneficiaries. It subsequently came to light that a small number of ineligible people received payments while others who should have received payments were missed. Both aspects of the issue generated extensive controversy during the First Assembly.
67 While no direct evidence is available to support the speculation about the lack of consequences for ministers who stray from the government position, the public record offers no indication of any sanctions.

9 Assembly Effectiveness I: Representation and Policymaking

1 For a discussion of legislative functions in a Canadian context, see David C. Docherty, *Legislatures* (Vancouver: UBC Press, 2005), 11–21.
2 Nunatsiavut Government, *Nunatsiavut Constitution Act*, CIL N-3, 2012, 4.1.3.
3 Hanna Pitkin, *The Concept of Representation* (Berkeley: University of California Press, 1967). Pitkin and others identify other forms of representation of lesser moment.

4 *Hansard*, 22 January 2019, 43.

5 Ibid., 7 June 2017, 98–100. The "Sixties Scoop" was a widespread, typically involuntary, removal of Indigenous children from their families and their placement in non-Indigenous homes for adoption.

6 On trustee and delegate models of representation, see Docherty, *Legislatures*, 13–15.

7 *Hansard*, 5 March 2008, 14.

8 Ibid., 8 April 2008, 14.

9 Ibid., 5 March 2008, 14.

10 Graham White, "The Territories," in *Big Worlds: Politics and Elections in the Canadian Provinces and Territories*, ed. Jared J. Wesley (Toronto: University of Toronto Press, 2016), tables 11.1 and 11.2.

11 Sikumiut Environmental Management, *Public Consultations Regarding a Moratorium on the Working, Production, Mining and Development of Uranium on Labrador Inuit Lands 2011* (Report for the Special Committee, 28 November 2011), 13, 22.

12 Gary N. Wilson, Christopher Alcantara, and Thierry Rodon, *Nested Federalism and Inuit Governance in the Canadian Arctic* (Vancouver: UBC Press, 2020), 140–57.

13 Docherty, *Legislatures*, 165–6.

14 *Hansard*, 2 February 2011, 32.

15 In a few instances, NG staff explained provisions of bills, sometimes at length, but members either only spoke minimally or did not speak at all; these are considered as minimal or no debate.

16 For a description of the land use planning process in Nunatsiavut, see Andrea Procter and Keith Chaulk, "Our Beautiful Land: Current Debates in Land Use Planning in Nunatsiavut," in *Settlement, Subsistence, and Change among the Labrador Inuit: The Nunatsiavummiut Experience*, ed. David C. Natcher, Lawrence Felt, and Andrea Procter (Winnipeg: University of Manitoba Press, 2012), 231–51. Procter and Chaulk's chapter was written before the draft plan was completed and the bill was introduced.

17 Section 8.4.3 requires the assembly to create laws setting out the notice and consultation process for prospective budget deficits. This has not yet been done.

18 In preparing this section, I reviewed in detail six complete budgetary processes between 2009 and 2022 and skimmed others. It is therefore possible that on rare occasion, minor deviations, such as a member entering the first reading debate, occurred. Overall, however, the process as outlined in the text is accurate.

19 Debate on the 2014–15 budget saw a number of questions about the government's housing policies, which engendered comments and responses from the first minister, whose portfolio includes housing, and the president, as well as brief interventions from the finance and culture ministers: *Hansard*, 5 March 2014, 142–68.

20 Ibid., 17 March 2011, 172–9. The minister of finance subsequently tried without success to reverse this decision by requiring some of the additional funds to come from a reduction of members' indemnities: ibid., 197–205.

21 The account of the historical background to the bill draws heavily on Andrea Procter, "The Prospects of Culture: Resource Management and the Production of Difference in Nunatsiavut, Labrador" (PhD diss., Memorial University of Newfoundland, 2012); Procter, "Uranium, Inuit Rights, and Emergent Neoliberalism in Labrador, 1956–2012," in *Mining and Communities in Northern Canada: History, Politics, and Memory*, ed. Ann Keeling and John Sandlos (Calgary: University of Calgary Press, 2015), 233–58; and Procter, "Uranium and the Boundaries of Indigeneity in Nunatsiavut, Labrador," *Extractive Industries and Society* 3 (2016): 288–96.

22 Ibid., 290.

23 Procter, "Prospects of Culture," 119.

24 Procter, "Uranium, Inuit Rights," 243.

25 Quoted in Procter, "Prospects of Culture," 135.

26 Procter, "Uranium, Inuit Rights," 244.

27 *Hansard*, 11 October 2007, 3.

28 Ibid., 5.

29 Ibid., 6–9.

30 Ibid., 5 March 2008, 13.

31 Ibid., 14–15.

32 Ibid., 8 April 2008, 13.

33 Procter, "Uranium and the Boundaries," 293.

34 *Hansard*, 8 April 2008, 15.

35 Ibid., 13 September 2011, 88.

36 For legislation requiring creation of administrative machinery or otherwise warranting delay before it becomes operational, the assembly may include a provision by which the act comes into force only when authorized by a presidential order. Similar provisions are standard in other legislatures.

37 See Golder Associates, "Nunavut Assembly and Staff Uranium Mining Risks and Benefits Workshop Report," September 2011.

38 *Hansard*, 13 September 2011, 90.

39 Patricia Kemuksigak, an Upper Lake Melville ordinary member, subsequently commented that attendance at the meetings in her area was sparse: ibid., 14 December 2011, 73. Attendance at the Happy Valley–Goose Bay meeting was thirty; at Northwest River, nineteen: Sikumiut Environmental Management, *Public Consultations*, 8.

40 Attendees were asked to complete post-meeting evaluation forms. Statements in the text reflect the results of these surveys; Sikumiut Environmental Management, *Public Consultations*.

41 In Postville, questionnaires were sent to all households; 57 of the 62 that were returned favoured lifting the moratorium, with 2 opposed and 3 undecided: ibid., 14. In Rigolet, 30 of 32 responses expressing an opinion were similarly inclined; 19 were undecided, while 50 had no comment or did not return their questionnaires: ibid., 18.

42 Ibid., 21–3.
43 *Hansard*, 13 December 2011, 41.
44 Ibid., 71–9.
45 "Aurora Energy Suspending Uranium Exploration in Labrador," CBC News,
   1 September 2015, https://www.cbc.ca/news/canada/newfoundland-labrador
   /aurora-energy-suspending-uranium-exploration-in-labrador-1.3209939.

10 Assembly Effectiveness II: Accountability

1 Christopher Alcantara, Zachary Spicer, and Roberto Leone, "Institutional Design
   and the Accountability Paradox: A Case Study of Three Aboriginal Accountability Regimes in Canada," *Canadian Public Administration* 55, no. 1 (March 2012):
   69–90; the Sechelt First Nation now refers to itself as shíshálh Nation.
2 This was consistently the case through 2019, 2020, 2021, and into 2022. When I began to study the assembly, in 2016, its website had photos of members and limited
   information about assembly activities. On enquiring why the earlier site had been
   taken down, I was told that concerns about hacking had prompted the move.
3 NG also puts out media releases for certain requests for proposals and for job ads.
   These are not included in the tabulations.
4 *Hansard*, 11 September 2012, 6.
5 Ibid., 11 June 2013.
6 The May 2017 open house recording was posted to the OK Society website in four
   segments: http://www.oksociety.com/2017/05/page/4/; http://www.oksociety
   .com/2017/05/page/3/; http://www.oksociety.com/2017/05/page/2/. The June 2018
   open house recording was posted in three segments: http://www.oksociety.com
   /2018/06/page/9/; http://www.oksociety.com/2018/06/page/8/; http://www
   .oksociety.com/2018/06/page/7/.
7 During the 2009 budget process, a few hours after the NG's auditors, Deloitte
   and Touche, had reported to the Assembly (*Hansard*, 17 March 2009, 57–76),
   one of the members pointed out that, despite the constitutional requirement,
   neither the Transitional Assembly nor the First Assembly had nominated an
   auditor for the president to appoint. It then came to light that the Department
   of Finance had put out and received tenders for auditors in early 2006 and NEC
   had made the appointment. A retroactive motion recommending Deloitte and
   Touche's appointment for the balance of their contracted term was then passed
   (ibid., 98–103).
8 On attest/financial and value-for-money/performance audits, see "What We Do,"
   Office of the Auditor General of Canada, accessed 28 July 2022, https://www.oag-
   bvg.gc.ca/internet/English/au_fs_e_371.html. A performance audit is described
   there as "an independent, objective and systematic assessment of how well government is managing its activities, responsibilities and resources."

9 Office of the Auditor General of Canada, *Reports of the Auditor General: Report 3 Implementing the Labrador Inuit Land Claims Agreement*, Fall 2015, https://www .oag-bvg.gc.ca/internet/English/parl_oag_201602_03_e_41060.html.

10 Ibid., 7.

11 *Nunatsiavut Constitution Act*, 8.11.7.

12 See, for example, Deloitte, "Independent Auditor's Report," in Nunatsiavut Government, *Consolidated Financial Statements of Nunatsiavut Government, March 31, 2019*, 2–3.

13 *Hansard*, 15 March 2011, 10–51.

14 Prior to bringing forward his motion, Russell attempted to table a petition about the need for an auditor general but was thwarted by a member's objection and a bizarre ruling from the speaker. As Russell was about to table the petition, a minister raised a point of order as to the acceptability of the petition in that members had not been given the opportunity to review it to ensure it was not unconstitutional. After some delay, the speaker ruled that the petition was in order but that the assembly should vote on whether to allow its tabling. Though they had not seen the petition, they voted 10–5 not to permit it to be tabled: ibid., 57–60.

15 Ibid, 89–109.

16 Labrador Inuit Land Claims Trust, "Labrador Inuit Land Claims Implementation Trust 2020," presentation to the Nunatsiavut Assembly, November 2021, 9 (Tabled Document 02-4(11)).

17 According to Isabella Pain, one of the trustees, the purpose of the trust is "to promote, advance, develop and improve the well-being of the eligible beneficiaries, to advance and develop Inuit culture, to provide assistance and means to advance education of eligible beneficiaries, to provide financial assistance for the delivery of social, health, recreational and housing facilities, services, and programs for eligible beneficiaries or to provide financial assistance for the promotion, advancement and development of financial, business, entrepreneurial and employment skills of eligible beneficiaries." *Hansard*, 20 November 2019, 140–1.

18 Labrador Inuit Land Claims Settlement Trust, "Labrador Inuit Land Claims Settlement Trust," presentation to Nunatsiavut Assembly, November 2021, 12 (Tabled Document 03-4(11)).

19 *Hansard*, 20 November 2019, 158–9.

20 Tasiujatsoak Trust, "Tasiujatsoak Trust," presentation to Nunatsiavut Assembly, November 2021, 8 (Tabled Document 04-4(11)).

21 For more details, see "Labrador Inuit Capital Strategy Trust," Nunatsiavut Group of Companies, accessed 28 July 2022, https://ngc-ng.ca/labrador-inuit-capital-strategy -trust/.

22 Some Canadian legislatures, such as the federal Parliament and the Legislative Assembly of Ontario, have committees on regulations and other "statutory instruments." They are of limited significance, however, in that they consider only the

form and legal status of regulations (does the regulation, for example, exceed the ambit of the authorizing legislation or have retroactive effect?) rather than their substance. In Ottawa, the Standing Joint [i.e., Senate-Commons] Committee for the Scrutiny of Regulations may recommend to Parliament disallowance of a regulation on technical or legal grounds, but not on its merits. See Gavin Murphy, "Extended Parliamentary Power over Regulations in Canada," *Statute Law Review* 26, no. 3 (January 2005): 161–70.

23 Recall that the term "question period" is not often used in the assembly.

24 *Nunatsiavut Government Organization (Transitional) Act*, CIL N-7 (09–03–2018), ss 15–16.

25 *Hansard*, 8 June 2021, 83.

26 Ibid., 17 March 2009, 47. At no point did the speaker explicitly say that the time allocated for question period had expired, but on several occasions he did indicate that question period had concluded: thus "apparently."

27 Ibid., 10 March 2010, 72.

28 Standing Order 32.

29 *Standing Orders and Procedures Respecting the Proceedings of the Nunatsiavut Assembly Made in Terms of Part 4.14 of the Labrador Inuit Constitution and Part 9 of the Nunatsiavut Assembly Act* (appendix A of the *Nunatsiavut Assembly Act*, IL 2005–09), Standing Order 56.

30 *Hansard*, 24 June 2009, 67.

31 Ibid., 7 June 2017.

32 Ibid., 17 September 2019, 51–4; 18 September 2019, 84–5. Offering ministers the opportunity to respond to questions about their former portfolios is, especially under the circumstances, sensible, but it is not in accordance with established Westminster parliamentary procedure, which holds current ministers responsible for activities of their departments, including actions of their predecessors.

33 Standing Orders 32(10) and 34(4). The original Standing Orders only required that written answers to oral or written questions be provided at "some future time" (Standing Order 64) or "some future date" (Standing Order 66).

34 *Hansard*, 26 October 2020, 94; 12 March 2021, 59; and 23 November 2021, 61. In one case, Speaker Marlene Winters-Wheeler ruled out of order a written question she herself had posed before becoming speaker.

35 Ibid., 19 November 2019, 75–85; 20 November 2019, 125–38.

36 This does not include the very brief emergency session of August 2007, called to pass urgently needed legislation.

37 Note that both periods extend over two assemblies and are thus not coterminous with the categories in subsequent tables, where data are arrayed by assembly.

38 These numbers are arrived at as follows: 2010–12 (70/(70 + 56 +36)); 2017–19 (83/(83 + 52 + 57)).

39 The First Assembly had only one member for the Canada Constituency, so that typically only two non-NEC ordinary members were able to pose questions. Given the relatively low number of questions in the First Assembly, this does not substantially affect the overall figures.

40 The first minister's department, Nunatsiavut Affairs, is responsible for providing funds and administrative support to the local enrolment committees and the Inuit Membership Appeal Board. However, the constitution clearly excludes the first minister, along with all assembly members, from involvement in specific enrolment cases. This has never stopped members from asking the first minister to explain, reverse, or intervene in particular cases.

41 CBC, *Labrador Morning*, podcast, https://www.cbc.ca/listen/live-radio/1-31-labrador -morning/clip/15910035-ageism-workplace-researching-wood-frogs-help -stroke-victims.

42 See "OKâlaKatiget Society," OKâlaKatiget Society, accessed 28 July 2022, http:// www.oksociety.com/.

43 Statements in this paragraph are based on a systematic review of all items posted to the OK Society website (typically, in recent years, 90–110 items a month) from January 2016 to mid-2022.

44 These are available at https://www.terracestandard.com/ and https://www .thenorthernview.com/. The figures cited here were gathered 17 December 2020. Sizeable contingents of Nisga'a citizens live in Terrace and Prince Rupert, though they only constitute small proportions of the total population of each city.

45 These publications can be consulted at https://nnsl.com/nwtnewsnorth/ and https://nnsl.com/yellowknifer/.

46 Nunavik, the Inuit region of northern Quebec, which is not (yet) self-governing as the term is used in this book, has a substantially larger population than Nunatsiavut. Its politics is covered by *Nunatsiaq News*.

47 "Communications," Nunatsiavut Government, accessed 28 July 2022, https:// nunatsiavut.com/department/nunatsiavut-secretariat/communications/.

48 All quotations and paraphrases come from *Hansard*, 7 March 2018, 197–200, 297–308.

11 Change, Continuity, and Self-Government in the Nunatsiavut Assembly

1 *Hansard*, 10 June 2014, 58.

2 Nunatsiavut Assembly, "Nunavut Legislative Assembly Visit to Iqaluit May 25–28, 2014," June 2014, 1.

3 Ibid., 2.

4 Ibid., 3.

5 Gary N. Wilson, "Nunavik and the Multiple Dimensions of Inuit Governance," *American Review of Canadian Studies* 47, no. 2 (2017): 151, 148.

6 Gordon, *Called Upstairs*, 269, 339, 342.

7 David C. Natcher, Lawrence Felt, and Andrea Procter, "Introduction" in *Settlement, Subsistence, and Change among the Labrador Inuit: The Nunatsiavummiut Experience*, ed. David C. Natcher, Lawrence Felt, and Andrea Procter (Winnipeg: University of Manitoba Press, 2012), 12. The other main challenges/opportunities they cited were "the ethnic basis of membership and … effective participation and relationships in wider levels of governance at regional, provincial national, and pan-ethnic levels."

8 Non-Inuit may vote for but are ineligible to serve as AngajukKât.

9 *Hansard*, 13 December 2011, 4.

Index

Alcantara, Christopher, 39, 42, 47

Alfred, Taiaiake, 45

Amaguk Inn, 12, 83

Andersen, Anthony (Tony), 74, 99, 101, 117, 118, 119, 127, 128, 133, 152, 194, 195, 196

Andersen, John, 152

Andersen, Toby, 63

Andersen, William III, 48, 61, 133, 155, 159, 254n14

AngajukKât

  absence from October 2022 session, 98

  assembly membership, rationale, 53, 97

  eligible voters for, 53

  exclusion from Members' Services Committee, 98

  influence, perceptions of, 99

  Joint Management Committee, members, 157

  NEC, ineligible for, 97

  ordinary members, relations with, 97–8

  relations among, 99

  role, 97–100

  voting cohesion, 167

Appleby, Humphrey, 93, 255n37

Assembly of the Nunatsiavut Government (the assembly)

  accountability function, 201, 226–7

  assessment, 235–6

  audio feed, 76, 121, 203, 221, 228

  auditor general, motion to establish, 208–9

  audit reports for, 207

  budget, 119, 120

  Canada Constituency, 69, 70, 71, 87, 88, 90, 93, 95, 96, 100, 102–3, 120–1, 152, 179–80, 224, 228, 271n39

  dissolution, 68

  educational function, 177–8, 198

  Euro-Canadian influence on, 6, 103–4, 122

  expulsions, 130–4

  functions, constitutional, 177

  information for public, 203, 222

  Inuit influence on, 6, 122, 140, 147, 158–63, 233–4

  Inuttut use, 79, 87, 121, 159–61, 163, 170

  isolation from other legislatures, 231

  legal advice for, 120

  policymaking function, 184–92, 198

  privilege, parliamentary, 76

  quasi-Westminster nature, 5, 6

  recordings, video, 122, 127, 203, 239n16

  regulations, scrutiny, 211–12

  representational function, 178–83, 198

Assembly of the Nunatsiavut
    Government (the assembly) (*cont.*)
  seating, 79–80
  session/sitting, definition, 76, 253n7,
    254n15
  sessions, frequency, length, 77, 83–5,
    190, 205, 254n16
  sessions, virtual, 77
  setting, 77
  sitting, emergency, 83, 254n14
  staff, 119–20
  structure, 6, 75, 76
  transparency, 224–6
  video feed, 77, 228
  weather, influence on, 83, 86–7
  website, 203, 204, 268n2
Assembly Act, amendment, 110, 114, 229
Assembly Act, provisions, 76, 84, 93, 95,
    99, 112, 115, 129, 115, 129, 190,
    255n27
assembly atmosphere
  ambiance, 162
  debate, tone, 80
  formality/informality, 81–2, 109, 123,
    143, 147, 162, 231, 235
  harsh words rare, 82
  livelier in early years, 81, 229–30
  unanimous consent, usually given,
    80–1, 85, 107, 109, 188, 189
Assembly Building, 77–80, 228, 235
assembly members
  background in LIA, 74, 81, 83, 102, 134
  Canada Constituency members, 87,
    90, 93, 102–3, 120, 121, 179, 228
  consensus values, adherence to, 230
  constituents, contact with, 181
  constituents, satisfaction with, 182–3
  deference to ministers, 191, 211
  delegate role, 181
  demographics, 87, 178
  dress, 80
  experience as bureaucrats, 88

Inuttut use, 79, 87, 121, 159–60, 161,
    163, 170
  leaves from, 89
  length of service, 90
  occupational backgrounds, 87
  orientation, 120–1
  quiescence, 191
  reporting of activities, 89
  representation, views on, 179
  residence requirement, 68, 87, 255n27
  salary and benefits, 88, 100, 118,
    121–2
  self-government, commitment to,
    197, 236
  turnover, 89–91
  turnover, implications of, 91
  workloads, 100, 116
  See also AngajukKât; first minister; In-
    uit community corporation chairs;
    ordinary members; president;
    speaker
assembly procedures
  abstention, 127, 259n7
  adjournment, 111
  bills: amendments, 187; assent, 111,
    257n9; budget, 185, 188–9; debate,
    110–11, 186–7; first reading, 109;
    notice of motion, 109, 110; order
    taken up, 110; private, 257n6;
    private members, 109–10; second
    reading, 109
  breaks, 85–6, 95, 108, 254n17
  budget, procedures 187–91
  committee of the whole, 81, 94, 109,
    111, 131, 125, 126, 148, 149, 150,
    186, 189, 193, 232, 234
  debate-limiting procedures, 147
  documents, tabling, 108, 257n4
  money bill rule, 75, 129, 189–90,
    259n19
  motions, 109
  notice of motion, 109

opening address by president, 106–7
orders of the day, 105–6
petitions, 108, 257n3, 269n14
prayer, 106, 256n1
question period: effectiveness, 220;
    rules, 107, 212–13
questions: by portfolio, 217–18;
    local-regional, 219–20; members'
    limited use of, 212, 214, 215–16;
    returns to, 107, 213; supplementa-
    ry, 214, 215; taken as notice, 213;
    written, 108, 213, 256n2
quorum, 106, 144
recorded votes, 129, 203
reports from committees, 108, 116
requirements, constitutional, 188
secret ballots, 126–9, 131, 132, 133,
    140
sitting, start, 106
Standing Orders, 50, 57, 95, 107, 108,
    109, 115, 116, 127, 129, 147, 148,
    187–9, 203, 212–13, 229; review/
    reform, 81, 85, 93, 94, 95, 99,
    109–10, 113–14, 116, 118, 127,
    128, 148, 215, 228–9; special, 114;
    waiving, 81, 85, 109, 111, 113, 123,
    126, 186, 189
statements: members, 107; ministers,
    107
visitors, recognition, 107
auditor general of Canada, 207
Aurora Energy Resources, 193, 194, 197

Barbour, William, 131, 135, 165, 193, 195
Belanger, Yale, 37, 44
Ben-Dor, Shmuel, 21
beneficiaries
    criteria for membership, 23, 35, 48–9,
        134, 238n12
    locations, 9
    membership decisions/appeals, 35, 49,
        169, 211, 271n40
    NG staff, 66
    numbers, 9
    revocation of membership, 134
    Settlers as, 23
Betasamosake Simpson, Leanne, 45
Blake, Max, 131
Blake, Nanette, 70, 252n62
Blake-Rudkowski, Edward, 86, 87, 95,
    96, 112, 113, 134, 155, 179, 213,
    252n62
Brice-Bennett, Carol, 16, 17, 18, 19, 57,
    137
Brody, Hugh, 21
Broomfield, Todd, 88, 94, 95, 96, 160,
    195, 255n42

Calder case, 245n4
Campbell-Higgs, Mina, 151
CBC, 27, 132, 155, 221, 223, 224
Clerk's Office, 107, 108, 120
Code of Conduct, 115, 134, 137, 235
    applied to Inuit community gov-
        ernments and Inuit community
        corporations, 262n55
    committee to establish, 109, 185
    discipline committees, 116, 131–3
    Ford, attempted removal, 133
    harshness, 138, 140, 233
    issues prior to passage, 103
    need for, 138–9
    Northwest Territories, 136–7
    offences against, 137
    Pamak dismissal, 136
    role of speaker, 94, 116
    Saunders expulsion, 132
    significance, 229, 236
committees
    caucus, 119, 145–6, 193, 197
    Code of Conduct Committee, 109,
        185
    Committee on Consensus, 94, 111,
        148, 186

committees (*cont.*)
  discipline committees, 116, 131–3
  Drug and Alcohol Committee, 100, 117, 118, 185
  evaluation, 108, 115, 118, 119, 184–5, 230
  Language Committee, 116, 160, 258n22
  legislation, special committees on, 111
  male-female balance, 57, 115, 116, 123
  Members' Services Committee, 88, 94, 99, 115, 116, 118, 120, 190, 230
  membership, 115
  non-assembly members, 57, 115
  number, appropriate, 118–19
  Nunatsiavut Business Centre Committee, 185
  powers, 115
  reports from, 108, 116
  review of administrative action, 115–16
  Rules and Procedures Committee, 85, 94, 95, 109, 113, 114, 116, 128, 148, 230
  Special Committee on Canada Constituency voting, 59, 71, 118, 230, 249n21
  Special Committee on Environmental Protection Bill, 185
  Special Committee on the Report of the Nunatsiavut Elections Officer, 118
  special committees, 118, 184–5
  staff, 118, 185
  uranium moratorium, special committee devoted to, 193, 195–6, 230
Commonwealth Parliamentary Association, 231
comprehensive land claims, 32–7, 44–6
consensus government
  absence of objection, 55
  assessment, 168–70, 234
  caucusing, 119, 145–6, 193, 197, 229
  concentration of power, 143–4, 169
  conflict avoidance, 144, 168, 169
  criticism of, 150
  expectations for, 143, 147–8
  expulsion of members, 136–7
  ideals of, 149–50
  limits on debates, 147
  mandate in constitution, 55
  members' views on, 149–50, 230
  opposition, absence of, 146–7
  opposition mentality, 146
  traditional decision making, 142, 147, 164
  See also political culture, Inuit
consensus government in the Northwest Territories and Nunavut, 75, 76, 81, 96, 119, 142–5, 146, 198, 263n4
constitution. *See* Labrador Inuit Constitution
Cornell, Stephen, 37
Corntassel, Jeff, 45
Coulthard, Glen, 37, 45
COVID-19
  budget session consequence, 83
  committee consultations limited, 71, 118, 249n21
  constitutional amendment on election timing, 62
  election, provincial effects, 253n66
  NG media releases on, 204–5
  presidential election 2020, effect on, 71, 251n44
  session cancellation, 158
  virtual sessions forced by, 71, 112–14
customary law, 36, 54–5

Deloitte, 207, 208
deputy speaker, 88, 93–4, 109, 134
Dicker, Joe, 257n3
Dubois, Janique, 42
Dunn, Lawrence, 23, 29

Edmunds, Tyler, 5, 86, 92
elections, 67–71, 74, 249n30, 250n33,
    251n53, 252n55, 253n66
Evans, Peter, 18, 26, 28

first minister, 125–6, 144, 218, 271n40
Flowers, Greg, 98
Flowers, Marjorie, 98
Ford, Patricia, 93, 133, 134
Freud, Sigmund, 141

Gordon, Tom, 232

Hamilton, David, 121, 229, 259n1
Hansard, 11, 106, 116, 122, 127, 160,
    203, 231, 239n16
Harper, Stephen, 40
Harvard Project, 43
Haysom, Veryan, 75, 76, 121, 138, 140,
    149, 229
Hebron, 21, 29, 192
Henderson, Ailsa, 17, 30
Hopedale Moravian Mission Church, 77
Huu-ay-aht First Nations, 52, 63
Hylton, John, 41, 42

Illusuak Cultural Centre, 145, 169
Implementation Trust, 209
Indian Act, 3, 38, 41
Innu, 15, 20, 23, 29, 36, 241n53
Innu Nation, 20, 24, 178
interpersonal dynamics
    Canada Constituency members, per-
        ceptions of, 102–3
    conflict, 91, 100, 101–2, 140, 150, 169
    division between powerful and less
        powerful, 102
    members as extended family, 82–3
    members' frequent interactions, 83
    mutual assistance, 100–1
    political elite, familiarity within, 83,
        102

Inuit community corporation chairs, 98,
    100, 167
Inuit community corporations, 9, 67
Inuit community governments, 53, 67
Inuit Court, 53, 55, 56, 64, 116, 202,
    257n9
Inuit Kaujummikatangit, 161
Inuit, Labrador
    Christianity, conversion to, 16, 17
    Confederation, effects on, 28–9
    demographics, 10
    distinctiveness, 8, 31
    diversity, 14
    elders, 22, 23, 27, 28, 54, 55, 57, 59, 61,
        132, 135, 137, 150, 162, 235
    elders' councils, 27–8, 43, 59, 150,
        164
    identity, 5, 30, 31
    Innu, relations with, 20
    Inuttut use, 10, 159, 163
    literacy, 17–18, 31
    men's meetings, 27, 28, 58, 164, 232
    Métis, 15
    Moravian influence, pushback against,
        18–19, 26–8
    Moravian influence on, 8, 15–19, 22,
        31
    NCC, relations with, 20
    political development, 29–30
    political traditions, 26–7, 58, 142, 147,
        149, 164, 233
    precursors, 7, 15
    settlement, adoption of, 16
    Settlers, interactions with, 21
    traditional political institutions,
        18–19, 26–8, 31, 159, 233
    women, role of, 19, 57
Inuitness, 8
Inuit Tapirisat Canada, 22
Inuttut, 51, 162, 205, 206, 222, 241n53,
    264n46
    decline, 29

Inuttut (*cont.*)
    encouragement by Moravians, 16, 17,
      21, 31
    fluency among Nunatsiavumiut, 8, 10,
      265n59
    president to speak and understand,
      61, 69, 159, 162–3, 169
    primacy in constitution, 52
    use in assembly, 79, 87, 121, 143,
      159–61, 170, 231
    use in presidential debate, 96, 110, 118

Jacque, Herb, 134, 196
James Bay and Northern Quebec
    Agreement, 33
Jenness, Diamond, 15, 16, 18
Joint Management Committee, 157

Kennedy, John C., 8, 18, 20, 21, 22, 23,
    24, 29, 192
King, Hayden, 45
Kleivan, Helge, 17, 18, 21, 27, 137

Labrador Inuit Association
    assembly members' roots in, 81, 83, 102
    choice of Westminster system, 60,
      103–4
    communications failings, 151
    constitution, development, 50–1, 57
    education, emphasis on, 31
    emergence, 29, 192
    existence, continuing, 245n6
    founding, 22
    land claim, 5, 30, 34, 36, 55, 209
    membership, 29, 49, 134, 241n53
    motivation for claim, 5
    president to speak Inuttut, 163
    relations with First Nations, 22
    relations with Settlers, 22–3, 163
    self-government, 52–3, 147–8
    standards of behaviour, 139
    Tasiujatsoak Trust, creation, 210

    transition to NG, 35, 73–4, 133
Labrador Inuit Capital Strategy Trust,
    10, 26, 96, 128, 170, 210
Labrador Inuit Constitution
    amendment, 58, 61–2, 68, 71, 163, 230
    aspirational elements, 51–2
    attitudes towards change, members',
      61–2, 230
    detail, level of, 50–1
    development, 50–1
    English text prevails, 54
    Euro-Canadian influences, 59–61
    expansion of LILCA, 48
    founding principles, 52
    Inuit influences, 54–6, 148, 162–3
    Inuit-made, 48
    Labrador Inuit Charter, 52, 55
    NG, auditing of, 206–8
    participation, provisions relating to,
      58–9
    preamble, 52
    ratification, 50
    rights of non-members, 53
    self-government, 52–4
    women, provisions relating to, 56–7
Labrador Inuit Land Claims Agreement
    co-management boards established,
      35, 48
    as constitutional "bible," 48
    emphasis on compromise, 48
    financial provisions, 34, 48, 188
    Inuit community corporations, 67
    Inuit community governments, 67
    membership criteria established,
      48–9
    negotiations, 30, 36, 60
    self-government provisions, 35
Labrador Inuit Land Claims Settlement
    Trust, 66, 128, 209, 209, 269n17
Labrador Inuit Settlement Area (LISA),
    34–5, 59, 66, 81, 103, 195, 204, 214
Labrador Metis Association, 23

Labrador Morning, 11, 24, 70, 132, 134, 211, 221

Lampe, Johannes, 24, 69, 70, 71, 88, 132, 135, 154, 156, 157, 159, 160, 162, 182, 206, 252n56

Land Claims Agreements Coalition, 36

Lane, Denise, 195

Language Strategy Committee, 160, 258n22

Leo, Sarah, 64, 69, 88, 93, 135, 136, 145, 156, 159, 205, 210

Lough, David, 28

Lyall, Jim, 96, 125, 127, 128, 131, 135, 156, 159, 182, 196, 220, 234

Lyall, Sean, 93, 96, 99, 134, 136, 146, 231

Macdonald, John A., 138

Mackenzie Valley Land and Water Board, 40

McLean, Carl, 195

McMahon, Nicole, 12

media, 204–5, 220–1, 223–5, 227

membership payment dispute, 117, 164, 169, 259n19, 265n66

Merrell, Andrew, 12

methods, research, 10–12

Michelin, Loretta, 120, 128

Mitchell, Gary, 100, 152, 162

Mitchell, Kate, 53, 68, 88, 92, 125, 126, 135, 156, 257n3

Moravians
  arrival in Labrador, 8, 15
  chapel servants, 18, 27
  culture, preservation of 16–17
  economics of Moravian Mission, 16
  expulsion of members, 25, 137
  influence on Labrador Inuit, 15–16, 18–19, 22, 31
  Inuttut, encouragement of, 16, 17, 21, 31
  literacy, emphasis on, 17–18
  men's privileged political position among, 57–8
  music, 232
  political institutions, establishment of, 27–8
  pushback against, 18–19
  Settlers, relationships with, 20–2
  women, influence on, 19, 57

Morrison, Jim, 130

music, Inuit, 232–3

Native Association of Newfoundland and Labrador, 22, 241n53

Newfoundland (and Labrador), Government of, 4, 17, 28, 29, 48, 63–4, 114

Nikolakis, William, 44

Nisga'a Lisims Government, 9, 224, 237n4

Nochasak, Susan, 135

Norn, Steve, 129

Nunatsiavut
  description, 7–10
  meaning, 4, 237n5

Nunatsiavumiut. *See* Inuit, Labrador

Nunatsiavut Executive Council
  accountability to people, 202
  cabinet solidarity, 75, 165, 168
  cohesion in voting, 165
  communications, criticisms of, 150–5
  composition, 76, 144
  concentration of power in, 76, 144
  finance minister and budget, 189
  ministers: demands on, 157; dismissal of, 134–6; lack of staff, 120, 154, 157; length of service, 91–3; must be ordinary members, 74, 76, 144; Nunatsiavut-wide perspective, 180; resignation, 134–5; selection, 126; shuffles, 91–3; turnover, 91–3
  non-NEC members, relations with, 82, 90, 91, 102, 146, 150–9, 165, 168, 230

Nunatsiavut Executive Council (*cont.*)
   open house meetings, 101, 153, 154,
      156, 157, 204, 205–6
   size, 6
Nunatsiavut Government
   access to information, 225
   administrative structure, 64–6
   appointments, transparency in, 226
   auditing of, 207–9, 268n7
   community liaison officers, 225
   decentralization, 66
   deputy ministers, 65, 189, 250n37
   documents, availability, 225
   expenditures, 66
   Facebook page, 11, 114, 205
   housing policy, 64
   journalists, relations with, 225
   jurisdictions, active in, 63–4
   Land Claims Agreements Coalition,
      member, 36
   language policies, 160–1
   LIA becomes NG, 35–6, 73–4, 133
   media releases, 204–5
   natural resource regulation, 64
   open houses, 101, 153, 154, 156, 157,
      204, 205–6
   power, "draw down" of, 63, 185
   relations with NCC, 24
   revenues, 66
   staff, demographics, 66
   staff, geographic distribution, 65–6
   transparency, 224–6
   website, 11, 113, 121, 122, 156, 160,
      203, 204, 211, 224, 225, 268n2
Nunatsiavut Government Research
      Advisory Committee, 12
Nunatsiavut Housing Commission, 64,
      150, 164, 214
NunatuKavut Community Council, 15,
      20, 22–3, 23–4, 178, 245n3
Nunavut, Government of
   as de facto Indigenous government, 39

assembly committees, 190
assembly staff, 145
assembly visit by Nunatsiavut speaker,
      146, 231–2
design, 65
dissatisfaction with, 63
elections, 182
Hansard, 160
Inuit staff, 66, 251n41
leadership selection, 125, 129, 144
legislation, 50–1
media coverage, 223–4
MLA expulsion, 129, 130, 138
public government, role as, 3, 52, 104
take-up of jurisdiction, 250n33
traditional decision making, 25
See also consensus government in the
      Northwest Territories and Nunavut
Nuqingaq, Samuel, 129
Nutak, 21, 29, 192

OK Society, 11, 127, 155, 156, 203, 221–3
Onalik, Susan, 87
ordinary members
   AngajukKât, relations with, 97–8,
      101
   assembly, seating in, 80
   beneficiaries only eligible as, 53
   Canada Constituency members, 87,
      102, 179
   candidates, number, 68
   constituency allowance, 88, 100, 121
   length of service, 90–1
   Members' Services Committee, mem-
      bers of, 115, 230
   NEC eligibility, 76, 94, 144
   qualifications, 68
   re-election rate, 182–3
   Transitional Assembly, 74, 253n1
   turnover, 91
   voting cohesion, 167
Our Footprints Are Everywhere, 21

Pain, Isabella, 147, 210, 226, 269n17
Paine, Robert, 19
Palliser, Carlene, 98
Palliser Treaty, 245n3
Palmater, Pamela, 45
Pamak, Richard, 135, 136, 138, 152, 257n3
Pauktuutit, 26, 57, 258n30
political culture, Inuit, 25–6, 30, 76, 137
political culture, Labrador Inuit
    adaptability, 26, 232
    assembly, influence on, 159, 197, 227, 232
    constitution, influence on, 54–6
    decision making, traditional, 27, 58, 72, 142, 147, 149, 164
    Inuit way, 161–2, 170
    unique elements, 26, 30
    values, 161
    willingness to push back, 26
political parties, 6, 61, 68, 71, 75, 82, 110, 115, 142, 146, 262n2
Ponniuk, Ben, 74
Pottle, Danny, 86, 101, 103, 135, 136, 138, 139, 154, 161, 162, 195, 220, 255n42
president
    assents to bills, 111, 257n9
    communications, letter regarding, 154
    constitutional petition, power to reject, 58
    election of, 68
    first minister, power to appoint, 143
    Inuttut capacity, 69, 162–3
    ministers, power to dismiss, 138
    opening address, 106–7
    questions to, 218–19
    speaker, nominates, 93, 126
    women candidates, responsibility to recruit, 68
Procter, Andrea, 18, 22, 192, 194

Rankin, Lisa, 15
regulations, 211–12, 267n36, 269n22

Richling, Barrett, 22, 26, 27
Riel, Louis, 130
Rodon, Thierry, 39, 42
Royal Commission on Aboriginal Peoples, 25, 37, 38, 43, 258n30
Russell, Keith, 135, 146, 147, 151, 162, 163, 164, 208, 220, 269n14
Russell, Todd, 24

Saunders, Kelly, 42
Saunders, Rachel, 132–3, 135
Saunders, Roland, 87, 102, 113, 152
self-determination, xi, 24, 29, 37
    for Labrador Inuit, 5, 28, 30, 31
self-government
    critiques, 44–6
    definitions, 37
    federal government role, 40, 42
    forms, 38–41
    Labrador Inuit, 52–4, 233–6
    literature, 41–6
Settlers, 18, 19–24, 28, 31, 163
Shaw, George Bernard, 152
Sheppard, Glen, 151, 195, 196
Shiwak, Darryl, 88, 156, 162
Sillet, Mary, 119, 120, 250n37, 258n29, 258n30
Simon, Mary, 109
simultaneous interpretation, 121, 122, 160, 206, 264n46
Sixties Scoop, 180, 266n5
speaker
    appointment to NEC, 94
    assembly business, involvement in, 95–6, 114, 255n42
    breaks, determines, 85–6, 95, 108, 254n17
    casting vote, 93
    committees, chairs, 94, 99, 113, 115
    consensus, determined by, 55
    deputy speaker selection, 93
    discretion over proceedings, 106

speaker (*cont.*)
  indemnity, 88
  must be ordinary member, 76
  nomination by president, 93, 126
  non-partisan, 6, 74, 93
  Nunavut visit, 146, 231
  OK Society, interviews, 203, 222
  powers, unusual, 94
  powers, usual, 94
  removal from office, attempted, 130, 133
  returns to oral/written questions, summarizes, 107–8
  role re Code of Conduct, 94, 116, 131, 132, 133–4
  secret ballots, and, 127, 128
  selection, 101, 126
  tolerance in question period, 213
  UKatti, 87
  visitors, recognizes, 107
split votes, 164, 165–7, 265n64
Stevenson, Marc, 25, 26

Tasiujatsoak Trust, 210
Tłı̨chǫ Government, 59, 224, 248n11
Torngat Fish Producers Co-operative Society, 111
Torngat Joint Fisheries Board, 35
Torngat Mountains National Park Co-Management Board, 35
Torngat Wildlife and Plants Co-Management Board, 35
Transitional Assembly, 74, 155, 186, 253n1
Trudeau, Justin, 20
trusts, 209–11
Twin Otter, 8, 83, 86, 254n19

United Nations Declaration on the Rights of Indigenous Peoples, xi
uranium moratorium
  bill, 181, 192–7, 257n7
  Brinex hearings, 29, 192
  proposals for mine, 29, 192–3
  public consultations, 195–6, 267n39
  public opinion, 196, 267nn40–1
  resolution, 193
  significance, 197

Vallee, F.G., 26

Webb/Tuglavina, Andrea, 71, 252n56, 252n62
Wesley, Angela, 52
Westminster system, 60, 74–7, 104, 165, 233, 238n7, 253n2
Whitfield, Greg, 47
Wilson, Gary, 39, 42
Winters-Wheeler, Marlene, 77, 256n2, 259n8, 270n34
Wolfrey, Charlotte, 98, 162
women
  assembly members, proportion of, 49, 51, 56–8, 115
  disrespectful comments on, 131
  Moravian influence on, 19
  NG staff, percentage of, 66
  representation on committees, 115–16, 123
  role in developing constitution, 57
  status of women, NG unit, 217–18
  traditional role, 19

Yukon Environmental and Socio-Economic Assessment Board, 40